C...
LIF...

CIVIL WAR

Spare time for a Civil War surgeon was always in short supply, yet Union surgeon George Thomas Stevens somehow found free moments in which to make notes for one of the earliest and best personal narratives of the War—one of only a handful written by doctors who served in the field. *Three Years in the Sixth Corps,* published in 1866, was the work of a remarkable man.

Stevens was born on July 25, 1832, in Essex County, New York, the son of a Congregationalist clergyman. He graduated in 1857 from Castleton Medical College in Vermont and began practicing medicine in Westport, New York. On October 8, 1861, the 29-year-old physician joined the Army at Saratoga Springs, and seven weeks later he was mustered into service as assistant surgeon of the 77th New York. Not long afterward, he was appointed chief operating surgeon for his brigade, "an exceptional honor," he recalled later, considering that all of his assistants were men with the full rank of surgeon. Soon promoted to surgeon, Stevens served the rest of his tour of duty as a chief of surgery and, for several months, medical inspector of the Sixth Corps. With the disbanding of the 77th New York in June 1865, he returned to civilian life.

He began work on *Three Years in the Sixth Corps* immediately after his discharge from service and spent most of 1865 researching and writing it. The first edition, illustrated with engravings from sketches Stevens had drawn in the field, was published the following year. A second, revised edition appeared four years later. Stevens' book, which he described as "the story of the grandest corps that ever faced a foe," contained such a comprehensive account of his unit's activities that its author was hailed as "the Sixth Corps historian."

While Stevens wrote about the major events of the War—the Peninsular Campaign, the great battles of Antietam and Gettysburg and others—he was also adept at zeroing in on small details. "Broken caissons, wheels, dismantled guns, thousands of muskets, blankets, haversacks and canteens, were scattered thickly over the field," he wrote of the scene after

TIME-LIFE BOOKS INC., ALEXANDRIA, VIRGINIA 22314

Antietam. "Hundreds of slain horses, bloated and with their feet turned toward the sky, added to the horror." Describing a march to Alexandria, Virginia, he summoned up the feel of the day: "The sky was hung with heavy clouds. A drizzling rain, now diminishing to a heavy mist, and now coming in fresh showers, made the marching heavy and unpleasant."

Like all soldiers, Stevens had his prejudices. He had little use for General George McClellan. In contrast, he regarded the Sixth Corps commander, John Sedgwick, as "one of the greatest soldiers of the age" and expressed admiration for the bungling General Ambrose Burnside.

Throughout Stevens' book are glimpses of what it was like to be in the medical service in a war where more than 200,000 soldiers on both sides died from battle wounds and twice that number perished from disease. In one of the most poignant passages, Stevens quotes from the letter of a surgeon—probably Stevens himself—that tells of doing nothing for four days and nights after the Wilderness Campaign but amputating mangled limbs. The more the surgeon toiled, the longer seemed to grow the line of those awaiting their turn. "It is a scene of horror such as I never saw. God forbid that I should see another."

After the War, Stevens resumed practicing medicine, in Albany, New York, and in 1870 became a professor of physiology and of diseases of the eye and ear at Albany Medical College. In 1880 he moved to New York City, where he became known for the diagnostic and surgical instruments he invented and for his new operating procedures: He was one of the first surgeons in America to remove a foreign object from an eye with a magnet.

Stevens was a prolific writer on a variety of subjects, from military matters and travel to botany. He was also an accomplished artist: His *Guide to Flowering Plants,* published in 1910, contains more than 1,800 of his own drawings. In all, he produced some two dozen books and pamphlets before his death at the age of 88 on January 30, 1921, at his New York home.

—THE EDITORS

MAJ.-GEN. JOHN SEDGWICK

THREE YEARS
in the

6ᵗʰ CORPS

FERGUSON.ALB.

THREE YEARS

IN THE

SIXTH CORPS.

A CONCISE NARRATIVE OF EVENTS IN THE ARMY OF THE POTOMAC, FROM 1861 TO THE CLOSE OF THE REBELLION, APRIL, 1865.

By GEORGE T. STEVENS,

SURGEON OF THE 77TH REGIMENT NEW YORK VOLUNTEERS.

ALBANY:
S. R. GRAY, PUBLISHER.
1866.

WEED, PARSONS AND COMPANY,
PRINTERS, STEREOTYPERS AND BOOKBINDERS,
ALBANY, N. Y.

PREFACE.

THE following pages are offered to my old comrades of the Sixth Corps, with the hope that they may pleasantly recall the many varied experiences of that unparalleled body of men. If much has been omitted which should have been written, or if anything has been said which should have been left out, I rely upon the generosity of brave men to treat with leniency the failings they may detect.

I have endeavored to present without exaggeration or embellishment of imagination, a truthful picture of army life in all its vicissitudes; its marches, its battles, its camps, and the sad scenes when the victims of war languish in hospitals. The story is written mostly from extensive notes taken by myself amid the scenes described; but official reports and letters from officers have been used freely in correcting these notes, and gathering fresh material. The narrative commences with the experiences of my own regiment; then when that regiment became a part of Smith's division, its incidents and history includes the whole. From the organization of the Sixth Corps to the close of the rebellion, I have endeavored without partiality to give the story of the Corps. If I have failed to do justice to any of the noble troops of the Corps, it has been from no want of desire to give to each regiment the praise due to it.

I cannot close without acknowledging my many obligations to the numerous friends, officers and soldiers of the Corps, and others who have favored me with their assistance. I take especial pleasure in acknowledging the kindness of Miss Emily Sedgwick, sister of our lamented commander; Vermont's honored son, Major-General L. A. Grant, Major-General Thomas H. Neill, Colonel James B. McKean, Colonel W. B. French, Chaplain Norman Fox, and Mr. Henry M. Myers. I am also indebted to the friends of Samuel S. Craig for the use of his diary, extending from the early history of the Army of the Potomac, to the death of the talented young soldier in the Wilderness.

The engravings are nearly all from sketches taken by myself on the ground, the others are from the pencil of the well known artist, Captain J. Hope, and all have been submitted to his finishing touch. Mr. Ferguson has executed the wood cuts in a style creditable to his art.

The typographical portion of the work has been done in a style of beauty and finish for which the work of Weed. Parsons and Company is so well known.

18 North Pearl Street, Albany, N. Y.

September 5, 1866.

LIST OF ILLUSTRATIONS.

CONTENTS.

THREE YEARS IN THE SIXTH CORPS.

CHAPTER I.

A NEW REGIMENT GOES TO THE WAR.

Organization of the Seventy-seventh N. Y. V. — Departure from Saratoga — Greetings by the way — New emotions — The noble dead — On board the Knickerbocker — At New York — Presentation of flags — Beauties of monopoly — Hospitality of Philadelphia — Incidents on the route — Arrival at Washington — In camp.

OUR regiment was organized at Saratoga Springs, the historic scene of the battle of Bemis Heights and the surrender of Burgoyne — hence its name, "The Bemis Heights Battalion." Hon. Jas. B. McKean, then member of congress, a gentleman of well known patriotism, was made our Colonel. We left our rendezvous on the 26th of November, 1861, Thanksgiving day, having been mustered into the United States service three days before.

As the long train of cars bore us from the station at Saratoga Springs, the thousands who had gathered to witness our departure united in cheer after cheer until all the groves and vales of that charming resort rang with the echoes of the tumultuous shouting.

The thousand brave fellows, who were about to try the stern realities of war, were by no means backward in replying to these hearty expressions of good wishes. Long after we had lost sight of the lovely village, the shouts of the multitude could be heard and the hills rang

1

again with the responding cheers of those in the cars. At each station, as we passed, crowds of people pressed to greet us, and loud and long were the cheers that bade us " God speed."

We were now fairly off for the war. We who had followed the various peaceful avocations of life, in the professions or in the workshops, in trade or in husbandry, had now turned away from the office, the desk, the shop and the plough, to join the Grand Army upon which the hopes of the nation were staked, and which we confidently believed was soon to sweep the rebellion to destruction.

Emotions hitherto unknown to us filled our hearts. We were soldiers, wearing for the first time the army blue, and perhaps soon to be called out to meet in deadly strife an enemy whose prestige for valor was already too well established.

Were we to return to the friends from whom we had just parted, bearing the chaplet of victory, or were we to find a last resting place on some field of the south, never again to meet with wife or sister, father or mother ? Four years have passed and those doubts have been solved. Many of those brave men have gone to their long rest.

" Their graves are severed far and wide."

Some sleep beneath the tall pines of Yorktown; and the bright azalia casts its purple blossoms over the graves of many who lie in the swamps of the Chickahominy. The Antietam murmurs a requiem to those who rest on its banks, and green is the turf above the noble ones who fell gloriously at Fredericksburgh. Some rest amid the wild tangles of the Wilderness, and upon the arid plain of Coal Harbor. Many of their graves are upon the banks of the Ny and the Po. The marble monument at Fort Stevens tells the names of some who gave their lives in the defense of the Capital, while the simple headboards of pine tell where repose many in the valley of the Shenandoah, and before Petersburgh. The remains of some have been brought back to the peaceful cemetery at home to rest beside the dust of loved ones.

> "'Tis little; but it looks in truth
> As if the quiet bones were blest
> Among familiar names to rest,
> And in the places of their youth."

Must it be said, many of the strongest yielded to the grim monster starvation in the rebel prison pens, and found relief from their tortures in lowly graves at Andersonville and Salisbury.

A little band, with bronzed faces and manly hearts, returned home. Their glorious and unspotted record had preceded them. They needed no song of victory, and they desired no greater marks of honor than their simple silver crosses, the badge of their corps.

No incident worthy of note occurred until we reached Albany, where we left the cars and embarked upon the steamer Knickerbocker, an old dismantled craft, unfit for any purpose but the transportation of soldiers; whose decks were covered with mud an inch in depth, and whose doors having been thrown overboard, a free circulation of the rough November air was allowed in every part. The men had no rations, and some of them became clamorous; but order was soon restored, and rations of bread and ham with coffee were distributed. They could not, however, all be brought to a perfect state of quietude. Some were determined not to submit, and passed the night in carousal, while those soberly inclined tried in vain to sleep. The officers found lodging in the after cabin, where some in berths and some on the floor, we passed a restless night.

As we approached New York in the morning, the sky was hung with heavy clouds, and as we left our rickety old craft for *terra firma*, the rain poured in fresh torrents

upon us. We marched through 14th street and Broadway
to the Park. We were to remain in New York until six
o'clock in the evening, and the Sons of Saratoga were to
present us with a stand of colors and guidons. They commenced by presenting us with an excellent dinner, at which
speeches were made by the committee, and responded to
by Colonel McKean and others on our part.

Dinner over, the regiment was drawn up in front of the
City Hall, where the ceremony of presenting the flags
took place. The banner was an exquisite piece of work,
of the richest fabric; a blue ground with elegant designs
in oil. On one side was represented an engagement in
which the American soldiers, led by Washington, were
fighting under the old flag — thirteen stripes and the
union jack. On the reverse was pictured the surrender
of Burgoyne, at Saratoga, under the new flag — the stars
and stripes — first unfurled in the goodly city of Albany,
and first baptized in blood at the decisive battle of Bemis
Heights, which resulted in the surrender of Burgoyne and
the virtual success of the Revolution.

We had already a beautiful national flag, the gift of the
patriotic young ladies of Mr. Beecher's seminary, at Saratoga.

The hour for departure arrived, and we crossed to
Amboy by ferry. We were in New Jersey. We had
heard disparaging things of the railroad management of
this State, but we were now to realize the beauties
of monopoly. We learned afterwards to respect New
Jersey's soldiers, many of whom fought shoulder to
shoulder with us, and were among the bravest of the
brave, but we never forgave her railroads. The men were
crowded into a number of shaky old cars, reeking with
filth, and redolent of most noisome odors. It was in vain
that we protested that these vehicles were unfit for transporting men; we were offered by the agent of the road

the alternative to take these cars or remain where we were. We concluded to go on.

At four o'clock we had passed over the whole of the Camden and Amboy road. Another ferry crossed, and we were in Philadelphia. Glorious, generous, enlightened Philadelphia! Many of our men were sick when we left Saratoga, and the unaccustomed hardships, with the cold and rain thus far on the route, had greatly prostrated them. Many others had also been seized with violent illness, so that our single medical officer had been taxed beyond his strength in looking after the wants of the sick, while the little case of medicines with which we started from Saratoga was exhausted. Among the first acts of kindness of these excellent people was the care of our sick. A gentleman, with countenance beaming with benevolence, said to the doctor, "If you will get your sick together, we will conduct them to comfortable quarters, and see that they are well cared for." The heart of the surgeon leaped with joy at finding some one who could and would help to care for the poor fellows.

The sick being collected, our friend mounted a barrel and called to the soldiers to hear him a moment. "You are welcome," said he, "to Philadelphia, and to show you that we are glad to see you, it gives us pleasure to invite every man of you to partake of a warm breakfast which will be ready for you in a few minutes." This speech was greeted by three hearty cheers for Philadelphia.

The doctor soon had his sick removed to the Soldiers' Retreat, a place fitted up by the noble-hearted people of Philadelphia for the entertainment of soldiers passing through their city. The upper part of the building was arranged with exquisite taste and order for a hospital. Here were many sick men left by the various regiments which had passed through the city. Our sick boys were placed in beds, with expressions of gratitude that, notwithstanding their illness, their lot had fallen in pleasant places.

Presently the men were marched into the long saloon, where all took their places at the well spread tables. The repast being over, Colonel McKean called upon the men for three cheers for the Philadelphians; remarking that there need be no fear of raising the roof, for even should such an accident occur he doubted not these generous people would willingly replace it. Then came the cheers; and such cheers! only to be surpassed by the three more and then three more that followed.

The long years of our campaignings never diminished the lively feelings of gratitude we experienced that morning, and to this day our veterans never speak of Philadelphia but with pleasing recollections of the friendly reception given them by the goodly inhabitants of the Quaker city.

The sun was up when we resumed our journey, and again we were met with surprises. All along the track of the railroad, men, women and children, filling the windows of the houses and thronging the wayside, cheered us on our way, shouting and waving flags and handkerchiefs. Children in the arms of their nurses waved little flags from the windows in great glee, while gray haired old men in piping tones cried "God bless our soldiers." This unlooked for, and to us surprising ovation continued until we had passed the limits of the city, and indeed did not cease till we had left the station many miles behind. In the train, the men kept up a continuous cheering; tears stood in the eyes of many, and the most enthusiastic expressions passed from lip to lip.

The experience of our regiment was only that of others who passed through this noble city, and often during our long campaigns, the soldiers of different regiments would gather round their camp fires, and relate to each other the kindnesses received by them in the City of Brotherly Love.

We were cordially welcomed in Delaware, the people waving banners and handkerchiefs, and when those were not at hand, newspapers or even articles from the clothes lines answered to show their good will; and the negroes in the fields swung their hats and their hoes with great spirit.

We reached Baltimore in the evening, where we were kindly received, furnished with supper and sent on our way. After many delays we reached Washington at four o'clock Sunday morning, and were assigned to temporary quarters near the station. Who would have suspected that it was the Sabbath? Now we began to see something of the circumstance of war. Horsemen were galloping in every direction; long trains of army wagons rattled over the pavements at every turn of the eye; squads of soldiers marched here and there; all was hurry, bustle and confusion.

It was night when we reached the ground for our encampment on Meridian Hill. The men had suffered much from cold, and what at that time was hardship. Not less than a hundred of them were sick. It was not long before tents were up, and for the first time the regiment was under canvas.

Our camp was pleasantly located, commanding a fine view of Washington, the Potomac, Alexandria and other points of interest. We were surrounded by the camps of other regiments, some arriving and some departing almost daily. We had not been two days here when we began to get a taste of camp rumors. One rumor declared that we were to have barracks erected, and we were to go into winter quarters, while another assured us that we were to have an immediate taste of actual warfare. These proved quite as reliable as the thousands of rumors which during all our years of service were afloat throughout the army, and acquired the expressive appellation of " Camp Yarns."

CHAPTER II.

Meridian Hill — Neighboring scenery — First Sunday in camp — Drills — Sickness — The Hospital — General Casey — "Why don't the army move?" — Washington blockaded — Burnside's heroes — Orders to move — Something of a train — Smith's division — Our first reconnoissance.

WE encamped on Meridian Hill December 1st, 1861, with 960 men.

Meridian Hill is the most delightful locality in the vicinity of Washington. The plain on which the city stands, extends northward from the Potomac about two miles where it is abruptly terminated by a line of hills. From the summit of these hills stretches back another plain, at an elevation of one or two hundred feet above the first. Along the margin of these eminences were some fine old suburban mansions. On our right towards Georgetown, was Kalorama, a charming spot, once the residence of Joel Barlow, the author of the famous poems "Hasty Pudding" and "The Columbiad." Now the building was converted by the government into a hospital. In close neighborhood to us was Columbia College, also used as a hospital, and to the east was the fine mansion of Colonel Stone, and other superb places, all of which, like Kalorama and the college, were full of sick men.

Meridian Hill was in the center of this line of once beautiful country residences, directly north of the President's house. It had been the residence of Commodore Porter, and the house still bore the name of "the Porter Mansion." The grounds had been elegantly laid out with box and juniper, while the rich groves of oak and chestnut surrounding lent additional charms to the locality. The hill was dotted with the white tents of a dozen regiments, but none were so pleasantly located as our own, under the shadow of those grand old trees.

The mansion itself became our hospital, and for a time also served as our head-quarters. From its broad piazza we could look upon the busy scenes of the city, and watch the vessels passing up and down upon the river. A week had passed before we were fairly established in our quarters, but we rapidly learned the mysteries of the soldier's life.

The weather was delightful; more like September than what we were accustomed to experience in December. Although heavy mists hung over us until nine or ten o'clock in the morning, they were dispelled by the warm sunshine, and then all was bright as midsummer. This lovely weather continued until about the first of January.

The country in rear of our encampment was charming. Fine groves, traversed by streams of pure, sweet water, and fields surrounded by hedges, stretched far to the northward. The dark green leaves of the magnolia were to be seen here and there among trees of larger growth, and the shining, ever-green laurel forming a dense undergrowth, gave the woods a lively and spring-like appearance. On the open plain might any day be seen a regiment of Lancers, wheeling and charging in their brilliant evolutions, their long lances with bright red pennons adding greatly to the beauty of the display, and, as we at that time vainly believed, to the efficacy of the troop.

The first Sunday came, and we had religious services. The regiment was formed in front of the mansion, every man being called out, unless on duty or excused on account of illness. This became an established rule with us for all time; every man was required to attend divine service

2

unless especially excused.   Chaplain Tully and the members of the staff occupied the piazza.   The chaplain offered
a prayer for the loved ones at home, and then we all sung
"Coronation," and after the sermon, we sung "Cambridge"
and "Old Hundred."   The men seemed deeply affected by
the simple service, and many a quivering lip betrayed the
emotions of the heart.

Drills became the order of the day.   Every morning
the hill rang from one end to the other with the sharp
commands of the company officers to "Order arms!"
"Shoulder arms!" as the men exercised by squads.
Besides the regular drill in the manual of arms, some of
the companies delighted in that system of military gym-
nastics called the bayonet exercise.   In the afternoon
Colonel McKean usually trained the regiment in the more
difficult exercises of the battalion drill.

But we began to feel the scourge of new regiments.
Disease became almost universal.   We had but a single
medical officer and he was tasked beyond his strength.
One hundred and fifty or two hundred men were pre-
scribed for every morning, aside from those so ill as to be
in the hospital.

The large parlors of the old mansion were neatly fitted
up for our hospital, for which they were admirably adapted.
The two principal wards were the large front parlors,
which communicated by folding doors; the ceilings were
high, and the large open fire places in either apartment
served the double purpose of supplying heat and ventila-
tion, so that while about fifty beds were always occupied,
the air was kept fresh and pure.   Typhoid fevers, typhoid
pneumonias, diphtheria, and remittent fevers were preva-
lent, while now and then the malaria manifested itself in
the form of the terrible spotted fever.   Besides, as usually
occurs when the last named disease prevails in camps,
some died suddenly from unknown causes.

By the tenth of the month the majority of the men were unfit for duty. In one company the three commissioned officers were in the hospital, and but twelve men could be mustered for evening parade. The labors of the medical officer who undertakes single-handed to minister to the wants of a regiment of recruits can only be known to those who have tried it. Our doctor was as much worn out by the perplexities of organizing his department as by the actual attendance on the sick. New demands came almost every hour of the day and night, and it was only when the violence of disease had subsided, and another officer was added to the medical staff, that our weary son of Galen found a degree of respite.

We were in the command of General Silas Casey, a noble specimen of a man and a soldier. His manly dignity and kindly bearing impressed all with profound respect for him, and although we were but a few weeks in his command we never ceased to remember him with pleasure. The provisional brigade and division to which we were attached was frequently reviewed and drilled by the general, and made a fine appearance.

Thus the time passed until the opening of the New Year. Our men, like most fresh soldiers, were anxious for a fight, and were heartily tired of what they considered inglorious inactivity. Many of them expressed great fears that they would be obliged to return home without ever hearing the sound of battle. How greatly they were mistaken we shall see as we trace the bloody campaigns of more than three years of hard fighting.

Our friends at home were not unmindful of us. Boxes of clothing and other comforts for the sick were sent in goodly numbers; so our sick were well supplied with bedding and changes of clothing, as well as jellies and other luxuries. Our friend, McMicheal, of Congress Hall, Saratoga, thinking we could better celebrate the New

Year with a good dinner, sent us one worthy of his fame as a landlord. Could Mack have heard the cheers of the boys that made the ground tremble as the four hundred pounds of cooked chickens and turkeys were distributed among them, his glory as a caterer would have been complete. With the New Year came stormy weather; rain was the rule, sunshine the exception. The mud became almost unfathomable and it was not uncommon to see the six mules attached to an army wagon tugging and striving with all their power to drag the empty wagon out of a mud hole. Boys who had plied the trade of bootblack gave up their profession and with pail and sponge in hand called to the passer by, " Wash your boots, sir ?" During the lovely month of December we had been impatient for action; but now the oft repeated question, " Why don't the Army of the Potomac move?" became ludicrous to our ears.

Thus passed another month in drills and camp duties. Some recruits came to us, while many of the men who came out at first were found unfit for field duty and were discharged.

Distrust arose among officers and enlisted men of our army about the capital, in regard to the manner in which the army was managed. A wilderness of men surrounded Washington, and yet we were blockaded by the rebels on all sides except one.

Government was paying enormous prices for fuel consumed by the army, because the Potomac was closed, and all wood had to be brought by rail from the sparsely wooded districts of Maryland. Provisions sold at fabulous prices, and Washington was in fact a beleagured city. Some rays of light from the west penetrated the thick darkness; but it cannot be concealed that while the Grand Army stationed about the capital panted for action and longed for the glory of the battle-field, a gloom possessed the spirits of the men, and a feeling, that all this splendid material was destined to a "masterly inactivity," prevailed. Our hopes were newly kindled when the affairs of the War Department passed into the hands of a live man, and when Mr. Stanton's practical energy began to be manifested both in the department and in the field. We heard from Burnside; first sad news, and then of success; and our hearts burned to be with him. Fort Donelson followed Roanoke; and Price's army was routed in Missouri. We envied the men who had been our nearest neighbors, but who had followed Burnside to the South. Glorious fellows! What cared they now for the fury of the waves or the hardships of short rations? We were afraid of being left as idle spectators of great things in which we should not be allowed to participate.

On the 15th of February came an order for us to move in a few days, and join Smith's division. This division lay upon the other side of the river, and although we had been anxious to move we did not wish to get permanently fixed in the mud by moving there. We knew little of General Smith or his division, only that the general had been trying very hard for some time past to get the regiment, and we had little hopes of good from the new arrangement. How little did we then suppose that the cross of that old division would be one of the proudest badges of honor that men could wear!

Sunday night came, and the order to move at once, came also. What a scene of confusion! We had never broken up camp before, and the excitement ran high. The pounding and tearing of boards, the shouting of men and braying of mules, combined in a grand uproar. Bonfires blazed from every part of the camp, and the whole night was spent in tearing down quarters and loading the stuff into army wagons as they presented themselves in great numbers. It was a rare sight. The camp glowing with a hundred fires, and the men and teams moving about among them like spectres. Morning came, and the teams were loaded, and the men ready to march. The teams drove out and formed a line reaching down 14th street from our camp nearly to the White House! One hundred and five six-mule teams constituted the train for our regimental baggage; and so much dissatisfaction prevailed among certain company officers that we were allowed twenty-five more teams next day! Rain had fallen nearly all night, and the prospect looked dreary. As the day advanced the rain came faster and faster, until it fairly poured. The men waded through mortar nearly to their knees.

It was three o'clock in the afternoon when we reached Smith's division and the ground on which we were to make our camp. The prospect was not cheering, and as two or three of our staff officers rode upon the ground, the place seemed forbidding enough. It had been recently the location of a thicket of scrub pines, but the trees had been cut down for fuel, and the stumps and brush remained, so that the mounted officers found much difficulty in reining their horses into the midst. Snow covered the ground to the depth of several inches. Here our men, tired and wet, cold and hungry, were to pitch their tents, cook their suppers, and make their beds.

The men fell to work heartily, and by dark they had cleared off the snow and brush enough to make room for their tents, and many cook fires blazed over the camp.

The regiments of the division showed us much hospitality, and a very pleasant acquaintance commenced on that day, which was destined to become earnest friendship. The next day was spent in putting the camp in order. As rain continued to fall, the mud in the company streets became knee-deep. Our sick, those unable to walk, had been left in our old hospital with a sufficient number of faithful nurses, under charge of the surgeon of one of the regiments that remained.

Let us for a moment glance at the composition of the division of which we now formed a part. We were assigned to the Third brigade. It comprised, beside our own, the Thirty-third New York, Colonel Taylor, a regiment whose gallantry at Yorktown, Williamsburgh and Fredricksburgh fully established its reputation as one of the best fighting regiments in the army. The Forty-ninth New York, Colonel Bidwell, a noble regiment with a noble commander, a regiment which could always be counted on to do all that men could do; the Seventh Maine, Colonel Mason, whose men were patterned after the pines of their own forests, tall, straight and powerful fellows, who never forgot their proclivities for hunting, and who were never so happy as when they could pick off a few rebel pickets with their rifles. The brigade was commanded by General Davidson, who afterwards made himself exceedingly disagreeable to the rebels, and famous at the north by his daring cavalry raids in the west. The first brigade included the Forty-third New York, Colonel Vinton; the Forty-ninth Pennsylvania, Colonel Irwin; the Sixth Maine, Colonel Knowles; and the Fifth Wisconsin, Colonel Cobb; all of them excellent regiments, under command of General Hancock, who has since placed his name high on the roll of fame as the commander of the old Second corps.

The Second brigade was composed entirely of Vermont troops, including the Second, Third, Fourth, Fifth and Sixth Vermont regiments, commanded respectively by Colonels Henry Whiting, B. N. Hyde, E. H. Stoughton, L. A. Grant and N. M. Lord, and known as the "Vermont Brigade," and nobly did they sustain the traditional reputation of the Green Mountain Boys, as stern patriots and hard fighters. They were commanded by General Brooks, who afterward commanded the Tenth corps.

General William F. Smith, or, as he was familiarly

known, "Baldy Smith," commanded the division. He is too well known to all who admire a true soldier to require more than a mention here, and his great fame has been well and faithfully earned.

No more splendid material, either for officers or men, ever entered into the composition of a division, and how nobly it played its part in the great drama of the war, it shall be part of our duty to record. Drills, regimental, brigade and division, were again in order, and picket duty now became a part of our routine.

This would not be a faithful chronicle of the doings of the new regiment, were we to forget to relate the history of our first expedition into the enemy's country.

An order came one evening in February for Colonel McKean to take his regiment and make a reconnoissance towards Vienna. His instructions were to pass the picket line, advance towards Vienna, make a thorough reconnoissance and return.

The news spread through the camp, and the regiment was ablaze with excitement. Some who had been on the sick list, and were excused from camp duty, sought from the surgeon permission to accompany the expedition, while a few who had been, up to this time, well, were earnest in their applications to be excused from the march.

The regiment was formed at ten o'clock at night; thick darkness, darkness of the blackest and most intense degree, prevailed. One could scarcely see his neighbor whose shoulder touched his own. We were miles away from the enemy, but the men were to be instructed in performing their movements in secresy; so the commands were passed along the line, as the companies were form-ing, in whisper. No lights were allowed, and we left our camp a column of blackness. We were presently joined by a guide who carried a lantern. We passed a great many regiments, all the while observing strict silence.

The mud was deep, very deep ; some of the men lost their shoes in the depths of the mire, and some even lost themselves, and were only discovered when they arrived in camp some hours earlier than the regiment. Through the darkness we plodded until we reached our destination, at daylight on the following morning. Here we found bough houses which had been used by rebel cavalry; and the tracks of many horses imprinted only a little while before, whether by the horses of our own cavalry; or by those of the enemy, we never knew. The battalion was halted and scouts were sent to the front and on the flanks. Some of the boys who had lost their shoes in the mud before we had advanced the first mile, had made the whole march in their stockings; while others, who had been sick, looked as though they could never get back to camp. The companies deployed and marched through the woods, but as the enemy was on the other side of Vienna we saw no rebels. It was noon when we reached our camp, tired and covered with mud. Those who went laughed at those who remained behind, and called them "dead beats!" The "beats" tauntingly demanded of the others what all their demonstration had amounted to.

The New York papers heralded the exploit as a grand advance on the enemy, and we said little about it.

3

CHAPTER III.

THE MANASSAS CAMPAIGN.

Orders to march — A grand spectacle — Bivouac near Fairfax Court House — The camps at night — Visits to Manassas and Centreville — Dissatisfaction in the army — A deserted country — Lawless soldiers — Fairfax Court House — A representative Southerner — Review by Gen. McClellan — March to Alexandria — "Camp Misery."

THE first week in March brought lovely weather: birds sang more sweetly, the sun shone more brightly, and bands played more merrily than usual, and friends passed from regiment to regiment seeking social pastime with friends.

We had known no such pleasant times in camp; still we were waiting for orders to advance. During the night of Sunday, the 8th of March, the order came: " This division will move at four o'clock in the morning with two days' rations in haversacks." Little rest we got that night; the hammer and the axe were plied vigorously in tearing down quarters and packing stores, and as the sun rose in the morning the whole army was in motion. It was a sublime spectacle: that immense line of troops pouring along hour after hour, stretching over the hills as far as the eye could reach; a hundred and twenty thousand troops on the move! Just beyond and above them, in the gray sky of the morning, hung a beautiful rainbow. At six our division commenced to march. Rain soon began to fall, and continued all day. We passed through Vienna and Lewinsville, each a hamlet of a dozen houses, and reached our camping ground at five o'clock in the afternoon, tired, and drenched, and hungry.

Great numbers of troops had already occupied the fields, and the whole country seemed alive with men and horses, artillery and wagons. We were in the vicinity of Fairfax Court House, about a mile to the northward, on what was called Flint Hill.

The army, for the first time, was under "*tentes d'abri*," or, as they are now called, shelter tents. Until now the enlisted men had occupied the spacious Sibley, or the comfortable wedge tents, and all officers were quartered in wall tents; now, line officers and enlisted men were to occupy shelter tents, which they were to carry on their shoulders; and although a small number of wall tents could be carried in the wagons for field and staff officers, yet so imperfect was the understanding, in or out of the quartermaster's department, of what could or ought to be done, that most regimental field and staff officers were left without any shelter at all.

The men proceeded to make themselves as comfortable as possible under their novel coverings, and as evening approached, the hills were magnificently illuminated with thousands of camp fires. Very few men occupied their new tents that night. They had not been accustomed to lie upon wet ground, with only a single blanket wrapped about them, so during all the night groups of soldiers stood about the camp fires, talking in low tones and wondering what was to happen in the morning. The sky was clear and bright when the sun rose, and as we looked out upon the hill tops, dotted with clean white tents, and bristling with stacks of shining muskets, we exulted in the thought that we were part of the Grand Army that was now at work. Soon we knew that we were not to fight here. The cavalry, and some of Porter's division, were returning from Manassas and Centreville, both places burned and deserted. Were we to pursue the retreating army, or were we to return to Washington to take a new start ? Parties from the division rode to Centreville and Manassas. The works were indeed formidable and the barracks extensive; and the old chestnut logs with blackened ends, that were mounted in some of the embrasures, had, at a distance, grim visages. The smoking ruins betokened the destructiveness of war. On the old battlefield lay bleaching the bones of horses and men, and here and there might be seen portions of human skeletons protruding from the shallow graves where some pretense had been made at burial. Fragments of shells, broken muskets and solid shot strewed the ground.

Head-quarters of the army were established at Fairfax Court House, and thither repaired the corps commanders to hold a council in regard to our future movements. The country about our camp was rolling and sparsely settled. Nearly all the houses were deserted, and most of them destroyed so far as any future usefulness was concerned. One house, the ruins of which stood not far from our camp, and which had been the most comfortable place in the whole section of country, had been the residence of a northern farmer. Although the house was completely stripped, and nothing of the barns and outhouses remained but the frames, yet there were many evidences of the thrift and comfort of the former occupant. A northern reaper, several horse rakes, ploughs of improved patterns, and other modern implements of agriculture, betokened a genuine farmer. We were told that he was driven from his home early in the war, and had now found refuge among his friends in New Hampshire. But the houses of the southerners had not been exempt from the general devastation, and some who had sought refuge in Richmond had left their homes to ruin. The people were evidently strongly " secesh," although some of them professed to be glad to see us.

It cannot be said that the presence of our army afforded

them great protection, for the men, unused to the strict discipline which afterward prevailed, coolly appropriated whatever articles seemed to them to be of use either for the present or the future.   It was amusing to see the soldiers of some of the divisions in which less than the usual discipline prevailed, peering and creeping about wherever there seemed a prospect of plunder.   Now one would pass with a pair of chickens; next, one bringing a clothes line; then one with part of an old table, and still another with half a dozen eggs.   This system of plunder was at length checked, in a measure at least.   Fowls, eggs and potatoes could be purchased of the people at fair rates, while rebel currency could be bought for silver at a very considerable discount.   Twenty-five cent and one cent shinplasters were brought into camp and laughed at by men who were afterward glad to get shinplasters from another manufactory.

To Fairfax Court House was but a short distance; and a ride to the village afforded a pleasant gallop of a morning. The place, and the country half a mile on each side, was occupied by McCall's division.   The village was pleasantly located on high ground, surrounded by fine groves. It contained some pretty residences, which were occupied by officers as head-quarters: their horses, in some instances, being picketed on the porticos, and in others in the kitchens.   The village was nearly deserted by its own people, not more than fifty of the original inhabitants being left, though the population of the town before the war was nearly six hundred.   Houses which were deserted were generally stripped of everything.   The court house was a solid old brick building of very limited dimensions, with a little bell swinging in a comical looking steeple. The court house was by no means an exception to the general rule of destruction; the seats were torn out, and the judge's bench had been split in pieces, and nearly all carried away by pockets full, as relics.   At one of the houses where the family still remained, a party reined up and made some inquiries of the *pater familias*, a hang-dog looking specimen, with an old slouched hat covered to the crown with rusty crape, a mark of second-hand gentility in these parts. He said that "this yer war" had caused such a famine among the people, that nearly all of them had been obliged to leave; some had gone to Washington and some to Richmond, "a right smart lot of them had gone to Richmond." He had "reckoned onct or twict" that he would have to go too, but he "had succeeded in hanging on so long."

Our division was reviewed by General McClellan, who was received with enthusiasm. Although many of us were familiar with the appearance of the Commander-in-Chief, this was his first appearance to us as a division. The General appeared a man below the medium height, with broad shoulders, full chest and a round pleasing face relieved by a heavy moustache. He sat his horse well and rode with great speed. While his appearance and address were pleasing, there seemed in his smooth face and mild eye nothing to indicate a man of brilliant genius or great purpose.

At length the council of corps commanders had rendered its decision, and the grand campaign of the Virginian Peninsula was planned. On the morning of the fourteenth of March, with buoyant hopes and exulting antici-pations of a "quick, sharp and decisive," and as we devoutly believed, a successful campaign, we left our camp at Flint Hill. It had few charms for us, and we were glad to leave it. How little we yet knew of real campaigning. Although we had notice several hours beforehand that we were to move by daylight, yet many, indeed, the majority of us, marched that morning without breakfast.

No morning sun cheered us as the day began, but the sky was hung with heavy clouds. A drizzling rain, now diminishing almost to a heavy mist, and now coming in fresh showers, made the marching heavy and unpleasant. Grandly appeared that majestic army as it filed down the turnpike to Alexandria. At times the elevation of the road afforded a view of the mighty column for miles to the front, and at other times we could see it pouring onward an endless stream of cavalry, infantry, artillery and wagons, far from the rear.

So grand a spectacle had never been witnessed on this continent before. Our march was rapid and we made no halt for dinner: those who went without breakfast had poor chance for coffee that day.

Towards evening the rain increased, and as we drew off into a piece of woods five miles out from Alexandria, the rain came down in sheets. Near our halting place were some deserted houses. No sooner had we stopped than began the work of destruction, afterward so familiar to us, and in less than an hour there was not a board or timber left of either building. The ground, although quite uneven and sloping, soon became so flooded that tents, even when they could be pitched, were untenable. The men attempted to build fires, but in most instances the floods of water quenched the flames. Some, however, succeeded in starting huge fires, and around these stood the men during the whole night, while the tempest poured in torrents upon them. A few of the officers of the division, among whom was one who afterward became noted for looking out for and providing good things for his regiment as quartermaster, sought refuge in a house not far off, where, for the moderate sum of twenty-five cents each, they were allowed by the people sleeping room upon the floor. Never since the times of Pharaoh was an army so thoroughly drenched. During more than three years campaigning in the field our boys never forgot that night; and to this day they frequently refer to the disagreeable experience in what they not inappropriately term " Camp Misery."   Here, in " Camp Misery," we remained several days, waiting to embark for Fortress Monroe.

Without doubt, the rebels all this time knew of our destination; for the people among whom we were encamped were by no means our friends or indifferent to the success of the rebels, and the point of our destination was well known and freely spoken of among them.

CHAPTER IV.

THE ARMY TRANSFERRED TO THE PENINSULA.

Embarking for the Peninsula — Mount Vernon — On the Potomac — Hampton — In camp — Orders to march — A night visit to Fortress Monroe — The advance — A sifting — A Quaker battery — At Newport News — Compliments of the Teaser.

On Sunday morning, March 23d, we marched to Alexandria. The whole of our division, and of the other divisions of Keyes' corps, were there, besides part of Heintzelman's corps and other troops. In the course of the afternoon, this great body of men was embarked upon the transports. The vessels having received their lading, swung out upon the river and laid at anchor during the night. Early in the morning the whole fleet was under way, steaming down the river. We passed Mount Vernon — the bells of the fleet tolling. The tomb lies in the midst of a clump of firs just south and a little below the house; the mansion and the grounds are nearly as they were left by Washington, and the whole looks down upon the river, calling upon the passer-by for a thought upon the great man whose dust lies beneath the fir trees. After passing Mount Vernon, nothing of special interest was seen except the broad expanse of waters of this magnificent stream. A few large mansions, a few inferior houses, and now and then a little hamlet, appeared on the banks; and at Aquia creek could be seen the insignificant earthworks that had covered the few field pieces which for so many months had kept up an efficient blockade of the Potomac.

How different was all this from our Hudson! The country bordering on the river is beautiful; nature has done everything for it, but a cursed institution has blighted it. There is not a country in the world where nature has been more lavish with its blessings, and yet it is forsaken, worn out, almost a wilderness. The magnificent rivers and unsurpassed harbors of Virginia, its natural fertility and the mildness of its climate, present natural advantages scarcely equaled by any country. As we stood upon the deck of the steamer, watching and admiring the ever-varying beauties of the noble stream, some one repeated these lines from Barlow's *Columbiad:*

> "Thy capes, Virginia, towering from the tide,
> Raise their blue banks, and slope thy barriers wide,
> To future sails unfold a fluvian way,
> And guard secure thy multifluvian bay,
> That drains uncounted realms and here unites
> The liquid mass from Alleganian hights.
> York leads his way embanked in flowery pride,
> And noble James falls winding by his side;
> Back to the hills, through many a silent vale,
> Wild Rappahannock seems to lure the sail ;
> Patapsco's bosom courts the hand of toil ;
> Dull Susquehanna laves a length of soil;
> But mightier far, in sea-like azure spread,
> Potowmac sweeps his earth disparting bed."

At night we were on the broad Chesapeake. A stiff breeze set our fleet rocking, but we slept quietly, leaving the waves to take care of themselves and the pilots to take care of the boats Reveille awoke us in the morning to discover on the one side of us the world-renowned Fortress Monroe and on the other the equally famous Monitor. At our bow lay the village of Hampton — or rather the chimneys and trees of what had been Hampton. Orders came for us to disembark here, and we were soon among the debris of the town. A sadder commentary on war could hardly be found than the ruins of this beautiful village. A forest of shade trees and chimneys marked the place where a few months before had stood one of the most ancient villages in America. Hyacinths and daffodils, peach trees and roses, were in bloom in the deserted and fenceless gardens; and the dark green leaves of the japonica and laurel covered many a heap of unsightly rubbish.

The walls of the old church, the most ancient in the State, stood like silent witnesses against the reckless spirit of destruction of the rebels. Although not large, the church had evidently been a fine old structure, having the form of a Greek cross. About it were the graves of the forefathers of the village, reposing under the shadow of those old trees. Many of the tablets were ancient, dating back as far as 1706.

THE OLD CHURCH AT HAMPTON.

The whole army was pouring out upon this shore, and at Fortress Monroe. Dense masses of infantry, long trains of artillery and thousands of cavalry, with unnumbered army wagons and mules, were mingled in grand confusion along the shore; the neighing of horses, the braying of mules, the rattle of wagons and artillery, and

the sound of many voices, mingled in one grand inhar-
monious concert.

Our division marched along a pleasant route to a field
about midway between Fortress Monroe and Newport
News. We rested until March 26th, when an order came
at midnight for the army to march very early in the morning. We were short of some medical stores and quartermasters' supplies, and officers at once mounted their horses
to ride through the thick darkness to Fortress Monroe, to
procure the needed articles. Along the road men were
already cooking their breakfasts, and artillery was hurrying towards Newport News. At short intervals along
the road, sentinels were posted; and as the sounds of the
horses' hoofs were heard, the sharp command rung out
through the darkness, "Halt! who comes there?" and the
galloping horses would suddenly halt at long distance from
the sentry.

"Friends with the countersign."

"Dismount and advance one; and give the countersign."

One of the parties, leaving his horse with the other,
would advance and give the required word, and on we
rode again until suddenly halted by a similar warning.
As we approached the fortress, the sentinels were more
frequent, until, as we came within half a mile of our destination, the guards were posted so frequently that we had
hardly passed one, before the sharp command to "Halt!"
was heard again. We crossed the drawbridge, and at
length found ourselves in the little village in rear of the
fort. Passing here many sentinels who examined us very
carefully, we reached the door of the citadel. Here we
were halted by a sentinel, and each examined for the
countersign. The sentinel called the corporal of the guard;
who after satisfying himself that we were Union officers
shouted to the sergeant. The great iron door ground

upon its massive hinges as it swung open just far enough
to permit the sergeant to squeeze through, and again it
was closed, and the heavy bolts rung as they flew back to
their places. The sergeant, after asking a few questions,
went back into the fort, and soon returned with the officer
of the guard, who, after receiving the countersign, questioned us closely as to our business, and who we were.
Satisfied, at length he ordered a soldier to take our horses,
the heavy door slowly opened, and we were admitted
within the walls. Such were the precautions in admitting
strangers to the stronghold.

At six o'clock the division was in line and on the road.
The morning was indescribably beautiful. The vapors
that rose from the broad expanse of waters were tinged
with a thousand gorgeous hues as they rolled away, dispersed by the morning sun; and the tall yellow pines
were crowned with rich golden coronals of light. The
road was perfectly level and dry, and the country delightful. Long rows of locusts and pines lined the sides of the
road, and the rich groves of oak just sending forth their
foliage, were beautifully interspersed with the holly, with
its bright red berries and rich evergreen leaves. Peach
orchards in full bloom added to the beauty of the scene,
and when at times we could see the lines of troops, two and
three miles in extent, their muskets glittering in the bright
sunlight, the enthusiasm of the men was unbounded.

All the bridges over the route had been destroyed by
the enemy, but pioneers advanced at the head of the
column, and as the bridges were all small they were
quickly repaired. A march of a few miles brought us in
sight of the James river; a noble stream, at least five
miles wide at this point. Not far from the shore appeared
the masts of the U. S. frigate Cumberland, sunk in the
memorable fight with the Merrimac. As our march led
us along the banks, the views were charming. On one

hand was the noble river, and on the other the orchards and groves. Deserted houses, and gardens blooming with hyacinths and other blossoms of early spring, were passed. On the opposite side of the river lay a rebel gunboat, watching our movements.

Our division, Smith's, had taken the lead on the James river road, while Porter's division had marched upon Great Bethel. After a march of fifteen miles, our division was drawn up in line of battle near Warwick. Porter's division had already reached Great Bethel, on our right, and we could see huge columns of smoke rising in that direction, and hear the roar of artillery. An aid dashed up and informed General Davidson that the enemy were in line of battle ready to receive us. Soon the order came to advance; the line swept onward through the woods and over a cleared field, but found no foe. A few cavalry pickets only were seen, and a shell from one of our Parrott guns set them flying towards Yorktown. We passed through the confederate encampments where their fires were still blazing, but soon turned round and bivouacked on ground last night occupied by rebels.

In this advance or reconnoissance of the whole army, the qualities of the individual soldiers composing it were brought out in bold relief. The effect on our own division was marked. During the months we had been in winter quarters, many officers and men had established marvelous reputations for bravery and hardihood, merely by constantly heralding their own heroism. But from this time these doughty heroes went back. Officers suddenly found cause for resigning; and enlisted men managed to get sent to the rear, and never showed their faces at the front again. On the contrary, some who were really invalids insisted on dragging themselves along with the column, fearful that an engagement might take place in which they would not participate. A sifting process was

thus commenced throughout the whole division, and to
its honor the poltroons were very soon sifted out, and from
that time forth, Smith's division never afforded a comfortable resting place for men of doubtful courage. "They
went out from us, because they were not of us."

Next morning we retired over the road upon which we
had advanced, and encamped near Newport News. As
we passed this place on our outward march, we saw at a
distance what appeared to be a heavy gun, but as we
approached it proved to be a large cart, on which was
mounted a great wooden mortar, which had, perhaps,
been used by negroes for cracking corn. When we returned
a hog's head was fixed in the mouth of the mortar.
"There," remarked an officer, "is the first Quaker we have
seen on the Peninsula." "You must sketch it," said the
colonel of the Seventy-seventh, and the officer obeyed.

THE QUAKER AT NEWPORT NEWS.

The division encamped upon a low plain covered with
sedges and reeds, a good enough encampment while the

dry weather lasted, but when the rain came in floods two
nights after we pitched our tents here, the whole division
was inundated, and we moved to higher and better
ground.

The masts of the Cumberland greeted our eyes whenever
we turned toward the river, and the rebel gunboats made
short excursions toward our side of the stream. One day
large numbers of men, mostly from the Vermont brigade,
were on the shoals of the river bathing and gathering
oysters. The gunboat Teazer discovering them, steamed
down toward them, and threw some heavy shells, shrieking and cracking among them, causing great consternation
among the bathers, and some confusion and much amusement on shore.

CHAPTER V.

YORKTOWN.

The advance to Yorktown — A thunder storm — "Reliable contrabands"— Facing the enemy — A strong position — The Union line — A rebel welcome — Digging — On picket — A dreary country — An enterprising planter — Active work — Battle of Lee's Mills — Charge of the Vermont brigade — Progress of the siege — Ravages of disease — A front seat — Short supplies — The rebels withdraw — Entering the strongholds — Infernal machines — March to Williamsburgh — Victims of disease.

At length, on the 4th of April, the army was put in motion for Yorktown. The General-in-Chief had arrived at Fortress Monroe the evening before, and at once the army became the scene of prodigious activity. Keyes' corps, our own division in advance, took the road along the banks of the James river. The rest of the army, headed by Porter's division, advanced on the more direct road to Yorktown, through Great Bethel, accompanied by General McClellan.

The day being clear and warm, the men soon began to realize the difficulty of transporting large amounts of clothing and camp equipage on their shoulders, and the roadsides were strewn with blankets and overcoats, dress coats and pants. The bushes and trees for miles along the route were thickly hung with articles of clothing, mostly new, and all good. Soldiers who had put on their marching suit would fall out of the ranks, the knapsack would quickly disgorge a new coat and pants, the wearers would as quickly divest themselves of the soiled garments and replace them with the new ones, the others being left on the ground. Whenever a halt was ordered this shifting process became general.

5

The roads, which at first were dry and firm, were as we advanced badly cut up, and great difficulty was experienced in getting the trains along.

An advance of ten miles brought us in front of Young's Mills, a strongly fortified position five or six miles from Yorktown. The corps was drawn up in line of battle and cavalry sent to reconnoiter the position. The works were deserted, but camp fires still blazed in them. Here we rested for the night. At daylight next morning the advance was renewed. The roads were even worse than the day before. Infantry could get along well enough, but artillery and army wagons had a hard time of it. Each piece of artillery made the road worse, until the axles dragged in a river of mud. We passed the little village of Warwick Court House. There were here a little brick court house, a jail and a clerk's office seven feet by ten, a store and a tavern. There were also two small dwelling houses.

After a march of three miles the division was drawn up in line of battle. We had reached the hostile works before the rest of the army. Skirmishers were sent to the front and we advanced slowly and cautiously through the woods. A terrific thunder storm burst upon us and the roar of the heavenly artillery seemed to mock any efforts at martial grandeur. Seldom, if ever, had we of the northern states witnessed such an exhibition of sublimity and terrible magnificence of the workings of the elements. The vivid lightning and terrific peals of thunder seemed to the men the presage of deadly work to come. The advance was very difficult, the woods being marshy and filled with tangles and briars. The men were scratched and bleeding. The long line of battle presently emerged from the woods and occupied a clearing, in the center of which was a mansion, the late residence of a rebel officer. Some scouts brought from the house a couple of negresses whom they led to General Keyes. They communicated their information with an earnestness that proved their sympathies were not with their late master. It was a picturesque scene; those tall negresses with their bright red turbans and long white woolen gowns, telling with earnest gestures what they knew of the position of the enemy, while the generals and their staffs listened eagerly to their words. They said that when we passed over the little hill just in front, we should be under fire from the batteries of the rebels, who were in large force; "but laws a massa, noting like all dese yer," said they, pointing to the troops of our division.

Cautiously the clearing was crossed, the long line of battle moving in beautiful order — Kennedy's, Ayres' and Wheeler's batteries each accompanying a brigade.

Again we entered a heavy pine wood in which the swamp was deeper than ever, and advancing through it we came face to face with the enemy. Warwick creek, a marshy stream which had been dammed by the rebels, raising its waters into ponds and deep morasses, was between us and their works, and the accessible points were guarded by artillery. Two regiments were at once deployed as skirmishers and sent in advance, and our batteries were planted along the edge of the wood with the line of the infantry. Only Smith's division was in line, the others were waiting on the road for orders to come up.

Along the road, for more than half the distance back to Young's Mills, the brigades of Couch's and Kearney's divisions were resting on their arms, while cannon by scores waited to be called into action.

The enemy was not slow to acknowledge our presence, and as a token of greeting sent some twelve-pound shells crashing among the trees about us. The firing now became brisk on our side, and the rebels replied spiritedly with their twelve-pounders. Hundreds of men were now called up from the rear brigades and detailed to build corduroy roads. Trees were cut down and trimmed of their branches, and laid side by side so as to form a kind of bridge over the swamp to enable more artillery to come up. The rapidity with which such roads were built was marvelous.

By this time the column on the right had reached the works in front of the town. The position here was also strong. Although the Warwick did not interpose, yet high bluffs, crowned with redoubts in which were mounted heavy guns, frowned upon the assailants. Thus far it appears that the leaders of our army had been totally ignorant of the position and strength of the enemy, and had led it up to the works, blindly feeling the way without maps or guides.* The defensive works were now found to consist of a series of redoubts and rifle pits stretching across the Peninsula, seven miles in extent, with high bluffs on the right and Warwick creek in their front on the left.

The position occupied by our division was known as Lee's Mills, and to our right, nearly three miles, was the village of Yorktown. The line of battle was now arranged in the following order from right to left: Heintzelman's corps, consisting of Porter's, Hooker's and Hamilton's divisions, were in front of the town; Sedgwick's division of Sumner's corps on the left of them, and Keyes' corps, comprising Smith's and Couch's division (Casey's division arrived in a few days), held the position on the Warwick at Lee's Mills.

The position of the enemy was, without doubt, one of great strength, and everything had been done to render it more formidable. Yet they were by no means too

---

* McClellan's Report.

strong or sufficiently well garrisoned to resist an assault from such a body of men as now appeared in their front. That there were weak points in this line of defenses, stretching seven miles, was afterwards demonstrated; and that the forces behind the works were by no means sufficiently numerous, at the time of our approach, to afford formidable resistance at all points in their extensive line, is now well known.

It appears from the official report of the rebel General Johnston, who then commanded all the rebel forces in Virginia, that at the time of the appearance of our army before Yorktown the works were defended by only about eleven thousand men, and that even after he had reinforced the garrisons by the troops which he was hurrying from Manassas, his army amounted to only fifty thousand men.

The artillery duel was kept up until night. We had lost some men during the day, but not so many as we had feared. First a poor fellow from the Seventh Maine, his heart and left lung torn out by a shell; then one from the Forty-ninth New York, shot in the head; the next was from our own regiment, Frank Jeffords, who had to suffer amputation of a leg; then a man from the Forty-ninth was sent to the rear with his heel crushed. In all, our loss did not exceed twenty men. The casualties in the other brigades were less than in our own.

As night approached, the firing gradually ceased, and nothing but the scattering shots of the skirmishers was heard. We lay down in the swamp with no tents, and many of us without food. Officers and men built platforms of logs and bark to keep out of the water where they were not fortunate enough to find a dry place. General Smith bivouacked near the line of battle, making his bed at the foot of a pine tree, with nothing but his overcoat for shelter. It may not be amiss to say here that General Smith, unlike most gentlemen with stars on their shoulders, was always in the habit of sleeping at the very front.

All the following day, and the next, the firing was kept up steadily on both sides. At night showers of cannister and grape would fall in our camp, and fortunate was he who had a good tree or stump between him and the rebel works against which to lay his head while he slept.

We at length became so accustomed to the continual skirmishing, that unless the firing was in fierce volleys we took no notice of it. The boys of the Thirty-third New York being on the skirmish line on the 8th, charged a rifle pit with shouts and hurrahs, and drove the rebels from it. An attempt was made to retake it, but the boys held their ground.

The men performed herculean labors on the roads, and in throwing up earthworks. No rest was allowed. When not on picket they were cutting down trees or throwing up earthworks or building bridges. Such constant labor soon began to exhaust the strength of the stoutest, and hundreds of them yielded to disease who supposed themselves capable of enduring any amount of hardships. Yet there was now and then a grimly gay episode in this hard routine. Here is an incident that occurred two or three days after we approached the works, and affords a good sample of picketing between us and the forts. Our pickets were within speaking distance of those of the enemy; each party kept, if possible, snugly behind some big stump or tree, out of the reach of his disagreeable neighbors. A good deal of hard talk had passed between one of our pickets and one of the "Johnnies." Finally the rebel thrust his hand beyond his tree holding in it a bottle, and shaking it, challenged the Yankee to come and take it—"*crack*" went the Yankee's rifle at the hand. "Ha, ha! why don't you hit it? What do you think of Bull Run?" "How do you like Fort Donelson?" responded the Yankee.

While this colloquy was going on, Yankee number two crept round behind a log, and drawing on the southerner, blazed away at him. The son of chivalry clapped his hand to his shoulder and ran off howling. "There, you fool," shouted Yankee number one, "I told you that blind man would be shooting you pretty soon."

The country about us was uncultivated and unhealthy. The lands were low and swampy, and mostly covered with a heavy growth of yellow pines. The few remaining inhabitants were mostly women, negresses and children; now and then a disabled specimen of poor white trash, or a farmer too infirm to be of service in the rebel army, was to be met with. All were alike destitute of enterprise, and the houses upon the "plantations" were of the meanest order, raised three or four feet above the ground upon posts without the usual foundation of stone. The "plantations" consisted usually of about ten or twenty acres of cleared land in the midst of the forest, with narrow roads among the pines leading to neighboring plantations.

The writer inquired of the proprietor of one of these isolated spots, who also had some forty negro women and children, how he managed to support so large a family from the proceeds of so little land. "Well," said he, "I could not support them from the proceeds of the land alone, but you see I sell a few negroes every year and buy corn with the money; so with what we raise and what we get for the sale of the negroes, we get along very well."

"But why do you not cut down some of this forest and till more land? You own a large tract of land which is entirely worthless as it now is."

"There is where you are greatly mistaken, said the enterprising southerner, my timber land is my best property."

But of what use do you make it? " Oh, I sell a great
deal of wood. I take it to Fortress Monroe and Hampton
and get two dollars and a half a cord for it!"

The reader will perhaps understand the profits drawn
from the wood lands, when it is remembered that Fortress
Monroe was twenty miles distant.

Night attacks by the enemy became common; and it
was not an unfrequent occurrence for the whole division
to be called suddenly to arms at midnight and stand in
line until morning. Skirmishes and sharpshooting continued with little intermission; bullets of rebel riflemen
whizzing through our camps or unceremoniously entering
our tents at all times. Rebel gunboats approached the
mouth of the Warwick and by their assistance the rebel
infantry attempted to turn our left flank, but the troops
of our division gallantly met their attack and drove them
back.

This state of affairs continued until the 16th of April.
That morning, word passed through the division that
we were to make an assault. Orders came to move, and
the division was massed near some ruins, known as " The
Chimneys," in front of one of the rebel forts; the Second
brigade holding the front line, supported by the First and
Third brigades. As we moved round to take our positions, an American eagle whirled above our heads in
elegant circles and at length floated away toward the
south, the boys swinging their hats and cheering the bird
with loud huzzahs.

The fort in our front covered the road from Newport
News to Williamsburgh, and could we get possession
of it we could turn the flanks of the enemy, obliging
him to abandon his position and enabling us either to
prevent his escape or to harass him in his flight. In
front of the fort the creek had been dammed and a deep
morass interposed between us and the works. General

CHARGE OF THE VERMONTERS AT LEE'S MILLS.

McClellan and his immense suite rode to the point from which the attack was to be made, and communicating a few minutes with Generals Keyes and Smith, left the field. Mott's battery was now brought into position on the open plateau and opened a fierce cannonade, to which the rebels replied with spirit, dismounting one of our guns and killing several of the gunners at the very start. Mott was reinforced by Kennedy's and Wheeler's batteries, and the hostile guns were soon silenced. Our batteries then advanced within five hundred yards of the fort, and the gray-coated rebels who were seen to fill the woods, were soon dispersed. Two companies of troops, from the Third Vermont, were now ordered forward. Down from the woods they came, rushed into the water to their waists, and gallantly made for the rebel rifle pits. The first line of the works was gained and then the second. The fort was empty, but a ditch to their left was filled with men. They poured a volley among them and the gray coats fled. Thus the fort was actually in their possession, and was held for some minutes by the noble fellows, but when they looked for support, none came. The three brigades stood upon the opposite bank, ready to plunge through the stream, and waiting with intense anxiety for the order, "forward;" but no order came, and the brave Green Mountain boys who had so nobly performed their part of the work, were forced to fall back under a galling fire from the rebels, who rushed back to their pits as soon the Vermonters had left them, pouring volley after volley into the retreating forces, who, their ammunition spent, could not reply to the rebel fire. Before they were able to reach the shelter of the woods, sad havoc was made in their ranks. Skirmishing was kept up for some hours, by other regiments, but with no result except the loss of men.

The following list of killed and wounded was obtained the next day after the battle:

2d   Vermont — 1 killed.
3d   Vermont — 24 killed, 7 mortally wounded, 56 wounded,
           1 missing.
4th Vermont — 3 killed, 30 wounded.
5th Vermont— 2 killed, 6 wounded.
6th Vermont — 11 killed, 77 wounded.

Total loss to the brigade, 218.

Thus ended the fight known as the "Battle of Lee's Mills," a battle in which two hundred men gallantly captured an important work of the enemy, and thousands of their companions burning with desire to share in their glory stood by and saw them abandon it! Why the other brigades were not ordered forward has never been explained satisfactorily. That General Smith would gladly have sent them forward we earnestly believe; but we now know that General McClellan desired that a general engagement should not be brought on at that time.

The wounded men exhibited the same bravery, while their wounds were being cared for, that characterized their brilliant charge. Men badly mutilated, with bullets in their heads, or breasts, or limbs, refused to receive attention from the surgeon who dressed their wounds, until their more unfortunate companions were cared for. "Don't mind me, doctor, there are others hurt worse than I am," said many a brave fellow, as he lay upon the ground bleeding from his wounds.

The following incident connected with this noble charge will be remembered by all who were at that time members of Smith's division, and by hundreds who saw accounts of it in the newspapers of the day:

Private William Scott, of Company K, Third Vermont, was, in the autumn of 1861, found asleep at his post on the picket line. It was a grave fault; but the weary soldier, inexperienced in the service, and unaccustomed to such night vigils, in an evil hour yielded to the demands of tired nature, little thinking that the lives of hundreds of his comrades were periled by his unfaithfulness. He was tried by a court-martial and sentenced to be shot. The sentence was approved, and at the appointed time he was brought forth to execution. General Smith, desiring to impress upon the minds of his men the terrible consequences of such an offense, formed his troops in line. The culprit was brought out before them, and led to the place of execution. The guard, with loaded muskets, stood ready to execute the dreadful sentence, which was read before all the troops. All waited in breathless expectation for the order to fire; but instead another paper was read. It was a pardon from the President! Then the wildest shouts of joy ran along the line. Shout after shout arose from the division, and hundreds blessed the name of President Lincoln.

There were many circumstances to render this a case of peculiar interest. It was the first sentence of the kind; it was at the beginning of the war, when a soldier's life was regarded of value, and when all eyes were riveted upon the army, and every incident was of interest. It was also the first instance of the kind in which the executive clemency had been exercised. So near had the hour of execution arrived when the President signed the pardon, that, fearing it might not be received in season, he took his carriage and drove to camp, to assure himself that the man's life should be spared.

"I will show President Lincoln that I am not afraid to die for my country," said the grateful soldier; and well did he fulfill his promise. Among the bravest of those two hundred heroes who crossed the swamp at Lee's Mills, was William Scott, of Company K, Third Vermont. But he was brought back a corpse. He had shown the President that he was not afraid to die for his country. He was one of the foremost in the charge, and one of the first to fall. His comrades made his grave under the shadow of the tall pines, and as they folded his blanket around him, and lowered him to his resting place, tears stood upon those brown cheeks; but the tears of sorrow were mingled with tears of joy, when they thought of his glorious death, and his narrow escape from an ignominious fate, and again, in their hearts, they blessed the man who was always the soldier's friend.

We resumed our place the next day after the battle, on the front line, and commenced digging.

Fierce night sorties were again made by the enemy and bravely resisted by our boys, who continued the work regardless of these annoyances. Only one fight occurred on our part of the line after the 16th, in which we lost any number of men. On the 28th the First brigade had a skirmish in which we lost one killed and half a dozen wounded. Among the latter was Lieutenant, afterward Colonel Milliken, of the Forty-third New York. A reconnoissance on the left about the same time, resulted in finding the rebels in considerable force, and a loss of two good soldiers to the Seventy-seventh New York. In the meantime earthworks of great strength were being thrown up on the right of the line before Yorktown, and everything was being put in a complete state of preparation for the grand bombardment. Enormous siege guns of one hundred and even two hundred pound calibre, and immense mortars were brought up and mounted in the earthworks, and it was thought that with the powerful means we were using the fall of Yorktown was only a question of time.

Our losses by the rebels before Yorktown were not great, but the ravages by disease were fearful. Many thousands of noble fellows who would gladly have braved the dangers of the battle-field, were carried to the rear with fevers engendered by the deadly malaria of the swamps, from which few ever recovered sufficiently to rejoin the ranks; and thousands of others were laid in humble graves along the marshy borders of the Warwick or about the hospitals at Young's Mills. For a month the men were almost continually under arms; often called in the middle of the night to resist the attempts of the enemy to force our line under cover of the thick darkness, standing in line of battle day after day and digging at earthworks night after night.

During the thirty days of the siege we had twenty days of rain. Thunder storms followed each other in quick succession, with lightnings more vivid than we had ever seen at the north. Men lay down to rest at night with their equipments buckled about them and wet to their skins. Men unaccustomed to the hardships of campaigning could not endure such exposure.

A few divisions of the army performed by far the greater part of the labor, either because they had at first reached positions which imposed greater toil, or because greater confidence was reposed in them. Our own division was one of those upon which the duties imposed were too great for men to perform; yet the men would have resented being sent to the rear, and it was said that General Smith remarked that "he had spoken for a front seat for his boys and he intended to keep it.

Added to all the exposures and hardships of the siege, there was a deplorable want of proper commissary and medical supplies. While the men were supplied with fair rations of hard bread, vegetables were unknown among us, and the supply of fresh meat wholly inadequate. In the Medical Department the greatest difficulty was experienced in obtaining supplies, and indeed it was impossible to get them. Not that regimental surgeons did not use their utmost endeavor to procure them, but as brigade and regimental commissaries could not obtain supplies of food which were not furnished to the army at all, so surgeons could not procure medicines and other necessaries which were locked in the storehouses in Washington. This subject will be more fully alluded to in another place, and it is to be hoped that the responsibility of this criminal negligence to supply the army with medical and hospital stores may fall where it belongs.

Thus, with their minds wrought up to a continual state of excitement, with constant exposure to tempests and malaria, with excessive and exhausting labors, and with improper food and scarcity of medicine, sickness and death swept over us like a pestilence.

At length, after a month of toil and exposure almost unprecedented, after losing nearly one-fifth of our magnificent army by disease and death, our batteries were finished, the enormous siege guns were mounted, and the thirteen inch mortars in position. The army looked anxiously for the grand *finale* of all these extensive preparations. Men had lost the enthusiasm which prevailed when we landed upon the Peninsula, and a smile was seldom seen; but a fixed and determined purpose to succeed still appeared in their faces. Now at length we were ready; and the countenances of the soldiers began to lighten up a little. But as the sun rose on the morning of the 4th of May, behold, the rebels had vanished, and with them our hopes of a brilliant victory! Unfortunately for our hopes of a great success at Yorktown, the rebel generals had shown themselves unwilling to afford us such an opportunity by waiting for us longer; and during the night of the 3d and 4th they had evacuated the place.

They had gained a month of time for strengthening the defenses about Richmond, and for concentrating their forces there. Now they were ready to fall back without testing our magnificent works and huge guns, and lead us into the swamps of Chickahominy; where they hoped that the fever would complete the ghastly work already commenced at Yorktown.

During the night of the evacuation, the roar of artillery exceeded anything that had been heard before. From one end of the line to the other the shells and shot poured into our camps, and the arches of fire that marked the courses of the shells, with flame spouting from the mouths of the guns, created a magnificent pyrotechnic display. But at daylight, orderlies flew from regiment to regiment with the startling intelligence that the beleagured works were deserted, and with orders to occupy them at once. Smith's division hastened to cross over the dam, and we found ourselves in the strongholds that we had so long invested. As the Seventy-seventh regiment passed along one of the roads leading among the intrenchments, a sharp report like that of a pistol was heard at the feet of those in the center of the column, and directly under the colors. The men scattered, and a piece of old cloth was seen lying on the ground at the point from which the report emanated. Colonel McKean, who was very near, lifted the cloth with the point of his sword, and discovered a torpedo carefully buried in the ground, except a nipple which had been filled with fulminating powder, which was covered by the old cloth. The fuse only had exploded. Had the machine itself exploded, it must have destroyed many of our men, our colonel among them. Other regiments were not so fortunate as we were. Very many men were killed in the streets and intrenchments by these torpedoes, which the enemy had planted in the street at either end of the bridges, about springs, and near the deserted guns. They were concealed beneath the ground with great care, the capped nipple only rising above the surface, and this, covered by an old rag or piece of bark thrown over it, exploded at the slightest touch. These infernal machines

were only one feature of the general plan of our enemies
to carry on a war by brutal, savage and cowardly means.
The starving of prisoners at Andersonville and Salisbury,
and the wholesale butchery at Fort Pillow, were other
parts of the same savage plan which was crowned by the
fearful tragedy at Ford's Theatre.

We made little delay among the rebel intrenchments;
only long enough to glance over the formidable works,
where the enemy had abandoned seventy-two pieces of
artillery, mostly of heavy caliber, with immense numbers
of shovels, picks, wheelbarrows and other paraphernalia of
an army.

The division was at nine o'clock sent forward on the
road toward Williamsburgh; encountering, before it had
proceeded far, a portion of the rear-guard of the confederate army, which hastily fell back before our advance.
General Smith informed the Commander-in-Chief of the
encounter, who ordered Stoneman, with a regiment of
cavalry, to give chase to the retiring body, and, if possible, cut it off; but, unfortunately, either from want of
proper information in regard to the roads, or from other
hindrances, this was not effected. The division pushed on
over the road lately traversed by the rebels, the men
overcoming all obstacles that had been thrown in their
way, in their anxiety to overtake the foe.

The scenery, as the troops passed, was indeed charming
beyond description. Magnificent forests of oak and pine,
interspersed with clearings, the residences of farmers,
with fine fields, covered with the green blades of the
newly springing wheat, met the view along the road;
while the woods were adorned with innumerable flowers.
The tall dogwood, with its clusters of large flowers like
swarms of white butterflies, mingled with the Judas tree,
whose leafless boughs were densely covered with racemes
of purple blossoms. The azalia and the honeysuckle

beneath formed a delightful contrast with the gorgeous floral display above.

Thus the division was hurried on, until at evening it came upon the rebel works at Williamsburgh. As our forces approached Williamsburgh, the cavalry came upon the enemy, and a sharp skirmish ensued, in which we lost about fifty in killed and wounded, and the rebels left as many on the field. The charge was made by the Sixth cavalry and Gibbon's battery, driving the rebels back. They, in their turn, being reinforced, forced our troops back; one of our guns, from which all the horses were shot, being abandoned. Each party strove hard for the possession of the gun, but night closed upon the contest, leaving it in possession of neither. In the meantime, the men of our division too sick to march were being cared for by our medical officers. Hundreds of the men of our division lay sick with typhoid fever and other equally dangerous maladies. These were all taken to the hospital which had been commenced a day or two previous, about a mile and a half from our camp. The whole day was occupied in removing these men. Of those sent to this hospital, as of the many previously sent to the hospital at Young's Mills and Fortress Monroe, few ever returned.

7

CHAPTER VI.

WILLIAMSBURGH.

EARLY on the morning of the 5th skirmishing commenced. The division of Hooker was posted on the left of the road from Lee's Mills to Williamsburgh, and our own division held the road, stretching mostly to the right of it. Fort Magruder was directly in front of us, commanding the road. All that part of the army which had advanced on the right, that is, on the road from Yorktown, were massed as fast as they arrived, awaiting orders. Great delay was experienced in getting the troops in position, as there seemed to be no harmony of action. Every general of a division seemed to do what pleased him, without orders from higher authority.

General Sumner was in command of the troops on the field, but from some cause seemed not to be able to combine his forces in such a manner as to bear effectually upon the lines of the enemy. One of the serious difficulties was getting artillery to the front. The roads had become very muddy from the rain during the night, and were blocked up with the immense multitude of wagons, so that artillery could not pass. Here was sadly exemplified the grand defect of our army — the want of organization.

Our army was an enormous heterogenous mass, without any pretense of a system to centralize and harmonize its movements. An army is not organized by throwing it into brigades and divisions; this is but the first and easiest step. The *departments* must be so organized that each performs well its part, without interference with another. In this case the quartermaster's department sadly interfered with the others. Every regimental quartermaster was for himself, and, as a natural result, the immense trains were thrown into great disorder, impeding the movements of all the other branches of the service. No one seemed at liberty to bring order out of this confusion; and thus artillery and wagons remained stuck in the mud. This same confusion prevailed in all the departments. We shall take the liberty here to quote at some length from the remarks of the Prince De Joinville, who was at that time a member of General McClellan's staff, an able soldier and an ardent friend of the Commander-in-Chief. Says the Prince:

"The American system of 'every man for himself,' individually applied by officers and soldiers of each corps to one another, is also applied by the corps themselves to their reciprocal relations. There is no special branch of the service whose duty it is to regulate, centralize and direct the movements of the army. In such a case as this of which we are speaking, we should have seen the general staff of a French army taking care that nothing should impede the advance of the troops; stopping a file of wagons here and ordering it out of the road to clear the way; sending on a detail of men there to repair the roadway, or draw a cannon out of the mud in order to communicate to every corps commander the orders of the general-in-chief. Here nothing of the sort is done. * *

"The want of a general staff was not less severely felt in obtaining and transmitting the information necessary, at the moment of an impending action. No one knew the country; the maps were so defective that they were use-

less. Little was known about the fortified battle-field on
which the army was about to be engaged. Yet this
battle-field had been seen and reconnoitered by the troops
which had taken part in Stoneman's skirmish. Enough
was surely known of it for us to combine a plan of attack,
and assign to every commander his own part of the work.
No, this was not so. Every one kept his observations to
himself; not from any ill-will, but because it was nobody's
special duty to do this general work. It was a defect in
the organization, and with the best elements in the world,
an army that is not organized cannot expect great success.
It is fortunate if it escapes disaster."

We may be pardoned for continuing this digression
from the narrative, to speak particularly of the disorder
in the medical department. The surgeons of regiments
were, as a general rule, men of ability, and who were
earnestly devoted to the duties of their position. Of
course, in so large an army, there were some who were
not fitted for their position, either by ability or moral
worth; these were exceptions. Yet, while there was a
general disposition prevailing in the department to make
any sacrifice or submit to any amount of fatigue, in order
to relieve the sufferings of those committed to their charge,
they labored under the greatest disadvantage from want
of proper combination and coöperation in the staff. Every
man was for himself. Each regimental surgeon was
expected to look out for the wants of his own men; to
erect his hospital tents; to see that the wounded of his
regiment were carried off the field; to administer food,
dress wounds, and attend to the operative surgery. With
all these divers cares, he could hardly be expected to perform any duties well. When any combination of action
was effected, the organization was voluntary and temporary, and, of course, wanting in order and efficiency.
Added to these difficulties, the medical officer found

himself destitute of supplies, and seemingly without any prospect of obtaining them.

It is true that the officers of the medical staff were generally inexperienced in the duties of military surgery, so different from the labors of the physician in civil life; yet, the great trouble was without doubt at head-quarters. The department was directed by an officer who had done good service in the Mexican war, but who by long connection with the regular army, seemed to have become so wedded to the formal precision of military routine, that no contingency was sufficient to move him from his established habits. Here was occasion for dispensing with formalities. Responsibilities should have been assumed, and, if necessary, supplies should have been thrown into the army broadcast, without thought of requisition or receipts. Under the direction of the efficient and gentlemanly surgeon of volunteers, Dr. Letterman, order was at length brought out of the confusion which existed until the battle of Antietam; from which time the medical staff became the most efficient ever known in any army.

To return to our narrative. By noon the battle raged furiously; Hooker's division contesting the field nobly against superior numbers, while our own division held the position on his right, but without coming to any direct engagement aside from being subjected to the fire of artillery. Hooker brought his men gallantly up to the work and at first forced the enemy back, but in turn was driven from the ground he had taken, and only by the most valorous fighting, prevented a rout.

The gallant general and his noble men held the ground alone until the division was fearfully cut up. At length General Kearney, at the head of his division, approached on the Lee's Mills road. General Sumner rode up to him and said quietly, "General, do you know that Hooker is badly cut up?" "No." "He is, and is falling back. Hurry

on your division as fast as possible." "How shall I reach
him?" said Kearney. " Through yonder strip of woods."
Kearney now led his men forward at a rapid pace and
very soon came to the relief of the exhausted division.
The troops of Hooker were holding their ground against
the enemy twenty thousand strong. They had fought for
hours with only nine thousand men.

General Hancock of our First brigade, at his own and
General Smith's request, was, at three o'clock, allowed to
take his own and a part of our Third brigade to the right
of the line, where the position of the enemy was very
strong by nature, and which was on that account secured
with less care than the rest of the line.

A steep wooded bluff rose to a great height in our front,
and a mill pond lying at the foot of the bluff and newly
dammed by the rebels, served as a moat. Spanning the
pond near the dam, was a bridge of logs which they had
neglected to destroy. Across this bridge and up a road
winding along the side of the bluff, the general led his
troops, finding the enemy upon the plateau above, occupying strong redoubts. Artillery was brought to bear upon
them and the rebels fled; our forces advancing and occupying the works. The enemy was now reinforced by a
brigade of North Carolina troops and charged upon the
federals. The Union troops allowed them to approach
very near, when they opened a tremendous fire of musketry and artillery upon them. Still the rebels came on
until they were within thirty yards of our men. "Now,
gentlemen, the bayonet!" cried Hancock, as he rode along
the line of battle close to the troops. The men charged
upon the rebels, who fell back before the shock, broke and
fled, leaving the broad, green wheat field strewed with their
dead and wounded.

While the fighting was going on, General Hancock had
sent for the remainder of our Third brigade. The order

CHARGE OF HANCOCK'S BRIGADE AT WILLIAMSBURGH

"forward, double quick" was received by the men with one of those wild exulting shouts, such as is only heard on the field of battle; and they rushed forward through the liquid mud, each regiment striving which should first reach the field. But as we reached the scene of conflict, the rebels had fled; leaving the victory with the men in blue.

The regiments engaged in this brilliant affair were, the Forty-third New York, the Forty-ninth Pennsylvania, the Sixth Maine and Fifth Wisconsin, of the First brigade, and the Thirty-third New York and Seventh Maine of the Third brigade.

The rebels, outflanked by the gallant movement of Smith's division, were glad to fall back from before Hooker and Kearney, and seek refuge behind their works. Meanwhile the great body of the army had remained entirely passive; not even having been brought into line of battle. Why some of these troops were not called to the assistance of Hooker, or to render the victory of Hancock more complete, we do not know.

Thus closed the battle of Williamsburgh; a battle fought by two divisions and a part of a third, while the mass of the army remained as idle spectators of the terrible scene. If less than twenty thousand men could drive the rebels from their strong works, what could not that grand army have done had it been brought into action!

General McClellan arrived on the field at five o'clock in the afternoon, and was received with shouts of applause; but the fighting was then over. The general had remained at Yorktown since the morning of the 4th, to superintend personally the shipment of Franklin's division of twelve thousand men; one-half of whom, in order that they might be in readiness at any moment to proceed up the river and head off the enemy, had never been allowed to disembark from the transports which brought them to Yorktown. General McClellan's conduct in spending nearly two days in overseeing personally the embarkation of half or even the whole of a division of men, while one of the most important battles of the war was in progress, leaving it to others to take care of the "little affair at the front," has, by some, been severely censured; while others have as earnestly claimed that the Commander-in-Chief had his own views of the necessity of getting those troops off at once, and the necessity of seeing that supplies of rations, ammunition and war material, were forwarded, was imperative; and that we are to remember that the advance was intrusted to General Sumner; a man in whose ability both he and the army confided. The general telegraphed that night to the Secretary of War: " After arranging for movements up the York river, I was sent for here. I find General Joe Johnston in front of me in strong force, probably greater a good deal than my own. * * * My entire force is *undoubtedly considerably inferior to that of the rebels*, who will fight well; but I will do all I can with the force at my disposal."

It was not known that night that we had won such a victory; but when, in the morning, we found the rebels all gone, he telegraphed: "Every hour proves our victory more complete."

In the light of this testimony of the Commander-in-Chief, what a noble record had those three divisions that day made for themselves! They had, according to these dispatches, fought with a force "greater a good deal" than our entire army, and had won a complete victory!

Night closed upon the battle-field. Our division bivouacked around one of the rebel redoubts. It was filled with rebel wounded, whose groans and cries made the night hideous. The ground was a bed of liquid mud, and the rain still poured. No fires were allowed, and the men stood shivering all night rather than lie down in the mud.

The sun rose clear and bright next morning, and the whole army filed into the works deserted by the enemy during the night, and occupied the town of Williams-burgh, a mile or more from the battle-field. All the pub-lic buildings in town were filled with the rebel wounded; and the inhabitants were actively engaged in ministering to their wants. Here the army remained three days, waiting for provisions to come up from Yorktown, a dis-tance of fifteen miles. It is a question, why troops, who were afterward accustomed to carry four or even six days' rations, were sent away from Yorktown with one.

8

CHAPTER VII.

THE MARCH UP THE PENINSULA AND THE ORGAN-IZATION OF THE SIXTH CORPS.

March up the Peninsula—Joy of the contrabands—Cumberland Landing—The Sixth Corps organized—At White House—On the Chickahominy—Fight at Mechanicsville—Battle of Hanover Court House.

On the ninth of May, after a delay of three days, the Army of the Potomac resumed the pursuit of Johnston's army. The day was fair and bright, and the journey of fifteen miles, to troops as yet little inured to the fatigues of long marches, bore severely upon them. We rested till three o'clock next morning; when orders came to fall into line, and at five we were again toiling over the road. After a hard day's march we halted near New Kent Court House; where General Stoneman, with his cavalry, had a day or two before overtaken the rear-guard of the enemy, who gave him battle. Evidences of the engagement were to be seen all about us, and many wounded cavalrymen were found in the neighboring farm houses. We remained here over the Sabbath and the next day; glad of rest, though anxious to be on the trail of the enemy.

General Franklin's division had already landed, and beaten the rebels at West Point; and the flotilla laden with supplies had also ascended the river thus far.

It was at New Kent Court House that the news of the destruction of the Merrimac, and the possession of Norfolk by General Wool's forces, first reached us, and our hearts swelled with joy at our successes. On the 13th we resumed the march; winding along the banks of the tortuous Pamunkey, enchanted by the lovely scenery which constantly met our gaze. The profusion of flowers in the forests, the bright green meadows, and the broad fields of newly springing wheat, offered a perpetual charm; and as we passed along, the women and negroes watched us with conflicting sentiments of interest. All the white men capable of bearing arms, and every able-bodied negro, had been swept along by the rebel army in its retreat, and none but women and children and aged negroes were now left along the route. At every house the alarmed white people threw out the white flag in token of submission, as though their protection from injury depended upon this symbol of peace.

Great numbers of negroes flocked to the roadside, to welcome the Union army. Their expressions of joy at seeing us were wild and amusing. All hoped we would shortly overtake and destroy the rebel army, their own masters included. Those who had hitherto regarded the relation of master and slave as one of mutual affection, had only to witness these unique demonstrations of rejoicing at our approach, and the seemingly certain destruction of the slave owners, to be convinced that the happiness and contentment claimed for those in servitude was but a worthless fiction. The negroes, gathering in crowds along the wayside, would grasp the hands of the Union soldiers, calling down all manner of blessings upon them, and leaping and dancing in their frantic delight.

One gray-haired old patriarch, surrounded by a numerous group of younger chattels, who were leaping and shouting, exclaimed, in a loud voice, "Bress de Lord! I'se been praying for yous all to come all dis time; and now I'se glad yous got so fur; and I pray de Lord dat yous may keep on, and conquer def and hell and de grabe!" All the others, joining in the chorus, cried, "Bress de Lord!" The master of the old man sat quietly watching the scene, offering no hindrance to these expressions of sympathy; but it is doubtful whether this conduct on the part of his servants was forgotten after the departure of our army. Whatever information the slaves could give concerning the movements, numbers, or probable intentions of the enemy, was communicated gladly, and although this information was not always reliable for accuracy, it was always given in sincerity, and was very often of great service.

Our march on the 13th, was an easy one of six miles. As we reached the brow of a hill overlooking the plain of Cumberland Landing, a scene of imposing beauty was spread out before us. Between us and the broad river, were thousands of troops, parks of artillery, squadrons of cavalry, divisions of infantry; some already in camp, others moving about in order, but seeming, from the distance, to be intermingled in most perfect confusion.

A broad plain stretched far away to the left, beautifully variegated with green pastures, rich groves and fields of grain. Beyond was the Pamunkey; here spreading out into a broad expanse of water, on which was riding the Union flotilla of gunboats and the transport fleet.

Upon this broad plain the whole army assembled. At no other time in the history of the Army of the Potomac, were all its forces gathered within a compass that the eye could take in at a single glance.

Early on the morning of the 14th, the cry, "Fall in!" resounded through the camps, and we proceeded up the river about four miles, and again encamped on its banks. A field of fresh clover served for our bivouac. In this pleasant spot we remained for several days; and while here, an event occurred of no less interest than THE ORGANIZATION OF THE SIXTH CORPS.

Just before the Army of the Potomac embarked for the Peninsula, it was divided, by order of President Lincoln, into five corps of three divisions each. These corps were placed under command, respectively, of Generals McDowell, Sumner, Heintzelman, Keyes and Banks. On leaving for the Peninsula, the First and Fifth corps had been left behind. Now two new corps were to be organized; the Fifth provisional, consisting of the divisions of Porter and Sykes, and the reserve artillery, under command of General Porter; and the SIXTH provisional corps, consisting of Franklin's division of the First and Smith's of the Fourth corps. General W. B. Franklin was assigned to the command of the corps.

Franklin's division, now the First division, Sixth corps, under command of H. W. Slocum, had been ordered away from the First corps, to join the army of the Potomac, while we were at Yorktown; and its recent exhibition of gallantry at West Point, had already established for it a reputation for valor. The regiments composing this division were, the First, Second, Third and Fourth New Jersey; regiments trained to the service by the knightly soldier and ardent patriot, Philip S. Kearney, now under command of Colonel Taylor, and afterwards so long and so ably led by General Torbert; the Sixteenth and Twenty-seventh New York, Fifth Maine and Ninety-Sixth Pennsylvania; General Slocum's own brigade; now commanded by Colonel Bartlett; and Newton's brigade; the Eighteenth, Thirty-first and Thirty-second New York, and Ninety-fifth Pennsylvania.

The history of the Second division, General Smith's, we have already traced. The bravery and extraordinary endurance of each of its brigades had been exhibited too often to be questioned.

With such splendid materials for a corps, a brilliant history of great achievements was to be anticipated, and nobly has it wrought out for itself such a history.

No other body of troops has ever made for itself so

proud a record. No corps, either in our own army or any other, ever met the enemy so frequently in general battle, and never were more glorious deeds accomplished by troops than were done by these. Never in the course of all their campaigns were either of these two divisions put to rout, and in almost all its encounters the corps held the field as victors.

We were now encamped on the old Custis place; at present owned by General Fitzhugh Lee, of the rebel cavalry service. On every side of us were immense fields of wheat, which, but for the presence of armies, promised an abundant harvest. Day after day passed, in quiet repose, and the Sabbath found us still waiting on the banks of the Pamunkey. It was marvelous that such silence could exist where a hundred thousand men were crowded together, yet almost absolute stillness reigned throughout the vast camp during the whole of this pleasant Sabbath. Save that here and there the notes of Old Hundred or some sacred air was heard from the band of some regiment whose chaplain had gathered his men for religious services, no sound disturbed the universal quiet.

Not far from us was the White House, at the head of navigation, on the Pamunkey. The house was a fine building, once the property of Washington, now in possession of the Lee family. Here the Richmond and York River railroad crossed the Pamunkey, and this was made the base of operations for the army. Here the transports poured out a vast amount of supplies, and under the protection of the flotilla of gunboats, the quartermasters and commissaries commenced their active operations.

Except that a few rails had been torn up, the railroad was in excellent order, and engines and cars were at once placed on the track ready to follow the army on its advance to Richmond.

The Sixth corps proceeded toward the Chickahominy, which it reached at a point several miles above the railroad crossing at Bottom's Bridge, occupying the extreme right of the Union line of battle as formed along that river. The position of the Union army was now as follows: Keyes' corps had crossed the Chickahominy at Bottom's Bridge, and Heintzelman had followed, taking a position between Keyes and the bridge. Sumner was on the railroad, and Franklin on the right near New Bridge; Stoneman's cavalry was on the right of the Sixth corps, and Porter's divisions were in the rear, within supporting distance.

On the 23d, General Stoneman with his cavalry pushed forward toward Mechanicsville, supported by Davidson's brigade. The brigade halted for the night near Beaver Dam creek, a marshy stream pouring into the Chickahominy. On the following morning the brigade again pushed forward, the men making their way with great difficulty through a swamp, then plunging through the stream, then forcing their way through brambles and briars, and again wading through the water; until the men seemed to have become amphibious. They at length found the enemy near the little village of Mechanicsville.

The brigade, with Wheeler's battery, formed in line of battle on some commanding grounds, and quietly rested for the night. On the morning of the 24th, the Seventy-seventh and part of the Thirty-third were ordered to advance toward the village and reconnoiter the position. Hardly had the advance commenced before the rebels opened upon the two commands a fierce cannonade, which forced our men to lie down, that the shells might pass over them. Wheeler's battery responded nobly to the rebel artillery, and presently General Davidson ordered Colonel McKean to charge the village with his regiment. The men rose to their feet and started forward with a yell.

Down the hill they rushed impetuously, cheering and yelling; but the two rebel regiments, the Seventh and Eighth Georgia, startled by the shouts, seized their muskets and ran; firing but one parting salute. Their battery also limbered up and beat a hasty retreat; and as our men reached the village they were seen lashing their horses into a run, and in a moment they disappeared altogether down the road.

In their haste the rebels forgot to carry off their knapsacks, canteens and haversacks; and our boys gathered them up to be kept till called for. They had also left a great many guns and cartridge boxes; and a flag, which the Seventy-seventh bore away in triumph.

On the 26th of May, the enemy was discovered in considerable force at Hanover Court House, to the right and rear of our army. A part of Porter's corps was sent to meet this rebel force, and if possible drive it from its position. After a fatiguing march through mud and rain, General Emory, with his own brigade, and other troops of the corps, came up with the enemy near Hanover Court House, and at once commenced advancing slowly against the line of the enemy, when, being reinforced by part of Martindale's brigade, a charge was ordered and the rebels were routed. They fled precipitately, leaving one of their guns in the hands of our troops.

Being reinforced, the rebels turned upon our troops, but were gallantly held by Martindale's brigade until General Porter brought a large force to the field. The rebels were again attacked and completely routed. They left about two hundred of their dead on the field to be buried by our men. Seven hundred prisoners were captured, beside two railroad trains, a twelve pound gun and many small arms. Our own loss amounted to about fifty killed and more than three hundred wounded and missing.

CHARGE OF THE 77TH NEW YORK AT MECHANICSVILLE.

CHAPTER VIII.

ON THE CHICKAHOMINY.

DAVIDSON's command was withdrawn from its position on Beaver Dam creek on the 26th of May. Moving down the river about five miles, it encamped with the rest of the Sixth corps on the farm of Dr. Gaines, a noted rebel, where it remained until June 5th. The camps were within easy range of the enemy's guns, which were planted on the opposite side of the river, and our pickets could observe those of the rebels as they walked their beats.

Few more charming places than Gaines' Farm could be found on the Peninsula. The broad wheat fields, alternating with wooded hills, afforded a scene of enchantment to the weary soldiers. A single wheat field contained four hundred and fifty acres, and a delightful grove in rear of the superb old mansion, furnished a cool retreat during the intense heat of the day. The extensive gardens were filled with rare exotics and most beautiful native plants and trees, and birds of varied and brilliant plumage sported among the flowering shrubs and charmed the air with their lively notes. Near the river side stood a large barn well filled with tobacco, from which the boys of the corps did not hesitate to lay in a full supply.

In the rear of the corps was Liberty Hall, the birthplace of Patrick Henry. Now it was used as a hospital, and hundreds of soldiers, worn out with fatigue or burning

9

with fevers, occupied the house and hospital tents surrounding it.

Our men were employed in doing picket duty, and in
building corduroy roads and bridges. The river, scarcely
restrained by banks, was rising rapidly from the continued
fall of rain, and at one time the pickets of our division,
including the Thirty-third New York, were found in the
morning surrounded by water; the rain having within
three hours risen so rapidly that many were standing in
water above their waists, while others were clinging
to bushes for support. Boats were procured, and the
drenched pickets were removed from their disagreeable
positions.

The army was divided into two wings, one on the south
and one on the north side of the Chickahominy. The line
of battle was in the form of a V : Keyes' and Heintzelman's corps on a line from Bottom's Bridge to Seven
Pines, forming the left arm of the V, and Franklin's,
Sumner's and Porter's on the north bank of the Chickahominy, from Bottom's Bridge to Gaines' Farm, the right
arm.

Keyes' corps, now composed of Casey's and Couch's
divisions, had crossed the river at Bottom's Bridge on the
24th, and after considerable skirmishing with the enemy,
had established itself on the road from Richmond to
Williamsburgh, about six miles from Richmond, and as
far from the Chickahominy, at a fork in the road called
Seven Pines. Heintzelman's corps had followed, and
occupied a position in the rear near the river. Casey's
division occupied an advance position, and Couch the
second line. One of the roads from this point, called
the nine-mile road to Richmond, crossed the Richmond
and York River railroad north of Seven Pines, at a place
called Fair Oaks. The country was wooded and marshy,
and General Casey was not able to throw his pickets out

more than a thousand yards in advance of his line of battle. Both divisions at once intrenched themselves, and slashed the forests, that any approach of the enemy might be discovered, and to widen the sweep of their guns. Here the two divisions remained, having occasional skirmishes with the enemy, until the morning of the 31st of May.

During the night before, the rain had fallen in torrents. Thunders rolled along the sky, and the heavens blazed with perpetual flashes of lightning. The morning found the earth drenched by the floods, and the men of Casey's division rose from their beds of mud to fight the battle of Seven Pines.

It became evident to General Casey early in the day that the enemy designed to attack him in force. He accordingly ordered his division under arms, and made such dispositions of his forces as seemed best calculated to resist the onset.

At half-past twelve the attack was commenced. Large bodies of rebels emerged from the cover of the woods, and at once commenced a brisk fire of musketry and artillery, driving in the picket line, and pressing forward against the Union line of intrenchments. The numbers of the enemy were now seen to be greatly disproportionate to those of the single division opposed to them, and General Casey called for help. Couch's division was under arms, acting as support, but not yet engaged. Some of the new troops, thus pressed by overwhelming numbers broke and retreated in disorder; but the division at large nobly withstood the mighty host which assailed it in front, flank and rear. The forces of the enemy constantly increased; and the single division was now fairly invested by the exultant foe, who pressed forward, unmindful of the losses inflicted by Casey's troops. Again and again the enemy came on in masses, receiving the shot and shells, which tore open their ranks, closing up the gaps, and pushing steadily on to the assault. Against these repeated attacks of superior numbers of confident troops, who constantly arrived in fresh numbers, and, forming under cover of the woods, rushed against our lines, Casey's division held its ground three hours, until almost half its number were destroyed. The execution done on the rebels was great. All means of transportation at their command, were brought into requisition to carry off the wounded to Richmond; and their dead lay piled upon the bloody field. The white-haired veteran, General Casey, was present wherever the danger seemed greatest. Riding along his lines, encouraging his troops, and making his dispositions for repelling the overwhelming assaults, his heroism inspired bravery in the hearts of the men, and prevented defeat from becoming a rout. General Keyes was directing the movements of the second line, held by General Couch. Portions of the division were rallied, and with the aid of Couch's troops and a brigade of Kearney's division, which that never tiring general had just led on to the scene of conflict, the attempt was made to retake the line of works just lost, but without success.

By this time General Heintzelman had arrived with his corps; and orders were given to fall back to a third line. The enemy made one more desperate attempt to crush the retreating division, but they were repulsed with fearful loss, and here commenced the turning of the tide in the conflict.

The line of battle as now formed was nearly two miles in the rear of the position of the morning, at Fair Oaks.

Heintzelman's and Keyes' corps at once proceeded to strengthen this position, and before dark the brave fellows of Sedgwick's division, of Sumner's corps, were on the ground, ready to assist in repelling the progress of the enemy. Richardson's division, not far behind, arrived at sunset; and now the Union army was prepared for any attempt which the rebels might see fit to make. The efforts which the enemy were now making to break through our flank on the left at White Oak Swamp, were, by this timely arrival of Sedgwick, thwarted. Had the confederates succeeded in this, the retreat of Keyes' corps and that part of Heintzelman's on the ground must have been cut off, and our army destroyed. The rebels, not satisfied with a partial victory, and determined to destroy the left wing of our army, then thrust beyond the river, renewed their assaults, and again and again pushed forward. Gathering in masses under cover of the forest, they would dash upon our lines with impetuous fury; only to be sent reeling back by a hurricane of leaden and iron hail. Sedgwick and the intrepid Kearney fought their divisions with greatest skill; and by their own example animated and encouraged their men. Night closed upon the scene; and at eight o'clock the fighting had ceased. The rebels, so exultant at their success in the early part of the day, were now hopeless of turning their victory to any good account; for their last assaults had met with such terrible repulses, that to renew the attack in force in the morning, would be but a useless waste of life to them. Still, they held their ground, and on the morning of June 1st, made some demonstrations against parts of our line, which were gallantly met.

Finally, General Hooker, who here sustained the enviable reputation he had so nobly earned at Williamsburgh, led his command across the open space in front of our line, a space not more than one-fourth of a mile wide, beyond which the ground was interrupted by forests, to attack the enemy.

With quick and steady step, the well trained division advanced across the field, deploying to the right and left;

and before half crossing the open space their pace was quickened to a run; constantly firing as they dashed forward on the enemy.

Presently the edge of the forest was reached; and here considerable opposition was met with; yet, after a moment's halt, the division again pushed forward into the woods. The din of arms was heard for a few moments, then the firing ceased, and our troops were in possession of the ground.

The rebels were, in their turn, now panic-stricken; and hundreds of them rushed back to the confederate capital, spreading the alarm, and declaring that the Yankees were about to walk into the city.

It was doubtless a sad mistake that this victory was not followed up. The rebels, who had greatly outnumbered us in the fight of the day before, were now themselves outnumbered. They had suffered severe repulses on the evening before, and on this day their rear-guard had been whipped by General Hooker.

A renewal of the attack in force on the part of the Union army would have probably resulted in the capture of the beleaguered city. As it was, the commander of the Union army was on the north side of the Chickahominy, many miles from the scene of action, and no order for a forward movement was given.

Such was the battle of Seven Pines or Fair Oaks. Fought for the most part, by a single division of less than six thousand men, against the combined forces of Longstreet, Hill, Smith and Huger; all under the immediate command of the Commander-in-Chief of the rebel army, General Johnston.

General Johnston had become satisfied, from the reports of his scouts, that only Keyes' corps, of two divisions, was across the Chickahominy. Believing that the bad state of the roads and the swollen condition of the Chickahominy, would effectually prevent reinforcements reaching this corps before he could fall upon it and crush it, he had determined to bring an overwhelming force against it. Accordingly, the divisions of Longstreet, Hill, Smith and Huger, were placed in position to make a sudden and destructive assault upon the front and flanks of Casey's exposed division, in the confident expectation of annihilating it. But, instead of giving way before this avalanche, as Johnston had contemplated, the regiments of the division, with few exceptions, manfully held their ground for three hours.

The Commander-in-Chief reported to the Secretary of War that Casey's division "gave way unaccountably and discreditably." Five days later he promised to modify his charge, if he found occasion; but it was only in his final report, made many months after leaving the army, he was constrained to acknowledge the good conduct of the division—an act of tardy justice to deserving men.

Notwithstanding the great disparity in the numbers of those engaged on the rebel and Union sides, the losses were nearly equal. The Union army lost four thousand five hundred and seventeen in killed and wounded, and one thousand two hundred and twenty-two missing. Nearly one-half of all these losses were from Casey's and Couch's divisions. General Johnston reported the rebel loss in Longstreet's and Hill's commands at four thousand two hundred and thirty-six.

Among the trophies of the enemy, were ten pieces of artillery and four stands of colors.

With these trophies, they were satisfied to boast their victory; regardless of the fact that they had been the assailants in superior numbers, and had been repulsed with fearful slaughter, and that the only fruit of their boasted victory was a few guns and colors, as an offset for the loss of thousands of their soldiers. General Johnston himself was among the rebel wounded, and was forced to give over the command to another.

On the other hand, the Union army might, had the corps on the north bank of the Chickahominy promptly followed that of General Sumner across the river, have easily entered Richmond. But the hesitancy which characterized the movements of the army lost to us all the advantages of success. Early next day the treacherous river had risen to such an extent as to render crossing almost impossible; so the army remained as the battle of Fair Oaks had left it; three corps on the south, and two on the north side of the Chickahominy, separated by an almost unsurmountable obstacle.

From our camp at Gaines' Farm, the men of the Sixth corps could see the smoke of battle and hear the roar of artillery and musketry; but were not able to go to the assistance of their fellows.

The distance from Gaines' Farm to Fair Oaks was, in a direct line, scarcely more than four miles, but as all communications with the opposite side of the river were by way of Bottom's Bridge, the distance was about fifteen miles. The Vermont brigade essayed a crossing in our own front on the afternoon of the second day of the fight, with the view of rendering assistance on the other side, but the attempt was abandoned.

General McClellan, with General Hancock and other officers, took a position in the line of our Third brigade, on Sunday, where they remained watching the progress of the battle from afar until darkness shut out the view.

On the day after the battle, rain poured in a continuous storm; deluging the roads and swelling what had been but rivulets the day before, into rivers. In the midst of this tempest of rain, Casey's division, destitute of tents and blankets, weary from fighting and disheartened by injustice, marched six miles to the rear to find a new encampment. On the 5th of June, Smith's division, of the Sixth corps, was ordered to cross the Chickahominy, and encamp on "Golden's Farm," nearly opposite. The Third brigade took the advance, followed by the rest of the division. Owing to the swollen state of the river, and the impossibility of bridging it, the division was forced to march to Dispatch Station before effecting a crossing. The march was a long and weary one to gain a distance less than three miles.

Some of our troops were found skirmishing with the enemy, and our batteries opened upon the gray coats, who quickly surrendered the ground and took to flight. Our Second division encamped in a pleasant locality, yet in close proximity to the swamp.

The Chickahominy wound its doubtful course among multitudes of islands scarcely raised above the surface, yet covered with trees, shrubs and vines in profusion, within a few rods of our camp. Beyond us, in our front, were forests of luxuriant growths of trees and climbing shrubs, and the country all about us was interrupted with rank growth of timber. The division at once proceeded, as did all the other divisions in the army, to throw up earthworks; making slow advances at certain points by pushing these works further toward the front. On the 18th, we were joined by the other division, Slocum's. The Sixth corps now formed the right of the new line of battle on the south of the river. The line reached from Golden's Farm to Fair Oaks. Day and night the men worked at the breastworks and bridges. One-third of the army was employed constantly at these works, and the immense lines of intrenchments were marvels of achievements in engineering. These were all constructed under the fire of the enemy; no day passing without its skirmish. Soldiers were daily brought to the hospitals with wounds, even in the most quiet times.

10

Everything combined to exhaust the energies of the men and produce fevers, diarrheas and scurvy. Day after day the men worked under a burning sun, throwing up the immense walls of earth, or toiled standing to their waists in water, building bridges. Night after night they were called to arms, to resist some threatened attack of the enemy. Their clothing and tents were drenched with frequent rains, and they often slept in beds of mud. With the hot weather, the malaria became more and more deadly. The whole country was alternately overflowed and drained; and the swamps were reeking with the poisoned air. The hospitals became daily more crowded. The strongest were constantly falling. Diarrhea, typhoid fever, and other miasmatic maladies, became almost universal. Men who worked at the breastworks one day would be found in the hospitals on the next, burning with fever, tormented with insatiable thirst, racked with pains, or wild with delirium; their parched lips, and teeth blackened with sordes, the hot breath and sunken eyes, the sallow skin and trembling pulse, all telling of the violent workings of these diseases.

Day after day, scores of brave men, who had left their northern homes to aid in the hour of their country's need, were borne to lowly graves along the banks of that fatal river; and at times one might sit in the door of his tent and see as many as six or seven funeral parties bearing comrades to their humble resting places.

Hospital steamers plied constantly from the White House to Washington, Alexandria and Philadelphia, bearing thousands of these victims of disease; and many, with stoic indifference, lay down in their shelter tents and gave themselves over to death, without even applying to comrades or surgeons for assistance.

Everywhere at the north, men were seen on cars and steamers, on the streets and in the houses, whose sallow countenances, emaciated appearance, and tottering steps, marked them as the victims of " Chickahominy fever." Express cars groaned with the weight of coffins containing the remains of youths who but a few months before had gone to the war in the pride of their strength, and had now yielded, not to the bullets of the enemy, but to the grim spirit which hovered over that river of death.

Our army seemed on the point of annihilation from disease; and matters were constantly growing worse. At White House landing, great temporary hospitals were established, where hundreds languished, and waited their turn to be sent north.

Thus, for nearly a month, the two armies looked each other in the face, each engaged in throwing up defenses against the approach of the other, but neither attempting to bring on any general engagement. The pickets of the two opposing forces were within speaking distance, but they contented themselves with watching each other, and, as a general rule, amicable relations existed between them. But occasionally, when a belligerent regiment would be on picket on one or the other side, some fellow, who imagined he had a capital chance to pick off an opposing picket, would blaze away; when in a moment the whole line on either side would flash with the discharge of musketry. Night demonstrations on the part of the enemy were so common, that it was a rare thing for our troops not to turn out at midnight, or at two or three o'clock in the morning, and stand under arms until after daylight.

The men of our Third brigade were a part of the time engaged in building a strong fort, near the river bank, which, in honor of our dashing brigadier, was named Fort Davidson.

A new regiment was added to Davidson's brigade during the month of June, the Twentieth New York. The regiment was composed entirely of German Turners.

Nearly every man had served his three years in the Prussian service.

They had been stationed in the works at Newport News, and their drill excelled anything in the army, either in the regular or volunteer branch of service. Their full ranks, and their unsoiled uniforms, were in striking contrast with the shattered and worn-out regiments forming the rest of the brigade.

Among the causes of discouragement and anxiety for the safety of our army, was the notorious raid of General Stuart in our rear. This energetic officer, with a body of about two thousand rebel cavalry, had swept round our entire rear, causing something of a panic, not only at White House, where all the shipping dropped down the river, but in the ranks of the army, where it was feared that our communications were destroyed, and we were liable to be hemmed in and overthrown at any time.

CHAPTER IX.

THE SEVEN DAYS' BATTLES.

At length, after great labor, the bridge across the river, near our own camps, was finished. It was an immense structure, spanning not only the river, but the swampy banks on either side to a great distance. Sumner's forces had also rebuilt and enlarged the bridge below, and now the two wings of the army, after weeks of separation, were united by means of these bridges. Communications were now rapid and easy, and there was no difficulty in reinforcing one wing with troops from the other.

General McClellan now determined to act; and an advance of our picket line was ordered on the 25th of June, preparatory to a general forward movement.

But General McClellan was not alone in deciding upon this particular time for commencing offensive operations.

General Lee, who had succeeded to the command of the rebel army when Johnston was wounded, aware of McClellan's intentions of approaching the city by regular approaches, and aware that it was in no condition long to withstand a siege, determined to act on the offensive.

The two armies were now about equal in numbers, each consisting of a little more than one hundred thousand men for duty.* Our own army had recently been reinforced by McCall's division, and five or six thousand troops from Fortress Monroe; and the rebel army had been strengthened by the accession of Jackson's force, of nearly twenty thousand, from the valley.

McClellan's first move was to advance the left wing, under Heintzelman, who occupied the ground on which had been fought the battle of Fair Oaks. General Hooker was ordered to advance his division about a mile across a clearing in his front. This the gallant general essayed to do.

In front of his camp, before reaching the clearing, was a thick entanglement of low pines and bushes, filled with swamps and ponds. This chaparral was about five hundred yards wide. Beyond was the clearing, in which were the rifle pits and strong redoubts of the enemy, and still farther on a forest. Hooker's brigades, commanded by Sickles, Grover and Robinson, protected on the left flank by Kearney's division, and on the right by a Massachusetts regiment, moved into the tangled forest, about eight o'clock on the morning of the 25th. Grover's pickets soon fell in with those of the enemy, and sharp skirmishing commenced; but the rebel picket line was steadily driven back into the clearing, where it was strengthened by their reserve. The fighting now became general. The woods rang with the sharp sounds of musketry and the deep tones of the artillery, and clouds of smoke obscured the scene from view. Ambulances were emerging from the woods bearing the wounded; and bloody forms on stretchers, and the less seriously wounded leaning on the shoulders of comrades, made up a melancholy procession.

The fire in the edge of the woods and in the open fields increased in intensity, until all of Hooker's and part of

* Our army had 115,000 men for duty.

Kearney's forces were brought into action. The rebels finally retreated across the field to the cover of their rifle pits. The retreat was slow and orderly, every foot of the way being disputed.

Our men were exultingly pushing forward, determined to drive them from their pits also, when an order from General McClellan directed General Hooker to retire with his division to the original position. Here was evidently a sad misconception of the state of affairs, for, when the Commander-in-Chief, an hour later, arrived on the field and consulted with General Hooker, the men were ordered forward once more to occupy the ground they had once taken and surrendered.

This time there was less resistance. The rebels steadily gave way, giving up their rifle pits and yielding the whole of the open field. Under cover of the forest beyond the field they made another stand, and late in the afternoon a brigade charged upon our lines; but they were bravely met by men of Grover's brigade, and driven back, leaving three hundred of their dead on the field.

By the action of this day, our line was advanced on the left nearly a mile. The victory, such as it was, cost us six hundred and forty men in killed and wounded. The men remained under arms all night, in readiness to meet the frequent sorties of the enemy, who intended nothing more serious than preventing reinforcements from being sent to the right of our line.

Little did General Lee heed these operations on our left. It was all the better for his plan that the attention of our army should be engaged in this direction. He was ready now to execute his plan of raising the siege of Richmond; and a tremendous force had been massed against our right, ready to advance upon it and our rear, with the hope of cutting the Union army off from its supplies, and placing it in the greatest jeopardy.

Let us, for a moment, recall the position of our army, which, since the first battle of Fair Oaks, has been somewhat changed. Porter's corps, consisting of McCall's, Morrell's and Sykes' divisions, still held the right, on the north bank of the Chickahominy, at Gaines' Farm and Mechanicsville. The several bridges which had been constructed since the 1st of June, formed avenues of communication between the two portions of the army separated by the river. Next, near the river, and opposite Porter's corps, was our own Sixth corps, Slocum's and Smith's divisions, Smith's nearest the stream. Then, on our left was Sumner's corps, Sedgwick's and Richardson's divisions; and finally, on the left of all, was Heintzelman, with his divisions under Hooker and Kearney, and Couch's division, of Keyes' corps. Casey's shattered division was in the rear, guarding Bottom's Bridge and the road to the White House.

The line stretched from Mechanicsville across the river to Golden's Farm, and thence to Fair Oaks.

The whole of this extensive line was protected by earthworks of marvelous magnitude, and whole forests of timber slashed in front of some parts of the line formed almost impenetrable abattis.

On the other hand, Lee's army had been as actively engaged in ditching and throwing up redoubts, and Richmond was surrounded by a cordon of most powerful works. Stonewall Jackson had been recalled from the Shenandoah Valley; and now, with an army of thirty thousand men, a very large proportion of them being men of his original army, he hung upon our right and rear, ready to come down upon our communications and flank like an avalanche.

Scarcely had General McClellan finished his dispatch to the Secretary of War, in which he announced the glad tidings that he had got his pickets in the right place, preparatory to a general advance, before he was aroused from his illusion by the intelligence that the pickets on the right were being driven in. He had already, during the day, learned something of Jackson's position, and it was now easy to divine the intention of that energetic chief.

During the night, Hill and Longstreet crossed the upper Chickahominy; and, by rapid marches, confronted the pickets of McCall's division at Mechanicsville before daylight on the morning of the 26th. Jackson, delayed by our skirmishers, was still behind. Without waiting for Jackson, Hill ordered an attack by daylight. Our pickets were forced back upon the main line, and the battle of Mechanicsville commenced. McCall's division, consisting of Reynolds', Meade's and Seymour's brigades, was strongly posted behind Beaver Dam creek; a stream about twelve feet wide, wooded on either side, with water waist deep, and a steep bank on the side held by the Union forces. Along this bank, timber had been felled, rifle pits dug, and other careful preparations made for meeting an attack. The only accessible places for artillery were the two roads which crossed the stream, one at Ellison's Mills, and the other a mile above. Against these two points the rebels directed their principal efforts. Hill's division made the first assault. Clearing their rifle pits, his men rushed forward with a yell, gaining the creek, within a hundred yards of our line. Here the creek and the almost impenetrable abattis checked their progress, and a murderous fire of shot, shells, cannister and musketry was opened upon them, which threw them into confusion, and repulsed them with fearful loss. Again and again the charge was renewed; each time with equal want of success. More and more grand and terrible the battle became, as the combatants struggled with each other at close range. Thus far there had been no such terrific artillery firing during the war. The uproar was incessant,

11

and sublime beyond description. Finding the position too strong to be carried by direct assault, the confederates fell back to their rifle pits; leaving their many dead and wounded on the ground. The men of McCall's division, securely posted behind their breastworks, had suffered comparatively little; our loss not exceeding three hundred in killed and wounded, out of the six thousand belonging to the brigades engaged.

On the other hand, the rebels had lost heavily. From their own official reports, it is known that of the twelve thousand engaged, the loss in killed and wounded was fifteen hundred; Ripley's single brigade losing five hundred and seventy-four men.

Both Davis and Lee were present on the field, directing in person the movements, and exposed to the fire where the battle was fiercest. General McClellan was at the head-quarters of General Porter, where he remained until the close of the battle, when he rode over the field.

From the camp of the Sixth corps, the battle-field was not more than four or five miles distant in a direct line, though by way of the bridge it was much farther.

We could watch the columns of smoke as they rolled up from the scene of carnage, and see the flashes of bursting shells, like sheets of lightning in dark thunder-clouds, and hear the tremendous roar of arms. In the afternoon, as the rebels charged upon a certain part of our lines, we could watch the movements of both armies. Our only part in the engagement was to stand to arms, ready to rush to the assistance of those on the other side of the river, at a moment's notice. In the evening, the news of our success spread through the army, creating the wildest joy. Men who had, by constant hardships, and by continually looking on death, almost forgotten the feelings of joy, now broke out in loud shouts of gladness; and for the first time in many weeks the bands played those heart-stirring national airs, which in times past had been wont to fill the hearts of the soldiers with enthusiasm.

The night passed in constant watchfulness, the men resting upon their arms; for a renewal of the attack might be expected at any moment. Still, the men of the whole of the left wing of the army were exulting in the glad hope that in the morning we were to march into Richmond, almost without opposition; and that their high hopes of success were to be speedily realized. The prize which they had so often been promised, seemed almost within their grasp. Men shook hands with each other, sung patriotic songs, and shouted in greatest glee.

Bands continued to ring out their notes of gladness until long after nightfall; general officers rode about announcing a grand victory; all was the most intense excitement; and the men lay down upon their arms to dream of reveling in the streets of Richmond before another night. For weeks, even the drum calls and the bugle notes had not been heard in our camps. Now, as if suddenly waked from a long slumber, the strains of the bugle and the roll of the drum were added to the general rejoicing.

It was known that the rebel troops engaged were not those of Jackson. He then must be working around to our rear. He was known to have a very large force; not less than thirty thousand. It was evident that our communications were in great danger, and that unless the main force of our army, now on the right bank of the Chickahominy, were hastily concentrated on the left bank, we could not expect to hold the line to the Pamunkey another day. If this were done, the rebels could easily prevent our retreat to the James river, and leave us on the banks of the Pamunkey. Accordingly, General McClellan gave up all hope of being able to maintain the position of that portion of the army on the north side of the Chickahominy, and at once issued orders with a view of preparing for a change of base. The quartermaster at White House was directed to "send cars to the last moment, and load them with provisions and ammunition." "Load every wagon you have," said the dispatch, "with subsistence, and send them to Savage's Station. If you are obliged to abandon White House, burn everything you cannot get off."

The quartermaster was directed, also, to throw all his supplies, not burned or sent to the army, up the James river, and there establish depots of supplies. General Casey, who was now in command of the guard at White House, was instructed to see these orders carried out. He burned immense quantities of stores, consisting of clothing, subsistence, and other war material, and then hastily marched his force to rejoin the army.

The evening of the 26th was passed in gladness over our victory; but while the army was rejoicing at this temporary success, it was losing one of the grandest opportunities ever presented it for entering the rebel capital. The whole plan of Lee had been based upon a false calculation; and had this mistake been improved by our commanders, the history of the war would have been entirely changed. Both Lee and Davis believed that the main body of our army was on the north side of the Chickahominy; whereas, of the five corps constituting our army, only one, that of Porter, remained on that side. Under this erroneous impression, Lee had brought nearly the whole of his army across the river to assail the Union army on its right. This was known to our generals, for while positive information had been received that Jackson, with his large army, was making for our rear, the prisoners taken during the day were from Hill's command, and from them it was known that the troops of A. P. Hill, Longstreet and D. H. Hill, were confronting us on the right. Thus, between our main force, of over seventy-six thousand men, and Richmond, less than twenty-five thousand rebels guarded their extensive line of works. A concentrated assault of the four corps on the south side of the river must have resulted in the utter rout of the force opposed to them, and the road to Richmond would have been opened.

But the error of General Lee was never suspected, and this grand opportunity was lost.

During the night of the 26th, the heavy artillery and baggage of Porter's corps was all sent across the river. McCall's whole division, except a line of pickets left as a blind, also fell back five miles below, to the vicinity of the bridge at Gaines' Farm, where the three divisions of the corps united.

The astonishment of the men on the south side of the river on discovering, in the morning, that Porter's corps had fallen back, was only equaled by their mortification and disappointment, as they saw the long lines of rebels advancing in the gray of the morning against our retreating column.

They had believed, when night came on, that our arms had achieved the first of a series of victories which was to give us the rebel capital. Now they saw that our army was already in retreat, and they gazed at the long train of artillery and wagons, which had parked near us, with downcast faces. From our camp, Porter's division could be distinctly seen, and we could watch the movements of the rebels as they arrived upon the highlands, formed their line on the range of hills opposite Porter, and planted their guns near the large barn on Dr. Gaines' farm.

The position of Porter's corps was a strong one; and he was ordered to hold it till night, and then to cross the bridge and burn it after him; the upper bridge having been burned during the night. The country between the two lines was rolling, somewhat wooded, but in parts cleared. Both parties went to work to cut down trees in their front.

The rebel forces, who supposed on the 26th that they were fighting our main army, were surprised, on the morning of the 27th, to find that only a picket line opposed them. They were early astir; and advancing against the slender line, drove it back. The whole rebel force advanced cautiously; A. P. Hill and Longstreet bearing to the right, while D. H. Hill turned to the left, to unite with Jackson, who was supposed to be coming in from the rear. Owing to the uneven country over which they were advancing, their march was slow; for they might fall upon a Union line of battle behind any rounding swell of land.

It was afternoon before the rebel army had fully formed its line on Gaines' Farm. The position of that army was nearly that of the same army when Grant attacked it at Coal Harbor two years later, only it was faced about. The battle opened about one o'clock, by skirmishing on both sides; but it was not till an hour later that Hill's division dashed across the open space, rushing through the swamp, and under a severe fire from our batteries and musketry, pushed up the slope on which was posted our line. The confederate troops advanced almost up to Sykes' line of battle on the right, and in other parts of the line actually forced back the Union troops; but they were able to hold their position only a short time, when they were forced back with great loss.

Longstreet now advanced against the left of our line, but he too met with a stern reception, and he withdrew to rearrange his plan of attack.

By this time Jackson was approaching, and now the overwhelming forces of the enemy promised to crush the single corps; but Slocum's division of our Sixth corps was ordered to the relief of the Fifth corps, and arrived at four o'clock. The division was sent into the fight at once, each brigade being ordered separately to strengthen the weak points of the line. Thus, while the division fought bravely, and suffered equally in proportion with the Fifth corps, its incorporation with that corps for the time deprived it of the honors to which it was justly entitled.

Bartlett, with his brigade, went to the aid of Sykes, who was doubtfully struggling to hold his line; but who now, by the aid of the gallant brigade, was able to hurl the assailants back from his front.

The rebel line being completed, Longstreet, A. P. Hill, and Jackson all up with their troops, a general advance was made.

The charge was made with great spirit, the rebels rushing over the open ground and floundering through the swamp under a most writhing fire, but the position of our forces was still too strong for them. At all points they were repulsed with terrible slaughter. First on the right, where Sykes' regulars, supported by Bartlett's brigade, withstood the onset of Hill, the disordered and disheartened confederates began to scatter in all directions.

One of the confederate generals reported that had not his men fallen back themselves he would have ordered it. "Men were leaving the field," says another general, "in every direction; two regiments * * * were actually marching back under fire. Men were skulking from the woods in a shameful manner. The woods on our left and rear were full of troops in safe cover, from which they never stirred." Such was the effect of the reception given by the regulars. On our left they met with no better success. These, too, fell back in disorder. Now a desperate attempt was made against our center. The tactics with which we afterwards became so familiar on the part of the rebels were brought to bear. This was in massing troops against certain parts of our line and making desperate onslaughts with a view of breaking the line. The forces of Jackson, Hill and Longstreet threw themselves fiercely against our works, but without being able to drive our men back.   Here it was that the First and Third brigades of Slocum's division saved the wavering line, and all the fury of the rebels was spent in vain.   General Porter directed Newton's brigade to its position in the center; Newton leading the Thirty-first New York and Ninety-fifth Pennsylvania into the woods on one side, and the gallant Colonel Matheson with the Eighteenth and Thirty-second entering on the other, both in the face of a destructive fire.   The rebels charged upon the brigade and gallantly the charge was met.   Newton, seeing the rebel line waver before the fire of his men, shouted "Forward!" and the impetuous regiments cleared the woods and drove the rebels more than seven hundred yards. But the confederates, reinforced, pressed hard upon them with overwhelming numbers, and Newton demanded aid. Regiments from the New Jersey brigade rushed to the assistance of their brothers of the Third brigade, cheering as they advanced, and the position was held until the left wing of Porter's corps gave way.   For two hours the conflict on this part of the line raged with terrible violence ; the columns surging backward and forward, neither party being able to gain any permanent advantage.   Never had we heard such volleys of musketry as now rolled along the borders of the swampy Chickahominy.   Artillery was less used ; a strip of pine woods intervening between the position occupied by some of our batteries and the rebel line preventing an accurate range.   The attempt to break our center was abandoned, and now immense forces were brought against the left.   The roar of battle became more loud than before.   The thousand continuous volleys of musketry mingled in one grand tumultuous concert of death ;

while the booming of artillery, which was now brought more into action, shook the earth for miles around. Under the pressure of overwhelming numbers, one brigade gave way; and another on the extreme left, finding itself out-flanked, fought its way back to the upper bridge, which had been partially destroyed during the night, and, cross-ing to the south side of the river, gathered its shattered regiments behind the breastworks of our Second division.

For two hours and a half the battle had raged fiercely on this part of the line, and as these brigades on the right gave way, the confusion spread all along. The rebels, seeing the disorder, and encouraged by their suc-cess on the left, came on with redoubled fury; and the whole line gave way, and fell back to some high grounds near the bridge. Here two brigades from the Third corps appeared as reinforcements, and the retreat was checked. The Fifth corps, with Slocum's division and the two brigades from the Third corps, were able to hold their position on the north side of the river till after dark.

But we had been beaten, and our losses were very great. Twenty-two pieces of artillery fell into the hands of the enemy. We lost two thousand prisoners, among whom was General Reynolds, commanding one of McCall's brigades; and our killed and wounded numbered about four thousand. The rebels had suffered greater losses in men, nine thousand five hundred having been killed or wounded. The action, on the part of the rebels, had been directed by General Lee in person, who was on the field during the whole action, controlling the movements of his troops, and attending to the details of the fight. On our part, the battle had been fought entirely under the direc-tion of General Porter. General McClellan, believing he could best watch the movements at all parts of his line from a central position, had remained during the day at the Trent House, five miles from the scene of action,

12

without deeming it necessary even to ride down to the river by the Woodbury bridge.*

Meantime, while the battle raged with fury on the north side of the Chickahominy, there was active work in our own front. Our Second division, at Golden's Farm, was joined on the left by Sedgwick's division, of the Third corps. The two divisions held the key to Richmond; for, had the brave men composing them, under the leadership of such men as Smith and Sedgwick, been ordered to break through the rebel line, there was no power in their front to restrain them. The rebels, aware of this, and designing to prevent reinforcements from going to Porter, made frequent feints all along our line. Now with pickets, and anon, gathering a considerable force, they would advance upon some part of our works. From the nature of the ground, they could appear in large force at one point, then withdrawing, pass under cover of the woods and reappear at another point; thus keeping up the idea of a large force.

These skirmishes and the artillery duels had been kept up all day, to the annoyance of all.

Just at sunset, Davidson's brigade was ordered to cross the river, by the Woodbury bridge, to reinforce the Fifth corps. Preparations for moving were not complete, when the enemy opened a fierce fire of artillery and musketry. The idea of reinforcing the Fifth corps was at once abandoned, and we hastily took refuge from the howling missiles behind our breastworks. The artillery firing increased, until the scene became in the highest degree exciting.

Our guns were answering the rebels with great spirit, hurling shells fast and furiously, and clouds of smoke rolled up from both the opposing lines. At length the

---

* McClellan's Report.

rebel infantry was brought forward to charge our line. Hancock's brigade of our Second division, and Burns' of Sedgwick's division, were farthest in advance. Hancock had taken up a critical position in front of the line of works, where his brigade was supporting a strong battery. Against these two advance brigades the enemy pounced with the hope of routing them by this sudden onset. Against Hancock they made the most desperate attempt, but with no success further than driving in the picket line. In return, the rebels were hurried back to the cover of the woods from whence they came, leaving many dead and wounded on the field. While the First brigade was thus bravely withstanding the assault of the rebels, the Third brigade and the Second occupied a second line, acting as support, but neither were actively engaged; yet several of the regiments in the second line lost men by the shells.

During the night our Third brigade relieved Hancock's regiments and remained in possession of the advanced position until afternoon next day. We had moved from our old position while the fight was in progress, and had left everything except arms and ammunition.

We could hear the sound of ambulances in the front where the rebels were gathering up their wounded, till after midnight; and toward morning they made a sally upon a part of the line, but were quickly repulsed.

June 28th, the men of Davidson's brigade who had been ordered the day before to leave haversacks, canteens, blankets and tents, found in the morning that their camp was occupied by another division, tired and hungry, who had lost their blankets in the fights of the two days before, and who had now appropriated the haversacks and blankets of our boys to their own use. Some confusion occurred upon making this discovery, but our boys soon helped themselves to substitutes and bore their loss on the whole very patiently.

Our picket line was relieved at 9 A. M., but before the whole line was changed the rebel batteries opened upon the moving companies a concentrated fire from twenty pieces of artillery, putting a stop to the process. Shot and shell came tearing through our camps in every direction, crashing through trees, throwing up great clouds of dust, riddling tents and alarming the cooks and contraband servants who remained in camp.

This artillery practice continued for an hour without eliciting much reply from our side, as our guns had been nearly all withdrawn from the front to join the train preparatory to the retreat.

The rebels ceased their fire and we inferred that they had withdrawn to some other point; but at two o'clock the mistake was discovered. A brigade of rebels was seen to leap over their breastworks and rush toward our line with yells and shouts like so many madmen. Our picket line was forced back before this impetuous charge, the pickets retreating to the main line.

The Thirty-third New York held the principal part of the picket line, but two companies from the Forty-ninth Pennsylvania of Hancock's brigade, and a detachment from the Seventy-seventh New York also guarded a part of the line in front of the Second division.

A part of the detachment from the Seventy-seventh held a small advance redoubt or lunette which had been thrown up by Hancock's men. Over this work the rebels rushed, unmindful of the bullets sent by the skirmishers, and the guard was compelled to retreat in haste.

But all did not leave that picket line.

One youth, as brave a boy as ever shouldered a musket, John Ham, of the Seventy-seventh regiment, had sworn never to retreat before the enemy. Faithful to his word, when the handful of pickets were compelled to retreat (and this was the first time that any part of his regiment had ever fallen back before the enemy), he stood his ground, loading and firing as rapidly as possible, alone defending the redoubt !

The rebels pressed upon him, and he fell riddled with bullets. When, later in the day, we had driven the confederates back to their works, we recovered his body, pierced by bullets and bayonets.

As the rebels neared our main line of battle, they were met by a withering fire from our men, and, after maintaining the contest for a few moments, they broke and fled in confusion, leaving the ground thickly strewed with dead and wounded. Not satisfied with this repulse, they reformed and came on again ; this time with less audacity than at first. Again a murderous fire compelled them to fall back, leaving more of their number on the field. Among their wounded was Colonel Lamar, who was in command of the charging regiments.

He was brought into our lines by Sergeant Bemis and another soldier of the Seventy-seventh. He had been formerly a mischievous member of congress from Georgia.

The final repulse of the rebels was made more complete and more fatal to them by the timely aid of a section of Mott's battery, which had come up and opened an enfilading fire upon them from the left. Joyous cheers went up from our men as they saw the rebels fleeing in all directions, and it was only by the peremptory orders of their commanders that they were restrained from following the flying enemy.

A company of about fifteen rebels threw out a white flag and voluntarily surrendered themselves. Fifty dead rebels and one hundred wounded remained in our front, whom their comrades were allowed to remove, under flag of truce.

The Thirty-third New York had, during this engagement, sustained the principal shock of the enemy's charge; and with that gallantry for which they bore during their two years of service an enviable reputation, they met the charge and repulsed the enemy.

By the retreat of the Fifth corps to the south side of the Chickahominy, which was accomplished during the night of the 27th and 28th, the rebel army was allowed to approach the river at Gaines' Farm. By this movement the camps of Davidson's brigade, which were upon the extreme right of our line, near the river, and the two forts we had erected, were rendered untenable; for the rebel guns shelled the whole position with ease. Our men went in squads and brought away the most valuable property, including regimental papers and the knapsacks and blankets. A few days before this, our whole corps, as well as the other corps of the army, had been supplied with an abundance of new tents. Staff and company officers had their wall tents, and the private soldiers their shelters. All these were destroyed by cutting them with knives; as it was known that any attempt to remove them would be discovered by the rebels, who would at once open all their batteries upon us.

Now, the feelings of the men underwent a terrible revolution. It was, for the first time, told them that.the army must *retreat* in all haste to the James river! Our brave fellows had looked with sad faces at Porter's retreating column; but that was felicity compared with what they now experienced. Even when the right wing was forced across the river, they still had faith that their bravery was to be rewarded with victory.

Now, they felt that all was lost. General Davidson rode through the camps, and announced to the commanding officers of his regiments the mysterious information, with directions to get off a few valuable articles and abandon all else.

Already, by Porter's retreat, the brave fellows in Liberty Hall Hospital, mangled and sick, groaning with wounds, and delirious with fevers, were abandoned, *deserted*, to fall into the hands of an enemy known to be merciless.

And now the siege of Richmond was to be abandoned, and the men who but two days before had exulted in the glad hope of a speedy entrance into the city, which even now lay just within our grasp, were to turn their backs as *fugitives* before their enemies! It was a time of humiliation and sorrow. Every man was weighed down with a terrible anxiety. Officers hurried to and fro, silently and hastily forwarding the preparations for the retreat. The great caravan of army trains was on its way under the direction of scores of officers, and with it were escorts of cavalry and infantry.

At three o'clock Sunday morning the 29th, the Sixth corps quietly evacuated its works and proceeded in the direction of Savage's Station. The men slung their knapsacks and quietly moved off. A scene of desolation met their view as they passed along. Tents cut to pieces, commissary stores thrown upon the ground or burning in heaps, blankets and clothing piled promiscuously about, not considered worth carrying away; all indicating a retreat under most disastrous circumstances.

We had been preceded by Keyes' corps, which had started at noon the day before, crossed White Oak creek and occupied the opposite side, acting as advance guard for our long trains which were now making all haste toward the James river.

The endless streams of army wagons, artillery trains and ambulances were all pouring down the roads from the various camps, and crowding into the narrow paths that led to the opposite side of the Peninsula. Porter's infantry mingled with the trains, and thousands of cattle driven along through the woods by the roadside made a strange scene. Franklin's, Sumner's and Heintzelman's corps were to guard the rear, and it was with secrecy that we had left the rifle pits; for the enemy was close upon us ready to take advantage of every movement. A picket guard was left to deceive the rebels, while regiment after regiment silently disappeared, leaving only the pickets to hold the long line of earthworks. These brave men waited hour after hour for the signal to retire. The gray lights of the morning broke upon them, yet there was no sign for them to join their commands. At length, when they had given up all hope of being relieved, they were signaled to leave the breastworks, and under cover of the morning mists, they quickly joined their comrades.

The Second division moved in the direction of Savage's Station, while the First kept on to the crossing of White Oak Swamp, acting as rear-guard to Porter's corps. We of the Second division kept along the high lands which skirt the Chickahominy, when, after marching about two miles, the division was brought to bay by the pursuing enemy. Facing about we waited in line of battle for our trains to get out of the way; when we again resumed the retreat. While here, General McClellan, with his immense staff, rode by us on his way toward Harrison's Landing. He passed White Oak Swamp the same day, and waited the arrival of the army; which, hindered by battles and innumerable difficulties, did not come up with its commander again till the 1st of July.

We arrived at Savage's Station at 4 P. M. Here trains and troops were crowded together in wonderful confusion. Immense heaps of commissary stores, arms and ammunition were waiting destruction lest they should fall into the hands of the enemy, and hundreds of sick and wounded men were taking sad leave of their friends; for it had been determined that these brave unfortunate men must be left to the tender mercies of the rebels. Again the division was formed in line of battle to protect our pioneers and the regiments which were engaged in the destruction of the stores. The long railroad bridge across the river at this point had been burned. The work of destruction went on at a marvelous rate. Boxes of hard bread, hundreds of barrels of flour, rice, sugar, coffee, salt and pork were thrown upon the burning piles and consigned to the flames. One heap of boxes of hard bread as large as a good sized dwelling made a part of the sacrifice. Boxes of clothing and shoes were opened and every man as he passed helped himself to whatever he thought worth carrying away. Notwithstanding thousands helped themselves, and huge boxes of clothing were cast into the flames, we found on our return to the Peninsula two years afterwards, that the inhabitants for a long distance around were clothed and shod with articles left by us at Savage's Station on the grand retreat. The people had also made large gains by gathering up the coats, pants, shirts and shoes left on the ground and selling them in Richmond and elsewhere.

It was easy thus to dispose of commissary and quartermaster's stores, but to destroy the immense magazines of cartridges, kegs of powder, and shells, required more care. These were loaded into cars; a long train was filled with these materials, and then, after setting fire to each car, the train was set in motion down the steep grade. With wildest fury the blazing train rushed; each revolution of the wheels adding new impetus to the flying monster, and new volumes to the flames. The distance to the bridge was two miles. On and on the burning train thundered like a frightful meteor. Now, the flames being communicated to the contents of the cars, terrific explosions of shells and kegs of powder lent new excitement to the scene. The air was full of shrieking, howling shells, the fragments of which tore through the trees and branches of the forest; and huge fragments of cars were seen whirling high in the air.

13

At length the train reached the river; and such was its momentum, that, notwithstanding the bridge was burned, the engine and the first car leaped over the first pier in the stream, and the cars hung suspended. While this destruction was going on, Smith's division moved back beyond Savage's Station, toward White Oak Swamp, marching, with frequent halts, three or four miles, when we were ordered to retrace our steps with all speed, to reinforce Sumner's corps, which was engaging the enemy. The heat of the day was most oppressive. Many of our men fell with sunstroke. Among those who thus suffered was General Davidson.

CHAPTER X.

THE GRAND RETREAT.

MEANWHILE the rebel army, finding no force in front of them, were at first at a loss to determine what course we had taken; but when it was discovered that we had withdrawn from before both wings of their army and that our base of supplies at White House had been abandoned, it was quickly divined that the Union army was retreating to the James river. Stuart, with his cavalry, had dashed down to White House and found only heaps of smouldering ruins; and from the absence of all motion in front of the right of their line, it was clear that no attempt was to be made on Richmond. Finding himself thus unexpectedly victorious, Lee at once ordered his forces, now on the north bank of the Chickahominy, to cross over and pursue the retreating army.

During the night of the 28th, they had been actively engaged in rebuilding the bridge destroyed by General Porter, and early on the morning of the 29th, the main body of Lee's army was pouring across the river. Hill and Longstreet moved rapidly so as to interpose between our army and Richmond, and to be able to strike us on the flank; two other divisions followed on the Charles City road, and Jackson, with his corps, moved down the bank of the Chickahominy, threatening our rear.

To resist any attack from these approaching columns, Sumner's and Heintzelman's corps, and our Second division of the Sixth corps, were formed in line of battle before Savage's Station.

For hours our division, with Sumner's corps, stood in the open field watching the enemy. Heintzelman withdrew his corps and left Sumner and Smith to stem the tide that was destined to pour upon us. It seems to have been the impression of General Heintzelman, who had listened with credulity to the stories of the immense superiority of the enemy in numbers, that all hope of resisting the power of Lee's army was gone, and that there remained nothing for us but to make the best of our way to the James river without stopping to give the enemy battle.

In the view that there was no safety but in retreat, he was guided by the opinion of the Commander-in-Chief, who had no thought of any further resistance than should suffice to bring the men and as much of the material of the army as could be brought by the teams across the Peninsula. Not so the old war horse Sumner. He would gladly have attempted, a few hours later, to have "pushed the rebels into the Chickahominy," had not his application for help been answered from beyond White Oak Swamp, "The rear-guard will follow the retreat of the main body of the army." If there was no hope for the army but rapid retreat, then it was right for Heintzelman to leave the road clear; for as it was, with only Sumner's corps and our own division, the road was packed so full that the men could scarcely march. But if there was an opportunity of inflicting great injury upon the rebels, as Sumner believed there was, then we are not surprised at the amazement of the veteran when he discovered, the battle having commenced, that one corps had left the line altogether. We were now as near our new base of supplies as the rebels were to theirs, and here we had enough to last the army

many days.   We were, as they had been, on the defensive;
and we had the advantage in position.   But there was
nothing left for those now on the line but to make the
best resistance possible under the circumstances, and then
fall back to the banks of the James.

About five o'clock the huge cloud of dust in the direction of the camps we had deserted, gave warning of the
approach of that part of the rebel army which was marching by the Charles City road; and at sunset the thunders
of their artillery burst upon us.   For an hour, only the
heavy roar of artillery was heard from both sides.   Shells
screamed from one side to the other, and the bright flashes
and sharp reports, as they burst in the air, mingled with
the noise and smoke of the battle, as battery responded
to battery.   Thus far no discharge of musketry was heard;
but suddenly Magruder's men, with yells and shouts, rushed
to the charge.   Streams of fire flashed along the two lines,
and the rattle of innumerable muskets told of closer work
than artillery duels.   The brave fellows of Sumner, and
of our Vermont brigade, met the assailants with defiant
shouts that rang out above the roar of muskets and
cannon.

Leaving Sumner's heroes to contend the ground on their
part of the line, let us glance more in detail at the part
borne by our own division in this battle of Savage's
Station.

The Vermont brigade having the advance of the division,
General Brooks at once threw his regiments to the front.
The Fifth and Sixth as skirmishers, supported by the
Third and Second in line of battle, the Fourth being
thrown upon the flank, the brigade advanced rapidly
through a wide strip of woods.   Suddenly, as the line of
skirmishers emerged from the woods they received the fire
of a battery and of a strong line of battle.   The Fifth at
once charged upon the force in front, which scattered in

all directions. The rebels were beaten back both from our own and from Sumner's front; but only to reform and press forward again from the cover of the woods to which they had retreated, to give battle with new vigor. Again the flash and roar of musketry mingled with the wild yells of the rebels and the manly shouts of the Unionists, and again nothing could be seen but the clouds of smoke, out of which sprung the vivid blaze of the cannon, and the quick flash of the rifles. Every now and then, fresh troops arriving upon the field would send up the shout above all the other noise of battle, and then nothing but the continuous din of arms could be heard. Three rebel regiments now advanced against the Fifth Vermont; but the brave fellows secured a good position and held it, in spite of every effort of the rebels to dislodge them. The other regiments were not so hotly engaged as the Fifth. Two hundred of the men of that regiment were killed, wounded or missing. Fifty of their dead bodies were left on the field. Davidson's and Hancock's brigades guarded important positions, but were not actively engaged.

The conflict raged till eight o'clock, when the confederates, repulsed at every point, beaten and discouraged, left the field, and no more was seen of them. The whole loss to the confederates in this engagement was about four hundred.

Before midnight, the rear-guard had turned toward White Oak Swamp, leaving many hundreds of our brave wounded and sick men lying upon the green sward, or collected under rude shelters. Here, large groups were gathered under the shade of some large tree; and there, long lines of staggering invalids, leaning upon their guns or staffs for support, tottered after the retreating column, in the hope of being able to reach with it a place of safety.

Surgeons were left to care for these unfortunate ones who could not get off; and a small amount out of the abundance of provisions that was condemned to destruction was saved for them. Of all the sad scenes which had made the Peninsula swarm with melancholy memories, nothing we had seen could compare with this most sorrowful of all. Twenty-five hundred of our sick and wounded were left to fall into the hands of the enemy.

At nine or ten in the evening, we withdrew from our position before Savage's Station, and marched rapidly toward White Oak Swamp. The road was completely filled with wagons, ambulances and artillery, mingled with horsemen and infantry, all crowding forward with utmost speed. Never had our men experienced so severe a march. They were obliged to pick their way among the teams, losing all organization, each man bent upon making his way forward regardless of others.

At length, toward morning, we crossed White Oak creek, ascended a little elevation on the further side, and lay down upon the grass completely exhausted and worn out.

The sun was shining brightly when we were roused from our heavy slumbers. The morning passed in perfect quiet except the rattle of the trains which had parked here over night, and now were hurrying along the narrow road, wagons and artillery rushing by with all speed to allow room for the immense collection to file out. This process continued till afternoon, and was the only source of excitement to us except the distant roar of battle on the left, where McCall and Hooker were hotly engaged. Thus matters continued until about two o'clock; the men seeking shelter among the pines or resting quietly after their weary night's march. A picket line composed of men from the various regiments of our Third brigade, Second division, guarding our extreme right flank. All

were listless and little dreaming of the tremendous storm
of iron hail which was gathering to break upon us in a
moment.

Suddenly, like a thunderbolt, seventy-five pieces of
artillery belched forth their sheets of flame and howling
shells; and in an instant, our whole division was thrown
into the most perfect confusion by the deadly missiles
which flew among us in every direction. Such cannonading had never before been heard by our army, and before
our batteries could reply with any effect, the horses were
killed, the gunners dispersed and the pieces disabled. It
was a most perfect surprise; no one was prepared; men
ran hither and thither seeking shelter behind any object
which seemed even sufficient to conceal them from the
view of the enemy.

It appeared that Jackson had effected a crossing of the
river, and with great secrecy made his way to the border
of White Oak creek, where, concealed by trees and underbrush, he had massed his batteries, and when all was in
perfect readiness had opened upon us this storm of death.
Unutterable confusion prevailed for a time; riderless horses
galloped madly to the rear; men rushed here and there;
officers wandered about without commands, and men were
left without directions how to act. Generals Smith and
Davidson occupied an old fashioned wooden house which
stood upon the brow of the elevation above and facing
the bridge. About it were many orderlies, holding their
horses, or lounging carelessly, or chatting with each other.
The very first volley riddled the house with shells; orderlies rushed from the place in consternation and the inmates
quickly appeared without, gazing in amazement toward
the source of this unexpected cause of the tumult. The
gray-haired owner of the house was cut in two as he stood
in the door, and several other persons were more or less
injured. General Smith, at the moment the cannonade

opened, was engaged at his rude toilette; his departure from the house was so hasty that he left his watch, which he did not recover. He coolly walked off to a less exposed position and devoted himself to restoring order. One regiment, as soon as the shells began to fly, rushed pell-mell to the rear, none of the men standing upon the order of their going.

During all this time a few of the regiments held their ground without moving. By active exertions, on the part of officers, order was restored and the whole division fell back a short distance, taking up a position at the edge of a strip of woods, which commanded an open field. General Smith, with his accustomed fearlessness, was to be seen riding along his lines exhorting his men to coolness, and by his own composure restoring confidence to them. The design of Jackson, to cross the stream, was frustrated. The firing soon ceased, and, as darkness came on, quiet again reigned, except now and then a little skirmishing.

At nine o'clock in the evening, under cover of the darkness, we silently and hastily withdrew. All orders were given in whispers; men refrained from conversation; and everything indicated the most intense anxiety on the part of our generals for the safety of the army. Thus, in silence, we hastened on our way; the weary and exhausted troops scarcely able to keep awake while they marched. No better illustration can be given of the intense state of anxiety, excitement and doubt which prevailed, than the following little incident, which occurred during this night march. Our Third brigade, leading the Second division, had halted where the narrow road passed through a piece of woods, waiting a moment for the road to clear, or for the guides to report the direction for the march. Generals Franklin and Davidson, with officers of Davidson's brigade, were grouped together near the head of the column, sitting upon their horses. The weary men, almost overcome by sleep, were leaning upon their muskets or lying in the road half asleep. Officers nodded and swung this way and that in their saddles. The stillness of death prevailed. In an instant, without any perceptible cause, as though a breath from some evil genius had swept the narrow track, every man was gone from the road. They stood in the woods looking with breathless wonder into the road for the unseen danger. After the first moment of surprise, the word passed along, in low tones, "Attention!" Not a living being could be seen in the road, and all was silence. Recovering from the first surprise, General Davidson looked for General Franklin, who, but a moment before, was dozing by his side. "General Franklin! General Franklin!" called the general in a loud whisper, but nothing could be found of him, and we saw no more of him that night. What was the cause of this sudden alarm we never knew. Possibly, a riderless horse might have suddenly startled those in front, or, quite as likely, there was no cause whatever; but the incident illustrates the state of feeling in the army that night.

At length, just as the gray light of the morning was streaking the skies, we came in sight of the majestic James river. Every man took a long breath, as though relieved of a heavy load of anxiety. Officers clasped their hands and exclaimed, "Thank God." The worn out men stepped lighter, for they had arrived at the haven of their hopes. Again they experienced a feeling of safety. We filed into a beautiful clover field, and there the exhausted columns sunk down for a brief rest. Brief it was to be, for scarcely had two hours passed when we were ordered into line of battle. We moved back through the woods, crossing a little stream, and formed in a wheat field, where the grain stood in shocks. Here we remained, watching the enemy, who stood in our front, contenting themselves with occasional sallies of their skirmishers, while the great battle of Malvern Hill was in progress on our left, where the booming of our field pieces and the dull roar of the heavy guns from the gunboats was heard for many hours. At length, as night came on, the sound of battle died away, and all was again quiet. Now we heard cheers on the left, and, looking in that direction, we saw, approaching at great speed, the commander of the Union army. Cheers greeted him as he rode along the line, and hats were thrown high in the air in honor of the chief.

As the leading corps of the army had fallen back from White Oak Swamp, they had occupied a superb position on the James river, called Malvern Hill. The wagons and other impedimentia of the army had also arrived there, and were secured behind the southern slope of the hill. The place was admirably adapted for a defensive battle. It was a lofty plateau, rising not less than one hundred and fifty feet above the plain, sloping gently toward the north and east, down to the border of the forest. The approach to this sloping field was rendered difficult by ravines, which ran along the front; and the enemy, if he approached, must do so by way of the roads which crossed them.

Upon the crest was posted the battery of siege guns which had escaped the hands of the enemy; and nearly three hundred field pieces were arranged along the heights, so that the fire might pass over the heads of the infantry, who were arranged upon the glacis, up which the enemy must charge, hidden, for the most part, by the tall wheat and corn. Here the main body of the army was posted. First, nearest the James, was Porter's corps; then Heintzelman's, Keyes', Sumner's and our Sixth corps, occupying the right flank, two or three miles from the position where the rebels must advance with their main force. The fleet of gunboats floated upon the river, on our left flank, ready to send their screaming monster shells into the ranks of the advancing enemy.

Against this position, naturally almost impregnable, Lee hurled his hosts, with the design of giving the final blow to the Union army, which should insure its destruction and capture. The rebel army confidently believed that the army of the north must now be compelled to surrender or be driven into the James.

If the rebels were confident and exultant, our own men were filled with the deepest despondency.

Exhausted by a month of constant labor and watchfulness, with fighting and marching and digging, now, as they believed, fleeing from the face of an enemy immensely superior to them in numbers, it is not to be wondered at that they were apprehensive of the worst results.

Paymasters sought refuge with their treasures in the gunboats on the river. The Prince De Joinville and his nephews, the Count De Paris and Count De Chartes, who had acted as aides de camp to General McClellan, who had been with us from the beginning, active, brave men, who were frequently where the danger was greatest, and who had entered our service with the determination of seeing it to the end, now departed; they, too, finding a respite from their toils upon one of the gunboats. The young men were accompanied on board by the staff and by the Commander-in-Chief himself. From the deck of the vessel he communicated his orders by the signal flags, to those left in command on shore. Here, with his young friends, and in consultation with the commander of the fleet, he remained until about five o'clock, when he rode down the lines to the rear of our corps, where he spent the time till darkness put an end to the fight.

Such was the sad state of feeling in our army. Yet, exhausted and depressed as they were, our men were as brave and determined as ever. They had yet a country;

and they knew that the fate of that country depended upon the result of this encounter, and they resolved to acquit themselves with heroism and even desperation.

Lee had marshaled his whole force in front of our strong position. He wrote to each of his division commanders ordering an assault, and directing, when they heard the yell of Armistead's troops, to charge also with yells.

The yell was heard, and some of the divisions, but not all, pressed forward to a wild charge.

The rebels came on heroically, but were sent reeling back down the slope in confusion and disorder. Again and again they renewed the charge from under cover of the woods which skirted the base of the slope. They would start across the open space, charging our batteries with wild yells, but the heavy fire of our guns and the steady volleys of our infantry sent them back as often to the shelter of the woods. At times our infantry would reserve their fire till the rebel columns had run the gauntlet of shot and shell from our batteries, almost reaching our lines, when with exultant cheers they would bound forward to seize the prize now almost within their grasp, when our men would open upon them a single volley, and, leaping over the breastworks, pursue the panic-stricken assailants, capturing prisoners and colors, and driving the rebels in confusion down the slope. Thus the battle raged with terrible fury; every attempt on the part of the enemy failing, until darkness set in, and the rebel chiefs were glad to let the battle subside; though it was not till nine o'clock the artillery firing ceased.

The weight of the attacks had been upon our center. Here Couch, Sumner and Heintzelman withstood the shock of battle for hours, only a part of Porter's corps being engaged, and neither our Sixth corps nor Casey's division of Keyes' corps being actively in the fight.

The rebel General Trimble thus describes the condition of their army on the morning after the battle:

"The next morning by dawn I went off to ask for orders, when I found the whole army in the utmost disorder. Thousands of straggling men were asking every passer-by for their regiments; ambulances, wagons and artillery obstructing every road; and altogether in a drenching rain presenting a scene of the most woful and heart-rending confusion."

Had but a show of an attack upon such an army been made, it must have resulted in defeat and utter rout to the rebels.

CHAPTER XI.

AT HARRISON'S LANDING.

OUR corps remained in line of battle in the wheat field till early next morning; changing position during the night just often enough to deprive us of rest. As we started out toward Harrison's Landing the rain was pouring in sheets; and throughout the day it continued to deluge the country. The roads were rivers of almost fathomless mud; and our tired men could scarcely drag themselves along. But at four in the afternoon we halted under cover of our gunboats, and bivouacked for the night. Such a deplorable scene as was here, was enough to melt the heart of the stoutest. As we debouched from a piece of woods skirting the plateau at Harrison's Landing, officers stood like hotel porters at a steamboat landing, calling out "This way for the Third corps;" "This way for the Fifth corps;" "This way for Slocum's division." All was confusion. The whole army seemed to be made of stragglers. Our little Brigadier Davidson rose in his saddle to an unusual height, as he looked back and saw with undisguised pride, his brigade marching in, almost unbroken.

The landscape before us was indescribably beautiful. There lay the James river, and spreading out between us and the river were the broad fields of wheat; the fine country houses; the long avenues and roads lined with rows of cedar trees; which last were almost in a moment stripped of their branches to make beds for the soldiers.

There, crowded together, were the immense caravans of wagons, ambulances, guns and pontoons, hugging the river, and the multitude of men swarming over the plain. Long processions of sick and wounded men, leaning on canes and crutches, their heavy steps and sunken faces now for a moment lighted up at the thought that their melancholy pilgrimage was nearly ended, filed by us; and battalions of cooks and special duty men were wandering about in search of their commands.

The river was full of transports and gunboats, giving it the appearance of the harbor of some commercial metropolis. Many of the hungry men, without waiting for their rations to be brought by the commissary, plunged into the stream, swam to the boats and there procured the coveted food. But the greater number of our men, their powers completely exhausted, without waiting for food, or to provide comfortable quarters, lay down in the bed of mud and were soon in heavy slumbers.

Again, after a poor night's rest, the corps was marched to a new position on the front line, where we remained to celebrate the anniversary of the nation's birthday. A gloomy "Fourth of July" was this to us, though every effort was made to keep up the spirits of the men. Early in the morning the enemy opened a fire upon parts of our line, to which our guns responded. A national salute had been ordered, and precisely at the hour appointed, while the fighting was in progress, the heavy guns were heard booming the salute. Our boys listened for a moment, and then, as if all inspired with new life, they made the welkin ring with their cheers. The bands, roused from their long inactivity, pealed forth stirring national airs, and the Commander-in-Chief issued an address to his army, in which he praised its gallantry and firmness, declared that he himself had established the new line, and that if the enemy would come upon us now we would convert his repulse into a final defeat.

At home, a heavy gloom hung over the nation. The news of our retreat and of the terrible battles, had been carried by the magic wires to the remotest parts of the north; but few yet knew the fate of their friends who were in the great army. It was enough that the siege of Richmond, which had cost so much time and money, and, above all, so many thousands of brave men, was abandoned, and the grand army, on which the hopes of the nation hung, was now beleaguered, defending itself in an unhealthy position, which offered little advantage for anything but defense. Sympathizers with the rebellion secretly rejoiced and openly prophesied the speedy destruction of our army by the scorching sun and poisoned air, even if left to itself by the rebels.

The cause of all these disastrous circumstances was by some attributed to unwise interference, on the part of the authorities in Washington, with the plans of the chief of our army. They claimed that the President, Secretary of War and the Major-General commanding all the armies of the Union, had, in the words of General McClellan, "done what they could to defeat this army." They complained loudly that reinforcements had been withheld, and that McDowell, with a large force, had been kept unemployed in the vicinity of Fredericksburgh, when his corps would have thrown the balance of strength upon our side. Others claimed that the whole campaign had been sadly misman-aged by a commander who had, as they insisted, never seen his army fight; who had invariably found employment elsewhere than on the field of battle when fighting was to to be done, and whose character as a soldier was made up of doubts and hesitancies.

15

Six weeks of camp life, dreary, sickly and monotonous, succeeded our arrival at Harrison's Bar.

Our corps proceeded to the work of throwing up strong intrenchments and mounting guns. Our Third brigade, Second division, constructed an extensive fort, in which several very heavy guns were mounted; each of the regiments taking their turn at the labor. In our front the forests were slashed for a great distance, and thousands of sturdy wood-cutters plied their heavy blows, sweltering under the burning rays of the sun.

Sickness became almost universal. The men were worn out with the tremendous labors which they had performed since their arrival on the Peninsula; they were burned by almost unendurable heat; they were nearly devoured by the countless myriads of flies and other annoying insects; and they were forced to drink impure and unwholesome water. It was not strange that hundreds died in camp, and that hundreds more, with the seeds of death implanted in their constitutions, went to their homes in the north to breathe out their lives in the midst of their friends, or languished in the large government hospitals at Washington, and other cities.

Leaves of absence were given freely, and thousands availed themselves of the opportunity of visiting their homes and recruiting their health. The men, with the patience which none but soldiers ever exhibit, went quietly to work to render their situation as tolerable as possible. Wells were dug in the camps, from which they procured better water than they were able to get at first, and small pines were brought and set among the tents, by which some degree of protection was afforded against the burning sun. On the morning of the 8th of July, the monotony was broken by the arrival of President Lincoln. The booming of artillery announced his coming, and the heartfelt cheers of the soldiers assured him of a welcome.

The President, after spending a few hours at the head-quarters of the army, proceeded to review the various corps. He was accompanied by General McClellan, and many officers of note. Everywhere he received an enthusiastic welcome from the men, who regarded him as their warm friend. He manifested great emotion as he rode along the lines and saw that the regiments, which but a few weeks before had left Washington with full ranks, were now mere skeletons of regiments. Evening drew its mantle over the scene, and the review was closed by moonlight.

Little occurred to relieve the monotony of the six weeks of camp life at Harrison's Bar, except the events of which we have spoken; a demonstration by the enemy during the night of the 31st, and an advance to Malvern Hill by General Hooker's division. On the former occasion, the troops were startled from their slumbers about midnight, by the sudden discharge of a battery of artillery from the south side of the James. The rebels had succeeded in getting a force in position there, and they now opened a vigorous fire upon our shipping and our camps. Their shells flew among us in disagreeable proximity, and the long lines of fire traced upon the midnight sky lent a certain charm to the dangerous business. Our gunboats answered the fire; and after two hours of exciting work drove the rebels from their position. Some infantry was taken across the river, who hastened the retreat of the enemy, burned the buildings near the shore, and cut down the trees, that they might not in future afford concealment for the rebels.

General Hooker's reconnoissance resulted in his occupying Malvern Hill for a day or two, having a brisk skirmish with the enemy and returning to camp.

Our active and gallant Brigadier-General Davidson was, early in August, relieved from the command of our

Third brigade, and ordered to the department of Missouri. Notwithstanding the severity of his discipline, and his occasional forgetfulness that men could not accomplish as much physical labor as horses — for the general had always been a cavalry officer — his never-tiring energy, his undoubted bravery, and his interest and pride in his brigade, had endeared him to the men. During the severe trials on the Chickahominy, and on the retreat, the general had taken an unusual interest in the brigade, and had made himself personally acquainted with nearly all the members of his command.

The general took command of a cavalry division in Missouri; where his name became a terror to all secessionists in that part of the country. The command devolved upon Lieutenant-Colonel Corning of the Thirty-third New York, then senior officer of the brigade, who was soon succeeded by Colonel W. H. Irwin, of the Forty-ninth Pennsylvania Volunteers.

Reinforcements began to arrive from Washington, and our army, in August, numbered one hundred and twenty thousand men. With these, and a few thousand more, General McClellan declared his belief that he could repel the enemy and advance into Richmond.

Let us for a moment turn to the fortunes of the regiment with which we left Saratoga, and whose early history we have traced. In all the stirring events which have transpired in the division and corps, the Seventy-seventh has acted an important and honorable part. Always ready to perform the duties demanded of it; always in its place when danger was greatest; ever cheerfully obeying the commands of superiors, it has assumed no honor above its fellows, but proudly claimed to be the peer of such noble regiments as the Sixth Maine, the Fifth Wisconsin, the Thirty-third New York, and other bright stars in the galaxy of the Sixth corps; ornaments to it and the army. "It is a little regiment," said General Davidson to a member of Governor Morgan's staff, who came to look after the interests of the New York troops, "but it is always in the right place." The general regarded the regiment with especial favor, and was accustomed to call it "my little Seventy-seventh." Since the arrival of the army on the Peninsula the experiences of the regiment have been varied. With the other regiments of Smith's division, it has spent a month at Yorktown, within musket shot of the enemy. At Williamsburgh it, with other regiments of its brigade, supported batteries in front of Fort Magruder, and when, in the afternoon, it received the order to go with the Forty-ninth to the assistance of Hancock, it started forward with cheers; the men going through the mud at double quick. But when the two regiments arrived on the field, their gallant brothers of Hancock's and of their own brigade, had nobly accomplished the work in which they would gladly have assisted. We have seen how gallantly the regiment routed the rebels at Mechanicsville; capturing a flag and other trophies; and when on the Chickahominy Smith's division held the line closest upon the enemy, it bravely assumed its part of the labor and danger. A portion of the regiment on picket on the 28th of June, exhibited sterling heroism, and we need hardly refer to the noble sacrifice of the brave young soldier John Ham.

Disease and exhaustion had made terrible inroads upon the Seventy-seventh. Instead of nearly a thousand men with which we came to the Peninsula, inspection in the middle of June showed only about two hundred and fifty men present for duty. Although this regiment had from the very beginning occupied an exposed position in the very front line; although it composed a part of Smith's division, which has already become famous both in the Union and rebel armies for being always in closest proximity to the enemy, yet it had thus far lost very few men in battle. All the rest of those now absent had been stricken down by fevers, or worn out by the exhausting labors and exposures of the campaign.

Among those attacked by typhoid fever was Colonel McKean. After suffering a few days in the vain hope of soon being able to place himself again at the head of his regiment, he was removed from the poisonous atmosphere of the swamps to Washington, and thence to his home in Saratoga. The men looked upon his departure with sincere regret, for they not only respected him as an able commander, but loved him for his never failing interest in their welfare. He had been to the regiment in the capacity of commander and father. His leave of the regiment was destined to be final; for except as an occasional visitor he never returned to it; and after many months of suffering, his constitution undermined, and his health permanently destroyed, he was forced to relinquish the command. But though forced to leave the field, the men of his regiment never ceased to cherish feelings of love and respect for their first commander. They had witnessed his bravery on the field, and they now knew that he was contending with disease with the same fortitude that had marked his course in the army. The departure of Colonel McKean from the service was not only a great loss to his regiment but to the whole corps; for he was not only a brave officer, but a gentleman of superior intellectual endowments. Another of the sufferers from typhoid fever was Lieutenant Bowe, a young man of fine abilities and greatly beloved by his regiment. After several weeks of absence, he returned to camp on the 18th of July restored to health. On the very next day, while standing with several officers in a tent, he was fatally wounded by an accidental shot from a pistol. His father, hearing of the sad occurrence, came for him and removed

James B. McKean
Col. 77 th Regt. N.Y.S.V.

him from camp; but only to see him expire in a few days.

Changes occurred among the officers. The lieutenant-colonel and major left the service, the first by resignation, the other by dismissal. Adjutant French was made major, and afterwards lieutenant-colonel, which office he held during the remainder of the term of the regiment. He assumed command of the regiment on his return to it after the battle of Antietam, and continued in command while it was a regiment. Captains and lieutenants also resigned. Chaplain Tully and Quartermaster Shurtliff departed for ther homes, having left the service. Lieutenant Hayward was made quartermaster, a position for which he was eminently qualified, and which he thenceforward held to the great satisfaction of the entire regiment.

CHAPTER XI.

RETREAT FROM THE PENINSULA, AND GENERAL POPE'S BULL RUN CAMPAIGN.

Premonitions of a change of base — The transfer commenced — Marching down the Peninsula — On board transports — A contrast — Arrival at Alexandria — Unaccountable delays — General Pope's campaign — An obstinate general — Causes of Pope's failure.

EARLY in August, rumors were floating about the army, that General McClellan had received positive orders to transfer the Army of the Potomac to the front of Washington, there to unite the forces of the two armies; and that this plan was strongly opposed by General McClellan, who insisted that he wanted only a few thousand more men to march into Richmond.

The army had received large reinforcements since arriving at Harrison's Landing, and now numbered more than one hundred thousand men; not by any means an inconsiderable force, yet too small, in General McClellan's opinion, to warrant another advance.

But, owing to the movements of the enemy in front of General Pope, the supposed impracticability of the route, and to some distrust as to the abilities of General McClellan by the authorities at Washington, peremptory orders had been sent to him to remove his army as quickly as possible from the Peninsula.

What the merits of the dispute in high places might be, the army at large was not able to decide; but the rumors gave rise to many spirited debates, in which the authorities at Washington and the authority at Harrison's Bar had each earnest advocates. At length it became known that the army was to leave the Peninsula, and preparations for this important movement commenced. The work of shipping the sick and wounded, numbering twelve thousand five hundred, began; but it was not carried on with a degree of alacrity satisfactory to the War Department or the President.

The wharves along the river side became the scene of immense activity. Ambulances crowded along the banks of the river, laden with sick and wounded, while those from the hospitals able to walk, tottered along with trembling steps, their wan faces and sunken eyes telling their story of suffering. Transports were in waiting for these, and were rapidly filled with their freight of suffering humanity. Everything not movable was ordered to be destroyed. Tents were struck and taken to the pickets who had left them behind, and everything betokened an important movement. Three or four days were spent in momentary expectation of the order to "fall in," but still the situation remained unchanged.

At length, on the 16th of August, all was ready and the men were ordered to pack their knapsacks; but the men of the Sixth corps remained in camp until the sun's rays became scorching; then the column moved rapidly eastward. A hard day's march on the 16th and another on the 17th, brought the corps in sight of the Chickahominy. It crossed a pontoon bridge of enormous extent, in the construction of which ninety boats were used, and the length of which was over two thousand feet. Thoroughly exhausted the men bivouacked on the eastern bank of the Chickahominy.

The rebels, now aware of the retreat, were following close at the heels of the Union army, but declined to make any offensive demonstrations, further than picking up stragglers and those that fell out by the way from

16

weakness and fatigue. The main portion of the rebel army was now occupied in important movements in another direction.

Another rapid march, under a burning sun, brought our corps to the ancient capital of the Old Dominion — Williamsburgh. Passing through its streets without halting, taking only time to glance at its now dilapidated buildings, we reached the familiar scenes of the old battle-field, which, three months before, we little expected to recross before the downfall of the rebellion. Here was the plain where a portion of our Second division had, by its gallantry, decided the fate of the battle; the scene of our bivouac in the rain and mud, and the redoubts where lay the wounded rebels, whose groans had rendered the night hideous. In the midst of these scenes we bivouacked again for the night.

At dawn the column moved again, and after a fatiguing march reached Yorktown; our Second division encamping in the works erected by Porter's division during our famous thirty days' siege of that place.

Many of the men had by this time become exhausted; and a long train of ambulances was filled with these and sent ahead on the morning of the 20th. The well ones soon followed toward Fortress Monroe, halting on the field of Big Bethel. This was the first visit of our corps to this disastrous field, and the men rambled about manifesting great interest in the spot rendered sacred by the blood of Winthrop and Greble.

Plums, peaches and sweet potatoes constituted novel additions to the diet of the men, and although the two former were unripe, their good effects were manifested in arresting multitudes of those troublesome cases of diarrhea which had resisted all treatment so long as the men were deprived of acid fruits. Another hard march on the 21st brought the corps again, after five months' absence, to the vicinity of the desolated village of Hampton, and the end of our march for the present. The whole army was crowded along the shores, waiting to embark for Aquia. Transports of every size and description were riding upon the bay or lashed to the wharves, and infantry, cavalry and artillery were crowding toward the beach ready to take their turn to embark. The scene was one of unusual activity, resembling only the one we had witnessed on embarking for the Peninsula months ago.

At length all were on board, and the transports swung out upon the bay and steamed up the Potomac. One of the transports on which a portion of the Second division was embarked, the "Vanderbilt," had been, in other days, an old friend, as she ploughed up and down the Hudson; now her magnificent saloons, which had been of dazzling beauty, were dismantled and disfigured. No gorgeous drapery or gilded mirrors adorned them, but desolation and filth prevailed.

The weather was charming, and, except for the crowded condition of the transports, the trip would have been a delightful one. What a contrast was there in the appear- ance of those same men now, and when they came down the river in April! Then our ranks were full; the men were healthy and in fresh vigor; their uniforms were new and clean, and their muskets and equipments were polished and glistening. Now, we looked about with sadness when we remembered how many of our former companions were absent, and how few present. We could bring to mind many who went to the Peninsula, full of hope, who had sunk as victims of the malarial poisons, and now rested in hum- ble graves at Yorktown or along the Chickahominy; and many others who had nobly fallen upon the field of strife; and yet others who now were wearing out tedious days of sickness in hospitals or at home.

The little band that remained could hardly be recognized as the same men who left the defenses of Washington but a few months since; their faces were now bronzed from constant exposure to the scorching rays of the sun, and their clothing was worn and soiled. Hats and caps of every description: hats of straw and of palm leaf, of brown wool, black wool, and what had been white wool. Caps military and caps not military, all alike in only one respect, that all were much the worse for wear. It would have puzzled a stranger to have determined from this diversity of apparel, what was the regular uniform of our troops.

We came up the river with feelings far less exultant and confidant than those experienced in our downward trip. Indeed a gloom hung over the minds of all. The army was satisfied that General McClellan would be removed from command, and it was said that General Pope or General Burnside would be his successor. Though they remembered the brilliant successes of the one in the west and of the other in the south, many expressed fears that the command of a large army might be as fatal to either of these as it had been to General McClellan.

At sunset of the 23d, the transports bearing the two divisions of the Sixth corps, were anchored just off Alexandria; but none of the men were allowed to go ashore. Spending another night in the crowded vessels, where the foul air prevailing between decks rendered breathing anything but a luxury, the men hailed the appearance of daylight as the time for their liberation from this close and unpleasant confinement.

The process of disembarking progressed rapidly, and the divisions were marched through the city to a field about a mile beyond its limits, where we encamped near Fort Ellsworth.

Although this was on Sunday morning, and it was known that Pope's army was fighting the enemy even before we left the Peninsula, and was in need of reinforcements; yet no signs of marching occurred until Thursday.

Let us now turn back for a moment and hastily glance at the movements of General Pope and his army, which had now for several days been actively engaged. The battle of Cedar Mountain was fought on Saturday, August 9th. General Banks, pushing his corps toward Cedar Mountain, and, finding the enemy in his front, had boldly attacked him. The confederate forces were led by General Jackson, and outnumbered the forces under General Banks. The field was hotly contested for an hour and a half, when our forces were obliged to fall back; but being reinforced by Rickett's division, they were able to prevent the enemy from occupying the field. During the night, Jackson withdrew his forces, leaving the ground in our hands, which was at once occupied by the Union forces.

The whole of Sunday was occupied in burying the dead and bringing off the wounded of both armies. Our men had behaved with great bravery, and the gallantry and zeal of General Banks was what might have been expected from that general. The field was yet in our hands; yet the battle could hardly be called a decided victory for our arms. Jackson retreated rapidly across the Rapidan, in the direction of Gordonsville, leaving many dead and wounded along the road from Cedar Mountain to Orange Court House. Except to follow up the enemy with cavalry as far as Orange Court House, no important move was made for several days by the forces under General Pope.

Reinforcements were constantly arriving for Jackson, and it became evident, by the 18th, that nearly the whole of Lee's army was assembling in front of General Pope, along the south side of the Rapidan. Among papers captured from the enemy at this time, was an autograph letter from General Robert Lee to General Stuart, stating his determination to overwhelm General Pope's army before it could be reinforced by any portion of the army of the Potomac.

The whole army was now ordered to fall back and occupy a stronger position behind the Rappahannock. The movement was executed on the 18th and 19th of August, without loss; the new line extending from Kelley's Ford to a point three miles above Rappahannock Station. The enemy appeared next day at the various fords, but, finding them strongly guarded, waited for all their forces to arrive from the Rapidan.

The whole of the 21st and 22d were spent by the enemy in efforts to cross the river, and a fierce artillery duel prevailed along the line for more than seven miles in extent, but the rebels were repulsed at every point, and withdrew with the intention of moving up the river and turning the flank of the Union army.

General Pope, appreciating the danger of this movement on the part of the rebels, telegraphed to Washington, and, in reply, was assured that, if he could hold out two days longer, he should be so strongly reinforced as to enable him, not only to hold his position, but to take the offensive.

It is needless to say that, with the exception of one or two small divisions, no reinforcements reached him within that time; and although General Porter reported to him by letter from Bealton on the 25th, it had been better for General Pope had he not come at all. On the night of the 26th, Jackson, coming through Thoroughfare Gap, got in the rear of Pope's army and cut the railroad at Kettle Run, near Warrenton Junction. Lee was still in front, in the vicinity of Sulphur Springs. General Pope, desiring at the same time to fall back toward Centreville and interpose his army between Jackson's and Lee's forces, ordered a retrograde movement. His troops were by this time fairly exhausted. In his report to the Secretary of War, he says: " From the 18th of August, until the morning of the 27th, the troops under my command had been continually marching and fighting night and day; and during the whole of that time there was scarcely an interval of an hour without the roar of artillery. The men had had little sleep, and were greatly worn down with fatigue; had had little time to get proper food or to eat it; had been engaged in constant battles and skirmishes, and had performed services, laborious, dangerous and excessive, beyond any previous experience in this country." Jackson had succeeded in burning fifty cars at Bristow Station, and a hundred more at Manassas Junction, heavily laden with ammunition and supplies. On the afternoon of the 27th, a severe engagement occurred between Hooker's division of Heintzelman's corps, which had arrived the evening before, and Ewell's division of Longstreet's corps, near Bristow Station. Ewell was driven back; the loss on each side being about three hundred. During the night, General McDowell with his corps, and Generals Reno and Kearney with their divisions, took such positions as effectually to interpose between Jackson's forces and Lee's, and no alternative was left Jackson but to turn upon Hooker and rout him, or to retreat by way of Centreville. Hooker's men had exhausted their ammunition, so that there were but five rounds per man left. General Pope, fearing that Hooker would be attacked, dispatched an aid to General Porter with orders to join Hooker at once. The aid was instructed to inform General Porter of the immediate necessity of moving at once, and to remain and guide him to the place. But Porter utterly refused to obey the order. Most fortunately for our army, Jackson, ignorant of Hooker's weakness, determined to retreat by way of Centreville; a mistake which prevented most serious consequences to us. Jackson in his retreat was hotly pursued, and on the 28th a severe battle took place between McDowell's corps and the retreating column, in which our forces gained decided advantages. On the 29th, Jackson was again near the old Bull Run battle-ground, and a terrific battle ensued, which lasted with great fury from daylight until dark. The rebels were driven from the field, which was occupied by our men. General Pope sent peremptory orders to Fitz John Porter to move at once upon Centreville; which would have cut off Jackson's retreat; but again this commander refused to obey orders, and Jackson was enabled to unite with Lee, who had by this time reached Thorough-fare Gap, and was pushing on toward him. Had the orders of General Pope been carried out, Jackson must without doubt have been crushed before Lee's forces could by any possibility have reached the field of action.

On the following day the whole of both armies were brought face to face with each other. General Pope, by this time hopeless of any aid from the fresh troops he had expected long before this from Washington, and aware of the disaffection of the largest and freshest corps in his command, although nearly discouraged, determined to give battle and inflict as much damage as possible upon the enemy. His force now, including Porter's corps, was about forty thousand. The whole of Lee's and Jackson's forces now pressed upon our lines with terrible effect.

The action raged with great fury for several hours; the rebels constantly massing heavy columns against our lines, especially upon the left, where McDowell's and Sigel's corps resisted the onset with great bravery, but were at length forced to yield, when an utter rout took place; the whole army falling back upon Centreville in great disorder. On this day, for the first time in all these long series of battles, Porter's corps was brought into action. The conduct of the corps, in the early part of the day, showed a determination on the part of its leaders not to fight, and the men fell back in disorder; but being rallied later in the day, the pride of the men overcame the obstinacy of their commanders and the corps did good service. Hooker's and Kearney's divisions, and Reynolds' Pennsylvania reserves had rendered most gallant services from the time they reached General Pope's army.

Returning now to our Sixth corps under General Franklin. The corps remained quietly at Alexandria, from the morning of the 24th until the afternoon of the 29th. Rations and ammunition were as well supplied when we reached Alexandria as when we left. The booming of cannon was heard on the 26th and 27th, and contrabands and white refugees informed us that terrible fighting was in progress beyond Manassas. We wondered that we were not ordered to go to the relief of the little army which we knew was resisting the whole of Lee's and Jackson's forces.

On Thursday afternoon, August 28th, the corps received marching orders. Tents were struck, knapsacks packed, rations provided, and many regiments, shouldering their knapsacks, stood in line ready to move. But sunset came and no further orders. The men waited impatiently, only a few venturing to unpack their knapsacks or pitch their tents, until long after dark.

Friday morning brought few indications of an advance. Head-quarter tents remained standing, artillery horses stood unharnessed, and everything showed an intentional delay. At length the corps moved. Marching quietly and easily, the old ground of Camp Misery was passed, and the corps reached Annandale, where it halted and encamped after an easy march of six miles. Saturday morning the corps again moved leisurely along, making very frequent halts. The firing in front indicated a hardly contested battle, and our men, knowing that Pope must be in need of reinforcements, were anxious to push forward rapidly. Every hour the corps halted for at least twenty minutes,

17

and sometimes even longer. At this snail pace we passed Fairfax Court House, the roar of musketry and artillery becoming constantly louder in front, and arrived at Centreville. Orders immediately came for the corps to proceed to Cub Run, about two miles beyond Centreville. Here, wounded men by hundreds and stragglers in greater numbers passed across the little bridge over the run, a dismal crowd, hastening toward Centreville.

As usual at such times, scores of cowardly villains were attempting to pass to the rear as wounded men.

An amusing encounter occurred between one of this class, a coward in captain's uniform, and one of our own officers, Captain Deyoe, as brave a fellow as ever drew a sword. The demoralized captain, his sword thrown away and its sheath after it, came hurriedly upon the bridge, where Deyoe was sitting, coolly filling his pipe. The fugitive captain turned his face, pale with fright, to the imperturbable Deyoe, and, striking him on the shoulder, said with as much composure as he could muster, " Captain, we have had hard times of it out there, but *don't be afraid, don't be afraid.*" Deyoe, turning his face toward that of the straggler with a look of unruffled coolness and unmitigated contempt, replied, " Well, who the d— *is* afraid? Oh, yes, I see, *you are.* Well, you had better get away from here then ! "

The corps remained at Cub Run until nightfall, when it was ordered to return to Centreville, where it encamped. Regiments from our Third brigade were sent to the rear of Centreville to arrest stragglers, who were hurrying toward Alexandria in great numbers.

The regiments were drawn up in line across the turnpike, where they remained all night, turning back hundreds of stragglers at the point of the bayonet.

The scene at Centreville on the next day was one of the utmost confusion. Thousands of stragglers wandered about without knowing or caring what had become of their commands; long columns of shattered regiments and batteries filed past to take up new positions, either within the intrenchments or on the flanks. The appearance of these skeletons of regiments and batteries gave evidence of the terrible experiences of this long series of engagements. Their ranks, thinned by the fortunes of battle, and still more by the disgraceful skulking which had become so universal, the worn and weary appearance of the men, their flags, each surrounded by only enough men to constitute a respectable color-guard, all showed that even the hard experiences of the Army of the Potomac had never had so demoralizing an effect as this.

The skulkers were loud-mouthed in their denunciations of General McDowell. Hundreds of them, who had in all probability not been near enough to the front during the whole retreat to know anything that was going on there, declared that they had seen him waving that mystic white hat as a signal to the rebels; and all knew that it was through his treachery that the army had been destroyed. Others declared positively that they had seen, with their own eyes, General McClellan, with a small body of faithful followers, dash against the advancing foe, and arrest the pursuit! Such wild and improbable stories filled the whole atmosphere, and, strangest of all, were believed by thousands, not only in the army, but throughout the whole north.

Long trains of ambulances were bringing from the battle-field wounded men, who had been, since Saturday, exposed to the burning sun and the storm which had prevailed during Sunday night.

Temporary hospitals were established, and surgeons were actively employed in ministering to the relief of the unfortunate. Monday evening the battle of Glendale or Chantilly was fought, in the midst of a terrific thunder

storm. The enemy, in attempting to turn our right, had
been met by Hooker, Reno, McDowell and Kearney, and
repulsed with heavy loss, from our entire front. But the
victory was a costly one for us. The brave, earnest and
accomplished soldier, Major-General Kearney, and the
gallant Stevens, were both killed while leading their commands against the enemy.

The Sixth corps, on Monday evening, was marched back
to Fairfax Court House; but early next morning returned
within a mile of Centreville, when it took possession of
the heights, and lay in line of battle until three o'clock
P. M., when orders were received to march back to our old
camp at Alexandria, which we reached at ten o'clock the
same night; thus making in a single evening, a distance
that had required two full days and a part of another, to
march, in going out.

Thus ended General Pope's campaign in Virginia.
Never was a campaign so misrepresented or so little
understood; and never were the motives of men so falsely
judged as were those of the generals connected with this
campaign.

General Pope had fallen a victim to the foulest treachery
of ambitious rivals, rather than to the strength of his
open foes. Any one who will in candor trace the movements and the handling of that little army, when beset
by an enemy now known to have been double its own
strength, must concede that his plans were well conceived,
and his generalship in this campaign fully equaled that
which had won him so great renown in the west.

That the defeat of General Pope was brought about by
the rivalry and jealousy of generals of the Union army
cannot now be doubted. We know why Porter withheld
the largest and freshest corps in the command from the
fights, while its eleven thousand men were within sight of
the battles; but why was the Sixth corps delayed? Some

one was equally culpable with Porter. Was it worse to keep a corps out of the fight, when on the field, than to keep another corps off from the field altogether without any good reason? There can be but one question — who was responsible for the criminal neglect to send the Sixth corps to the assistance of Pope's army?

CHAPTER XIII.

THE MARYLAND CAMPAIGN.

GENERAL POPE, at his own request, was relieved from the command of the army, and General McClellan resumed the direction. Whatever might have been the real fitness of General Pope to command, his usefulness with the army just driven back upon the defenses of Washington, had departed. The return of General McClellan was hailed with joy by a large portion of the army.

On the 5th of September, Lee crossed the Potomac into Maryland, and occupied Frederick City. General McClellan was ordered to push forward at once and meet him. It was on the evening of the 6th that orders were issued to move. It was but short work to pack up our limited supply of clothing, cooking utensils and the few other articles which constituted our store of worldly goods, and prepare to march. We left Alexandria, and proceeding toward Washington, passed Fort Albany and crossed the Long Bridge, the moon and stars shining with a brilliancy seldom equaled, rendering the night march a pleasant one. As the steady tramp of the soldiers upon the pavements was heard by the citizens of Washington, they crowded upon the walks, eager to get a glance, even by moonlight, of the veterans who had passed through such untold hardships. Many were the questions regarding our destination, but we could only answer, "We are going to meet the rebels." Passing through Georgetown, we reached the little village of Tanleytown, where, weary from the short but rapid march, we spent the remainder of the night in sleep. The morning passed without orders to move, and it was not until five o'clock in the afternoon that we again commenced the march, when, having proceeded six miles, we halted. At daybreak on the morning of the 8th, the corps was moving again, and passing through Rockville we halted, after an easy stage of six miles.

On the 9th we marched three miles, making our camp at Johnstown. On the following morning, at 9 o'clock, we were again on the move, driving before us small bodies of rebel cavalry, and reaching Barnesville, a small village, ten miles from our encampment of the night before. Our Third brigade, of the Second division, was quartered on the plantation of a noted secessionist, who, on our approach, had suddenly decamped, leaving at our disposal a very large orchard, whose trees were loaded with delicious fruit, and his poultry yard well stocked with choice fowls. Our boys were not slow to appropriate to their own use these luxuries, which, they declared, were great improvements on pork and hard tack. In the enjoyment of ease and abundance, we remained here until the morning of the 12th, when we resumed the march, proceeding ten miles farther, halting near Urbana, at Monocacy bridge, which had been destroyed by the rebels, but was now rebuilt. On the same day General Burnside, having the advance, entered Frederick, encountering a few skirmishers of the enemy, which he drove. On the 13th, we arrived at the lovely village of Jefferson, having made ten miles more, and having driven a detachment of rebels through Jefferson Pass.

The advance was sounded at ten o'clock on the morning of the 14th, and at three we found ourselves near the foot of the South Mountain range, having marched about fifty miles in eight days. Upon the advance of Burnside into Frederick, the rebel force had fallen back, taking the two roads which led through Middletown and Burkettsville, and which crossed the South Mountains through deep gorges, the northern called South Mountain or Turner's Pass, and the other, six miles south of it, Crampton Pass.

These passes the rebels had strongly fortified, and had arranged their batteries on the crests of neighboring hills. The Sixth corps came to a halt when within about a mile and a half of Crampton Pass, and a reconnoissance was ordered.

General Franklin was now directed to force the pass with the Sixth corps, while the remaining corps should push on to the South Mountain Pass and drive the enemy through it. We formed in line of battle and advanced. Before us lay the little village of Burkettsville, nestling under the shadow of those rugged mountains, its white houses gleaming out of the dark green foliage. Beyond were the South Mountains; their summits crowned with batteries of artillery and gray lines of rebels, while the heavily wooded sides concealed great numbers of the enemy.

A winding road, leading up the mountain side and through a narrow defile, known as Crampton's Gap, constituted one of the two passages to the other side of the range; South Mountain Gap being the other. The enemy had planted batteries and posted troops behind barricades, and in such positions as most effectually to dispute our passage.

At the foot of the mountain, was a stone wall, behind which was the first rebel line of battle, while their skirmishers held the ground for some distance in front. The position was a strong one; admirably calculated for defense, and could be held by a small force against a much larger one.

CHARGE OF THE SIXTH CORPS AT BURKETTSVILLE.

The day was far advanced when the attack was ordered. No sooner had the lines of blue uniforms emerged from the cover of the woods, than the batteries on the hill tops opened upon them. The mountains, like huge volcanoes, belched forth fire and smoke. The earth trembled beneath us, and the air was filled with the howling of shells which flew over our heads, and ploughed the earth at our feet. At the same time, the line of battle behind the stone wall opened upon us a fierce fire of musketry. In the face of this storm of shells and bullets, the corps pressed forward at double quick, over the ploughed grounds and through the corn fields, halting for a few moments at the village. The citizens, regardless of the shells which were crashing through their houses, welcomed us heartily, bringing water to fill the canteens, and supplying us liberally from the scanty store left them by the marauding rebels.

Patriotic ladies cheered the Union boys and brought them food; and well might they rejoice at the approach of the Union army, after their recent experience with the rebels, who had robbed them of almost everything they possessed in the way of movable property.

After a few minutes, in which our soldiers took breath, the advance was once more sounded, and again we pushed on in face of a murderous fire, at the same time pouring into the face of the foe a storm of leaden hail. Slocum's division, of the Sixth corps, advanced on the right of the turnpike, while Smith's division pushed directly forward on the road and on the left of it. After severe fighting by both divisions, having driven the enemy from point to point, Slocum's troops, about three o'clock, succeeded in seizing the pass, while our Second division pressed up the wooded sides of the mountain, charging a battery at the left of the pass and capturing two of its guns. The confederates fled precipitately down the west side of the mountain, and our flags were waved in triumph

18

from the heights which had so lately thundered destruction upon us. As we advanced, we wondered, not that the foe had offered such stubborn resistance, but that the position had been yielded at all. Their dead strewed our path, and great care was required, as we passed along the road, to avoid treading upon the lifeless remains which lay thickly upon the ground. On every side the evidences of the fearful conflict multiplied. Trees were literally cut to pieces by shells and bullets ; a continual procession of rebel wounded and prisoners lined the roadsides, while knapsacks, guns, canteens and haversacks were scattered in great confusion. The rebel force made its way into Pleasant Valley, leaving in our hands their dead and wounded, three stand of colors, two pieces of artillery and many prisoners. Our troops scoured the woods until midnight, bringing in large numbers of stragglers.

We had lost quite heavily ; some of our best men had fallen. Colonel Mathison, who commanded the Third brigade of Slocum's division, whose heroism at Gaines' Farm, and bravery in all our campaign on the Peninsula, had endeared him to his division, was among the killed.

The corps moved down the road to the western side of the mountains, our men resting on their arms for the night, expecting that the battle would be renewed at dawn. But the morning revealed no enemy in our front ; we were in quiet possession of the valley.

Meanwhile on the right, at South Mountain Pass, a still more sanguinary battle had been in progress.

On the morning of the 14th, the Ninth corps, Burnside's veterans, the heroes of Roanoke and Newbern, under the command of the gallant Reno, advanced from Middletown ; and coming near the base of the mountains, found the enemy strongly posted on the crests of the hills, thronging the thickly wooded sides, and crowding in the gap. No matter what position the brave boys occupied, they were submitted to a murderous fire from the crests and sides of the mountains. Unaer this galling fire, the First division of the corps formed in line of battle, and advanced toward the frowning heights. It was an undertaking requiring more than ordinary valor, to attempt to wrest from an enemy strong in numbers, a position so formidable for defense; but the men approaching those rugged mountain sides had become accustomed to overcome obstacles, and to regard all things as possible which they were commanded to do. Under cover of a storm of shells, thrown upward to the heights, the line of battle advanced, with courage and firmness, in face of terrible resistance, gaining much ground and driving the rebels from their first line of defenses. Now, the corps of Hooker rushed to the assistance of the Ninth. As the gallant general and his staff rode along the lines, enthusiastic cheers for " Fighting Joe Hooker," greeted him everywhere. Forming his divisions hastily, he pushed them on the enemy's lines at once.

Thus far, the battle had been principally maintained by artillery; the rattle of musketry coming occasionally from one or another part of Reno's line. But now, the whole line was pushing against the rebel line, and the continued roll of musketry told of close work for the infantry. Reno's troops on the left and Hooker's on the right, were doing noble fighting. The advancing line never wavered; but pressing steadily forward, pouring volley after volley into the enemy's ranks, it at last forced the rebels to break and fly precipitately to the crests, and, leaving their splendid position on the summit to retreat in great haste down the other slope of the mountain. The engagement had been of three hours duration; and the bravery of the Union troops was rewarded by the possession of the mountain tops. Darkness put an end to the pursuit.

Thus the two chief passes through the mountains were in the possession of the Union army.

While his corps was striving to dislodge the enemy from the stronghold, the gallant Reno was struck by a minie ball, and expired. The loss of this hero threw a gloom not only over his own corps, but throughout the army.

In the many battles in which he had taken a brilliant part, he had won an enviable fame, and his private virtues and kindly qualities of heart added lustre to the brilliancy of his military record.

While the fight was in progress in Crampton Pass, the booming of guns at Harper's Ferry, only seven miles distant, told us of an attempt, on the part of the rebels, to capture that important point; and while we lay upon our arms on the morning of the 15th, two miles nearer than we were on the day before, the firing was heard to be still more fierce. Our Sixth corps was ordered to press forward to the relief of the beleaguered place; but before we had started the firing suddenly died away. General Franklin concluded that the place had been surrendered; and his conclusion was verified by reconnoissances. So the corps remained in Pleasant Valley, at rest, all of the 15th and 16th.

The surrender of Harper's Ferry was a terrible blow to our cause. Had it continued in our possession it must have insured, with any respectable energy on the part of our commanders, the destruction of the rebel army in its retreat. As it was, our loss was over eleven thousand men, and a vast amount of war material.

Of course, the surrender of Harper's Ferry, at this critical period, was owing directly to the imbecility and cowardice, not to say treachery, of the officers in command at Harper's Ferry and on Maryland Heights. But, while we condemn the weakness and cowardice of these commanders, can we relieve from a share in the responsibility, the general who marched his army in pursuit of the enemy at a snail pace, traveling but six miles a day upon an average, when by a few brisk marches this important point might have been reinforced?

Early on the morning of the 17th, the Sixth corps was on its way, hastening to the scene of conflict which had commenced on the banks of Antietam creek. A part of the Seventy-seventh had constituted one-third of the picket line which had extended across the valley between the corps and Harper's Ferry.

These companies, by a hard march, much of it at double quick, succeeded in overtaking the division just as the Third brigade was making a charge over ground already thrice won and lost by Sumner's troops. Without waiting to form the companies, the detachment joined the command, and, all out of breath and faint from their forced march, rushed with their companies against the foe.

CHAPTER XIV.

THE BATTLE OF ANTIETAM.

AMONG the delightful and fertile valleys which beautify the State of Maryland, none is more charming than the one through which the Antietam winds its tortuous course. Looking from some elevation down upon its green fields, where herds of sleek cattle graze, its yellow harvests glowing and ripening in the September sun; its undulating meadows and richly laden orchards; its comfortable farm houses, some standing out boldly upon eminences, which rise here and there, others half hidden by vines or fruit trees; the ranges of hills, rising on either side of the stream, diversified by charming vales or deep gullies; the turnpikes winding along the sides of the hills and through the valleys; the lovely stream itself, now flowing smoothly over its dark bed and anon tumbling noisily in rapids over a stony bottom, winding here far up to one range of hills and then turning back to kiss the base of the other; the whole scene is one of surpassing beauty, upon which the eye rests with untiring delight. Who would have selected this lovely valley as the scene of one of the most bloody struggles ever recorded? Who, looking down from some height of land on the morning of the 13th of September, would have dreamed that those stacks of grain, which dotted the fields here and there, would soon become the only protection from the heat of the sun and the storm of battle, to thousands of wounded, bleeding men? or, that from those lovely groves of oak and maple, now reposing like spots of beauty upon the landscape, were to belch forth fire and smoke, carrying destruction to thousands? Yet, here on these smiling fields, and among these delightful groves, one of the grand battles which should decide the march of events in the history, not only of our own country but of the world, was to be fought. These green pastures were to be stained with blood, and these peaceful groves marred and torn by shot and shell.

Driven from the towns along the Potomac, from Frederick, from Hagerstown, and from Boonsboro'; and forced from the strong passes in the South Mountains, the detached portions of the rebel army were concentrated along the banks of the Antietam creek, in the vicinity of the little town of Sharpsburgh. Hither Jackson and Longstreet, Hill and Stuart, with their hosts, had gathered to offer combined resistance to the Union army; boastfully proclaiming that now, upon northern soil, they would hurl our army to final destruction. One hundred thousand men, flushed with recent victories, and eager for one grand crowning success, proudly defied the Union army.

Their position was well chosen. A line of steep hills, forming a half circle, with the convexity in front, rising at some distance back from the creek, and nearly parallel with it, afforded admirable advantages for posting batteries, in such a manner as to sweep the plain below, from right to left. Upon their left, wooded fields afforded protection to their infantry; while upon their right, the undulating nature of the grounds near the base of the hills, covered them from the fire of our guns. In their rear was Sharpsburgh; and two fine roads leading to the Potomac, afforded safe lines of retreat in case of disaster. From the crest of the hills, on which Lee had thus posted his army, the ground sloped gently back; concealing the movements of his forces from the view of the army in their front, allowing them to maneuver unobserved by their opponents. Owing also to the form of their line of battle, it was an easy matter to throw troops from one part to another. Thus, strongly posted and confidently anticipating victory, they waited the approach of the Union army.

Our own forces were also gathering toward this point. Richardson's division of the Second corps, pressing closely upon the heels of the retreating rebels, had passed through Boonsboro' and Keedeysville, and had overtaken them here.

Porter, with his regulars, was close at hand, and took position. Then came Burnside, with his favorite Ninth corps; and the white-haired veteran, Sumner, with troops worthy of their leader; fighting Joe Hooker and his gallant men; and Mansfield, with Banks' corps. The afternoon and most of the night was spent in getting into position. Brisk skirmishes were occurring with sufficient frequency to excite the men on both sides; but no general engagement took place. The morning of the 16th found our army ready to give battle. On our right was Hooker; then Sumner with his own and the Twelfth, Mansfield's corps; and far to the left was Burnside. Porter's corps, secure behind an elevation in the rear, was held in reserve.

The night had passed with but now and then a little picket firing; but all felt that, before many hours, must commence a battle, which must determine the fate at least of that campaign.

Crossing the Antietam, in front of the line of our army, were three bridges. The first, on the Hagerstown road; the next on the road to Sharpsburgh; and the third on

the left, three miles below, on the road from Harper's
Ferry to Sharpsburgh.

This last bridge, crossed the stream at a point where
steep and high hills crowded closely on every side; the
summits of those on the western side of the stream,
crowned with rebel batteries, and their steeply falling
sides covered with infantry.   Over the first of these
bridges, on the right, Hooker was to cross his forces;
while on the left, Burnside was to attempt to dislodge the
enemy from his commanding position.   Far in the rear, a
prominent hill rose above the surrounding country; here
was a signal station, and here the commander of the army
established his quarters.   Hour after hour of the 16th
passed away, the two armies facing each other, watching
and waiting; troops moving this way and that, maneuvering like two giant wrestlers, each willing to try the movements and feel the gripe of the other before coming to the
sharp grapple.   At four o'clock, Hooker crossed his corps
and occupied a position on the west side of the creek, and
Mansfield soon followed; a little fighting, but not severe,
and then darkness closed over the scene again.   The skirmishes and artillery practice here, developed, to the quick
eye of General Hooker, the position of the enemy in his
front, and their plan of defense.   Satisfied with this knowledge, he was willing to allow his corps to rest until
morning.   Our lines were now very near those of the
rebels; so near that the pickets of the opposing forces
could hear conversation from one line to the other.

At an early hour on the morning of the 17th, the great
battle commenced in earnest.   Hooker formed his line
with Doubleday on the right, Meade in the center, and
Ricketts on the left.   Opposed to him was Stonewall
Jackson's corps.   First, Meade's Pennsylvania reserves,
of Hooker's corps, opened upon the enemy, and in a
few moments the firing became rapid and general along

19

the line of both Meade's and Rickett's divisions. The rebel line of battle was just beyond the woods, in a cornfield. The hostile lines poured into each other more and more deadly volleys; batteries were brought up on each side which did terrible execution. Each line stood firm and immovable. Although great gaps were made in them, they were closed up, and the opposing forces continued to pour fearful destruction into each other's ranks. General Hooker, riding everywhere along the front line, knew exactly the position and the work of every regiment in his command. Cheer after cheer greeted him as he passed along the line, inspiring the men by his presence. Thus for half an hour the two lines stood face to face in deadly conflict; at length the general directed a battery to be placed in a commanding position, and the shells and shrapnell were seen to work fearful havoc in the rebel ranks. The gray line wavered; then back through the cornfield and over the fences the confederates rushed, seeking shelter from the terrible storm, under cover of the woods, on the other side of the field. "Forward!" shouted General Hooker, and his divisions pressed rapidly through the cornfield, up to the very edge of the wood, while the welkin rang with their cheers. Here, the fleeing foe, reinforced by fresh troops, made a determined stand. Terrific volleys poured from the woods, thinning out the Union ranks at a fearful rate. Unable to sustain the deadly fire, they fell back — this time the rebels following with yells and shouts; but before the cornfield was crossed, our troops made another stand, and the swarthy foe was brought to bay; yet the thinned line seemed hardly able to sustain the fearful shock much longer. Hooker, fearing that his center was doomed to destruction, sent to his right for a brigade, although his right was hard pressed and in danger of being flanked.

The fresh brigade pressed steadily to the front, and the

rebel line again fell back to the woods. Mansfield's corps now came to the support of the right wing, and well did those troops, so lately demoralized at Bull Run, stand their ground. General Mansfield received here his mortal wound.

It was at this time, when Hooker saw his forces gaining a decided advantage and felt that their part of the work was well done, that a rifle ball passed through his foot inflicting a painful wound. Lamenting that he could not remain to see the end of what he hoped would prove a great victory, he left the field. The battle lulled at this point; but in the center it raged with terrible energy. There, Sumner the white-haired veteran, led his corps into the very jaws of death. If he seemed reckless of the lives of his men, he had no more care of his own. Across the ploughed ground, over ditches and fences, with unsurpassed ardor, sweeping over all obstacles, the corps pushed forward, driving the enemy before it; but the right became hard pressed, and a terrible fire on that part of the line and on the center, forced the corps back. Again the ground was taken; and again the enemy, with wild yells of triumph, drove our men back. Still determined to win, the veteran hero ordered a third charge; and the third time the field was ours, but only to be lost again. The brave General Sedgwick, who then led one division of Sumner's corps, whom we were afterward proud to call the commander of the Sixth corps, thrice wounded, was at length obliged to leave the field. Richardson and Crawford were carried wounded to the hospitals.

It was at this critical moment, when Sumner's troops, weary and almost out of ammunition, were for the third time repulsed; the remnants of the shattered regiments no longer able to resist the overwhelming forces opposed to them; the artillery alone, unsupported, holding the enemy for a moment in check; that the Sixth corps, our second division in advance, arrived upon the field.

The scene before us was awful. On the left, as far as the eye could reach, the lines of the contending forces, stretching over hills and through valleys, stood face to face; in places, not more than thirty yards apart. The roar of musketry rolled along the whole extent of the battle-field. The field upon which we had now entered, thrice hotly contested, was strewed with the bodies of friend and foe.

Without waiting to take breath, each regiment as soon as it arrives on the field, is ordered to charge independently of the others. The third brigade is first; and first of its regiments, the Twentieth New York, with their sabre bayonets, are ready; and the shout, " Forward, double quick!" rings along the line. The Germans waver for a moment; but presently with a yell they rush down the hill, suddenly receiving a volley from a rebel line concealed behind a fence; but the Germans, regardless of the storm of bullets, rush forward; the rebels breaking and flying to the rear in confusion, while the Germans hotly pursue them. Next, on the left of the Twentieth, the gallant Seventh Maine charges; rushing forward into the midst of the cornfield, they, too, are met by concealed foes. Although they are concealed from our view, the crashing of musketry tells us of the struggle which they maintain.

The gallant regiment makes its way down the slope, almost to the earthworks of the enemy, when the men throw themselves upon the ground behind a rail fence. Here, subjected to the shells from the Union and rebel batteries, the regiment can neither advance or retreat; but our batteries, finding that their shots are as fatal to our men as to the rebels, allow the remaining fragments of the regiment to retire from the perilous position.

On the right of the Seventh Maine comes the glorious Forty-ninth and our own Seventy-seventh, Captain Babcock in command. On the right of all is the old Thirty-third, within supporting distance. The men of the

Seventy-seventh rush forward over their fallen comrades, making toward a small school house which stands upon the Sharpsburgh and Hagerstown turnpike, behind which is a grove swarming with rebel troops. Our boys are almost on the road, when, at a distance of less than thirty yards, they find themselves confronted by over-whelming numbers, who pour a withering fire into their ranks. The Seventy-seventh receives the fire nobly, and, although far ahead of all the other regiments, stands its ground and returns the fire with spirit, although it is but death to remain thus in the advance. The brave color-bearer, Joseph Murer, falls, shot through the head; but the colors scarcely touch the ground when they are seized and again flaunted in the face of the enemy. Volley after volley crashes through our ranks; our comrades fall on every side; yet the little band stands firm as a rock, refusing to yield an inch. At this juncture, General Smith, riding along the line and discovering the advanced and unprotected position of the regiment, exclaims, "There's a regiment gone," and sends an aid to order it to retire. The order was timely, for the rebels were planting a battery within twenty yards of the left of the regiment, which would, in a moment longer, have swept it to destruction.

The regiment reformed behind the crest, in line with the other regiments of the brigade, all of which had been forced to fall back; but the line held was far in advance of that held by Sumner's troops when the division arrived. Thirty-three of the little band had fallen; they were less than two hundred men when they came upon the field. In the Seventh Maine the loss was still greater; of the one hundred and seventy men who went into the fight, one-half were killed or wounded; more than eighty of those noble forms were prostrated like the slashings in their own forests. The Thirty-third lost fifty in killed and wounded. The total loss to our Third brigade was three hundred and forty-three; of the Second division, three hundred and seventy-three; of the corps, four hundred and thirty-eight.

Our men lay down behind the ridge to protect themselves from the rebel batteries; yet even here the shells came, carrying death to many of our number. The Vermont brigade was sent to the assistance of French's division, who, having expended their ammunition, were making feeble resistance to the enemy. The Vermonters behaved with their usual gallantry, resisting the advance of the enemy; and although frequently subjected to the fire of artillery, they held their ground bravely. The brigade was composed of men who could always be depended on to do what they were ordered to do.

The advent of the Sixth corps upon the field had decided the contest upon the right of the line, and after the first charge by the Third brigade the battle lulled. Of all the brilliant charges made in the army on that memorable day, none was more gallant or more important in its results than this noble charge of the Third brigade of Smith's division. Although the infantry on both sides became comparatively quiet, artillery thundered from every eminence in possession of our own or the enemy's batteries. Shells and cannister tore through the Union ranks, making in parts of the line fearful havoc. Thus, for nine long hours, our Sixth corps endured this fiery ordeal, when darkness closed over the field of strife.

Meanwhile, on the left, Burnside became hotly engaged. At nine o'clock in the morning, his troops moved down toward the stone bridge, over which they hoped to cross. The hills on either side slope down almost to the water's edge; the road leading to the bridge winding through a ravine, and then on the other side ascending through another ravine to the highlands. No sooner had the head of the column descended into this amphitheater of hills, than the rebels opened a destructive fire from behind defenses which they had thrown up along the hillsides. Rifle pits, and breastworks of rails and stones, concealed thousands of infantry, who, from their secure position, poured volley after volley into the advancing column; while batteries, placed upon the heights, brought an enfilading fire upon the bridge and its approaches. In the face of this reception, the Ninth corps formed in line of battle. One brigade with fixed bayonets charged upon the bridge; but the concentrated fire of the enemy forced it back. Charge after charge was ordered and executed by different portions of the command with like success. At length a battery was brought to bear directly upon the enemy's position at the farthest end of the bridge, and, aided by these guns, fresh troops charged with great enthusiasm, carrying the bridge and planting their colors on the opposite side of the stream. Sturgis' division immediately advanced up the slope, driving the enemy before it. Meanwhile Rodman's division had succeeded, after a desperate fight, in crossing the stream below, and had also gained a position along the crest of the hills. The enemy having the range perfectly, made the position along the crest of the hills untenable, and the men were forced to fall back a little; lying close upon the ground to avoid the shells that burst about them.

At length, at three o'clock, General Burnside ordered a general advance. The divisions moved in fine order, but were soon met by the enemy in overpowering numbers. The whole line became hotly engaged. All the reserves were brought into action, and still the rebels poured upon the Union men in increasing numbers; pressing their flank and turning the attack into a doubtful defense. It seemed impossible for the corps to hold its position against the overwhelming force opposed to it. At this juncture General Burnside sent to General McClellan for aid. Porter's troops were still in reserve; but McClellan refused to relieve the hardly pressed corps. Again Burnside sends word, "I cannot hold my position half an hour longer, unless I am reinforced;" and again the appeal is met with refusal. Contrary to his own expectations, Burnside's forces held their ground until darkness put an end to the strife.

Thus our own Sixth corps, and Burnside's corps, held the ground they had each by most desperate fighting wrested from the hands of the enemy; and in spite of the peril which had threatened the right, when Hooker's braves were forced back, the center, where Sumner's brave men fell back for the third time with empty cartridge boxes, and the left, where Burnside was so hardly pressed, the advantage remained with our army; and the weary soldiers lay down in the expectation of renewing the battle in the morning.

Their valor had saved them from defeat; they hoped to make the battle that should come, a complete victory.

But the battle was ended. Toward morning, it was known to officers of our corps that the rebels were moving back, and the fact was reported; but no attention was paid to it. A truce, under pretense of burying the dead, gave the rebels a quiet day, in which to prepare for their escape, by sending their trains and much of their artillery to the rear; and on the night of the 18th, the whole rebel army disappeared. So this memorable and sanguinary battle ended. A defeat for the rebels, but not the decided victory to our arms that could have been hoped for.

The Second division of the Sixth corps was relieved soon after noon of the 18th by Couch's division, which was soon afterward joined to the Sixth corps. Until now our corps had consisted of but two divisions, the First and Second. Our men were glad to fall back enough to allow them to cook their coffee once more, and they proceeded to the work of preparing a good meal with great spirit.

The scene on the battle-field was past description. The mangled forms of our own comrades lay stretched upon the ground, side by side with those of the rebels. On almost every rod of ground over one hundred acres, the dead and wounded, some clad in the Union blue and some in confederate gray, were lying. A ghastly sight, presenting all the horrible features of death which are to be seen on such a field. At one point in our own front, for more than half a mile, the rebels lay so thickly as almost to touch each other. On the field where Hooker's men had won and lost the field, the dead and dying were scattered thickly among the broken cornstalks, their eyes protruding and their faces blackened by the sun. Wherever the lines of battle had surged too and fro, these vestiges of the terrible work were left. In the edge of the wood, where the rebels had made a stand against Hooker's advancing divisions, the bodies lay in perfect line, as though they had fallen while on dress parade. Further to the left there was a narrow road, not more than fifteen feet wide, with high fences on either side. Here a regiment of rebels was posted; when our batteries getting an enfilading fire upon them, and the infantry at the same time opening a murderous fire, the regiment was literally destroyed; not more than twenty of their number escaping. Their bodies filled the narrow road. Some were shot while attempting to get over the fence; and their remains hung upon the boards. A more fearful picture than we saw here, could not be conceived.

Broken caissons, wheels, dismounted guns, thousands of muskets, blankets, haversacks and canteens, were scattered thickly over the field; and hundreds of slain horses, bloated and with feet turned toward the sky, added to the horror of the scene.

20

While the excitement of battle lasts, and we hear the roar of artillery, and the shock of contending armies, the terrible reality of the occasion hardly presents itself to our minds, and it is only when we survey the bloody field, strewed with the mangled, lifeless remains of friend and foe, or walk through the hospitals, where the unfortunate victims of battle writhe in the agony of their wounds, that we realize the terrible nature of a great battle.

Sickening as is the sight of the battle-field, the scenes about the hospitals are worse, except to those who are actually engaged in ministering to the relief of the wounded. To these the excitement and labor incident to their duties, crowd out the thoughts of the ghastly surroundings. They see only so many demands upon them for assistance, and have no time to indulge in sentimental emotions.

Here in the rear of the army for miles, was a succession of hospitals. Every house, and barn, and haystack, formed the nucleus of a hospital, where men, shot through the head, through the limbs, through the body; with every conceivable variety of wounds, lay groaning in anguish. Surgeons toiled day and night with never lagging zeal to relieve these sufferings, but all their labor could only afford slight relief. The labors of medical officers after a great battle are immense, and there is no respite from their toils so long as a wounded man remains uncared for. While others find repose from the fatigues of battle in sleep, the surgeons are still at work; there is no sleep for them so long as work remains to be done.

The rebel army had fallen back; yet a skirmish line had been left to cover the movement. At length even this suddenly disappeared, and, firing a few solid shots, as a parting salute, the enemy took a final leave of the field. Our forces were ordered on. We passed over the scene of carnage, where hundreds of dead lay still unburied; and pioneers were on every part of the field throwing the mangled, disfigured forms into shallow graves. Along the roadsides, under the fences, and where the confederate hospitals had been, still these gory objects met our view. We reached Sharpsburgh, and here the evidences of the terrible conflict were to be seen everywhere. Houses riddled by shells and bullets; some of them destroyed by fire, and some battered into shapeless masses; the streets filled with disabled wagons; horses galloping about without riders; knapsacks, guns and equipments cast away in the hasty flight; churches filled with rebel wounded; all helped to make up a scene of destruction such as has been rarely witnessed. The people of the village welcomed us as their deliverers, and brought water, and such other refreshments as they had been able to conceal from the rebels. We passed the village and bivouacked for the night.

On the 20th, we, of the Sixth corps, retraced our steps, passing again over the battle-field, where the stench was now unendurable. We reached Williamsport at daylight, where Couch's division was face to face with the enemy, who were said to be recrossing the river, and who had last night forced back part of the division.

The rebel force had, however, consisted of about four thousand cavalry, who, finding the Unionists in force, quickly returned to the south side of the Potomac. Here we found an immense division of Pennsylvania militia drawn up in line of battle. Its regiments were larger than our brigades. They were armed with every variety of fire-arms, from light sporting shot-guns to Sharpe's rifles. Their uniforms had quite as little uniformity as their arms. Some were dressed in gray pants and jackets, others in light blue; and still others in the various fashions which constituted the wearing apparel at home. Grave gentleman in spectacles, studious young men in green glasses, pale young men who were evidently more at home behind the counter than in line of battle, roughs who had not been tamed by the discipline of military life, and boys who, for the first time, had left the paternal mansion, made up the heterogeneous division.

Remaining at Williamsport until the morning of the 23d, we marched on the Hagerstown turnpike to Bakersville, where we remained about three weeks. Here it was that Couch's division was joined to the Sixth corps.* On the 3d of October the corps was ordered out for review by President Lincoln. The line was formed on a fine plain, and the booming of cannon announced the approach of the Commander-in-Chief of the armies of the United States. The illustrious visitor was accompanied by Generals McClellan, Franklin, Smith and other notable men, with an immense retinue. Conscious of the fatigues already endured by these veterans, the President simply passed along the line of the divisions, acknowledging the salutations which greeted him, without requiring the columns to march in review. The soldiers manifested their appreciation of the interest taken by the Chief Magistrate in their welfare, by loud and repeated cheers. Sumner's, Burnside's and Porter's corps had already been reviewed by the President.

While at this camp, large accessions were made to our thinned ranks. Before the army left Harrison's Landing, efforts had been set on foot for filling up the skeleton regiments of our army. Recruiting officers had been detailed from every regiment, to go to the localities from which their respective regiments had been raised, and bring in recruits, to fill the places made vacant by death and disease. The critical condition of affairs when the army

---

* The regiments of this division were, the 36th, 55th, 62d, 65th, 67th and 122d New York; the 23d, 82d, 93d, 98th and 102d Pennsylvania; the 7th, 10th and 37th Massachusetts, and the 2d Rhode Island.

was withdrawn from the Peninsula, and, afterward, when Pope was so disastrously forced back upon the defenses of Washington, had roused to most earnest action, many patriots, who hoped to avert further disaster by forwarding men to the field. Under these influences, and as the result of these patriotic efforts, many recruits offered themselves; but after the battle of Antietam, new life was added to the recruiting service. Many who then supposed that the war was nearly ended, gladly accepted the large bounties, and in the hope of soon being "in at the death" of the rebellion, enrolled themselves among the soldiers of the Union. War meetings were held in every town, and the utmost enthusiasm was created. In Saratoga, a large concourse of people, among whom were many of the visitors at the Springs, gathered for a war meeting. Stirring speeches were made. Ladies offered their diamond rings, their watch chains, their watches and other valuables to those who should come forward and enter the service. Under the influence of such enthusiasm, many came forward and enrolled their names, and received the jewels from the fair hands of the patriotic donors. By such efforts as these, all over the country, from two to three hundred recruits were raised for each regiment in our corps, and large accessions were made to the ranks of the whole army.

The advent of the new comers was hailed with joy by the veterans, who had become sadly discouraged by their small and constantly decreasing numbers.

Our men were enjoying the welcome rest and the abundant supply of food obtained in this delightful country, and many varieties of diet, well remembered as familiar in former years, but unknown to them since their campaigns commenced, adorned their humble mess tables. Among other luxuries, "hasty pudding" and johnny cake became common articles of diet. The process of producing these articles, was after the rude manner of men who must invent the working materials as they are needed.   One-half of an unserviceable canteen, or a tin plate perforated by means of a nail or the sharp point of a bayonet, served the purpose of a grater or mill for grinding the corn.   The neighboring cornfields, although guarded, yielded abundance of rich yellow ears; which, without passing through the process of "shelling," were rubbed across the grater, yielding a finer meal than is usually ground at the grist mills.   The meal being obtained, it was mixed with a large or small quantity of water, as mush or cake was desired, and cooked.

The men complained of want of proper and sufficient clothing, and many of them were absolutely barefooted. On whom the blame for the long delay in furnishing these necessary articles should rest, we can only refer to the controversy between the Major-General commanding the armies of the United States and the Major-General commanding the Army of the Potomac.

Soon after midnight, October 11th, the corps was ordered to move to Hagerstown.   In the .midst of a heavy shower the march was made, and Hagerstown was reached soon after daylight.   Here a new cause of excitement occurred.   Stuart, with his cavalry, was in our rear; Chambersburgh was burned, and other towns sacked.   The Vermont brigade was hastily loaded into cars and sent to Chambersburgh in pursuit of the cavalry, which was already far on its way to the Potomac.   Of course they could only return, having had an excursion through the country at government expense.   The Third brigade of Smith's division marched hastily to the Maryland and Pennsylvania line, to where a stone bridge crossed the Antietam; a battery of artillery was also here, and the brigades and battery prepared to defend the crossing.   But no enemy appeared, and the two brigades returned to Hagerstown; the Vermonters to occupy the town as provost guard, the other to encamp in a delightful grove a mile beyond.

Thus ended the famous campaign of Antietam; which had humbled the pride of the boastful confederates, and had turned back their hordes to their mountain fastnesses in Virginia for safety. A campaign which, while conducted with great hesitancy and a total want of that celerity of movement usually considered absolutely necessary to brilliant success in military operations, yet had preserved the north from imminent and immediate danger which threatened it. Our losses in killed, wounded and missing, in this campaign, amounted to fifteen thousand two hundred and twenty.

The army was posted, two corps, the Second and Twelfth, at Harper's Ferry; the remaining corps along the Potomac, above and below that point, for twenty miles. Here, six weeks were spent in getting ready for another campaign; the President, meanwhile, constantly ordering an advance across the river; General McClellan, constantly offering excuses for delay. It is not our purpose to discuss the merits of these excuses, but it may not be out of place to mention, that although the Sixth corps was represented as being in worse condition, in regard to clothing and shoes, than any other corps, that corps finally crossed the river before it received its clothing, showing that even the corps least supplied with these important articles could undertake the campaign even after another month's wear of the old clothes and the advent of the cold weather. On the 18th of October, that portion of the Third brigade able to perform duty, was marched to Clear Spring to perform picket duty, leaving in camp the recruits, who were unarmed, and the invalids. Thus the brigade occupied two distinct camps several miles apart. The duty on picket was by no means severe, and

the country was delightful. The boys found little difficulty in procuring abundant supplies of luxuries, such as
soft bread, hoe cakes and other articles, from the farmers;
and as the enemy was at Winchester, they were not in
great alarm from rebel raids.

The Hagerstown camp was indeed a pleasant one. The
people were generally loyal, and seemed glad to furnish the
soldiers with all the comforts possible. There was little
duty, and the invalids had time for recovering their
exhausted strength, while the recruits were afforded an
opportunity for drill.

General Slocum, who had commanded the First division
of our corps since the corps was organized, was assigned
to the command of the Twelfth corps, in place of General
Mansfield, who lost his life at Antietam.

In the Vermont brigade an important change occurred,
General Brooks, the old and tried commander of the
brigade, was assigned to the command of the first division of the corps, succeeding General Slocum, who took
command of the Twelfth corps. General Brooks was
one of the most energetic and brave brigade commanders
in our army, and notwithstanding his abrupt and sometimes very stern manners, had endeared himself by his
excellent discipline and fighting qualities, not only to
his brigade, but to the whole division.

An amusing incident, well calculated to illustrate the
mingled sentiments of love and fear entertained for the
general by even those in his own command, occurred
at a meeting of the officers of the brigade, immediately
after the order for the transfer. The object of the meeting, was to make arrangements for presenting the general
with a suitable testimonial of their regard. Some dis-
cussion occurred in regard to the character of the gift.
Some proposed a silver service, some a sword. At length
it was proposed, that a fine horse and equipments be pur-

chased.   An officer rose and said that it was all very well to talk about buying a horse for General Brooks, but he would like to know who would be so bold as to undertake to present it to him! Another officer suggested that the horse might be saddled and bridled and hitched in front of the general's quarters during the night, with a note tied to the bridle stating for whom it was designed, and by whom presented.

A magnificent silver service was finally presented to the general, who, forgetting his rough manners, received the beautiful gift of his loved brigade with tears standing on his brown cheeks.

21

CHAPTER XV.

THE SECOND ADVANCE INTO VIRGINIA, AND THE BATTLE OF FREDERICKSBURGH.

Marching in Maryland—Arrival at New Baltimore—General McClellan superseded by General Burnside—Thanksgiving in camp—The grand divisions organized—The march resumed—Fatal delays—In order of battle—The crossing—
Fredericksburgh bombarded—Situation of Fredericksburgh—Scenes of activity
—The Bernard house—Scenes at the hospital—The battle on the right—Charges
of the Pennsylvania reserves—The river recrossed—Reflections.

THUS, for nearly six weeks, the army remained at Hagerstown, and on the line of the Potomac, resting and waiting
for clothing. On the 28th of October, orders came to clear
all the camps of sick; and all from our Sixth corps were
sent to hospitals in Hagerstown. At dark, we set out, and
making a night march of a few miles, reached Williamsport, where we bivouacked and remained two days, and
thence went to Boonsboro'.

The march from Williamsport to Boonsboro' led us
through a magnificent country. On either side of the
road, the long lines of corn shocks and the vine-clad houses,
formed a picture of wealth and comfort. We halted at
Boonsboro' in sight of the field of Antietam, and passed
our bi-monthly muster. At daybreak in the morning we
were again on the road. The first part of our way led
through a beautiful open country, but we were soon winding among the hills that form the slopes of "Pleasant
Valley."

The forests on the hillsides, glowing with the brilliant
colors of autumn, the fine old residences, appearing here
and there among the trees, and the plethoric stacks of hay

and grain, combined, indeed, to make it a "pleasant valley," and, as the lines of troops filed along the roads, the
spectacle was beautifully picturesque. We passed South
Mountain, where the rebels had met with such a bloody
reception from our forces, and not long after we were on
the ground of the battle of Burkettsville, where our Sixth
corps had charged up the hill and had driven the enemy
in confusion. Every tree bore lasting marks of a terrible
fight. For more than a mile, the forest was completely
scarred by bullets and shells; not a tree had escaped, and
many of them were pierced like the cover of a pepper-box.
We halted near Berlin, in a charming valley, where we
staid over Sunday. Monday morning, we crossed the
Potomac to Virginia, on pontoon bridges, passed through
the little towns of Lovettsville and Purcellville, Union
Town and Upperville, then crossing the valley almost
from west to east, from the Blue Ridge to the Kittoctan
mountains, at length, on Thursday, reached White Plains,
a station on the Front Royal and Manassas railroad, not
far from Thoroughfare Gap. Here we were overtaken by
a cold storm of rain, sleet and snow, gloomy enough, but
not so gloomy as was the news that here reached us of
the elections in New York. Whatever the attitude of the
political parties may have been before or since that time
in reference to the war, in our army the result of the New
York elections was regarded, at that time, as a repudiation
of the war.

We reached New Baltimore on the 9th, and the next
morning we were notified that, by order of the President,
General McClellan was relieved from the command of the
army of the Potomac, to be superseded by Major-General
Burnside.

No sooner had the farewell order of General McClellan
been read to the troops, than the whole army was ordered
into line for review by corps. The retiring and the incom-

ing generals, each with his long train of followers, galloped along the whole of the line of the army, while batteries fired salutes and bands played "The Star Spangled Banner" and "Hail to the Chief." Many of the regiments cheered the departing general with great enthusiasm, while others observed a studied silence.

A week was spent at New Baltimore, and then another week on the banks of Aquia creek, not far from Stafford Court House.

The 27th of November was Thanksgiving day, in nearly all the loyal States, and doubtless our friends at home, as they gathered in many a family circle that day, to partake bounteous Thanksgiving dinners, spoke of those who were away at the war, and thought, that with them, Thanksgiving could only be a hard day's march in the rain or mud, with rations of hard bread and pork; and so, many kind hearts pitied the soldiers as they thought that we were deprived of the luxuries which they were enjoying.

But we, too, enjoyed a pleasant Thanksgiving. In the morning, throughout the corps, there was brigade inspection; we put on our good clothes and presented ourselves to our generals, looking our best; then as we marched back into the various camps, we found dinner smoking in many a cook-tent, and the odor of roast meats rising throughout the whole corps like an odor of sweet incense. Fresh sheep pelts hanging here and there in considerable profusion, told of good cheer among all the men.

As evening approached, the voice of singing was heard from all the camps, and groups were gathered under the shadow of the chestnut trees, where many pairs of government shoes were shuffling to the music of violins. Throughout the limits of the corps, good humor and mirth prevailed; the sick forgot their pains, and the home-sick ones, for the time, looked bright, as they yielded to the general feeling of happiness.

General Burnside, immediately upon taking command, consolidated the army into three grand divisions, of two corps each. The Right, to consist of the Second corps, General Couch, and the Ninth, General Wilcox; General Sumner to command the grand division. General Hooker was placed in command of the Center division, which consisted of the Third corps, General Stoneman, and the Fifth, General Butterfield. The Left grand division consisted of the Sixth corps, under General Smith, and the First corps, under General Reynolds; General Franklin was assigned to the command.

The command of the Second division, Sixth corps, was given to Brigadier-General A. P. Howe.

At length, we resumed our march, reaching Brooks' Station the first night; then, after a day's delay, we started again. The weather was intensely cold, and the mud almost unfathomable. The troops, with much difficulty, moved about six miles, reaching the rear of Falmouth Station, opposite Fredericksburgh; but the trains, at midnight, had only proceeded two miles. In the ambulances, the sick suffered beyond description. Six soldiers from the Third brigade, Second division, died in the ambulances that night. Even the well men in camp could hardly manage to keep warm. Few persons in that vast army slept, and the ring of hundreds of axes and the falling of trees, which were to be piled on the fires, were heard all night.

The Right and Center grand divisions, had arrived in the vicinity of Falmouth several days before; and it had been the design of General Burnside to cross his army over the Rappahannock, seize the heights of Fredericksburgh, and push on toward Richmond, before the enemy could throw a sufficiently strong force in his front, to offer serious resistance. In this, doubtless, he would have been successful, but " some one had blundered," and the Commander-in-Chief suffered the mortification of seeing his plans foiled, and his series of forced marches a failure, because the pontoons which were to meet him on his arrival before Fredericksburgh were still at Washington; and this through the criminal neglect of some one. This campaign, which promised more than any previous campaign of the Army of the Potomac, was now destined to prove a failure.

From the time that the first troops appeared in front of Fredericksburgh, nearly three weeks were spent in waiting for pontoons; while General Lee had abundant time to bring together all his forces and post them in such positions, as to dispute our passage at any point, for twenty miles up and down the river. In guarding this extensive front, General Lee had stretched out his army to such an extent, that Burnside hoped, by throwing his whole army across at one point, to pierce the weak line before his enemy could concentrate his forces.

On the morning of the 11th of December, we marched to a point about two miles below Fredericksburgh. The whole army was in motion. The ground had become hardened by frost, and a light coating of snow lay upon it. The wheels no longer sunk in the mire; but artillery rolled easily over the frozen ground.

The Right grand division, Sumner's, had already taken its position immediately in front and above the city of Fredericksburgh; the Center, Hooker's, and the Left division, Franklin's, now took position below the town.

As we descended from the heights of Stafford, into the valley of the Rappahannock, dense clouds of fog obscured the view of the opposite bank, and it was only at noon that we could distinguish objects on the farther side of the river. Engineers were hard at work laying pontoon bridges, being submitted to a brisk musketry fire from the rebel skirmishers, who at times charged upon them, killing and wounding several of the workmen, and greatly hindering the work. A few volleys from our batteries, which were brought forward presently, put these troublesome parties to flight, and the work went on. Still, during all the day, the enemy strove with artillery and infantry to prevent the laying of the bridge, but to no avail.

On the right, where the veteran Sumner commanded, the task of throwing the bridges across, was far more difficult than at the lower crossing. In the storehouses and dwellings along the banks of the river, swarms of rebel soldiers were concealed; and these, by pouring murderous volleys into the midst of the pontoniers, compelled them to desist from the attempt to finish their bridge. Determined no longer to be thwarted by these concealed foes, General Burnside, having previously notified the civil authorities of the town, that if the houses were used as covers for men who were shooting our soldiers, the town must suffer the consequences, ordered our batteries to concentrate their fire upon it and batter down the walls. Soon after noon, the bombardment commenced. One hundred and seventy cannon belched forth the huge iron missiles upon the devoted city. The roar of the artillery was terrific, and as the winds rolled away the huge columns of smoke, we saw that the city was on fire, the flames leaping to the skies. The spectacle was one of awful grandeur. The bursting bombs, shooting forth their flashing coruscations from the columns of smoke, the great tongues of flame from the burning buildings, leaping to the heavens, the clamor of the bursting shells and the shock of the artillery which shook the earth, made up one of the most terribly magnificent of scenes.

In the midst of all this direful tumult, and while the conflagration of the city drove the confederates out of their places of concealment, Sumner's forces succeeded in laying their bridge and crossing troops; not, however,

until two brave regiments had crossed in boats and captured or dispersed the rebel sharpshooters, who had given
so much trouble.   Hooker also effected a crossing at the
same time.   We had now bridges across at three points;
"Franklin's Crossing" being nearly two miles below the
town.

The city of Fredericksburgh is upon the south bank of
the Rappahannock river.   Fronting the city, on the north
side of the stream, rises a steep bluff — Stafford Heights —
which approaches near the river above and opposite the
town, and gradually recedes from it below.   This was the
side held by our army.   Behind the town, on the south,
the ground rises in several successive terraces until it
reaches an elevation called "the mountain."   Each ter-
race commands all below it, and the whole forms a position
of unsurpassed advantages for defense.   Here, between
these high grounds, and stretching on either side of the
river, is the valley of the Rappahannock — almost a level
plain of six miles in length, and averaging two and a half
miles in breadth, narrowing in front of the town to less
than a mile, and spreading out, at the point where our
lower bridges were thrown across, to at least three miles.
On the crest of the heights, north of the river, were posted
our batteries in great numbers.   On the plain and on each
of the terraces south of the river, the enemy was intrenched
in most formidable positions.

The advance of the enemy fell back, as our forces crossed
the river, leaving us in possession of the plain on both
sides, and of the town.   Night came on, and the spectacle
was unutterably grand, as the sheets of fire burst from the
mouths of the opposing batteries; but at length the roar
of battle subsided, and except the firing of pickets, all
was quiet.   Franklin threw but a small force across the
river; a strong picket line, well supported, holding a
semi-circular tract of the plain.   The Eighteenth and

Thirty-first New York were the first of the Sixth corps to cross the bridge.

The Sixth corps returned to the heights and bivouacked for the night, leaving a few regiments to hold the plain in front of the bridge. It was the intention of the commanding general to press the enemy closely in front with the Right and Center grand divisions, while the Left division was to make a flank movement on the right of the enemy's line, seizing the road to Bowling Green, and rendering the rebel position untenable.

Before dawn on the following morning, we made our way again to the river. Thousands crowded upon the banks, or hurriedly dashed across the bridge. The rumble of wheels upon the frozen ground, the tramp of thousands of men, the neighing of innumerable horses, mingled with the roar of musketry. The sun rose in splendor, and the spires of the city, two miles to our right, shone brightly, for only the lower part of the town had been destroyed by the conflagration of the day before, and tens of thousands of muskets gleamed in the morning light. The broad plain, on the south bank, swarmed with the hosts of Franklin and Hooker. Musketry fire became more and more brisk, as our forces moved into position, but no general engagement came on. Shells from the rebel batteries came bursting in our midst, and in reply, our own guns on Stafford Heights sent their shells screaming over our heads, to burst in the midst of the rebel artillerists.

A fine stone mansion of large dimensions, situated on the south bank of the river, and a little below the bridge, was taken by the surgeons of our Second division, for a hospital. The position was exposed to the rebel fire, but it was the best that could be found. Just in front of it the gallant General Bayard, of the cavalry, was struck by a shell, and killed instantly. Others, some of whom had been previously been wounded, received fatal shots at the

22

very doors of the house. The owner of this magnificent mansion still remained in it. He was an old secesh bachelor, very aristocratic in his notions, and highly incensed at the use his house was put to by the "hireling Yankees." But he was taken care of by a guard. His servants cooked for the wounded and our surgeons; his fine larder furnished us delicacies and his cellar rich old wines.

Doubtless his feelings on delivering to us the keys of his wine cellar were not unlike those of Sir Hugh Berkley in "The Wagoner;" who

> "—only knew they drank his wine;
> Would they might hang, a scarecrow line,
> On the next lightning blasted tree."

Saturday, the sun appeared, bright and warm as on a spring morning. The battle now commenced in terrible earnest. First, on the left, the booming of heavy guns and the rattle of musketry told of hot work in our own front. Then gradually the battle rolled on to the right; and while it thundered there, our forces on the left remained comparatively quiet. Then, back again came the roar of cannon, the shrieking and cracking of shells and the din of musketry.

The hills in our front were thickly wooded, and in these woods "Stonewall" Jackson had concealed his forces. General Meade, with his division of Pennsylvania reserves, and Gibbons, with his division, both of Reynolds' First corps, were sent to take and hold the Bowling Green road, which lay in the edge of the wood. Gallantly and in splendid order, the two divisions moved up toward the edge of the wood. Gibbons' division halted at the railroad, near the wood, Meade's pressed forward, and presently disappeared among the trees. Although considerable resistance was met with, the gallant division continued to press forward, the rebels steadily giving way. Suddenly, the roar of cannon became awful, and the fire of musketry almost deafening. The rebels had opened an enfilading fire upon the division, which made fearful havoc. The men who had so gallantly marched into the woods, came hurrying back in disorder; not, however, until they had succeeded in capturing several hundred prisoners from the enemy. A flag, one or two mounted officers, and a squad of a dozen or twenty men were all that could be recognized as a regimental organization; all others had fallen before the deadly fire that met them, or had lost their commands. The men quickly rallied about their flags and again charged into the woods, and again they were sent back in disorder. They were now withdrawn, and the rebels charged upon the line of the Sixth corps. The troops of our Second division were lying down behind a slight elevation of ground, and, as the rebels charged down furiously upon us, our men suddenly rose and poured a deadly volley into them. At the same time the troops of the First division met their attack with spirit, and sent them reeling back to their cover in the forest.

The wounded poured into our hospitals, and well did those surgeons, who had seized the stone mansion, earn that day, lasting gratitude from their division.

Never had wounded men been so quickly or so well cared for. It was the beginning of an era of *organized* labor in that department. Among the earliest of the wounded was General Vinton, commanding the Third brigade, Second division. A ball had passed into the abdomen, and was cut out from his back. The unfortunate men were stowed in every part of the great house, and in the smaller buildings surrounding it, and tents furnished shelter for those unable to find room in the buildings. After General Vinton was wounded, Brigadier-General Thomas H. Neill was ordered to assume the command of our brigade, which he did on the battle-field.

Meanwhile, on the right, Sumner's and Hooker's forces were striving, with herculean efforts, to dislodge the enemy from his strongholds, but to no avail. His position was impregnable, and the Union forces only advanced against the works to meet with deadly repulse from the savage fire of the concealed foe, and to fall back with fearful losses. Thus the struggle lasted until evening, when the roar of battle was hushed, and our tired troops slumbered upon their arms.

On Sunday morning the rattle of musketry and the thunder of artillery commenced again, but, as little reply was made by the enemy, the demonstration on our part soon ceased, and the day was spent in comparative quiet. It was said that General Burnside, unwilling to give up the struggle, had ordered an advance of the Ninth corps, which he was personally to lead, against one of the rebel strongholds, but that he had yielded to the advice of the grand division commanders to refrain from the attempt.

Monday still found us on the battle-field. The thumping of artillery was renewed, but not fiercely. Our wounded were removed to the other side of the river. A kind providence had favored them, for the weather had been delightful. Had such weather prevailed as we experienced a few days before, many of the wounded, faint and exhausted from the loss of blood, must have perished with the cold. During the night the whole army was withdrawn, with as much secrecy as possible, across the pontoon bridges. No sooner had the troops crossed to the north side of the river than the bridges were taken up, and the two armies were again separated by the Rappahannock. As the bridges were being taken up, the rebels rushed to the bank and fired into the pontoniers, but were repelled by the men of the Seventy-seventh New York. That regiment formed a picket line along the bank of the river, but were ordered not to fire unless the enemy did. " A pretty order," said Terry Gray, of Company B, " to wait till a man is killed before he can fire his gun !" The army went into camp on a line from Falmouth to Belle Plain; the Sixth corps occupying nearly the center of the line, at a place called White Oak Church, from a little whitewashed meeting house, without bell or steeple, in the midst of a clump of white oak trees.

The attempt to capture the heights of Fredericksburgh by a direct assault was indeed a daring undertaking, and one involving a fearful risk. The only hope of success lay in the active and hearty coöperation of all the commands of the army. Such coöperation was not to be had. To the Left grand division was assigned an important work which it failed to accomplish; not because it was defeated in the attempt, but because the attempt was not made in earnest. The troops were brave and eager to meet the enemy. None were ever more brave or more desirous to test their valor. The heroic deeds of those who did advance against the enemy will ever redound to the glory of our arms; and had all the forces of the Left grand division been brought fairly into action, the result might have been different. Surely such troops as composed the grand old Sixth corps were fitted for a nobler work than standing upon an open plain, exposed to fierce artillery fire, without ever being allowed to turn upon the enemy. Our defeat had cost us more than twelve thousand men, in killed, wounded and missing.

CHAPTER XVI.

THE WINTER AT FALMOUTH.

Camp at White Oak Church—"The mud march"—Return to camp—General
Neill—General Hooker supersedes General Burnside—Burnside's magnanimity
—General Hooker as a soldier—Reconstruction—The cavalry organized—Busi-
ness departments renovated—The medical department—Ambulance system—
Quartermasters' and commissary departments—Life in camp—Snowball bat-
tles—In the Seventy-seventh—The Light division—Review by General Hooker
—General John Sedgwick—Scene at head-quarters—Review of the army by the
President—Preparing for the campaign.

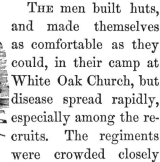

White Oak Church, Va.

THE men built huts, and made themselves as comfortable as they could, in their camp at White Oak Church, but disease spread rapidly, especially among the recruits. The regiments were crowded closely together on ground too low and wet for good camping ground, and the men, having never before erected winter quarters from shelter tents, were not so expert as they became in the succeeding winters; so they suffered from inconvenient quarters, as well as from the low ground and crowded camps.

Our army was now composed in large part, of the recruits sent from the north during the preceding summer and autumn, and thousands of these had never had any idea of fighting or of suffering the privations of army life.

They had enlisted for the large bounties which were paid at that time, with the determination to leave the service as soon as their bounties were paid, and a favorable opportunity offered itself for escape. Desertions became alarmingly frequent; indeed, when a few weeks later General Hooker assumed command, there were more than eighty-four thousand absentees, with and without authority. The great number of desertions, we think, should be attributed to the fact that so large a proportion of the new recruits had enlisted for money, rather than to the demoralization of the army.

Notwithstanding the inconveniences to which the men were subjected, and the advance to midwinter, the weather was in our favor. The sun shone brightly, the days were warm and the roads dry. It became evident that General Burnside was determined not to allow the delightful weather and the excellent roads to pass unimproved. Indications of a general movement crowded upon us, and on the 20th of January came the order to march.

The whole army broke camp and moved toward Banks' Ford, two miles up the river from White Oak Church. On the march, an order from the commanding general was read to the troops, announcing to them that the auspicious moment had at length arrived when we were to reap the glorious fruits of our long toils. At five o'clock we halted in the thick woods at Banks' Ford, the point selected for crossing the river, and in a few minutes were quietly and comfortably bivouacked out of sight of rebels on the opposite side. Scarcely had we settled ourselves for a comfortable night's rest, when the clouds, which had been gathering since morning, broke in rain, and the delightful Indian summer gave way to the rainy winter of the south. All night long the rain poured, and all the next day. It was evident we had waited too long. But the commander was determined not to abandon his effort to outflank the enemy. By morning, the roads were so softened by the rain, that horses could not haul artillery or pontoons into position. Men took the place of horses. The whole Vermont brigade was detailed to drag the pontoons and guns to the river. All day long, working and tugging with the mud above their knees; here a hundred men pulling at a pontoon boat, there a party prying a cannon out of the mire with long levers, and still other parties laying strips of corduroy road. The Vermonters passed a disagreeable day.

General Burnside was not idle all this while. Riding from one point to another, now personally superintending the placing of a battery in position on the bank of the river, now encouraging the men who lugged at the boats and guns, and now selecting places to cut new roads, he passed the night and the day in fatiguing and anxious labor. As he rode through the camp of our division in the afternoon, with only two staff officers, himself and his horse completely covered with mud, the rim of his hat turned down to shed the rain, his face careworn with this unexpected disarrangement of his plans, we could but think that the soldier on foot, arm oppressed with the weight of knapsack, haversack and gun, bore an easy load compared with that of the commander of the army, who now saw departing his hopes of redeeming the prestige he had lost at Fredericksburgh.

Men were detailed from each of the regiments of the corps to return to Falmouth, a distance of five miles, to bring on their backs two days' rations; those brought by the men being nearly exhausted. But during the night it was determined to abandon the attempt to cross the river. The enemy, by this time fully aware of our intention, was prepared for us, and a crossing could only be made at great sacrifice, perhaps with defeat. So at sunrise in the morning we were on the road back to our old camp; this time for permanent winter quarters. All along the road lay a multitude of dead horses and mules, which had fallen in the tremendous but unavailing efforts of the day before. Artillery and wagons still stuck fast in the mud, and cannoniers and teamsters lifted and tugged with rails and with poles to raise the piece or the wagon from the mire.

The mud was deep, the day was gloomy and the men were discouraged. They straggled badly. Regiments were not to be distinguished. The whole column became an unorganized crowd, pressing toward the old camps. Tired and discouraged as were the men, they kept up their lively sallies and jokes, as though all was smooth work. Toward evening the troops of our corps arrived on their old ground, now to be our home until the opening of spring, and at once fell to work to restore to some degree of comfort that most desolate of scenes, an abandoned camp. Unfortunately, on leaving the place, little thinking that they were so soon to return, they had burned everything combustible, and thus a strip of board or a piece of timber could hardly be found within the limits of the corps. Nevertheless, comfortable quarters were soon erected, and the routine of drills and picket was resumed.

Brigadier-General Neill, who was assigned to the command of the Third brigade, was active in encouraging his men to provide good quarters, and in furnishing every facility in his power to make them comfortable. The general was a portly gentleman, with light red hair and whiskers, and a small blue eye, ceremonious in his style, and a perfect pattern of courtliness. He had, at West Point, won the appellation of " Beau Neill," a title which never left him. He was a good commander in camp. He orginated the brigade dress parade that winter, often calling out the brigade on fine evenings, and substituting the brigade for the regimental parade. The custom was at

23

length adopted in many brigades in the army of the Potomac; but few gave credit for the improved parade to the
originator of it.

The second failure of General Burnside rendered his
removal from the command of the army a thing to be
expected; and no one was surprised when the order came
relieving him, and assigning General Hooker to the command. It must be confessed that our failure at Bank's
Ford had done much to demoralize the army and destroy
the confidence in the commanding general so absolutely
necessary to success. On our way back from Bank's Ford,
as we passed Fredericksburgh, we saw huge placards posted
up by the rebels with taunting inscriptions, such as " Burnside stuck in the mud," printed in conspicuous letters.
The men caught up the words, and " Burnside stuck in the
mud " passed from one end of the disordered column to
the other. When we had failed at Fredericksburgh, the
men were as willing as ever to try again under the same
commander. They believed him to be at least earnest and
brave. They knew that he was noble and self-sacrificing.
In the noble letter to General Halleck, in which he assumed
all the responsibility for the failure at Fredericksburgh,
they found renewed assurance that he had all the qualities
of a true soldier — bravery, integrity and true manhood;
but an army must have success, or it cannot long repose
confidence in the general. So, while the Army of the
Potomac regarded General Burnside with great respect, it
gladly welcomed the advent of " Fighting Joe Hooker "
to the command.

General Hooker had fairly won the title of " Fighting
Joe " at the slaughter of Williamsburgh, where, almost
single-handed with his division, he had stemmed the tide
of battle for hours, until reinforced by Kearney, and then,
with the help of that hero, had held the whole rebel army
until it was outflanked by our Second division.

In all the battles of the Peninsula he had been conspicuous, and at South Mountain and Antietam his fighting
propensities were exhibited in more than their wonted
splendor. In person he was of large stature, with fine
features, brilliant eye, his side whiskers and ruddy countenance giving a more youthful appearance than his light
gray hair would indicate. His gleaming eye told of the
spirit which animated the man, and his determined air
betokened the persistent and fearless soldier. In battle
or on review he rode a magnificent milk white steed, a
powerful animal and of extraordinary fleetness. Mounted
on this superb war horse, he was the most conspicuous, as
he was always one of the handsomest men in the army.

The energy of the new commander soon began to be
manifested in the reconstruction and reorganization of
the whole army. The first step in the progress of reconstruction, was the revocation of the order making three
grand divisions of the army. By the abolition of the grand
divisions, Generals Sumner and Franklin were relieved
from their commands; and the corps commanders, no
longer subject to intermediate commanders, were again
directly responsible to the general-in-chief of the army.
Doubtless General Hooker had seen that the creation of
these grand divisions had much to do with the failures
of General Burnside.

The cavalry next engaged the attention of the general.
The whole force was thoroughly reorganized and put in
an efficient condition, under command of Major-General
Stoneman. Hereafter, men were not to ask, "Who ever
saw a dead cavalryman?" To General Hooker, the cavalry of the Army of the Potomac owes its efficiency and
the glorious record it from that time made for itself.

The superiority of the rebel cavalry, in the early part
of the war, was generally attributed to the supposed fact
that the young men of the south were so much better

horsemen than those of the north. In reality, this had little, if anything, to do with it. It is even very doubtful if there was any difference in favor of the superior horsemanship of the southern cavalry. Their strength lay in their union. The rebel cavalry was organized from the beginning; ours was an incoherent mass of men, having no proper relations or dependencies within itself. From the day that it became organized, the superiority of the rebel cavalry passed away forever. We had always better horses, and our men were certainly never inferior to the rebels. All that was needed was the proper combination of action; and, as soon as this was secured, our cavalry became the finest in the world.

The business departments were also thoroughly renovated. The changes in the medical, quartermasters' and commissary departments were such as to bring each to a standard of perfection, which had never before been reached by those departments of any army in the field. No army had ever been provisioned as was ours that winter. Soft bread, potatoes, beets, carrots, onions, fresh beef, flour, sugar and coffee, constituted the regular rations of the men, and facilities were afforded for procuring luxuries not in the regular supply.

The medical department became so thoroughly systematized, that wounded and sick men were cared for better than they had ever been in an army before. This radical change had commenced under General Burnside; but was perfected under General Hooker, by the efficient and earnest medical director of the army, Dr. Letterman; to whom belongs the honor of bringing about this most desirable change.

By the new system, the surgeons were enabled to accomplish a far greater amount of work, and in much better order than under the old; and the wounded were better and more quickly cared for. By this system the hospital of the division was the unit. From the division, a medical officer of good executive ability was selected, to whom was assigned the general oversight of the hospital. One or more surgeons of well known skill and experience were detailed from the medical force of the division, who were known as "operating surgeons;" to each of whom was assigned three assistants, also known to be skillful men, who were either surgeons or assistant surgeons. To the operating surgeons all cases requiring surgical operations were brought, and thus the wounded men had the benefit of the very best talent and experience in the division, in the decision of the question whether he should be submitted to the use of the knife, and in the performance of the operation in case one was required. It was a mistaken impression among those at home, that each medical officer was the operating surgeon for his own men. Only about one in fifteen of the medical officers was intrusted with operations.

From each brigade an assistant surgeon was detailed to provide food and shelter for the wounded. His duty was to superintend the erection of hospital tents as soon as there was a prospect of an engagement, and to have hot coffee and rations of food ready for the wounded as soon as they came to the hospital; he was to attend to their clothing, bedding and rations as long as they remained in the hospital.

Another assistant surgeon from each brigade was selected to keep the records; to take the name and character of wound of every one who was brought to the hospital, with the operation, if any; and the list of deaths, the place of burial, and all other matters necessary to record. An assistant surgeon was to remain with each regiment, and attend to getting the wounded from the field into the ambulances, and to arrest hemorrhage in case of necessity.

Thus, all labor was systematized. Every officer and nurse knew exactly what to do: each had his own part of the work assigned to him, and there was no conflicting of orders or clashing of opinions.

Our ambulance system was also very perfect — so complete, indeed, that, after a year of trial in the Army of the Potomac, congress adopted it as the ambulance system of the United States. To Doctor Letterman, also, belongs the honor of originating this system.

The ambulances of each corps were under command of a captain, who acted under directions from the medical director of the corps. A lieutenant commanded the ambulances of a division, and a second lieutenant those of a brigade. To each ambulance was assigned a driver, and two stretcher-bearers; and to three ambulances a sergeant, mounted. The ambulances of a division always went together, behind the division, and on the march were attended by a surgeon, an assistant surgeon, a hospital steward, a cook, and three or more nurses, who were to attend to the wants of the sick in the ambulances, and at night, if any were unable to return to their regiments, to erect tents for them, and supply them with food and bedding. In an engagement, the stretcher-bearers of each regiment, with the sergeant, reported to the assistant surgeon in attendance with the regiment. As soon as a man was wounded, he was brought to the medical officer, put into an ambulance, and taken to the division hospital. By this means, ordinarily, every man was carried to the hospital of his own division.

The improvements in the quartermasters' department were nearly as great; and we have already alluded to the abundant supplies furnished by the commissary department.

Great difficulty was experienced by the troops of our corps in getting wood. The men of our Second division lugged wood on their backs a mile and a half, with which to do their cooking and warm their tents. But notwithstanding the hardships they endured, the inclemency of the winter, and their severe picket duty, the men were gay. In many of the regiments, the sounds of the guitar and accordion could be heard every evening; and on pleasant afternoons and evenings, parties assembled in the company streets and danced cotillions, and polkas, and jigs, to the music of violins. When snow covered the ground, mimic battles with snowballs were a frequent amusement. At times, one regiment would challenge another, and a general melee would follow. Snowballing was, particularly, a favorite amusement with our friends of the Twenty-first New Jersey, who never let an opportunity pass for indulging in their favorite sport. Each party carried its flags and was led by officers chosen for the occasion. The capture of a flag, or of a number of prisoners, from an opposite party, caused great glee among the victors. A good deal of interest was excited throughout the Second division by a snowball battle between one of the Vermont regiments and the Twenty-sixth New Jersey. Both regiments formed in line of battle, each officered by its line and field officers, the latter mounted. At the signal, the battle commenced; charges and counter-charges were made, prisoners were taken on either side, the air was filled with the white missiles, and stentorian cheers went up as one or other party gained an advantage. At length victory rested with the Vermonters, and the Jersey boys surrendered the field, defeated.

Another favorite amusement in the corps was the game of base ball. There were many excellent players in the different regiments, and it was common for the ball-players of one regiment or brigade to challenge another regiment or brigade. These matches were watched by great crowds of soldiers with intense interest.

In our Seventy-seventh regiment, matters went on much the same as in other regiments of the corps. We had our share of disease and desertions. We had our ball-players and our violinists; our singers and our story-tellers, as every regiment had. At regimental head-quarters, matters went on gaily. It was the custom of the officers of the field and staff to collect in one of the tents as evening came on, and, in company with friends from other regiments, pass the hours in lively converse, in singing and relating amusing stories.

We had a glee book and an old copy of the "Carmina Sacra," and then our friend, Colonel, now Major-General, Connor, was never at a loss for a song, and Colonel French often displayed his genius with the violin, and our friend, the chaplain, could always tell a good story or perpetrate a joke. Chaplain Norman Fox was an accession to our staff, who joined us when we first encamped at White Oak Church. He was a gentleman of enterprise and talent, who, soon after his arrival in camp, instituted a series of religious meetings on week days, in addition to the regular services of the Sabbath, and a good deal of religious interest was awakened among the men.

Among other changes, we lost one of our most valuable and beloved officers. Dr. Campbell, who had for weeks been declining in health, was obliged to resign. The doctor was a most genial and companionable man, and an excellent officer. We greatly missed his hearty laugh, his fund of stories and ready wit in our social gatherings. The doctor was afterward appointed surgeon of the Fortieth New York, but was attacked with spotted fever, from which he recovered only after a long illness, during which he again resigned.

The First brigade, Second division, which for some time past had been under command of General Calvin A. Pratt, was broken up, and a new brigade, called the "Light division," was formed from the regiments of the First brigade, and one regiment from each the First and Third divisions. The regiments were, the Fifth Wisconsin, the Sixth Maine, the Thirty-first and Forty-third New York, and the Sixty-first Pennsylvania. Colonel Burnham, of the Sixth Maine, was placed in command.

Among other reviews in the Sixth corps during the winter, was one by General Hooker, of our Second division and the Light division. The troops were formed in line, and the general and staff were escorted to the ground by the Twentieth New York, of Neill's brigade, in splendid style. The regiment was composed entirely of German Turners. Their drill surpassed that of any regiment of regulars, and the exquisite neatness they displayed in their dress and in the care of their equipments, together with the perfection of their movements, made them the finest appearing regiment in the service, when on parade. It is to be regretted that the prestige of the regiment was not always sustained on the battle-field. As the regiment and cavalcade appeared on the field, it was a brilliant pageant; first came our brigade band, one of the finest in the army, then the pioneers of the Twentieth, their axes, shovels and picks polished so that they glistened in the sunlight like burnished silver; then the Twentieth regiment, in column by company, marching with step as perfect as though all were directed by a single will; following the regiment, rode General Hooker on his superb white horse, a head and shoulders above all his cavalcade. The immense suite, consisting of General Hooker's own staff, and a large number of major-generals and their staffs, completed the brilliant column. The division was drawn up in a line, stretching a half a mile across the field, straight as the flight of an arrow, with artillery on either flank. The general and his brilliant retinue, rode to the right of the line, and advanced slowly along the front of

24

the whole division, inspecting closely each regiment as he passed, the bands playing " Hail to the Chief," the colors dipping, and the bugles pealing notes of welcome. Having passed the entire front of the line, the chief now rode at a rapid pace along its rear to the point of beginning. He then, with his attendants, took a position on a slight elevation of ground at a distance from the line, when the whole division, in column, marching to the place, passed in review before him, and the pageant was ended.

An important change in the command of our corps occurred about this time. General Smith, who had so long commanded our division, and for some time past our Sixth corps, was relieved of his command, and ordered to the department of North Carolina. His successor was General John Sedgwick, then well known as one of our best division commanders, and one of the sternest soldiers in the Army of the Potomac. Bred as a soldier, he had served with great distinction in Mexico, and at the breaking out of the rebellion he had joined the Union army, and was soon placed in command of a division in Sumner's corps, which, under his command, became the best division of the corps, as the Sixth corps became the best in the army. Modest and retiring in his ordinary intercourse with his fellows, he exhibited the most brilliant qualities in time of battle. The dignity of his bearing fitted him to command, and he needed not the insignia of rank to command the deference of those about him.

None who witnessed the farewell reception of General Smith, will forget the scene at corps head-quarters. The two generals, the old and loved leader of the Second division and of the corps, and the new commander, stood side by side. General Smith, tall, well dressed, his regulation coat buttoned closely about him, his easy and graceful manner and conversation; General Sedgwick, of stouter build, wearing a loose blouse and coarse blue pants, such as are furnished the private soldier, strong and manly in his appearance, and somewhat abrupt in his manner. Officers returned to their camps satisfied that although the corps had lost a favorite commander, it had also gained a brave leader.

One of the grand events of the winter was the review of the whole army by President Lincoln. The review continued two days. The first was occupied in reviewing the Second, Fifth, Sixth and Third corps; the second of the remaining corps. It was a most imposing spectacle, never to be forgotten by those who were actors or spectators. The President, in his civilian's dress and tall hat, accompanied by General Hooker, and followed by an immense suite, was welcomed by the thundering of artillery as it fired the national salute. The different corps were drawn up in line, each occupying a plain within sight of the others. Riding in front of the corps, the President and the immense cavalcade passed along the whole line, inspecting carefully each regiment, then returned in the rear. This inspection over, the President and staff stationed themselves in some favorable position, and the whole corps passed in review before him.. The same process was repeated with each corps.

How one unaccustomed to such physical fatigues could endure such labor, commencing early in the morning and only resting at dark, was a wonder. It seemed as if the President's physical, like his mental constitution, could bear up under the most trying and continued labors. As the warm weather of spring appeared, the men adorned their camps with evergreen trees and beautiful arches, so that the camps presented a pleasant appearance; but we had little time to enjoy these, for as soon as the roads began to be passable, preparations were pushed forward for the spring campaign.

CHAPTER XVII.

THE CHANCELLORSVILLE CAMPAIGN.

Orders to move — The river crossed — Sedgwick's command — The First corps withdrawn — Gallant conduct of the Light division — Advancing to the heights — The line of battle — The columns of attack — Attack of Howe's columns — Of Newton's column — Of Burnham's — Misfortune following victory — Fight of Bartlett's brigade — The First division at work — A critical position — The Sixth corps surrounded — Savage fight of Neill's brigade — The corps withdraws to Banks' Ford — Recrosses the river — Hooker's operations on the right — Position of the corps — Rout of the Eleventh corps — The rebels repulsed — Jackson renews the attack — The rebels again repulsed — Hooker recrosses the river.

ON Tuesday, the 28th of April, the Sixth corps received orders to break up its camp and be ready to march at a moment's notice. Eight days' rations had been issued to the men, who were in the highest spirits, having forgotten all their former discouragements, and were now only anxious for an encounter with the enemy. A storm of rain of some violence set in on the morning of the 28th, which rendered marching difficult. At twelve o'clock we received the order to "fall in," and in five minutes we were on our way to take our place in the line of battle. A march of six miles through thickets and bogs, brought us to the rear of Falmouth Station, at a short distance from the river. Here we bivouacked for the night, and were awakened before daylight in the morning by the sound of artillery and musketry at the river, where Russell's brigade, of the First division, was forcing a passage across the stream. The Second division only had been allowed to rest quietly during the night. The men of the Light brigade had toiled from dark until nearly dawn, carrying the pontoon boats on their shoulders to the river side, and launching them in the stream. So noiselessly had they conducted their operations, that the pickets of the enemy took no alarm until they suddenly saw the braves of Russell's brigade approaching in the boats, just as dawn was breaking. The astonished confederates fired a few volleys of musketry, and our guns threw among them a few charges of cannister, and the rebels fled precipitately. A number of prisoners were captured, among them the officer of the picket-guard. Colonel Irwin, of the Forty-ninth Pennsylvania, who had, at Antietam, commanded the Third brigade of the Second division, was among the wounded on our side.

At sunrise the Second division filed down to the river side, and took position in line of battle. Our horses cropped the green blades which had sprung from the grain scattered for their food nearly five months before. The division was upon the very spot where it lay before, at the first battle of Fredericksburgh. The bridge also was in the same place that Franklin's bridge had been. The point was known as Franklin's Crossing.

The First division of our corps (Brook's) was on the other side of the river, holding the plain for some distance. The pickets of that division formed the half of a circle of about three-fourths of a mile in diameter, the center being at the pontoon bridge, where some earthworks were thrown up. At our left, about a mile down the river, the First corps had also effected a crossing. The rebels had offered strong resistance, but the crossing was gallantly accomplished by Wadsworth's division in boats. Like the First division of our own corps, Wadsworth's division was holding a semi-circular portion of the plateau; but being able to maintain the position by some fighting.

Sickles' Third corps was upon the high ground in the rear, ready to come to the assistance of the corps at the river. The three corps, First, Third and Sixth, were under command of General Sedgwick.

The rebels spent the day in throwing up intrenchments and shelling Reynolds' position. Toward night the artillery practice ceased, and the First and Sixth corps bivouacked where they had stood during the day, but Sickles and his corps were ordered to the assistance of Hooker, on the right.

The morning of the 30th was lowery, but the clouds dispersed as the day advanced. About noon the troops were massed by brigades, and a congratulatory order from General Hooker was read to them, amid great cheering. "The enemy," said the order, "must now come out and fight us on our ground, or retreat ingloriously." Nothing more of interest occurred that day; but, in the afternoon of the following day, the First corps became engaged in a fierce artillery duel with the enemy, in which the corps lost a large number of its men in killed and wounded. At sunset an order came from General Hooker, at Chancellorsville, for General Sedgwick to assume a threatening attitude — to make a severe demonstration — but to make no attack. There was much marching and getting into position, and regiments and divisions were marched and countermarched in such a manner as to convey to the rebels the impression that a grand attack was to be made at that point. The enemy was evidently deceived by these maneuvers, and heavy columns of rebel infantry commenced to form upon the old battle-field. While we stood in line of battle, one of our bands near the skirmish line struck up the air, "Dixie." The rebels, hearing the strains, set up defiant cheers, which were answered by our army in the most tremendous shouts imaginable. The contest seemed for the time to depend on strength of lung, and our boys certainly beat them at shouting.

As the sun disappeared behind the hills, when Hooker's guns were thundering, we retired to our tents. All day long the earth had been shaken by tremendous firing of artillery on the right; and now, as darkness gathered over the scenes of conflict, the thundering of the guns and the trembling of the earth seemed like a succession of earthquakes. The spirit of our boys rose, as the battle on the right progressed, and there seemed to be indications of work for them. Groups might be seen at any time, when we were not standing in line of battle, telling yarns, singing songs, playing ball and pitching quoits, while they momentarily looked for the order to advance upon the heights, into the very jaws of death.

Saturday morning, May 2d, the First corps was withdrawn from its position; its bridges were taken up, and the corps moved past us up the river to join the main body of the army under Hooker, on the right. The Seventy-seventh was sent to do picket duty on the ground occupied by the First corps the night before. Our reserve was posted a little way from the river, in a pleasant field, where the fresh clover furnished a soft bed for the men, and a dainty bite for our horses. Just in front of us was a lovely spot — the residence of Doctor Morson, for fifteen years a surgeon in the United States navy. The place was in remarkable order; the gardens in full bloom, the mocking birds building their nests, and the greenlets warbling sweetly among the flowering shrubs.

We strolled along the banks of the beautiful river, gathering flowers and glancing at our "secesh" neighbors on the opposite bank, only a few yards distant; or we lounged in the shade of our tents, enjoying the charms of a lovely May day, while the terrible din of battle on the right, where Hooker's forces were contending, shook the ground beneath us, and we knew that ere the sun set, thousands of our brave comrades must be sacrificed.

As the evening drew near, we who were on the north side of the river saw our skirmishers, of the "Light division," drive back the skirmish line of the enemy. It was a gallant feat, and finely executed. Our hearts leaped for joy as we watched our brave fellows, their line as perfect as though on drill, advance, firing rapidly, and pressing the enemy at "double-quick." They made no halt until they had crossed the whole breadth of the plain and reached the base of the hills.

Few who were then in the Sixth corps will ever forget that scene. The sun, just sinking behind the hills where Hooker was at work, threw a beautiful golden light over the plain, and crowned the heights with brilliant hues. It was one of those evenings of surpassing loveliness, such as gladdened our hearts only at long intervals. Prominent in the foreground of the beautiful scene was a noble white steed, with its gallant rider, dashing from one end of the skirmish line to the other. None who witnessed the spectacle will forget the white horse and the fearless rider; and few of the Second or Light divisions need be reminded that the horseman was Colonel Baker, of the Forty-third New York, who was then in charge of the skirmish line.

The "Light division" was, as we have before stated, the First brigade of our Second division, with regiments from the First and Third divisions which had been, a short time before leaving camp, detached to form an independent organization. The arrangement was broken up immediately after this battle, and the regiments put in the First and Second divisions again.

Immediately after the brilliant advance of the "Light division," the Seventy-seventh regiment was ordered to leave the picket line and join its brigade. The Second division crossed the river and took position, the Third brigade in front, the Vermont brigade in rear. The Thirty third and Forty-ninth New York, of the Third brigade, went forward as pickets in front of the hills, relieving pickets of the "Light division," which moved to the right.

We remained in line all night, sometimes throwing ourselves upon the ground to catch a moment's sleep, then roused in expectancy of an advance.

At four o'clock in the morning we did advance. Straight across the plain we went, until we came nearly to the base of the heights, where the hosts of the enemy awaited us, then taking the Bowling Green road, filed to the right and proceeded to the rear of Fredericksburgh; the Seventy-seventh in front, the Twenty-first New Jersey, the Forty-ninth New York, Twentieth New York, Seventh Maine and Thirty-third New York, constituting the Third brigade, under command of General Neill, following in the order mentioned. Then came the Vermont brigade, Colonel L. A. Grant commanding; these two brigades forming the whole of Howe's (Second) division of the Sixth corps since the First brigade was detached.

As we gained the rear of the eastern part of the town, the batteries of the enemy opened upon us, and swarms of infantry rose up in our front and poured volleys of bullets into our ranks. The " Light division " and Newton's Third division of our corps had passed through the streets of the town, and were now on our right. The skirmishers from Wheaton's and Shaler's brigades had struck those of the enemy near a large mansion, where, each party dodging behind the garden fence, the cherry trees and the outhouses, they kept up a lively engagement for several minutes, but Newton's advance was forced to yield the ground.

In the meantime, the long line of rifled cannon which surmounted Stafford Heights, on the north side of the river, as at the first battle of Fredericksburgh, were throwing huge shells across the wide valley and stream into the works of the enemy. One or two field batteries near the head of our own column, and some attached to the other divisions, got into position and opened a fierce cannonade.

25

General Howe quickly formed his troops in line, as did the other division commanders.

The line of battle of the corps extended from the pontoon bridge at Franklin's Crossing to the right of the town of Fredericksburgh. First, on the left, Brooks' division held the plain in front of the crossing. Next, on the right, in front of Marye's Heights, was Howe's Second division; then the "Light division," Colonel Burnham; and on the extreme right was Newton's Third division. Gibbon's division of the Second corps, which, because its encampment was in plain view of the enemy, had been left behind, also crossed into the town by a bridge which it threw over, and took position on the right of the corps.

General Sedgwick, finding that the heights could only be carried by direct assault, directed storming columns to be formed in the Second and Third divisions and the Light division, which order was at once carried into execution.

In the Second division, General Howe directed General Neill to lead the advance. The plan of attack of the division was in two lines of battle of three regiments each.

The first line consisted of the Thirty-third New York, Colonel Taylor, the Seventh Maine, Colonel Connor, and the Twenty-first New Jersey, Colonel Van Houten, preceded by the Seventy-seventh New York, Colonel French, as skirmishers. The line was commanded by General Neill.* The second line consisted of the Sixth Vermont, Colonel Barney, the Twenty-sixth New Jersey, Colonel Morrison, and the Second Vermont, Colonel Walbridge, and was under command of Colonel L. A. Grant. Both lines were arranged from right to left, in the order above mentioned.

---

* "I was ordered to form three regiments as the *advance of a column of assault* against the heights of Marye's Hill, back of Fredericksburgh. I led the Thirty-third New York, Twenty-first New Jersey and Seventh Maine Volunteers, preceded by the Seventy-seventh New York, who were acting as skirmishers, under a heavy fire of shot and shell."—*Neill's Report.*

The Forty-ninth and Twentieth New York formed the right reserve, and the Third, Fourth and Fifth Vermont, under Colonel Seavor, the left reserve.

The next column was composed of the Seventh Massachusetts, Colonel Jones, and the Thirty-sixth New York, Colonel Walsh; both under the command of Colonel Jones — the Fifth Wisconsin, Colonel Allen, acting as skirmishers. Supporting the column, in line of battle, were the Sixth Maine, Colonel Harris, Thirty-first New York, Colonel Jones, and the Twenty-third Pennsylvania, Colonel Ely.

The right column of all consisted of the Forty-third New York, Colonel Baker, and the Sixty-first Pennsylvania, Colonel Spear — the two regiments under command of the latter officer, who fell, mortally wounded, while leading the charge. The Sixty-seventh New York, Colonel Cross, and the Eighty-second Pennsylvania, Major Bassett, under command of Colonel Shaler, supported this right column.

At half-past ten, the arrangements for storming the heights were completed, and Newton's batteries opened upon the enemy. At the sound of Newton's first gun, General Howe ordered his batteries to direct their fire upon the heights, and then ordered the storming column forward.

The division advanced toward the bold bluffs, which, bare of trees as well as the plain below, allowed the enemy an excellent view of all our movements. A railroad traversed the plain near the bluffs, and in a deep cut through which the road passed, were rebels. They rose up as we advanced, and poured showers of leaden hail into our line; but one of our batteries, getting an enfilading fire on the road, sent the gray-coated occupants hurriedly to the rear. For a moment we halted, the batteries on either side playing into each other with spirit.

It was a moment of contending emotions of pride, hope and sadness, as our gallant boys stood face to face with those heights, ready to charge upon them. At double-quick, and in splendid style, they crossed the plain. Our line was perfect. The men could not have made a more orderly appearance had they been on drill. Proud of their commands, Generals Howe and Neill, and Colonel Grant, cheered the men onward, while Lieutenant-Colonel French, in charge of the skirmish line, inspired, by his own intrepid behavior, the utmost confidence and bravery in his men. They took the matter as coolly as though on parade.

Just in rear of the division, three batteries of Parrott guns were playing into the works of the enemy, while from the heights above, all the opposing batteries poured a terrible and destructive fire upon the advancing lines. Having gained the rifle pits at the base of the hills, they pushed forward to capture the heights.

A more grand spectacle cannot be imagined. There were the hills, enough to fatigue any man to climb them without a load and with no one to oppose. At the foot of the hills were thousands of the enemy, pouring into them volleys of musketry, and on the heights were their lines of earthworks, with their artillery, from which poured grape and cannister in a frightful storm. But the boys pushed nobly, steadily on, the rebels steadily retreating, the division coming up in splendid style. Generals Howe and Neill and Colonel Grant directing the movements and cheering on the men, as they pressed undauntedly against the murderous storm of iron and lead that met them from above. Our men were falling in every direction, but the lines were immediately closed, and on they passed. With shouts and cheers that drowned the roar of artillery, the noble division, with bayonets fixed, mounted the heights, the rebels retreating in confusion. Of that noble column the skirmishers of the Seventy-seventh first reached the

STORMING OF MARYE'S HEIGHTS BY HOWE'S DIVISION.

heights of Marye's Hill, the Thirty-third New York, in line of battle, followed, and then the Sixth Vermont,* the other regiments of the two brigades being but a moment behind. But the work was not all done yet. On our left was an earthwork of strong profile, from which now the rebels turned their guns upon us. Against this the column turned, and soon gained possession of it also. A third stronghold then fell into our hands, and we were in undisputed possession of the heights. While the troops under Neill and Grant had thus nobly stormed the works in front, Colonel Seaver, with his three regiments, had scaled the heights further to the left.

With one or two exceptions, every regiment in the division had behaved with great gallantry.

The Seventy-seventh New York captured a stand of colors belonging to the Eighteenth Mississippi regiment, two heavy guns, a large number of prisoners, among whom was Colonel Luce of the Eighteenth Mississippi, and great numbers of small arms.

As the regiment reached the heights, and took possession of the guns, General Howe rode up, and, taking off his hat, exclaimed: "Noble Seventy-seventh! you have covered yourselves with glory!" The general's words were greeted with tumultuous cheers.

In the second work, the Thirty-third New York captured a piece of heavy ordnance and a number of prisoners. The regiment had exhibited great spirit and bravery. Six color-bearers had been shot down successively.

It was at the signal of the first gun in Newton's front that General Howe had ordered the charge of the Second divi-

---

* General L. A. Grant, in his report, does unintentional injustice to a brave regiment. He says: "The Sixth Vermont followed the Thirty-third New York, *and was the second* to gain the heights of Fredericksburgh." The Thirty-third was not the first to gain the heights on that part of the line. The testimony of General Neill, as well as of the members of the regiment, and the many trophies it captured, fully establish the claim of the Seventy-seventh to the honor.

sion. The Third division and the Light division had not been idle while the events we have described were going on. It will be remembered that the column on the right consisted of the Forty-third New York and the Sixty-first Pennsylvania, supported by a line of battle; and that the other column consisted of the Seventh Massachusetts and Thirty-sixth New York, also supported by other regiments.

The ascent in front of the Third and Light divisions, though steep, was less precipitous than in front of Howe's column, and a good road led to the heights. But a stone wall skirted the base of the hills, behind which the rebels swarmed in great numbers.

Under the fire of the rebel batteries, Newton's and Burnham's regiments lay, some in the outskirts of the town, some in the cemetery, until General Sedgwick gave the order for the advance. Then, almost at the same time, both commands moved up the glacis towards the heights. Colonel Jones, with his two regiments, the Seventh Massachusetts and Thirty-sixth New York, pushed forward up the telegraph road, against the stone wall, bearing to the right of the road; their knapsacks and haversacks were left behind that they might be unincumbered with needless burdens. As they approached within three hundred yards of the wall, a murderous volley checked the advance, and threw the head of the column into disorder. In two minutes the men were rallied, and again they approached the wall, this time nearer than before; but again they were broken. A third time they were rallied; this time they pushed straight forward to the works.

The column under Colonel Spear started briskly forward, divested, like the others, of knapsacks and haversacks. Sallying from the town at double quick, in column of four ranks, they crossed the bridge just outside the city, when the gallant Colonel Spear received his mortal wound, and fell at the head of his men. The Sixty-first, which led the column, shocked at the death of their beloved leader, broke, and in confusion turned toward the town. This unfortunate confusion spread to the men of the Forty-third, who, checked by the disordered mass in front, and submitted to a galling fire, also commenced falling back. Finding any attempt to get the men through the disordered mass in front, the gallant Wilson drew his colors to the right and rallied his regiment around them. Then, bounding forward, the regiment reached the heights scarcely behind any of the regiments on the left, capturing a gun and many prisoners.

The line of battle under Colonel Burnham advanced on the left of the road; the Fifth Wisconsin on the skirmish line, the Sixth Maine, the Thirty-first New York, and the Twenty-third Pennsylvania in line. Four more gallant regiments could not be found in the service. Leaving everything but guns and ammunition, they started forward, encountering a shower of bullets, grape and canister, as soon as they rose above the slight knoll which had concealed them. We of the Second division looked with admiration upon the advancing line; our flag—it was the flag of the Sixth Maine—in advance of the others, its brave color-guard bounding forward, then halting a moment while the men came up, then dashing forward again, and finally gaining the heights before us all! It was a noble spectacle, and filled our hearts with pride for our brave comrades of the Light division. The Light division secured as trophies about seven hundred prisoners and five cannon.

Thus the heights were won. It was a glorious day for the Sixth corps. Never was a charge more gallantly made. But it was a sad day, for many scores of our brave comrades lay stretched in death, along the glacis, and on the steep ascent, in the ravines and along the road.

The Seventh Massachusetts, the Sixth Maine, the Fifth Wisconsin, the Second Vermont, and the Seventy-seventh,

Thirty-third and Forty-third New York, were among the greatest losers. The Sixth Maine reached the rebel works with the loss of six captains and the major, and a proportional number of enlisted men. Two color-bearers and Lieutenant-Colonel Newman were shot in the Thirty-first, and Colonel Jones, of the Seventh Massachusetts, was seriously wounded, while one hundred and twelve of his brave men were either killed or wounded.

The wounded had been taken to the city, where they were kindly cared for by the surgeons of the corps, who had seized the town for hospital purposes. Churches and private dwellings swarmed with the unfortunate men, whose mangled forms told of the fearful work of the day. Surgeons were hard at work ministering relief to the suffering, binding up the wounds or removing the mangled limbs which offered no hope of recovery; while nurses administered food and coffee, and prepared beds, such as could be extemporized from blankets spread upon the floors. More than three thousand wounded were brought into the city before nightfall.

Upon the very heels of the brilliant success of the corps commenced disaster. An order from General Hooker had directed General Sedgwick to advance toward Chancellorsville, and form a junction with the main army. So the corps which had so nobly won the heights pressed on for further achievements. The heights were left behind. Brooks' division, which now took the lead, had advanced as far as Salem Church, on the Chancellorsville pike, when, instead of meeting any portion of Hooker's army, a few shells from rebel guns warned the division of the presence of the enemy.

A dense thicket was in front, and Bartlett's brigade, which had the advance, was deployed to skirmish and ascertain the position of the concealed foe. Presently, having fallen upon a strong line of skirmishers, the bri-

gade was formed in line of battle; the Twenty-seventh
New York on the right, then the Fifth Maine, then the
One Hundred and Twenty-first New York, and on the
left the Ninety-sixth Pennsylvania; the Sixteenth New
York holding the skirmish line in front. General Bartlett
advanced his line to the thicket, the Sixteenth driving the
rebel skirmishers, the brigade following closely. At
the edge of the thicket General Bartlett halted the line,
but being ordered by General Brooks to advance rapidly,
he pushed on again.

Advancing through the thicket about thirty rods, the
brigade suddenly found itself face to face with a rebel
line. The confederates were lying down in a road which
traversed the thicket; and, when the Union line was within
twenty yards, they suddenly discharged a volley, which,
had it been well aimed, must have almost annihilated the
brigade; but the fire was returned with effect, and presently, the confederates were glad to leave the road, which
was almost filled with their dead and wounded, and seek
shelter behind rifle pits. The rifle pits were but a few
yards in rear of the road, and here a very strong force
was posted. The Union forces occupied the road, and
directed their fire against the works; but the rebel fire
cut down their unprotected ranks like grass before the
scythe. For fifteen minutes the gallant regiments endured
this murderous fire, and then fell back in good order, having lost, within twenty minutes, nearly seven hundred
men; of whom two hundred and seventy-three were from
the One Hundred and Twenty-first New York.

The New Jersey brigade, and the whole division, had
by this time been brought into action, and great slaughter
was made in almost every regiment. Newton's division
was also fiercely engaged on the right, Wheaton's brigade
holding its position only by the most stubborn fighting.
The enemy having forced the First division to retire,

advanced against our line; but the batteries under Williston, Rigby and Parsons, by splendid practice, repulsed the
onset.   The Second division, forming the rear of the column, had not been brought into the engagement.

Darkness came to the relief of the corps, and the men
slept soundly on their arms after the arduous duties of the
day; but there were many misgivings among officers in
regard to what to-morrow might bring forth.

While we rested, the enemy was bringing up reinforcements from the direction of Richmond.   Very early in the
morning the siege guns on Stafford Heights, opposite the
town, sent some shells screaming across the valley to
the heights of Marye's Hill, giving the alarm to those in the
town and to those who had so recently left it.   Lines of
rebels were seen all along the outskirts of the town and on
the crests above.   Fifteen thousand confederate troops
were between the Sixth corps and Fredericksburgh Heights.
The surgeons immediately prepared to send the wounded
across the river, but, supposing that to accomplish the
whole before the rebels should take possession of the town
would be impossible, made every preparation for being
themselves taken prisoners.   A small detachment of Gibbon's division still guarded the town, but nearly all his
troops had recrossed the river and were on Stafford Heights.
But the small force in the town seemed sufficient to convey
to the rebels the impression that it was well guarded, for
they made no attempt to seize the immense amount of
hospital stores which was at their mercy, or to molest the
wounded or the surgeons.

The Sixth corps was now in a critical position; its communications entirely cut off, and surrounded by hosts of
the enemy.   The corps was sandwiched between the rebels
on the heights and Lee's whole army; while on its left was
a strong force, and on its right an impassable river.   Dispositions were at once made to meet the emergency.

Brooks' division was drawn back, and Howe's, still in the rear, changed front and quickly extended the line of battle to the river, so as to include Banks' Ford, six miles above the city, over which communications were at once established.

The whole of Early's rebel division occupied the crest of Marye's and Cemetery Hills; the divisions of Anderson and McLaws were on our flank; and the brigades of Hays, Hoke and Lawton, supported by Lee's whole army, were in our rear. We were in the vicinity of Salem Church, and our only line of retreat was upon the road leading to Banks' Ford.

The first demonstration of the rebels, on the morning of the 4th, was against the position held by Neill's brigade. A company from the Seventh Maine, and two companies from the Forty-ninth New York, in conjunction with a part of Martin's battery, and supported by the remaining companies of the Forty-ninth, gallantly repulsed and routed a whole brigade of rebels, capturing two hundred prisoners, and the colors of the Fifty-eighth Virginia regiment; which last trophy was borne off by the men of the Forty-ninth, and was the second stand of colors taken by that gallant brigade in this engagement, the Seventy-seventh having captured the other.

The day wore away with little fighting till five o'clock. General Howe had so disposed his troops as to occupy two positions.

In front was the Third brigade, holding a crest which overlooked a ravine through which the rebels must pass. Behind the brigade was another ravine, in which was a thin skirt of woods. In rear of this second ravine, and behind a swell of ground, the Vermont brigade was strongly posted, forming the second line of battle. There were in each of these two brigades about three thousand men.

Now came the most fearful struggle of the campaign. At five o'clock the rebel hordes came, with deafening yells, upon the division. The divisions of Early, Anderson and McLaws rushed upon the single brigade of less than three thousand men, massing their troops in the ravine, and charging with impetuous fury. But the noble regiments heroically withstood the shock, the Germans of the Twentieth only going to the rear in confusion. The stubborn resistance of the brigade prevented the rebels from piercing our lines, and cutting off our retreat, and thus, by its gallantry, enabled the corps to cross at Banks' Ford. But one thousand men — more than one-third of the brigade — fell on that crest. Colonel Van Houghton, of the Twenty-first New Jersey, was mortally wounded, and many other choice spirits were among the fallen. General Neill was injured by the fall of his horse, which was shot. General Howe now ordered the brigade to fall back, and the decimated regiments left the front line, and fell behind the strong position held by the Vermonters. The rebels, thinking this a retreat, followed with yells of exultation, but were met by the second line of battle, which, from its position behind the swell of ground, was concealed, with a murderous fire, which sent them reeling back to the cover of the first ravine. Their charge had inflicted little damage upon the Union line. It was now nearly dark, and the reception which the rebels had received had so completely routed and broken them, that they made no further attempt upon our lines.

About nine o'clock, the division was ordered to fall back to Banks' Ford, now two miles distant from us. We fell back quietly, and found that the other divisions had preceded us, and were snugly behind rifle pits. They had fallen back as soon as it was dark, leaving the Second division to cover the retreat.

Meantime, comparatively little fighting had been done

by the other divisions, though a constant skirmish was kept up, and in the evening the confederates managed to get in the rear of a part of the picket of the Light division, capturing a large number of prisoners from the Forty-third and Thirty-first New York, and Sixty-first Pennsylvania.

The position at Banks' Ford might have been held until reinforcements could have reached the corps from Hooker; but, unfortunately, that general, receiving from General Sedgwick first, intelligence that he could not safely hold the position, then that he could, ordered the corps to be withdrawn, and afterward countermanded the order; but the last order was only received when the movement had been accomplished.

Toward morning the corps recrossed the Rappahannock on pontoon bridges; not without the utmost difficulty; one bridge being destroyed by rebel artillery, and the other barely saved from destruction long enough to allow the troops hurriedly to pass over.

The corps had passed through a fearful ordeal, and had shown itself to be made of heroic material. No two more brilliant feats had been performed during the war, than the storming of the heights of Fredericksburgh, and the splendid resistance when surrounded and attacked by overwhelming forces. The men came out of the fight, not demoralized, but as ready to scale those terrible heights again, if called upon, as they had been on the 3d of May.

General Sedgwick had manifested during the fights, those masterly qualities which made him one of the greatest soldiers of the age. His conduct on the retreat was cool and unimpassioned. Personally examining every part of the ground in front and rear, riding from one end of the line to the other, now ordering a battery placed at some commanding point, and now looking out a new position to which his troops might fall back in case of necessity, he was everywhere present, full of energy, as determined to save as he had been to win.

Throughout the land the glorious deeds of the Sixth corps became household words; but its glory had been dearly purchased. Five thousand of the heroes who crossed the Rappahannock on the 2d of May, were either dead or wounded. Colonel Van Houghton, one of New Jersey's bravest sons, had received a mortal wound, from which he died in the hands of the enemy. Captain Luther M. Wheeler, of the Seventy-seventh, was shot while we halted at the foot of Marye's Hill. It was a sad loss to his regiment, and the corps. Few more gifted young men could be found in the army. He was one of our bravest and most efficient officers. Gentle in his relations with his fellows, cool and daring in battle; his youthful face beaming with fortitude, was a continual joy to his men in time of danger. He died as he had lived, a hero.

The Forty-third had lost Captain Knickerbocker and Lieutenant Koonz. Two young men of brilliant promise, greatly loved and respected in their regiment and in their native city, Albany.

The wounded men in the hospitals exhibited the same heroic fortitude in their sufferings that they had manifested in the charge and in the retreat. A few instances are given as illustrations of many: Erskine Branch of Company D, Seventy-seventh New York, when his leg was torn to shreds by a shell, hobbled off on the sound one and his gun, singing "The Star Spangled Banner." Corporal Henry West was shot through the thigh, and he was brought to the rear. "I guess," said he "that old Joe West's son has lost a leg." The corporal died soon after. While in the hospital, suffering from extreme anguish, a wounded man at his side lamented that he had come to the war. "I am not sorry that I came," instantly responded the brave corporal.

Let us now turn back and glance hastily at the maneuvers of the main army at Chancellorsville. We, of the
Sixth corps, could only see by the balloon which, like
some huge bird, hovered over the army, where it held its
position, and the unceasing roar of artillery told us of a
severe struggle with its foe; while rumor brought, now
reports of brilliant success, and anon tales of sad defeat.
We knew little of the true state of affairs at the right,
and it was only when we mingled with our comrades of
the other corps that we learned the details of the battle
of Chancellorsville. We now repeat it as it was given to
us. On the day that the army broke up its winter camp,
General Hooker led the Fifth, Eleventh, Twelfth and
Second corps, except Gibbon's division of the latter, up
the river, until he reached Kelley's Ford, about twenty
miles above Fredericksburgh. Here he crossed his whole
force, and pushing southward and eastward, uncovered
the United States Ford eight miles below, which was
guarded by a brigade of rebels, and struck the intersection of the Gordonsville plank road with the Orange
county turnpike, about five miles from United States
Ford; having by great exertions crossed two rivers and
marched twenty miles. At the crossing of the two roads,
west of the turnpike, and south of the plank road, stood
a single large mansion, the Chancellor house. Here General Hooker made his head-quarters, and from this point
he disposed the corps of the army so as to form a line of
battle, which should face south and east, with a single
corps to guard against an advance from the west. The
Third and First corps soon joined Hooker's forces, and
the corps were posted as follows: The Eleventh corps,
under General Howard, was on the right of the line, three
miles southwest of Chancellorsville, facing westward;
next, to the left of Howard, but far to the south, and holding the turnpike five miles in front of Chancellorsville, was

Sickles with his Third corps; back almost to the plank road, and left of the turnpike, was Slocum with the Twelfth corps; and still to the right, and behind the plank road, the Fifth corps, under General Meade, faced toward the southwest; behind Meade and Slocum, the Second corps was posted, one division guarding the approach to the bridge. The country was densely wooded. Except an open space about the house, it was a tangled wilderness. The ground was low and marshy, and nearly level. Earthworks were thrown up in front of all the corps, and everything seemed in readiness for the enemy, for whom General Hooker now waited, hoping, that by fruitless assaults upon what seemed an impregnable position, the enemy would be so exhausted that he might turn upon him with fresh divisions, and rout the retreating forces. His programme was to secure a position in the rear of the rebel positions at the fords, while that portion of the army left at Fredericksburgh was to divert attention from the principal movement. Stoneman, with the cavalry, was to make a grand raid on the communications of the rebel army, burning the bridges and tearing up railroads. The main body of the army having secured its position, and accomplished its work, the Sixth corps was to press forward and harass them in their retreat toward Richmond.

Saturday afternoon, almost at dark, the First corps, Reynolds', which had that morning parted company with the Sixth corps, crossed the river and took position near the ford, four miles in rear of Howard.

The rebel army had been on the southeast of ours. Sickles, on the afternoon of Saturday, discovered a train of wagons and ambulances moving across the pike far in his front. He sent a force to cut it in two, and was successful in taking a large number of prisoners and in creating a panic in the train. He advanced, and was met by a strong force of the enemy. He now sent to General Howard for reinforcements. General Howard led a brigade to his assistance in person, and then at full speed galloped back to his corps. He was just in time. Bursting shells on the right of his line told of the presence of the enemy. "Stonewall" Jackson, with an immense force, had passed round our army, and now came like an avalanche upon the right division of the Eleventh corps, General Devins. The men were cooking their coffee, when suddenly the whizzing of innumerable bullets aroused them from their culinary engagements. The hosts of Jackson, with yells and shouts, fell like a thunderbolt upon the astonished division, and it melted away like a snowflake in summer. The next division, Shurz, tried to maintain the ground, and did what men could do, but could not withstand the shock of fifty thousand men. General Hooker, fearing that the flying Germans would stampede the whole army, directed the cavalry which was with him, to charge upon the fugitives and arrest their flight; but no power could halt them. The commanding general at once directed General Sickles to attack the enemy on the flank, and, if possible, check his farther advance.

General Howard, with great presence of mind and perseverance, succeeded in stopping the rout at a stone wall, behind which he posted his line. Forty pieces of artillery were also, by General Hooker's order, concentrated to oppose the confederates, who again rushed forward with mad desperation, and were met with terrific fire from this long line of guns. They staggered back, but soon rallied, and again charged, and again met with a terrible repulse. The conflict now ceased for the night. Hooker drew in his lines, making them more compact, changed the disposition of some of the corps: throwing the Eleventh corps from the right to the left of the line, and bringing Meade,

with the Fifth corps, to the right. Sickles and Slocum, with
the Third and Twelfth corps, were near the Chancellor
house. Artillery was massed to command the approaches
to the turnpike, and earthworks went up in the night as if
by magic. At daylight, Sunday morning, Jackson, with
all his forces, advanced on the turnpike, against the Chancellor place, not with the thin line of battle, but in solid
mass. His men poured from the woods like a torrent,
their shouts and yells making a pandemonium of the wilderness. Suddenly, from the mouths of forty cannon was
hurled against them a cruel storm of grape and canister,
which ploughed through the advancing column, carrying
death and destruction in its course, while the infantry
from the Third corps poured into the faces of the desperate foe a terrible hail storm of bullets which almost
decimated the heavy column. With the desperation of
madness, the rebels rushed against this terrible fire, almost
reaching the muzzles of the guns, only to be hurled back
again by the fearful tornado in front. The Third corps
seemed hardly able to hold its position, but now General
Hooker sent two divisions of the Second corps to attack
the enemy in the flank. These, with the Fifth corps, came
with great force upon the left of the column. It reeled,
the huge mass wavered to and fro, and then fell back in
flight. The troops at the house, however, had been forced
back, and General Hooker again shortened his lines,
making his forces still more compact.

Again, in the afternoon, the rebels came on exultingly,
but not with the desperation that marked the attack of
the morning. Hour after hour they strove to drive back
or break in two the Union line, but it was immovable.
Artillery poured into the ranks of the assailants the most
deadly fire, until they fell back, long before nightfall, disheartened and defeated. Hooker had at length succeeded
in accomplishing a part of his object. He had allowed his

enemy to fight him until his army was exhausted and dispirited, while he himself had half his army fresh and ready to charge upon the weakened foe. Now came the time for action. If he now succeeded in putting the enemy to flight, the rebel cause was destroyed; if, on the contrary, he suffered a repulse, what would be the result? The river was swelling rapidly; the pontoons could even now with difficulty be held together. If, haply, they were to be swept away, all means of retreat would be cut off, and a repulse would amount to annihilation. Sedgwick and the Sixth corps were driven back, and Stoneman, who had gone with his cavalry toward Richmond, was not heard from. In the midst of these doubts, he called a council of corps commanders, who agreed, not unanimously, that it was advisable to recross the river. So the army, on Wednesday, was withdrawn across the river, when victory seemed ready to rest on our banners.* Without doubt, had the general known of the panic created by the cavalry in the rear, or had he been sure that his communications would remain intact, the result would have been far different.

The loss to the whole army, in this campaign, was over seventeen thousand in killed and wounded.† Very many of these were left in the hands of the enemy.

---

* The author makes no attempt to discuss the merits of the controversy, which grew out of this battle, between two of the best soldiers of our army. The reader will find, in the Report on the Conduct of the War, 1865, all the facts and arguments on both sides, by those most competent to give them—Generals Hooker and Sedgwick.

† The following statement exhibits the loss to the various corps in killed, wounded and missing:

1st,	292	6th,	4,925
2d,	2,025	11th,	2,508
3d,	4,039	12th,	2,883
5th,	699	Cavalry,	145

CHAPTER XVIII.

SECOND ENCAMPMENT AT WHITE OAK CHURCH AND THE PENNSYLVANIA CAMPAIGN.

The army in its old position—A trip to Dixie—The wounded at the hospitals—Introduction of army badges—Adornments of the camps—The "Third crossing"—The Barnard mansion—Exchanging papers—A broken lieutenant—The Pennsylvania campaign commenced—Restriction of baggage—A severe march—An army bathing—At Centreville—Bristow Station—March to Maryland—General Hooker succeeded by General Meade—Position of the army.

THE army now turned back to its old position, encamping in line nearly as before, only all the troops which had encamped on our left, between the Sixth corps and Belle Plain, were placed far to the right, leaving the Sixth corps on the left of the army, instead of being nearly in its center. The corps occupied a line nearly a mile in rear of the old camp, where the ground had been unoccupied, and where a growth of young pines, and, in places, considerable groves of oak timber, afforded far more attractive surroundings than the old quarters.

The wounded were taken to an immense field hospital at Potomac creek, where hospital tents sufficient to accommodate eight thousand wounded men were erected in a locality where cool breezes could play freely among the encampments, and where pure water could be obtained. On the 9th, many of our wounded were brought to the side of the river at Fredericksburgh and sent over to us by the enemy, in pontoon boats, under flags of truce. On the morning of the 10th, the surgeon of the Seventy-seventh was ordered to proceed at once to Banks' Ford to receive wounded officers who were to be removed from the enemy's lines. The doctor was soon at the ford, where he found a boat and a flag of truce at his disposal. He crossed the river and met the officer in command, who received him courteously, but declared that he knew nothing of any officers to come there. The surgeon addressed a note to General Wilcox, commanding the brigade at Banks' Ford, but he knew as little about it as the officer at the river. "There are plenty of federal officers here," said he, "and we shall be glad to send them across to your lines at any time when General Hooker shall apply to General Lee for them; but I know of no arrangement of the kind now." Believing that some arrangements had been made for the transfer of the wounded officers, but that the order had not yet reached General Wilcox, the surgeon spent the day among the rebels, conversing with their officers, while his boatmen, having with them a canteen of brandy, soon made themselves very popular with the crowd of rebel soldiers who gathered about, dressed in motley colors, buff, blue, gray, butternut, and colors indescribable. They were all in good humor and lively, and the hours passed pleasantly, as the men from the two opposing armies chatted in the shade of some oak trees. Finding little prospect of executing his peaceful mission, the surgeon obtained permission from General Wilcox to get the remains of Colonel Van Houghten, of the Twenty-first New Jersey regiment, who was shot at Salem Church, and died from his wound next day. Doctor McNiel, of the Twenty-first, with a party of men, proceeded to the place where the colonel was buried, a mile and a half from the ford, and brought the remains to the river and across to our own lines. On reporting at General Hooker's head-quarters, the surgeon found that no agreement had been concluded until late in the day for the delivery of the wounded officers; so he had spent the day in rebeldom to little effect, except the restoration of the body of the colonel to his friends, and leaving a company of nurses to assist our surgeons who were already in attendance upon our prisoners.

Nearly all our wounded were at length returned to us, and were sent to Potomac Creek, or to Washington. At Potomac Creek, the coöperation of the Sanitary Commission was of great assistance to the surgeons; and many comforts and luxuries, the gifts of our friends at home, cheered the hearts of the wounded and suffering heroes. Sheets, pillow cases, handkerchiefs, with jellies and canned fruits, were distributed in profusion. Here was the place for manifesting the overflowing interest and noble generosity of the people of the north, and thousands blessed them for their munificence.

A mistaken idea prevailed among friends at home, that the agents of the Sanitary Commission resorted to the battle-field, ministering to the wants of the wounded, dressing the wounds, bringing the crippled from the field, and feeding the hungry. Our illustrated papers were filled with fine engravings, representing these acts of mercy on the battle-field. These were pictures of the imagination. Nothing of the sort was done. No Sanitary or Christian Commission agents frequented the battle-field. All wounded were brought from the field by soldiers, placed in ambulances of the government and taken to the field hospitals, where all the wounds were dressed by surgeons or their nurses, and where all were fed by officers selected for this special duty. The Sanitary and Christian Commissions had a great mission. They were the representatives of the lively interest felt by the people of the north, for the army it had sent forth to maintain the institutions of their country. They found abundant opportunity for accomplishing their mission at the large hospitals after the roar of battles had passed away; but they had nothing to do with the care of the wounded on the battle-field.

Just before leaving camp for the campaign just closed, General Hooker had issued an order assigning to each corps and division its badge, which was to be worn by every officer and soldier connected with either of the corps. The men of the Sixth corps now regarded their cross with greater pride than had ever ancient knight looked upon the heraldry which emblazoned his arms. It had been baptized in blood, and amid wonderful achievements of heroism. Every member of the noble corps felt an exulting pride in his relation to it, and regarded his badge as a mark of great honor.

The introduction of these badges became of great service to the army. Every man could easily recognize the corps and division of any other one in the army; and each corps learned to feel a pride in its own badge.

We had seven corps in the army; First, Second, Third, Fifth, Sixth, Eleventh and Twelfth. The badge of the First corps was a lozenge, that of the Second a shamrock, of the Third a diamond, of the Fifth a Maltese cross, of the Sixth a Greek cross, the Eleventh a lunette, and of the Twelfth a star. The badge of the First division of each corps was red, that of the Second white, and of the Third blue. All wagons and ambulances were marked with their appropriate badge, and the sick soldier who fell to the rear with a pass to the ambulances, had no difficulty in finding his own train; and quartermasters and others connected with the trains were greatly assisted in their duties by this ingenious device.

The camps of all the regiments of our divisions were pleasantly located, and great pains were taken in laying them out and in decorating them. When regiments were not sheltered in groves, pines were transplanted in the company streets in great profusion; and arches and bowers of the most elaborate and elegant designs, formed of the boughs of the red cedar and pine, exquisitely entwined with the bright green holly, formed a most attractive and beautiful feature of our second camp at White Oak Church. At division head-quarters, General Howe had caused to be erected a most elegant hall of these rural materials, which was a wonder of architectual beauty as well as exquisite taste and ingenuity. Its alcoves, its vestibules and its arches, were marvels of elegance. Here came officers, high in command, and brilliant dames, and passed a night in the service of Terpsichore, while bands discoursed stirring music.

In the camp of the Seventy-seventh, the adornments were profuse and beautiful. At head-quarters, a palace of green arose among the trees near our tents. For days, mule teams hauled huge loads of cedar boughs, which were woven into massive pillars or elegantly turned arches, and the structure rose like one of those fair bowers we read of in fairy tales. Our surgeon and quartermaster were preparing the elegant structure for the reception of their wives. It was almost complete, needing only a few finishing touches, and the anxiously awaited guests were expected on the following day; when, alas for the expectations of men, an order came to be ready to march at daylight next morning! The ladies, although too late to enjoy this rustic palace, arrived in time to find the corps in line of battle, and witness fierce artillery duels between the opposing armies. In their eagerness to watch the flight of the shells, they sometimes manifested greater bravery than their companions, whose experience had taught them to regard with suspicion the shrieking missiles.

We had passed a pleasant month at this camp, and the men were eager, notwithstanding their comfortable quarters, for active campaigning. The health and spirits of the soldiers of the corps had never been better, and in spite of the failure at Chancellorsville, they felt a great deal of confidence. So the order to move was received with pleasure, and we turned away from our pleasant camps willingly.

We left camp on the morning of June 5th, one of the loveliest of days, and, taking the road we had already trod on two occasions, halted in the valley of the Rappahannock, on the very spot where we had rested at the first and second battles of Fredericksburgh, and prepared, for a third time within six months, to cross the river. A correspondent of one of the daily journals, writing from head-quarters of the army, says: "Howe's splendid division of the fighting Sixth corps was selected for the work of crossing, and the point for laying the bridges was just below the mouth of Deep Run, at the identical spot where we had crossed twice before."

Pontoons and batteries of artillery formed long lines behind the little ridge which runs parallel with the river, and the infantry marched and countermarched to get in right positions. Here, behind the little ridge, we rested, until about five o'clock in the afternoon, our men mounting the ridge, and gazing across the river, where the enemy had turned the rifle pits thrown up by our First division, to their own use; and, in return, the rebels raised their heads above the breastworks, or ventured to the river side, wondering what could be the intention of the army, so recently driven from these grounds, in making such preparations for another crossing. There seemed but a small force opposed to us; a strong picket on the bank, and the reserve posted behind the breastworks, were all that could be seen, though we well knew that the heights beyond swarmed with opposing hosts, as they had twice before. At length the engineers drew the pontoons to the edge of the river, the Seventy-seventh being detailed to assist in unloading. The rebels betook themselves to the rifle pits, and opened a brisk fire; but presently they were glad to draw their heads behind the earthworks, for five of our batteries, Williston's, McCartney's, Cowen's, Haines' and McCarthey's, were run out upon the plain, and opened a fierce fire, whole batteries firing by volleys, until the whole plain, on the further side, was a sheet of flame from the bursting shells, and huge clouds of dust, plowed up by the shrieking missiles, rose so as to obscure the heights. The rebels could only load, and thrust their guns above the earthworks, firing at random, for no man could raise his head without coming in the way of the fiery messengers of death, which filled the air. Still their fire, although at random, was annoying, and it was evident that the safest method was to cross men in boats, enough to drive the rebels from their pits, or capture them, and then build the bridge without opposition.

The Twenty-sixth New Jersey and Fifth Vermont regiments leaped into the boats, quickly crossed, and, rushing from the bank, charged upon the pits. The rebels were now, for the first time offered an opportunity for flight; for while the artillery was filling the whole plain with bursting shells, there remained no alternative but to hug the earth behind the rifle pits; now that the artillery ceased, they scattered across the plain in hot haste, before the rapid charge of our boys. The two regiments pursued the fugitives, and many of them threw down their arms; we captured about seventy-five prisoners; of these, thirty-six were captured by Captain Davenport, who, with eighteen of his men, was marching up the ravine through which passes the Deep Run, when they came upon the rebels, whom they obliged to surrender, their captain delivering his sword to Captain Davenport. Five or six men of the engineers were killed, and some wounded. The Vermonters and New Jerseymen, also, had a few men wounded.

The Seventy-seventh had one man killed. Sergeant Rex Haines was shot through the head. He was a brave man, and one of the best soldiers in the regiment. He had, until that very day, been confined to the hospital with severe illness. A few of our men, also, received slight wounds.

The engineers proceeded at once to lay the bridges, and on the following morning the whole division crossed. Our picket reserve made their rendezvous at the ruins of the fine mansion which we had used for our Second division hospital at the first battle. Now nothing but the bare walls and heaps of rubbish marked the place where the beautiful residence had stood. A regiment of Mississippians had occupied the place, and had ruthlessly and willfully burned it. Yet the fine chestnuts and broad-spreading oaks afforded as luxurious a shade as in the palmy days when the old bachelor proprietor lounged beneath their shadow.

The picket line extended nearly to the railroad, and, as before, formed a semi-circle, radiating from the pontoon bridge. The enemy had also formed a strong picket to oppose us, and the two lines of skirmishers were within a few yards of each other.

It was a beautiful Sabbath, and all day long the troops lay upon the plain, wondering what was to be done. There were the frowning batteries of the enemy on the hills in front, apparently able to blow the whole division into the air, and we could, with our glasses, discover great numbers of infantry at the base of the hills, half hidden by the low growth of pines. The main body of our army still remained in camp; only our Sixth corps had moved. Evidently the enemy concluded that the advance was rather one of observation than attack, and quietly awaited our movements. Some firing was for a time kept up on the skirmish line, and now and then a shell would come crashing through some of the houses at the right, where our pickets were concealed; but at length, by mutual consent, the pickets of each army watched the movements of their opponents without molesting them. During this quasi-truce, a spirit of sociability manifested itself, and our boys soon struck up an acquaintance with their dangerous neighbors. At length an exchange of papers was proposed, and upon mutual agreement of temporary amity, a Yankee and a Johnnie would step into the open space between the two lines, shake hands, inquire each other's regiment, trade papers and retire.

There came at this time, to each company of one regiment, a copy of the New York Observer, Independent, Christian Examiner, Evangelist and other papers, and Mr. Alvord, the agent of the Tract Society, had just been among the men, distributing copies of the American Messenger. These were soon collected and carried over to be exchanged for copies of the Richmond Enquirer, Sentinel, and Examiner. The trade was not kept wholly within the limits of literary exchange, but sugar and coffee passed into the rebels' hands in return for plugs of tobacco. At length an order came from division head-quarters, stopping this illicit practice. Our boys declared that they were acting the part of colporteurs to the barbarian rebels, and, if they had been allowed to continue the distribution of religious papers among them, they would soon be convinced of the error of their ways, and desist from further fighting.

During the night of the 8th, our division was withdrawn to the north side of the river, our place being taken by the Third division. We retired to Stafford Heights and bivouacked. Our bivouac became our encampment for a week. There we lay, wondering what was next to be done, while the artillery on either side exchanged shots. The 32-pounders on our hills sending their huge shot across to the opposite heights, and the rebel guns replying, sometimes with shells of most improved pattern, and at other times throwing over huge pieces of railroad iron.

An incident of much interest to Neill's brigade occurred while we were here. A lieutentant, belonging to the Twenty-first New Jersey regiment, had been tried by a court-martial, and convicted of cowardice at the battle on May 3d. The whole brigade was brought out at the hour for evening parade, and formed in a hollow square. To the center of the inclosure the culprit was brought. His sentence was then read to him, which was that he be dismissed the service in disgrace. The adjutant-general of the brigade then proceeded to execute the details of the sentence. The sword of the cowardly officer was taken from him and broken over his head; his shoulder-straps and buttons were then cut off, and his pistol broken and thrown away. The sentence, and the manner of its execution, were ordered to be published in the newspapers of the county where the regiment was raised. A similar sentence was executed in the Seventy-seventh regiment on the same evening. Lewis Burke, of Company F, was convicted of cowardice at the same battle. He was brought before the regiment, which stood in line; his sentence read, his buttons and the blue cord on his coat cut off, and a placard marked "COWARD" hung to his back. A guard, with fixed bayonets pointing at his back, then marched him off, the band playing "The Rogues' March." Burke went to serve out his time at the Dry Tortugas at hard labor, without pay or allowance.

As we looked upon the execution of these humiliating sentences, we could not help feeling how much better it would have been to have fallen nobly on that field of battle, honored and lamented, than to live to be thus degraded and despised. It had never been so forcibly impressed upon our minds, how much better it was to die nobly than to live in disgrace. When we thought of the noble Wheeler and his brave companions, who had given their lives for their country on yonder heights, and then turned to the sickening scene before us, we could but exclaim, "How are the dead to be envied!"

At length, on Saturday night, June 13th, we withdrew from Fredericksburgh, and commenced the memorable Pennsylvania campaign. There had been, for several days, indications that General Lee was throwing his army to our right, and was crossing the Rappahannock in the vicinity of Culpepper. At length this had become a certainty; and the whole army was quickly moved to come up with him. All day long the hurrying of trains, the movements of troops, the intense activity at the railroad station, where everything was being hastily thrown into cars, had indicated a sudden leave-taking.

At length the trains were off, and the whole army in motion. Our own corps being rear-guard, started at ten o'clock at night. The darkness was intense, and a thunder shower prevailed. Our route for a long time lay through a thick woods, where the branches of the trees, meeting over our heads, shut out the little light that might have penetrated the thunder clouds, and the column was shut in perfect darkness. The road was terribly muddy, and the batteries which were trying to pass over the same route, were frequently stuck in the mire. Our men stumbled over stones and fallen trees, often falling beneath the feet of the horses. Men fell over logs and stones, breaking their legs and arms. Thus we continued the hasty and difficult march, while the rain poured in torrents upon us. Later in the night the road became more open, and the rain ceased. The darkness was not so black, still it was difficult to see the road. We were passing over corduroy; some of the logs were a foot, and others a foot and a half through. They were slippery from the rain, and the men, heavily laden with knapsacks, guns and cartridges, tumbled headlong, many of them going off at the side, and rolling far down the steep embankments.

A laugh from the comrades of the luckless ones, while some one would call out, "Have you a pass to go down there?" was the only notice taken of such accidents; and the dark column hurried on, until at three o'clock in the morning, we halted at Potomac creek, where we slept soundly upon the ground until morning.

The following day was Sunday. Our corps did not march until evening; we lay resting from the fatigues of the night before, and watching the immense army trains hurrying by, the horses and mules lashed to their full speed, or viewing the destruction of the great hospitals which had been established here.

There were here immense quantities of stores; bedding, glass and earthenware, instruments and medicines, with cooking and other utensils which could not, in the haste of breaking up, be transported; so they were thrown in great heaps and burned.

All day long the trains crowded by, four and five wagons abreast; the drivers shouting and lashing their beasts to their greatest speed. No one who has not seen the train of an army in motion, can form any just conception of its magnitude, and of the difficulties attending its movements. It was said that the train of the Army of the Potomac, including artillery, at the time of which we speak, if placed in a single line, the teams at the distance necessary for the march, would extend over seventy miles.

At Fairfax Court House, soon after this, the trains were greatly reduced, and again at Fairfax Station; and after General Meade took command of the army they were still further reduced. Yet, notwithstanding all these curtailments, our trains were said to be between thirty and forty miles long.

How little did the impatient people, who clamored at all times, in winter as well as summer, for an immediate "advance" of the army, consider that this immense body must always advance with the army; that it must always be protected; that the army on every march and at every halt must be so disposed as to prevent the enemy from reaching it from front, flank or rear; and that when an advance was commenced, if the trains were to become blocked up, or stuck fast in mud, the whole army must wait for them, no matter whether it had reached a favorable position for a halt or not. It was no small undertaking to move an army with such a train; yet there were many at home who thought the army could move from one place to another with the greatest ease.

It is true that the enemy got along with smaller trains than ours, and it is true that the rebel army on that account was more easily moved than our own. It was one of the disadvantages of too liberal a government that our movements for two years were weighed down with these cumbersome trains; and even after so long an experience of their evil it was with strong feelings of opposition that the reduction was acquiesced in.

A captain or lieutenant of the line was allowed a small valise, in which to carry his company books and his clothing; and a staff officer was but little better off. Must this little be reduced? Surely the ammunition and the commissary trains could suffer no diminution. The amount of hospital supplies carried in the wagons was already limited; could it be reduced? The people were clamoring to have wagons of the Sanitary and Christian Commissions admitted to the hospital trains, to carry articles which, although they were gratefully received by the soldiers, yet were not absolutely necessary. The ambulance train was surely not too large, and we could spare no artillery.

Yet the train was reduced. Small as was the valise of the line officers, it must be still smaller; little as was the baggage of the staff officer, it must be less; and inconveniently contracted as was the size of the mess chests, they must be still further reduced.

Thus, through the day, we watched the hurrying trains as they swept by with immense clatter and tumult; and the files of troops, guards to the trains, pressing forward, amid the clouds of dust and the rattle and noise of the wagons. As the sun sunk in the west, we gathered about a green knoll, in the shade of a pine grove, and sung old familiar hymns; then the chaplain made a prayer; thus was offered the evening sacrifice for the Sabbath. Few who gathered —

> " Where through the long drawn aisle or fretted vault,
> The pealing anthem swells the note of praise,

offered more heartfelt thanksgiving, or more earnest supplications for future protection, than the band of veterans seated on that mossy bank, while about them was the confusion of a great army, pressing to meet its foe.

At length, at nine o'clock at night, we took the road, and, joining the mighty column, marched rapidly forward. The night was dark, and the roads uneven, yet the men pressed forward with wonderful spirit. They had heard during the day that Lee with his army, avoiding us on the right, and moving with secrecy, had already eluded us, and was rapidly making his way into Maryland, taking his route through the Shenandoah Valley. This was enough to stimulate men whose greatest desire was to meet their opponents in open fight, even on rebel ground. But now the rebels were invading northern soil; Maryland, Pennsylvania, and even New York, were threatened, and the men knew no limit to their enthusiasm. "We can whip them on our own soil," said they. "There is no man who cannot fight the better when it is for his own home." Such expressions passed from lip to lip as the dark column pushed on during the whole night. At times

29

there would be a halt; not for rest, for the men, expecting momentarily to move on, would stand in the ranks; then, on again. Here and there were the camps of troops who had occupied the extreme right of the army. Fine arbors and avenues had been erected from the cedar boughs; these were set on fire, and the whole heavens were aglow with the flames. Morning dawned, the march was becoming tedious. The men were faint, and wanted rest and coffee; but there was no halt.

Faint and weary, yet with determination, the masses of men toiled along. At length, as the morning advanced, the heat of the sun was almost intolerable, and the dust suffocating. Not a leaf stirred on the trees. Vegetation drooped under the scorching rays, and the clouds of dust was so dense, that one could not see half the length of a regiment.

The men at length began to fall from exhaustion. One after another, with faces burning with a glow of crimson, and panting for breath, would turn to the surgeons of their regiments, and receive passes to the ambulances and a draught from the surgeon's flask; but at length no more passes could be given; the ambulances were crowded, and so many were falling on every side, that it became useless to require or attempt to give passes, or even for the surgeons to attempt to relieve the sufferers.

In every corner of the rail fences, and under every tree and bush, groups of men, with faces glowing with redness, some with streams of perspiration rolling down their cheeks, and others with their red faces dry and feverish, strewed the wayside and lined the hedges. Here the color-bearer of a regiment, his color lying beside him, lay gasping for breath; there a colonel, his horse tied to the fence, strove to fan the air into a little life with his broad-brimmed hat. Under one little clump of cedars might be seen an exhausted group of line officers, captains and lieutenants, and under the next, a number of enlisted men who could no longer keep the road. The spectacle along the roadside became appalling. Regiments became like companies, and companies lost their identity; men were dying with sunstroke; and still the march was continued.

This could not last much longer, for the brave men who still held out were fast losing strength, and soon there would be no troops able to move. At length, at nearly three o'clock, we came in sight of the little, old, depopulated town of Dumfries. Here, to the joy of all, we saw men filing into the fields for a halt. There was no cheer, no expression of gladness; for the tired men, with feet blistered and raw, worn out by seventeen hours' constant march, almost melted and smothered, cared little for demonstrations. Throwing themselves upon the ground, they rested for half an hour, and then, rousing long enough to cook their coffee, they refreshed themselves with their hard tack, pork and coffee, and were ready to sleep. Here the Vermont brigade was drawn up in line, and some half a dozen men, skulkers, principally from the Twenty-sixth New Jersey, were drummed out of camp, the bands of the brigade playing "The Rogues' March." All who were participants of that day's work, remember it as the most trying march of the Army of the Potomac. Very grateful to the weary army was sleep that night, but, at two o'clock in the morning, the shout passed along the line, "fall in! fall in!" And so, without coffee, we rolled our blankets and fell into line. But, as often happens, when the whole army is to move, some parts must wait long before the others are out of the way. So we of the Sixth corps waited until four o'clock, and got our coffee finally before the rest of the column had made way for us. It was another hot, dusty day, but not so intolerable as the day before, and about two or three o'clock we arrived at Occoquan creek, crossing at Wolf Run Shoals

Here we had two or three hours' rest. The men had no sooner halted than they plunged into the stream, and the wide creek was soon alive with swarms of men splashing and diving in the cooling element.

It was a novel sight. An army bathing. A brigade of nine months Vermont troops, had been stationed here during the winter. They were full regiments, never thinned by exhausting labors, hard campaigns or the trying ordeal of battle. They now bade farewell to their comfortable quarters and picket duty, and joined the Grand Army on a real campaign. Although we had already made a long march, at four o'clock we were again on the road, and before dark we reached Fairfax Station, six miles from Wolf Run Shoals. This was a more cheerful march than the others. The men, refreshed by their bath, and strengthened by a good dinner and two hours' rest, now went shouting, singing and laughing, as though marching was but play.

This day we heard that some part of Lee's army was in Pennsylvania! The men were as anxious to go forward as were their commanders. The corps bivouacked in groves on the turnpike, which led from Fairfax to Manassas, resting for the night and the following day. Here our train underwent a process of purging. Needless articles, and many useful ones, which could be disposed of, were sent to the rear. The trains were to go with smaller loads, and many teams were to be taken from them.

We had marched, since setting out from before Fredericksburgh, through a country, well enough by nature, but neglected, barren and depopulated. How large a portion of this great State was in this sad condition? Its naturally rich fields were grown up to scrub pines, mugworts and wormwood. Its fair valleys desolate of inhabitants, or inhabited by low white trash, as idle as ignorant. The groves and fields where we now rested were pleasant for a bivouac, but the fields were waste land, and the oak timber was all that seemed of any value, as far as we could see. Yet we were now within a few miles of Washington, where articles of food brought fabulous prices, and wood could scarcely be procured. Why were these fine lands desolate? Was it because agriculture was unprofitable? Surely, with Washington and Alexandria so near, and Baltimore at a short distance farther, there should be a good market for produce. Was it because the war had put a stop to agricultural pursuits? The scrub pines and dwarf oaks growing upon deserted tobacco fields, where the ridges were still plainly visible, showed that before the war indolence prevailed.

At five o'clock on the morning of June 19th, we were again on the march, reaching Fairfax Court House before noon. Again our train was overhauled, baggage reduced, and teams sent to the rear. By this time the train began to assume more reasonable dimensions. General officers were strictly forbidden the use of ambulances, henceforth all ambulances were to be used for their legitimate purposes, and general officers and their staffs were to get along with a more reasonable amount of baggage, while regimental officers were to be allowed only the most limited amount of transportation. A single small valise only was the extent of baggage for each regimental officer, and a mess chest of the size of a cracker box, was to be the allowance for all officers of a single company.

About Fairfax Court House was stationed a division of cavalry and some infantry, under the command of General Stahl. These troops, like the brigade of Vermont troops, had been employed in guarding the country against the inroads of guerilla bands. These were now also to join the Army of the Potomac, and their gallant conduct at Falling Waters, a few days after, showed them to be composed of the best material.

General Hooker, unwilling to favor General Lee, by uncovering the capital, and wisely judging of his wary enemy's motives, instead of pushing rapidly forward to Maryland, as Lee desired, threw the different corps into positions, which should at once be favorable for watching his movements, and resisting any attack. Accordingly, our own corps, turning partly back from our line of march, on the 20th, marched towards Bristow Station.

We passed through Centreville, its powerful forts and redoubts garrisoned by large regiments of men, who wore bright new uniforms, and whose officers had red tufts upon their caps. These new uniforms were soon to be as grimy and dusty as those of the veterans, at whom they now gazed with so much interest, and the full regiments were soon to find their ranks thinned by the same terrible process which had made those passing by them only fragments of regiments.

The works about Centreville were of most powerful character, having been made even stronger than at the last battle of Bull Run. In the forts and redoubts upon the commanding positions, was mounted heavy artillery, and the long lines of trenches and breastworks, stretching far to the flanks, and commanding declivities where musketry and artillery could sweep an advancing force with terrible effect, rendered the position impregnable from any direct assault. The few dilapidated houses still remaining to mark the site of the village, presented a forlorn and pitiful appearance. Deserted by their owners, occupied as stables and storehouses, some of them falling in ruins, and all dirty and dilapidated, they were a mournful commentary on the ruthless destruction which follows in the footsteps of war. Still further on, our route led us along the Manassas Gap railroad. Here were more sad pictures of the havoc of war. The track was torn up, the ties burnt. Every now and then, numbers of car wheels and axles, iron bands and braces, couplings and reaches, showed where whole trains had been burned.

Here and there, the incombustible materials among the debris showed the lading of particular cars. The remains of fruit cans, tin plates, blacking boxes and glassware, told of sutlers who had disposed of their wares at less than the usual exorbitant prices. Heaps of spikes and handleless hammers, and iron bars, reminded us of disconcerted plans in railroad extension, while numberless solid shot, bullets and fragments of shells, showed where car loads of ammunition had been consumed in harmless explosions.

At length, after a hard day's march, we arrived at Bristow Station, where the corps turned into the fields and bivouacked.

The tower and wind-mill which had been used for raising water to the tank, remained alone to show where the station had been; all the other buildings being destroyed, except where still remained the dismantled ruins of what had once been a hotel.

Here, as for miles back on the road, were the remains of ruined cars and their contents.

The surrounding country was delightful. A mile or two south of us was a little church in the midst of an oak grove. It is an agreeable peculiarity with the southern people, that they are accustomed to locate their country churches in the midst of pleasant groves, sometimes at a distance from any residence. In this respect, they certainly exhibit better taste than the people of most of our northern States, who have such a propensity for setting the church on the summit of some high hill where not a tree or shrub adorns the grounds, and the aspiring steeple seems, like Babel, to be striving vainly to reach the heavens.

On the morning after our arrival here, we heard the sounds of cannonading not far off, and learned that the cavalry under General Pleasanton were hotly engaged at Aldee and Upperville, with Stuart's rebel cavalry, and that our forces were getting the best of the desperate encounter, winning laurels for themselves and gaining another of that series of victories which was destined to remove the derision in which that arm of the service had been held, not from any previous want of good fighting qualities on the part of our cavalry. General Pleasanton had attacked Stuart's forces near Middleburgh, driving the rebels in confusion through Upperville to Ashby's Gap, taking some pieces of artillery and a large number of prisoners. General Kilpatrick, in this engagement, had exhibited fighting qualities of the first order, riding in front of the men and leading the way when they hesitated. His gallant conduct inspired for him the confidence and admiration of his men. It was the commencement of a brilliant career which made him one of the first cavalry commanders in the army. His dashing ride from the Peninsula to Fredericksburgh, with but a handful of men, eluding the watchfulness of the wily Stuart, had already established his talent for bold adventure, and his conduct on this occasion proved his personal bravery. These are the two great qualities needed for a cavalry officer, and Kilpatrick's name at once became a tower of strength among his men.

In this pleasant locality the corps remained, an outpost for the army, guarding the passes from the Shenandoah, for five days. The weather was delightful, and the men enjoyed, to the utmost, the needed rest. They lounged in the shade of their tents or in the neighboring groves, or strolled along the railroad track, examining curiously the ruined remains of the trains. In a delightful spot at a distance from the camps, almost surrounded by a grove of oak trees, the hospital tents of our Second division were erected. To this quiet and lovely spot, where cool breezes always played, were brought the sick and weary, and carefully nursed.

But General Lee despaired of inducing General Hooker to uncover the capital, so, leaving Virginia with his whole army, he pushed toward Pennsylvania, determined at least to draw our army as far away from Washington as possible, and to reap rich harvests of spoils among the overflowing granaries of the Keystone State.   No sooner had the movement of the main body of Lee's army into Maryland commenced, than General Hooker, with his forces, commenced the pursuit.

30

CHAPTER XIX.

THE GETTYSBURGH CAMPAIGN.

The rebels in Pennsylvania — Panic at Harrisburgh — Alarm at Baltimore and Washington — Sixth corps leaves Bristow Station — A surprise — General Meade takes command — Position of the army — Marching through Pennsylvania — An unprecedented march — Exciting news — Battle of Gettysburgh — Death of Reynolds — First and Eleventh corps fall back — Second day's battle — The battlefield — Fighting at Round Top — On the right — The grand onset — The battle decided — Rebel and Union wounded.

MEANWHILE, great excitement prevailed at the north, especially in Maryland and Pennsylvania, on account of the invasion of the rebel army. As early as the 15th of the month, more than a thousand rebel cavalry had reached Chambersburgh, which they had sacked. Two days before, the battle of Winchester was closed. Ewell, with overwhelming numbers had fallen upon General Milroy's force, which had unwisely been, by order of somebody, thrust far away from its base, and out of the reach of reinforcements, routing the division, and in its flight capturing its artillery and a large portion of the infantry.

Nothing now opposed the march of the invaders through the Shenandoah Valley. In Harrisburgh, the excitement rose almost to a panic. All the paintings, books, papers, and other valuable articles, were removed from the capitol, packed in boxes and loaded into cars, ready to be sent off at the first sign of immediate danger. The citizens formed themselves into military companies, and worked day and night throwing up redoubts and rifle pits about the city. Men unaccustomed to manual labor vigorously plied the pick and the spade, and kept up their unwonted toil with an earnestness worthy of veteran soldiers. To add to this confusion and alarm, the trains of Milroy's division that had escaped capture were rattling through the streets in search of a resting place. Throughout the State of Pennsylvania business was suspended. The governor was calling loudly for men to rush to arms in defense of their homes; and General Couch was striving to organize the militia which presented itself.

Baltimore and Washington were like besieged cities. Stuart was threatening the Baltimore and Ohio road, and bodies of rebel cavalry had penetrated within half a dozen miles of Washington. Bells rung out the alarm, and the affrighted citizens rushed to arms. Loyal leagues were now of service, forming the nucleus of many an improvised company of defenders. All these facts we learned from the newspapers, a few stray copies of which fell within the path of the army, and from the highly colored accounts of citizens, who, with expressions of the utmost alarm and anxiety, related what they had heard or seen.

On the night of the 26th of June, the Sixth corps left Bristow Station. The darkness was intense, and a drizzling rain rendered marching disagreeable. The march was rapid, and some of the men fell behind, and were next day collected and marched off to Richmond, by the guerilla parties that constantly hung upon our flanks and rear. Before daylight we halted at Centreville. The men threw themselves upon the wet ground, and slept for two hours, while the rain beat upon them. Then, at six o'clock, they were again roused, by the order to be ready to move at once. While taking our coffee, and waiting for the final order to march, some villain, belonging to the troops stationed at Centreville, set fire to the little Episcopal chapel that stood not far from us, and was the only building remaining in the little village which pretended to any appearance of modern architecture. Those vandals who follow an army, bent on nothing but destruction, are among the unavoidable evils of war, and even the most severe discipline is insufficient to effectually arrest all mischief of the kind.

Our march was a severe one for men who had been on the road all night, and the men were glad when we bivouacked a little before dark, in a beautiful oak grove near Drainsville. Very early next morning, descending into the lovely valley of the Potomac, we reached Edwards' Ferry, where troops were crossing; after a delay of one or two hours, waiting for troops of another corps to cross the pontoon bridge, we followed, and were in Maryland again. All day long troops were passing over the bridges and taking their positions upon the neighboring hills, ready for starting anew in the morning; for nearly the whole army was crossing at this point, and as the process was necessarily slow, those who went over first waited for those behind.

On Sunday, we left Edwards' Ferry; marched through Poolesville and Barnstown to Hyattstown. A halt was made at Barnstown for dinner, and the Sixth corps left the road and occupied a pleasant valley, where the chestnut trees afforded a grateful shade for the men. They had just unslung knapsacks, when we were all startled by the sound of a church bell, which seemed in our midst. The boys gazed for a moment in mute astonishment in the direction from which the sound came, when they discovered at a short distance from them, a little church half hidden among the trees, and the parishioners gathering for service. When the first surprise was over, the word passed from one to another, "It is Sunday!" "It is Sunday!" and they set up a shout that demonstrated that they had not forgotten to love the institutions of civilization, even after so long an absence from a civilized country. Few who were present at this time, will ever forget the thrill of pleasurable surprise which we all experienced at hearing once more the sounds which so forcibly reminded us of home.

Some of the men attended the service. It was a Catholic church, a small edifice which had once been white, but, by the action of the weather for many years, it had now become brown. The seats and altar had never been painted, and the plaster of the inner wall had, in places, fallen from the lath. The parishioners seemed quite devout people, and the pastor a sincere man. In his prayers he remembered the President and the government, and he supplicated for peace. The reverend father said that, owing to the confusion in town, there would be no sermon, but he wished the good people to pray for sister A., who was at the point of death, and for the repose of the soul of brother B., who was already dead. Some of our officers engaged in a pleasant conversation with the pastor after service. He was an agreeable, shrewd man, and professed to be a good Unionist.

It was at Hyattstown that we first learned that General Hooker had been superseded, in the command of the army, by General George B. Meade. The announcement of this unexpected change at such a time, was received with astonishment, and by many with indignation. To deprive the leader of a great army of his command just upon the eve of a great battle, when, by the most brilliant marches and masterly strategy, he had thrown this army face to face with his enemy, thwarting his designs of moving upon the capital, without some offense of a grave character, was an act unheard of before in the history of warfare. It seemed, from later information regarding this extraordinary measure, that a difference had arisen between General Hooker and his superior at Washington in regard to the disposition of troops at Harper's Ferry, and that, each refusing to surrender his opinion, General Hooker was relieved. His successor demanded the same disposition on the very next day, and it was granted!

The army was not dissatisfied with the appointment of General Meade; the soldiers would as readily fight under Meade as under Hooker. They were anxious to retrieve what had been lost at Chancellorsville, and would have been glad could General Hooker have shared in the victory which they believed they were about to achieve; but the men of the Union army fought for their country and not for their leaders. So they at once transferred their hopes and their obedience to the new commander. General Meade was well known to the army as a good soldier, the brave general who had, with his single division, dashed upon the rebels at the first Fredericksburgh, and as the leader of a corps which behaved gallantly at Chancellorsville. All were willing to try him, and hoped for the best.

The movement from Fredericksburgh had been conducted with consummate skill and energy, and now the army was moving in several columns by roads nearly parallel, with the twofold object of greater rapidity of movement, and of sweeping a greater extent of country.

The Sixth corps was now upon the extreme right, marching toward Manchester; next, on our left, was the Twelfth corps, at Taneytown, a little hamlet named in honor of the chief justice of the United States, whose residence was there. At a point a dozen miles north and west of us, was the head-quarters of the army, and the Second and Third Corps. Further to the left, at Emmitsburgh, were the First, Fifth and Eleventh corps. Upon either flank of this line, extending twenty miles, was cavalry. Thus the army was guarding a great extent of country, at the same time that the different corps were within supporting distance of each other.

The rebel army under General Lee, one hundred thousand strong, occupied an equally extended line to the north and west of us, stretching from Harrisburgh through Chambersburgh and Cashtown.

At five o'clock, Monday morning, 28th, the corps marched again, passing through Monroville, New Market, Ridgeville and Mount Airy Station, halting for the night at Sam's creek. As the corps passed through Westminster on the following day, the people welcomed us with demonstrations of joy, which were all the more earnest, as the rebel cavalry had, but two hours before, taken a hasty leave of them. At night we were at Manchester, at least twenty miles from the left of the army, and between the line of march of the enemy and Baltimore. We rested here until evening of the next day. The plot was thickening, and the hostile forces were moving cautiously, each watching the movements of the other, and each ready to seize any opportunity for rushing upon its enemy to destroy it. Thus far our marches had been of most fatiguing character. We had, in the last four days, passed over one hundred miles of road. It is to be remembered that these marches were made under burning suns, and that each soldier carried with him his gun, knapsack, haversack, containing five days' provisions, and forty rounds of cartridges. The men had kept up wonderfully during this trying campaign, but the great march of all, in which this magnificent corps was to outdo all that was ever recorded of wonderful marches, was yet in store for it.

We waited at Manchester until evening. The inhabitants were well supplied with rye whisky, and it must be confessed that soldiers have a way of finding out the existence of that luxury, and of supplying themselves with it; and as the men of the old Sixth corps were in no respect behind their comrades of the other corps, many of our brave fellows became, long before dark, considerably inebriated.

At nine o'clock in the evening of the 1st of July, we

were on the road, but it was eleven before we were fairly under headway. Those who during the day had indulged so freely in the rye whisky of the farmers, as to disable them from marching or even standing in line, were quietly thrown into the clumps of bushes by the roadside, and left to be gathered up by cavalry squads that were scouring the country for stragglers. Those that were left by our own provost-guards were picked up by rebel scouts.

The column now pushed rapidly on; all night the weary march was kept up. A halt of ten minutes for breakfast, and then on again. Now we heard that a part of the army, the First corps, had already engaged the enemy at Gettysburgh, with doubtful issue, and that its commander, General Reynolds, was killed.

New ardor was now kindled in the breasts of the men of the Sixth corps at these tidings, and they pressed forward at a pace unusual, even for them. The day was bright, the sun pouring scalding rays from a cloudless sky. The men strove hard to keep in the ranks, for few in that corps were willing to be left behind in a fight.

Yet some gave out from exhaustion, but even these, at a slower pace, followed the rapidly moving column.

At the houses on the roadsides, the citizens, their wives and daughters, were bringing water, from which the soldiers filled their canteens as they passed. At Little-town we saw citizens bringing the wounded from the field in their carriages, and many wounded soldiers who could walk were making their way to the village. The marching was more rapid. Our friends were waiting for us. Soon we saw above the valley that lay before us, clouds of smoke and the white puffs of bursting shells. As yet we could distinguish little of the sound of battle, but those small fleecy clouds which appeared so suddenly, flashing forked lightning, told us of work ahead. It was five o'clock when the Sixth corps arrived on the battle-field, having made an unprecedented march of thirty-four miles! We halted in reserve, not to rest, but to wait a few moments until our place should be assigned us in front. We had more marching to do! Four miles more of marching and countermarching that night, made thirty-eight miles in a single day. Such marching as had been done by the Sixth corps since leaving Bristow Station, is unparalleled in the history of armies.

The roar of battle was terrific. On our left, where rose a hill covered with timber on the top and side, a fearful struggle seemed in progress, and the roll of musketry and the rapid discharge of artillery was almost deafening.

Let us now turn back and review the operations of the First and the Eleventh corps since yesterday morning. We give it as it was related to us by members of the First and Eleventh corps. General Buford, commanding the cavalry on the left flank of the army, had advanced north of the town of Gettysburgh, and had fallen in with large bodies of cavalry, supported by infantry. He became hotly engaged with this force, and at once reported the information to General Meade that he had found the enemy in large force. General Reynolds, who, with the First corps had by this time reached Marsh creek, within easy striking distance of Gettysburgh, was directed to urge his troops forward to Gettysburgh as rapidly as possible. The corps pushed on, and reaching Gettysburgh, filed through the town, leaving it to the rear. General Buford was found fiercely struggling to maintain his position against the infantry of the enemy. At once, General Reynolds proceeded to select a position for his line of battle. Without a moment's hesitation, the corps was deployed; the division of Wadsworth, leading the van, was in position; a battery which had been brought to the front was slowly forced back, but the gallant Wadsworth, bringing more infantry into line, arrested the retreat, and in turn forced back the hostile forces, who were now found to be in large numbers. It was at this time that General Reynolds, riding forward with a few members of his staff, to inspect the field with the view of bringing the rest of his troops into favorable position, was shot through the neck, the enemy having, at the moment, opened a full volley of musketry. The noble commander, feeling the wound, turned to his soldiers and shouted, "Forward men! for God's sake, forward!" and fell, dying, into the arms of one of his companions.

This sad loss only fired the hearts of the soldiers to more desperate determination, and they rushed into line upon the run, burning to avenge their beloved leader. General Doubleday, of the Second division of the corps, was next in rank, and took command. The encounter was sharp, and the rebels were giving way. Three hundred prisoners were brought in, and the corps was put into position to hold its ground. The force of the enemy now engaged, proved to be the corps of General A. P. Hill, and the prisoners declared that the rest of the confederate army was close at hand. A column of the enemy now moved toward the left of our line, debouching from a piece of woods, and occupying a close proximity to our forces. Volley after volley was poured into the advancing column, without avail, except to stretch many of its men upon the ground, wounded and dying.

At length the brigades of Doubleday's own division were ordered to charge upon the obstinate line. They obeyed with alacrity, their cheers and shouts ringing above the roar of musketry. The rebels gave way before this impetuous charge, and several hundred more prisoners were brought in.

Thus far the First corps was victorious, but its ranks were becoming terribly thinned.

In the meantime, General Howard, with the Eleventh corps, was hastening to the assistance of the First.   Just before receiving his fatal wound, General Reynolds had sent a messenger to Howard, who, with his corps, was ten miles behind, to hasten forward as rapidly as possible.

The men of that corps were burning to wipe out the unfortunate record of Chancellorsville, and the roar of artillery before them, inspired vigor in their movements and urged them forward; but the noise of the battle was heard by others.

Ewell, with his confederates, was but three miles off; and while the Unionists looked for the coming of help, a fresh corps reinforced the rebels.   But the opposing forces were, for the time, willing to allow a lull in the battle.   So, from ten o'clock until half-past two the First corps held the enemy at bay.   By this time a division of the Eleventh corps was on the ground and another on the other side of Gettysburgh.   General Howard took command.   The Union reinforcements were just arriving; those of the rebels had already taken their position, and were ready for a desperate charge.

Suddenly, rushing from the cover of the woods in which they had debouched from the York road, the old corps of Stonewall Jackson, now under Ewell, charged, with yells, down upon the Eleventh.   The Germans, this time stood their ground, returning with spirit, the volleys of their old antagonists.

On the left, Hill was also charging fiercely upon the First corps, and the sturdy divisions of Wadsworth and Cutler were almost destroyed.

The rebel line now overlapped that of the Union forces on either flank, and the two corps under Howard were in danger of being surrounded by the greater numbers of their adversaries.   The lines began to waver under the fearful storm of lead and iron, and the order was given to fall back. The lines retired in good order until they reached the town. There, in passing through the streets, the Germans became confused and alarmed, and the retreat of the corps became a rout. Twelve hundred were taken prisoners in the streets. The First corps maintained its line of battle and held its foe at a distance in spite of the deadly fire which was decimating its ranks. The heroic Wadsworth cheered and encouraged his men by his own noble example, while the messengers of death shrieked thickly about him. On the right of the corps, Hill had already forced back the line, and now the Eleventh corps having left him, both flanks of his division were exposed. It was useless to protract the hopeless struggle, and these sturdy troops also fell back, retiring slowly and firmly, while the rebels, flushed with victory, were pouring into front and flank the most deadly fire. It was a moment of vital importance to our army and our cause. A rout of these two corps, while the remaining two-thirds of the army was separated in columns far distant from each other, must insure the destruction of each column in detail, and give to the rebels undisputed sway throughout the north. But the christian hero, whose empty sleeve testified of hard fought fields before, was still sufficient for the crisis. Halting the retreating divisions as they reached the line of hills upon the south side of the town, and selecting a ridge called Cemetery Hill for his second line of battle, he reformed his disordered ranks, and planting batteries so as to sweep the declivity in front and on right and left, awaited the onset of the victorious hosts. On they came, until half through the town, when, from the whole line of guns on the crest, burst a murderous fire, from which the assailants staggered in consternation.

The tide was turned; for now a part of Hancock's Second corps was coming up, and in half an hour the rebels retired, and the one-armed general was master of the situation.

But the day had been a fearful one for the two corps.

The First corps had lost its general, loved and admired for his bravery. Hundreds from the ranks of the corps, lay beyond the village stretched in death. Of those who went into the fight in the morning, but one-half remained.

The havoc was almost as fearful in the Eleventh corps. Hundreds had been killed and a greater number captured. Yet there was no faltering among those veterans, and when, toward evening, the Third and Twelfth corps arrived upon the field, their confidence and hope rose, and all now believed that our army was yet destined to achieve a grand victory.

No further demonstrations were made on either side that night. Each party was gathering its strength for the grand conflict. Late in the evening General Meade arrived on the field, and with General Howard proceeded to inspect the ground, and make arrangements for posting the troops of the army.

The Eleventh corps was still to occupy Cemetery Hill, just opposite the town. Upon a knoll to the right of the Eleventh corps was the First corps, and still farther, and forming the extreme right of the army, was the Twelfth corps, General Slocum. On the left of Cemetery Hill, occupying the extension of the ridge and a prominent hill, Round Top, the Third corps, General Sickles, was posted, and the Second corps, General Hancock. The Fifth corps was to be held in reserve until the arrival of the Sixth corps. Thus through the night, the two armies lay upon their arms, each watching the other, to wake to a contest more fearful than the last.

At daylight Thursday morning, July 2d, the rebel skirmishers opened fire upon parts of our lines of pickets, but there was little betokening any general engagement. Occasionally a few of the skirmishers of the enemy, would make a charge upon parts of our line forcing back the pickets, but a gun from some one of our batteries would hastily send them to the rear again. Doubtless it was for the purpose of disclosing the positions of our batteries, that their dashes were made. Thus the day wore on until four o'clock.

General Sickles, with the Third corps, had moved out beyond the general line of battle nearly a mile, and had come upon the advance of the enemy, where Longstreet, with one-third of the rebel army, was concentrating his forces against the left flank, with the hope of turning it and seizing the ridge.

The battle opened at once. Seven batteries of artillery opened upon front and flank of the exposed corps, and large bodies of infantry in column by division. The corps withstood the shock heroically, and was soon strengthened by troops from the Second corps. Our artillery now opened upon the rebels from the ridge, and hurled destruction upon them. The valley was filled with bursting missiles, and the smoke rolled up in huge columns. It was at this stage of the great battle that the Sixth corps arrived on the ground, after its unparalleled march, and the Fifth corps was at once ordered into the fight. For an hour the Sixth corps was the reserve of the army, but even this reserve was soon called into action.

The writer, while our corps waited for orders, rode along the front, from where the Second and Third corps were engaged in their deadly struggle with the enemy, across Cemetery Ridge and to the hill where, on the right of the line, Slocum had established his head-quarters, and he will attempt to describe the field as he saw it.

To form a correct idea of the position of the armies, one should imagine two ranges of hills, between which was the valley and the village of Gettysburgh.

These ridges are nearly parallel, and are from a mile to a mile and a half asunder. Their course is not a direct line but curving. The ridge on which our forces are posted, bend outward and backward, so that the line is in the form of a half circle, fronting from the center, while the rebels were forced to occupy an exterior line facing towards the center.

At Gettysburgh several roads converge, first, on the right is the Baltimore turnpike, next is the road to Taney-town, and further to the left is the Emmitsburgh road. These all meet at Cemetery Hill, which is the key to the whole situation.

Cemetery Hill is in the center of a range of hills running south and west from Gettysburgh, and considerably in front of the others. Standing upon its summit, the spectator looks down upon the village, a little to his right and upon the long declivity stretching between the crest and the town.

The crest of this ridge is bristling with batteries, which are so arranged as to sweep the declivity, the valley below, and the opposite range of hills. Here, by the side of the Baltimore pike, General Howard has his head-quarters, and just in front lie long lines of infantry, who wear the crescent badge, which distinguishes the Eleventh corps.

Stretching to the left and rear, Cemetery Ridge gradually diminishes in elevation, until it reaches an abrupt peak which rises considerably above the other hills of the range. This is Round Top. It is covered with timber at its summit, its sides are rugged, and, toward the enemy, quite steep. On the north slope of Round Top, the Second and Third corps are maintaining the unequal struggle with one-third of the rebel army. The roar of musketry is awful beyond description, and the whole valley trembles with the thunder of the artillery. On the right of Cemetery Ridge is another elevation, Slocum's Hill, where the commander of the Twelfth corps sits among the huge fragments of rock, watching his own and the enemy's line in his front, and where is another battery, which from time to time is sending its screaming messengers to the hills beyond or across a little stream which winds along the right of his position.

In rear of Slocum's Hill is a little whitewashed cottage, surrounded by a picket fence. There are two or three wall tents in the yard, and many horses are tied to the fence. This is the head-quarters of the army. From this point General Meade is directing all the movements of the Union forces.

It will be seen that our troops could be sent from one point to another of the line, easily and quickly, while the rebels, who occupied the exterior of the circle, must make long circuits in order to reinforce one part of the field with troops from another. For the first time since Malvern Hill, our forces had the advantage of position.

The rebel lines which had so fiercely attacked the Third corps, steadily advanced, pouring destruction before them, while the two corps, unable to resist the weight of the advancing columns, steadily fell back. At the moment that the Sixth corps reached the field, the Fifth were rushing to the assistance of the wavering lines on Round Top. It was a glorious spectacle, as the veteran wearers of the St. Andrew's cross rushed along the rear of the peak and among the rocks, at double-quick, and then suddenly moving by the flank, formed in line of battle. Through the woods and down the slope they rush, fall upon the advancing columns, and check their progress. The Union line now advance upon the rebels, who fall back more. Shot and shells pour in a fearful storm from the rebel batteries, sweeping the slope of Round Top and the crest of Cemetery Hill. Here, near Howard's quarters, a train of ambulances and army wagons attract the fire of the enemy, and the bursting shells soon send them hurrying through the narrow defile in the rocks through which the road passes, panic stricken. For more than two hours the desperate battle rages on the left, while the right, except that on either side artillery belches forth its thunders, is quiet. The Sixth corps, the only reserve of the army, is also put into the line on the left; only one brigade, Neill's, is sent to the right to reinforce Slocum, who has also sent a great portion of his corps to the left, and against whom the rebels are now charging. The doubtful contest ceases as darkness gathers over the battle-field, leaving the rebels still in possession of some of the ground occupied by Sickles' corps at four o'clock.

Both armies again lay upon their arms, waiting for daylight, by which to renew the contest. The losses in the Second and Third corps had been fearful, and scarcely less were those of the Fifth. From our own Sixth corps, there were many killed and wounded, but compared with these others, the loss was slight. General Sickles had been wounded early in the fight, and suffered amputation of a leg. The morning of July 3d dawned brightly, and at once the rattle of musketry told of the renewal of strife. On the right, where Slocum with a single division of his own troops and our Third brigade of Howe's division, Sixth corps, held the long line, an attempt was made to retake the rifle pits which the rebels had captured yesterday. The rebels in turn charged furiously. They had possession of some of our pits, and now they hoped to turn our flank and rout the army; but the small force replied to the desperate charge of the whole of Ewell's corps with the most stubborn resistance. Charge after charge was made, but to no avail. At length Neill's brigade passed far to the right of the rebel line, and poured an enfilading volley into the gray-coats. They, supposing that a heavy force had got on their flank withdrew, when our forces charging in turn, drove them with great loss from the rifle pits, which were held during the remainder of the engage-

32

ment in spite of repeated efforts to dislodge our forces.
By noon quiet prevailed along the whole line, except that
now and then a shot from some of our batteries screamed
across the valley, but eliciting no reply. The rebel lines
could be seen moving here and there as if preparing for a
desperate struggle. The men at our batteries declared
that so completely had they got the range of the other
crests that the rebels dare not open a piece. Little did
they imagine that more than a hundred guns were concentrating just behind the little strip of woods below them.

This unwonted silence continued until about one o'clock,
when suddenly, as though pandemonium had broken loose,
the air was filled with the shrieks, screams, howls and
clangor of bursting shells. The sky was filled with smoke,
amid which flames darted in every direction, and the valley and hills quaked with the thunders of artillery. Never
on this continent had been heard such cannonading as this.
For two hours this storm of shell and shot raged in all its
fury. At the first opening of the storm, parts of our line
were forced back, but they quickly advanced again. Horses
and men fell together, mangled and torn by the screaming
missiles. In some of our batteries every horse was destroyed, and the men drew back the pieces by hand to save
them from capture. One hundred and twenty-five guns
were concentrated against our left center, which continued
for two hours to belch forth death and destruction. At
length, when it was supposed that our guns were silenced,
and our infantry confused by the fearful cannonade, came
the expected charge of infantry. Longstreet's corps,
massed, with Picket's division in front, rushed forward with
the well known yells, which rang above the clangor of musketry and artillery, and threw themselves with utmost fury
upon the Union lines. Our men had waited the onset with
unflinching courage, and now poured into the assailants a
most murderous fire, which hurled them back and strewed

the ground with their dead and dying. Again, with the fierceness of desperation, they rush forward, and again are met with the same deadly reception. Hundreds from the attacking columns, in order to escape the certain doom, threw down their arms and came in as prisoners. The tide of battle lulled for a time.

Again artillery did its work alone, until about four o'clock, when the last desperate charge was made, the grand effort which was to sweep the Union lines in confusion, or result in the total defeat of the rebel army.

The heavy masses swept up as before, with the desperation of madness. They advanced until they were fairly on our lines, and, at some points, actually pushed them back. Then they were met with enfilading fires, from which the carnage exceeded all that had been before. Nearly the whole of Picket's division, finding itself unable to retreat through the fiery storm, was captured, and the remaining divisions reeled back in confusion, leaving the ground literally covered with dead.

This decided the fate of the battle. The enemy had staked all upon this last desperate charge, and had been hurled back in confusion and with enormous losses.

No pursuit was attempted, but, although the rebels were not at once driven from their position, they had suffered a terrible defeat, and they must retreat with all speed to their defenses in Virginia, or submit to the destruction of their army. Our wounded were collected in great numbers in and about the field hospitals, which were composed chiefly of hospital tents, some farm house with its large barns, serving as a nucleus for each. To these, thousands of our brave comrades were brought with mangled limbs, torn bodies or bleeding heads, yet, notwithstanding their terrible wounds, exhibiting their accustomed heroism. Long trains of ambulances were bringing in crowds of poor fellows with arms or legs torn to shreds, yet who never uttered a word of complaint, and who, indeed, appeared cheerful, and some even gay.

In this respect there was the greatest contrast between the wounded of the Union and the rebel armies. A Union soldier, if so severely wounded that he could by no possibility assume a cheerful countenance, would shut his teeth close together and say nothing. While a rebel, if he could boast of only a flesh wound, would whine and cry like a sick child. One unaccustomed to such scenes as can only be witnessed about a field hospital in time of battle, would be filled with astonishment at the stoical bravery manifested by the northern troops. If one had passed along where our men were lying in rows, he would only now and then have heard a groan escape from some poor fellow who had received a bullet through the abdomen or some such fatal and painful wound. But let a group of wounded rebels be placed in some part of the hospital, and their groans were heartrending. This contrast is not over-drawn. Every surgeon who has had opportunities to observe the difference in the bearing of wounded men of the two armies, can testify to the greater heroism of the northern soldier at such times.

CHAPTER XX.

PURSUIT OF LEE'S ARMY.

Scenes of the field of Gettysburgh — The rebel hospitals — The sightless rebel soldier boy — The Sixth corps at Fairfield — "Hurrah for the Union" — Kilpatrick's handiwork — At Waynesboro' — On picket — A division of militia — The Vermonters at Funkstown — The army at Funkstown — Meade's failure to attack — New York riots — Return to Virginia.

THE battle was over and the invading army which had suffered such a crushing defeat, had only to gather up its shattered remnants and hastily retrace its steps southward. We were in no condition to renew immediate hostilities. Every man and every gun had been brought into service. Never before had all of our army been fought at once. At Gettysburgh, every man of the infantry reserve, and every gun of the reserve artillery had been brought into action. The men were exhausted by their tedious marches and hard fighting, while our ammunition was well nigh spent.

During the night of the 4th of July, Lee's army retreated, and on the morning of the 5th, our Sixth corps, Sedgwick's cavalry as the corps was called, was sent in pursuit on the Fairfield road. The battle-field was horrible. Dead men were thickly strewed over the fields with their faces blackened, and eyes starting from their sockets; and upturned, swollen horses lay, sometimes in groups of six or eight, showing where some battery had suffered fearfully. As we passed the scene of the conflict on the left, at the foot of Round Top, was a scene more than usually hideous. Blackened ruins marked the spot where, on the morning of the third, stood a large barn. It had been used as a hospital. It had taken fire from the shells of the hostile batteries, and had quickly burned to the ground. Those of the wounded not able to help themselves were destroyed by the flames, which in a moment spread through the straw and dry material of the building. The crisped and blackened limbs, heads and other portions of bodies lying half consumed among the heaps of ruins and ashes, made up one of the most ghastly pictures ever witnessed, even on the field of battle. But we passed these direful scenes to meet with others of less shocking but still sad character. Every house and barn from Gettysburgh to Fairfield was a hospital; and about most of the large barns, numbers of dilapidated hospital tents served to increase the accommodations for the wounded.

All of the worst cases were left in these hospitals, the number being estimated, by the rebel surgeons in charge, at no less than fifteen thousand. Never had we witnessed such sad scenes as we were passing through to-day. The confederate surgeons were doing what they could for their wounded, but they were destitute of medicines and surgical appliances, and even food sufficient to supply those in their charge. At one of these barns some of our officers stopped, and as they passed among the gray-clad sufferers who were lying in rows upon the barn floors, one, a boy apparently not more than sixteen years of age, attracted the notice of one of the company, a surgeon. The lad looked more like a delicate girl than a soldier; his hair fell from his fair forehead in long flaxen curls upon his pillow of straw, some of them matted with blood; his cheek was rosy, and his soft white hand told of a youth spent amid more tender scenes than those of the camp. A piece of linen laid across his face covered a ghastly wound where a ball had passed through his face, and had torn both his eyes from their sockets.

The surgeon spoke a kind word to the youth, who stretched out his hand, saying, "Come near me, I want to touch you." The doctor stooped over him, and the boy, pressing his hand in his own, said, "You are a friend, are you not?" "Yes, I am a friend to all the unfortunate." "But are you not a confederate?" "No." The boy clung to the hand of the surgeon in silence for a moment, and then said slowly, "I did not think a federal would speak so kindly to me; your voice sounds like that of a friend, and your hand feels like one; will you not stay with me?" When the other told him that he must follow his command, he replied: "Oh! I shall never hear any one speak so kindly to me again; my mother lives in North Carolina, but she will not see me. Can you not stay?" The doctor was far from being a rebel sympathizer, yet he turned away from the poor boy, with a sad face and a deep drawn sigh, to join the moving column.

Early next morning we passed through the somewhat dilapidated village of Fairfield. Our advance threw a few shells down the street, scattering a body of cavalry, which had been left in town, and killing some of the horses attached to their battery. A mile beyond the town the South Mountain range rose in our front, the road running through a narrow pass. Here the rear guard of the rebel army was strongly posted. Neill's and the Jersey brigade advanced against the rebel skirmishers, but after losing some six or eight men they were ordered to halt. General Sedgwick deeming the position too strong to assault with his corps from the front, reported to General Meade that the pass was very strong, and one in which a small force of the enemy could hold in check for a considerable time, a force much larger than its own. The main body of the army, therefore, was moved around their flank by way of Frederick; while Neill's brigade, with Colonel McIntosh's brigade of cavalry and two light batteries, all under command of General Neill, were made to form a flying division to harass the enemy in the rear.

Our march over the mountain that day was by a wild, romantic route, than which none more charming could be asked by tourist in search of nature's wildest moods. Before each little log house by the roadside would stand a wondering group, astonished at seeing such multitudes of men in those secluded regions, where scarcely a dozen travelers usually passed in a week. At one place, as the column was passing a cottage half hidden by sunflowers and flowering beans, those at the head of the column were heard cheering heartily; and, as we advanced, other voices took up the cheer, exciting the curiosity of those behind. In the midst of the noise, sounded a shrill voice; and as we approached, we saw, sitting upon the fence in front of the cottage, a little boy, about four years old, his face flushed with excitement, his flaxen hair flying in the wind, as he was waving his little hat, and with childlike indistinctness shouting in his shrill tones, "Hurrah for 'e Union! Hurrah for 'e Union!"

Soon those in the rear of the line heard those ahead shouting again, and another shrill voice was heard between the cheers of the men. There by the roadside stood an old man, over whom more than eighty years had passed, with voice indistinct with the tremor of age, all excited as the little boy had been, his hair tossed about by the breeze, as with hat swinging he too was shouting, "Hurrah for the Union! Hurrah for the Union!" And the cheers of the multitude again rang in response to the old man's shout. We could but note the similarity and the disparity. One vaguely dreamed of those blessings which the other had fully realized, and for which he had struggled; and the same shout was lifted up by those two children—the one of four, and the other of fourscore—the one with the flaxen curls of childhood, and the other with the white locks of age—the one voice with the shrill treble of infancy, and the other with the high-keyed tones of decrepitude. Those people, who had seen the rebel army pass a few hours before, now felt the value of the Union.

On the summit of the mountain we passed Monterey Springs, a charming summer retreat, where the Pennsylvanians resort to indulge in the sports of trout-fishing and deer-hunting. Passing down the western slope of the mountain, the handiwork of Kilpatrick was strewed along the roadside for miles. As the battle of Gettysburgh drew to a close, and General Meade knew that Lee must retreat toward Virginia, he had sent the dashing Kilpatrick with his brigade of cavalry to harass the rebels in their flight. Reaching these mountains, the cavalry had come upon a long rebel train of wagons and ambulances, hastening with all speed, with their lading of stolen goods and provisions and their wounded men, towards the Potomac. With shouts and cheers the horsemen dashed from the cover of the woods, upon the flying train, shot the leading horses and mules, captured the drivers and remaining animals, appropriated the stolen goods to their own use, and burned the wagons. Now, as we marched down the forest road, the wildness of the scene was heightened by the remains of the ruined wagons which lined the wayside, some burned, some with the wheels disabled by cutting the spokes, others tumbled off the steep embankment. For more than three miles, these remnants of the rebel trains met our view.

It was near the middle of the afternoon when the column, the army under General Neill, descended into the beautiful Cumberland valley, and arrived at the village of Waynesboro. The people gave our little army a joyous reception, and we encamped at a little distance from the village. One regiment, the Seventy-seventh, was sent on picket on the banks of the Antietam creek, and so pleasant was the duty that the regiment petitioned to be allowed to remain until the army moved, to which request General Neill very graciously assented. Our picketing on

33

the Antietam became one of the bright sports in the history of our campaigning. We were a mile in advance of the other troops, and the picket line was two miles long, so that we were not at all crowded. The weather was fine, the country delightful, and the people kind and hospitable. The most friendly relations sprang up at once between the people and the soldiers, the inhabitants supplying the boys with luxuries, and taking them into their houses as welcome guests, the soldiers on their part guarding the people against the depredations of stragglers and militia.

The grain was ripe for the harvest, and the farmers were short of help; but the boys laid aside their guns, and swung the cradle and the scythe with a zest that showed that they worked with a good will. Day after day the boys of the Seventy-seventh reaped and bound in the fields, while the good ladies worked day and night to make bread and cakes for the veterans, who had so long been accustomed to diet on pork and hard tack. Soft bread, milk, poultry and the staple luxury of Pennsylvania, apple butter, was a glorious improvement on the usual bill of camp fare, and kind sympathizing Union people were much better calculated to render our stay among them agreeable, than the bitter rebels among whom we had so long been.

The left wing of our extended picket line was under command of Major Babcock, who, with the line officers of his part of the picket, established head-quarters at the house of a miller, whose comfortable rooms and well filled larder afforded substantial inducements to our friends; but the great attractions at the miller's house were doubtless the three charming daughters, whose merry faces and bewitching eyes rejoiced the hearts of our gay major and his associates. Word came to the right of the line that our friends on the left were in the enjoyment of far more than the usual allowance of pleasure for men on picket, and thither started the colonel and the doctor, and our friend, Colonel Connor, of the Seventh Maine, to investigate the matter. Riding through a lovely region, now rising to the summit of some gentle eminence, from whence they could look away upon the surrounding country, its rich fields of grain ready for the harvest, its charming groves of oak, and its neat farm houses, making up a most delightful landscape, now descending into some green valley where babbling brooks danced over pebbly beds, and now reining up to listen to the complaint of some cottagers, who said that " the militia were robbing them of their pigs and their poultry, and but for the old soldiers, who were perfect gentlemen, they would be stripped of everything they had;" now fording the bright waters of the Antietam, and anon halting to converse with some group of men who were reclining beneath the shadow of some clump of chestnuts or oaks, doing picket duty as amateurs, the party at length arrived at the miller's house, nestled in a pleasant grove by the side of the beautiful river. Here was the major, and here were the happy line officers, and here was the main reserve of the left wing of the picket, all exhibiting the most abundant good humor. Here, also, they found our chaplain, and Chaplain Osborn, of the Forty-third New York. It was evident, at a glance, that the reports of gay soldiering which had reached the right of the line were in no way exaggerated. The miller took the horses, and the party was ushered into the house, when the good lady and her merry daughters welcomed them heartily. The miller brought out his best wines and his biggest apples. The ladies were smiling, the wines were good, and the apples delicious, and the hearts of the soldiers were gladdened. The ladies retired, leaving the gentlemen in possession of the airy sitting-room. They sung Old Hundred, and Coronation, and Lenox, and Cambridge. Now our friend,

Colonel Connor, would lead off in a rollicking soldiers' song; then our chaplain would follow with "Benny Havens, Oh!" and all would join in the chorus. Chaplain Osborn, of the Forty-third, could tell a good story, and relish a glass of wine; and so they passed a happy hour, singing and chatting, till called to dinner, where the long table was loaded from the abundance of the miller's stores. Dinner over, the company strolled among the fruit trees and along the banks of the river; but at length, as an end must come to all pleasures, our party, who had left the right of the line in the morning, galloped back to their quarters, satisfied that picket duty was not necessarily the most vexatious in the service.

The Forty-ninth was provost guard for the town, and a merry time the men had of it. Here in the principal hotel, General Neill established his head-quarters, and in regal style amid flowers and fruits he received the homage of the citizens and soldiers. The remaining regiments of the brigade were stationed in a lovely grove half way between the town and the picket line. They lounged in the shade of their beautiful camp, or strolled to the village or to the picket line on the Antietam. They purchased from the people fruit and bread, apple butter and other luxuries, enjoying a pleasant respite from labors, while the Forty-ninth guarded the town and the Seventy-seventh the river. But notwithstanding all the pleasures of this bright episode in our campaign, the boys were not without a source of annoyance.

Soon after our arrival at Waynesboro, we were joined by a large division of New York and Pennsylvania militia, under our old commander General W. F. Smith, who still held a prominent place in the affections of the boys. The militia was composed mostly of young gentlemen who had left their places behind the counter or at the desk, for the double purpose of lending their aid to their country in its hour of need, and of enjoying a month of what they hoped would be amateur soldiering.

On the evening of their arrival, they were all complaining bitterly of the terrible marches they had endured, and swore they would shoot the general if they ever got into a fight. They had marched all the way from Harrisburgh, to which point they had been brought in cars, at the rate of from eight to fifteen miles a day! In addition to the severe marches, they had been subjected to great privations; many of them had not tasted any *butter* for more than a week, and nearly all declared that they had absolutely nothing to eat for several days. The writer, who listened to these grievous complaints from some who had been his friends in civil life, pointed to their trains of wagons loaded with boxes of hard bread. "What," replied the militia-men, "You don't expect us to eat that hard tack do you?"

These regiments of militia were undisciplined and unaccustomed to the hard fare of the soldier's life, and the majority of the men took to plundering the inhabitants of the neighboring country, and perpetrating other depredations equally dishonorable in the eyes of the old soldiers. As the veterans constituted the picket and the guard of the town, and were intrusted to guard many of the houses of the citizens outside of the village, they found great annoyance in attempting to resist the incursions of the militia, and rather frequent collisions resulted, in which the old soldiers usually got the best of the encounter.

The citizens very soon learned to look upon the veterans as their friends and their protectors, while they regarded with dread any squad of soldiers that might approach, if they were clad in new uniforms.

But, on the 11th of July, we drew in our picket line, the brigade assembled, and at dark the troops, veterans and militia, were fording the Antietam, the water nearly to their waists. We marched rapidly all night, halting at a place called Leytirsburgh. At daylight next morning, we were again marching. The day was extremely hot, and large numbers of the men fell by the wayside from sun-stroke. At Smithville we fell in with the First corps, which was moving towards Hagerstown, and the hearts of the men were gladdened by the sight of the old familiar flags of the Army of the Potomac. We had been absent from the main body of the army for a week, and it seemed now as though we had fallen in with old friends from whom we had been long separated. Falling in the rear of the First corps, we marched toward Hagerstown. At 2 o'clock a most terrific thunder-storm arose, such as had never over-taken our army, even in Virginia. Huge black clouds rose from the north and from the west and south, and meeting overhead poured down great volumes of water, until the road through which we were marching, and which was bordered by high banks on either side, was filled with a mad torrent which reached to the knees, and in places to the waists of the men. At sunset we reached Funkstown, where the main body of our corps was in line of battle, having yesterday met the rebels and driven them more than a mile. Our friends of the Vermont brigade had, as usual, given a good account of themselves; and the head-boards of pine, here and there among the trees, showed that the victory had not been gained without a struggle.

In marching from Boonsboro' towards Funkstown, the Vermont brigade in advance of the corps, the little stream, Beaver Creek, was passed, and General Howe found Buford's cavalry in his advance holding a strong position against the skirmishers of the rebel infantry. At General Buford's request, General Howe sought and obtained per-mission to send the Vermont brigade to relieve the cavalry. Colonel Lewis with his Fifth Vermont and part of the

Second, and Colonel Barney with the Sixth regiment, at once deployed as skirmishers, forming their line two miles long. The Third and Fourth regiments were supporting a battery, and the balance of the Second was held in reserve. They saw the rebel infantry approach a strip of woods in front, and at once advanced and occupied it themselves. Against this long thin line of skirmishers, the rebels opened a severe fire of artillery and musketry, and advanced to drive the skirmishers from their position; but the brave mountaineers never dreaming that a Sixth corps skirmish line could not hold a rebel line of battle, resolutely refused to leave and sent the presumptious rebel line of battle to the rear in confusion; not, however, until Colonel Stoughton with the Fourth and Colonel Seaver with the Third, came forward to the support of the Fifth and Sixth. Again, the rebels, disgusted at being repulsed by a skirmish line, came up in several lines of battle and charged upon the Vermonters and they again went to the rear in confusion. A third charge was made against the obstinate skirmish line, and a third time the attack was broken. Meanwhile a strong force attempting to cross the Antietam and come in on the flank, was repelled by the Second Vermont.

The gallant brigade had repelled Anderson's brigade, of seven large regiments, from its front, and another from its flank.

An instance of a skirmish line, a mile and a half from any support, resisting repeated attacks of troops in line of battle, is rarely found in the history of armies.

The men used from sixty to eighty rounds of cartridge, and when the first supply was exhausted, a fresh one was brought to the front on stretchers.

The victory cost the brigade a loss of nine men killed and fifty-nine wounded, while the enemy lost more than two hundred men.

The men of Neill's brigade were rejoiced to find themselves once more with the glorious old corps, and when their brigade flag, bearing the insignia of the Greek cross, was once more thrown to the breeze, it was greeted with vociferous cheers.   Brisk skirmishing was going on along the line, and frequent charges were made by our Union pickets upon the rebel line, which usually resulted in the capture of a greater or less number of the enemy's pickets.   All things indicated a great battle on the morrow.   The two armies were facing each other in a line in front of Hagerstown, near a hamlet called Funkstown, the line of battle extending several miles.   The rebels had occupied the higher grounds, and had thrown up strong earthworks to dispute our progress.   Night came on with rain, and all expected to be roused early by the sound of battle.   But morning came and passed, and the day wore on with little activity on our part.   Here and there skirmishers kept up a rattle of musketry, but no general engagement came on.   Much as the veterans, who knew too well the risks of battle, usually dreaded a general engagement, this time there seemed a universal desire, on the part of the men, now to strike a blow which should destroy their adversaries before they should be able to cross the river again.

Deserters and prisoners from the rebel army represented it in a deplorable condition; and the men of the ranks in our army believed that this was the grand opportunity for striking a final blow.   And notwithstanding the assertion of general officers that the Potomac was so swollen as to prevent the crossing of the rebel army, there were few privates in our ranks who were not ready to declare that, unless we gave battle at once, the prey would surely escape.   Thus, as the day wore on, great dissatisfaction was expressed all along the ranks — men openly and freely cursing the hesitancy which held them back, as they believed, from a certain victory.   So, when they arose on the morning of the 14th, to find that there was no enemy in our front, they were more incensed than surprised. There was certainly a very general ill-feeling pervading our army at this easy escape of the rebel army, which even the glorious news of Vicksburg and Port Hudson failed to pacify.

Brisk firing in the vicinity of the Potomac, however, warned us that there were still rebels enough left on the north side of the river to offer some resistance. We learned, late in the day, that the firing was caused by a brilliant charge of Kilpatrick's cavalry upon the rear guard of the rebels at Falling Waters, where they captured several hundreds of prisoners; thus adding one more brilliant success to their many daring achievements during this campaign. Marching until nightfall, we reached Williamsport, and encamped very near the spot that had been our resting-place on a former occasion, nearly a year before.

Why General Lee and his army were allowed to cross the Potomac unmolested, we do not attempt to explain; nor do we condemn the determination of General Meade not to give battle. When men of such well-known military ability and bravery as General Sedgwick advise against a movement, it may be well to hesitate; yet it will doubtless be the verdict of history, that the hesitancy of General Meade at this time was his great mistake.

A hard march on the 15th brought the Sixth corps to Boonsboro', where our Second division encamped on precisely the same ground that we had occupied on the 31st of October last. Neill's brigade made the march at a breakneck pace, leaving the Vermonters far to the rear, who declared that the recent associations of the former with the cavalry had transformed them into a flying brigade. While resting here, a large body of rebel prisoners was marched past. They were mostly those who had been captured by Kilpatrick's men at Falling Waters. The rebels were hungry and destitute of rations. Our men at

34

once divided their rations of hard bread and coffee with them, who, officers and all, declared that it was the best meal they had enjoyed for several days, and expressed themselves greatly pleased with the generosity of their guardians.

Notwithstanding our glorious success at Gettysburgh, and the good news from the west, we were now hearing news that made our hearts sick, and caused the cheeks of the New York soldiers to burn for the disgrace of their native State. It was a source of the deepest mortification to the brave New Yorkers, to feel that their own State and the great metropolis had been outraged by the most disgraceful riot that had ever stained the annals of any State or city in the Union, all for the purpose of over-awing the government in its efforts to subdue the rebellion. Our companions from other States, with the generosity that characterizes soldiers, never derided us with this disgrace, but alluded to the riot as an uprising of foreigners, who had for the moment overpowered the native element. Even the fact that the governor of that great State had, in the midst of these terrible scenes, addressed the miscreants as his "friends," was alluded to with a delicacy that won our hearts.

It was one of the pleasant indications of a union of hearts as well as of States, that the soldiers of our sister States looked upon these riots in the light of a general calamity, rather than a disgrace to a particular State.

Crossing the South Mountain range, from Boonsboro' to Middletown, the Sixth corps reached Petersville, three or four miles north of Berlin, where the army was to cross the Potomac. Here, nearly the whole army was crowded into a space of not more than three miles, all waiting for the orders to cross. The men were universally eager to push forward, and the necessary delay caused by crossing the men and material of so large an army seemed to them a wearisome expenditure of time. While waiting here, the Second division was honored by the presence of several ladies, wives of officers of different regiments, who had been waiting in Washington an opportunity of visiting their husbands, and had met them here. As a memento of this brief visit, the Seventy-seventh New York received from the wife of the surgeon the gift of a pair of beautiful guidons, which the regiment boasted were unequaled in the army. The design was a white cross, the badge of our division, upon a ground of deep blue silk. In the center of the cross were wrought the figures " 77." These beautiful guidons were carried by the regiment until its final discharge from the service, when, with the old banner, the tattered national flag, and the magnificent new flag which was presented afterward by the ladies of Saratoga, they were presented to the State of New York, on the Fourth of July, 1865, in the presence of General Grant and a great concourse of illustrious men.

On Sunday, the 19th, the Sixth corps crossed the pontoon bridge to Virginia, the bands playing " O carry me back." As usual, while the corps was crossing a bridge or passing a difficult place, General Sedgwick stood at the farther end of the bridge preventing confusion and hurrying up teams which might obstruct the way. We climbed the rocky defile, and, at four o'clock, found ourselves well on the Virginia side of the Potomac. On our march we passed through the little village of Lovettsville, and, much to the surprise of all, the doors and windows of the dwellings were filled with ladies, whose hair and dresses were decked with ribbons of red, white and blue, and scores of Union flags waved a welcome to our soldiers. Such a sight had not greeted us before in Dixie, and it was most refreshing to witness such a demonstration of loyalty in Virginia.

The corps encamped about ten miles from the river, near a beautiful clear stream of water, which was very soon filled with bathers. Here orders came for each regiment in the army to send, to the State in which the regiment was raised, a certain number of commissioned officers and enlisted men for recruiting duty.

The march on the 20th was slow and through groves and pleasant meadows. Twelve miles were made, and we halted for the night and the next day. Wednesday we passed through Union town and Snickersville, reaching the base of Cobbler's mountain, a high spur from the Blue Ridge, not far from Ashby's Gap. Thursday the Sixth corps proceeded to Ashby's Gap, and, halting there for a few hours in a most delightful valley, again started southward. Vines of the trailing blackberry covered the ground, and the delicious fruit grew in such profusion that the men enjoyed a continual feast. Never had we, in our wanderings in the south, found such an abundance of fruit, and the effect upon the health of the men was marvelous. By the time that we reached Warrenton the occupation of the surgeons was almost gone. At no time, perhaps, in the history of the Army of the Potomac, did the medical reports exhibit a more general state of health than during our stay in the vicinity of Warrenton.

Thus, marching along at the foot of Blue Ridge, now turning aside to enter some mountain pass, and again proceeding on the general course, the army, on the 25th of July, reached the vicinity of Warrenton, our Sixth corps occupying a line from Warrenton to Waterloo, the scene of some of the early engagements of General Pope's army at the first rebel invasion. The First division was stationed in and about Warrenton; the Jersey brigade being provost guard of the town, where the gentlemanly conduct of the men, and the strict order preserved in the town, won for them the good opinions of the town's people, as well as of army officers. The Third division was in the rear of the other two divisions, and guarding the flank. The Second division encamped about an old Baptist church, which, inclosed by a thick growth of trees, large and small, had been, before the war, the only house of worship for miles around. No paint had ever stained its seats or casings, and no steeple from its roof had ever pointed toward heaven. The pulpit, the white folks' seats and the black folks' seats, were all in ruins now. The Rappahannock river was but a half a mile distant, and the Seventy-seventh and Fifth Vermont were sent to perform picket duty along its banks. On the following day the camps of the two regiments were moved to the vicinity of the river, in front of the remainder of the division, and we were ordered to perform picket duty while the division remained in its present camp. The camp of the Fifth Vermont was established a fourth of a mile from that of the Seventy seventh, its lines joining ours on the left. On the bank of the river just below our camp, was the residence of Mr. Hart and a grist-mill; hence the place was called " Hart's Mills."

CHAPTER XXI.

CAMPS AT WARRENTON, THE CENTREVILLE CAMPAIGN AND THE BATTLE OF RAPPAHANNOCK STATION.

THE camp at Hart's Mills was truly a pleasant one. It was situated in the midst of a most delightful oak grove, on a projecting hill, around whose base the Rappahannock coursed in a beautiful curve. Along its banks was our picket line. Westward the view extended over a charming valley to the Blue Ridge, some ten miles away; and at evening, when the sun sank behind those fine hills, tinging them and the clouds with gorgeous colors, the prospect was truly delightful. The village of Warrenton was some four miles distant, and the celebrated Warrenton Sulphur Springs about three miles down the river.

Under the direction of Chaplain Fox, a place in the grove was selected, a speaker's stand was erected, surrounded by rows of log seats, and here services were held on the Sabbath; and on other days of the week there were other regimental gatherings, which the men greatly enjoyed. At evening, the place would be lighted by Chinese lanterns of various colors, hung among the boughs of the oak trees, giving to the grove a most romantic appearance.

On one evening the regiment, with many invited guests from the division, assembled in this lovely spot and listened to speeches from several gentlemen of eloquence, the brigade band lending the aid of fine music to the evening's entertainment.

Thus pleasantly passed the time of the two regiments — the Seventy-seventh and Fifth Vermont — in doing picket duty for the Second division, along the banks of the Rappahannock. Our friends of the Fifth Vermont were, in addition to the pleasant location of their camp and their easy picket duty, favored with the presence of the wives of some of their officers. A ride to the Sulphur Springs was always a pleasant pastime; and we recall with pleasure one of these excursions. A small party, including one of these ladies, enjoying a morning's drive, turned their horses' heads towards the Springs. A merry gallop across three miles of delightful country, through pleasant groves and over rolling meadows, fording clear sparkling streams and leaping fences, brought the party to the former Saratoga of the south.

The morning had been cool and cloudy, but as our friends reached the little settlement the clouds were breaking away, and the sun began to pour blazing rays upon them. They secured their horses and walked into the grounds, in the midst of which General Birney, commanding a division of the Third corps, had established his head-quarters; and as it was then the dinner hour, the general and his staff were gathered around the board under the shade of the chestnut trees, while a band discoursed sweet music for the benefit of those at table.

Oak, chestnut and ailanthus trees form a rich and grateful shade for the grounds, which dip so as to form a kind of basin, in the center of which rises the cupola which covers the spring. As we step down into the inclosure of the cupola, indeed as we approach it at a distance, a strong sulphurous odor is perceived; but there is a delightful coolness as we sit down upon the benches which are placed around the area of the cupola. Several Vermont officers

greeted our friends as they approached, offering the odorous
drink to the lady. There are two springs or vats within
the cupola, each inclosed by marble sides; and the water
stands so high that we may dip it ourselves, thus dispensing with the necessity of the "dippers," such as take our
dimes at Saratoga.

A glass of the sparkling fluid was presented to our lady
friend, who raised it to her lips, and then turning her face
away, with an expression of infinite disgust, and saying,
with a good deal of energy, "I don't want any," handed
back the glass. The gentlemen endeavored to convince
her that the water was good; but even after adding a little
fine brandy, she could not be induced to quaff the liquid,
which she declared carried with it such powerful sugges-
tions of unserviceable eggs.

Our friends lingered about the grounds for some hours,
enjoying the cool shade and examining the old buildings,
the principal one of which was originally a fine structure,
but it had been burned the year before by our soldiers.
The massive columns and high walls were still suggestive
of the hilarious old times when the chivalry used to congre-
gate here in all its glory. Encircling the grounds was a
row of long one and two story buildings, most of them
painted yellow. These were divided into small apart-
ments which had been used as lodging rooms. There were
a dozen or more of these buildings, all dilapidated by age
rather than suffering from the ruthless usage of war.
They inclosed the grove which occupied ten or twelve
acres of land.

Except the circle of buildings immediately surrounding
the grove and springs, there were but very few dwellings
in the neighborhood, those evidently intended for the
purpose of receiving summer boarders. It was said that
about five hundred boarders used to spend the summer
here every year, and double that number of visitors took

rooms at Warrenton, a mile and a half distant, from which place they rode to the springs morning and evening to quaff the odorous fluid, or to stroll about the groves. The new White Sulphur Springs in the Shenandoah Valley had, for some years past, diverted the patronage from the Warrenton springs, and thither, at the foot of the Blue Ridge mountains, great numbers of fashionable southerners had resorted.

It was evidently a blessing that this resort had been despoiled by war. It sadly needed renovating and modernizing, and so long as the old buildings stood, no southerner had the enterprise to pull them down and replace them with better ones. A few thousands of dollars in the hands of an enterprising Yankee would soon make this one of the most delightful resorts in the southern states.

One of the characteristic features of our picket duty on the Rappahannock, was the great number of contrabands who came through our lines.

Squads of gray-headed old negroes, young negro women and children, carrying in bundles all their worldly store, constantly applied for permission to enter the lines on their way to the north. The cavalry who scouted in front on the south side of the river, returned with wagons loaded with little darkies, whose mothers and elder sisters and grandsires trudged along on foot. All wagons going to Warrenton without other lading were filled with these refugees from slavery, old and young, some black, some olive and some white; some with black curly wool, some with wavy black hair, and some with brown ringlets.

Our northern soldiers had, by this time, begun to look upon slavery in its true light. They had also learned that the negroes were their friends. It required a long schooling to teach them this lesson, but it was thoroughly learned at last. We heard now no jeering and hooting when a negro or wagon load of negroes went by. The

35

soldiers treated them with the greatest kindness, and aided them in every way to get off to the north.

While our boys did not hesitate long to take from the white inhabitants any articles that they thought they were in need of, it was considered an act of outrageous meanness to take a chicken or any other property from the negro people.

While passing through Orleans, on our way to the present camp, a great many slave children were standing along the streets watching us. Many of these children were nearly white. The attention of one our captains, who was one of the last relics among us of that class of men who were loyal to their country but despised the negro, was fixed upon a beautiful child of olive complexion and wavy hair, who stood gazing in innocent wonder at the passing column. The child was indeed a picture of unadorned beauty, in her long coarse garment of "negro cloth." The captain turned to a staff officer and as a tear stole down his rough cheek at the thought of the degradation of the beautiful child, he exclaimed, "Is'nt it horrible."

It is hardly necessary to say that the captain's sentiments from that moment underwent a radical change, and ever after there were none more ready to afford assistance to the needy refugees, than our generous but hitherto prejudiced captain.

Many of these colored refugees had the greatest faith in what they deemed the promises of the Bible. There was an almost universal faith in the ultimate overthrow of the south by the north, and this belief was founded in most cases upon their supposed Bible promises.

One of these people, a gray-haired negro, bent with age and leaning heavily upon his staff, who hoped to spend the evening of his life in freedom, said to the writer: " Our massas tell us dat dey goin to whip de Yankees and

"WHAT'LL OLE MISSUS DO NOW?"

dat Jeff. Davis will rule de norf. But we knowd it warnt
so cause de Bible don't say so. De Bible says that de
souf shall prevail for a time and den de norf shall rise
up and obertrow dem."

Where the old man found this strange prophecy he did
not say, but many of the slaves declared this to be Bible
truth and all asserted it in the same way.*

Among those who were thus fleeing from bondage, were
two fine boys, each about twelve years of age and from
the same plantation. Each gave his name as John, and
as they were both remarkably bright little fellows, they
were at once adopted into our head-quarters family.
Their sprightly manners, their ready wit and their
kindly good nature soon brought them into general favor.
We were very early one morning startled by an extraordinary commotion in front of head-quarters, where
the two Johns stood swinging their hats, leaping and
dancing in most fantastic manner, and screaming at the
top of their voices the wildest exclamations of delight.
Looking in the direction to which their attention was
turned, we saw a group of eight or ten negro women and
small children accompanied by an aged colored patriarch.
One of the Johns suddenly forgetting his ecstacy of delight,
rolling up the whites of his eyes and holding his hands
above his head, exclaimed with impressive gravity, "Oh
my Lor a massa! What'l ole missus do now?"

The party consisted of the mothers and younger brothers
and sisters of the two boys with their grandfather. Forgetting for a moment their joy at the escape of their
friends from slavery, the boys were overpowered with the
vision of "ole missus" left desolate, without a slave to
minister to her many wants.

---

* Since the above paragraph was in print, a friend has called my attention to the
passage in Daniel, chap. xi, verses 13-15, as the probable origin of this belief among
the negroes. He further assures me that he is informed that the negroes in North
Carolina entertained the same belief.

On the morning of the 6th of August, we were astonished to find the camp of our neighbors of the Fifth Vermont deserted, and their picket line occupied by a regiment from the Third division. The surprise was still greater when we learned that the whole of the Second brigade had been ordered to New York city to guard against any resistance which might be offered to the enforcement of the draft. The order had reached the brigade after midnight, and at three o'clock it was on its way to the north. Thus the Third brigade was now all that was left of the Second division of the Sixth corps. Up to this time General Howe had kept the division, except the two regiments on picket, hard at work at division drills. It is safe to say that no division in the army performed more labor in drills than Howe's during the time that it was under command of that officer. The whole division was encamped in one of those charming localities which make this part of Virginia more beautiful than almost any other, and aside from the continual round of drills, the time passed most agreeably. The Jersey boys here spent the time in pleasant alternation of guard duties and social enjoyments; a part of the time being devoted to military affairs, and a much greater part spent in agreeable attentions to the winning young ladies of Warrenton.

But, like every other brief respite for the army of the Potomac, this was destined to come to an end. On the 15th of September the army moved toward Culpepper, which was reached on the 16th; the Sixth corps taking position at a place called Stonehouse Mountain, three miles west of Culpepper.

Here we remained three weeks; the camps were by no means so delightful as those about Warrenton and Waterloo, and the weather was becoming quite cold, so that our three weeks stay at Stonehouse Mountain had little about it to make us desire to make it longer. Some pleasing incidents, however, relieved the monotony of our stay at this place, the presentation of an elegant sword to Colonel French, by the line officers of the Seventy-seventh, was the first. The presentation was followed by festivity and merriment, and in the evening our friends of the Seventh Maine, forming a torchlight procession, marched to the camp of the Seventy-seventh to congratulate the colonel and line officers upon the mutual trust and confidence existing between them. The next was the return of the Vermont brigade from New York. The Third brigade was drawn up in line to receive our returning comrades, and with much ceremony welcomed them back to the division. It must be acknowledged that both brigades would have been better pleased with the unrestrained welcome which would have been expressed in cheers than by the formal military salute.

On Monday, October 5th, the Sixth corps marched to Cedar Mountain on the Rapidan, the scene of General Banks' conflict with Jackson. The First corps was already stationed in the vicinity of Raccoon Ford, and the two corps now occupied a line of five or six miles along the bend of the river, holding the roads to Culpepper and Stevensburgh. The two corps were thus thrown out ten miles in front of the main army, having little communication with the rear. Few wagons were allowed to follow us, and those were ordered to the rear under a strong escort. On Friday, the 11th, the signal officers stationed on the summit of Cedar Mountain, while watching the rebel signals, read the message sent by their flags: "I am at James City. J. E. B. S." Thus it was known that Stuart was making for our rear, and as long trains of wagons had also been discovered moving in the direction of James City, it became evident that Lee was endeavoring to throw his whole army in the rear of our own. General Meade determined to draw the rebel army back if possible; accordingly the Sixth and First corps were ordered to build extensive fires and be in readiness to march at a moment's notice. On the following morning, Buford, with a division of cavalry, appeared at Germania Ford, some twelve miles below us, while our infantry advanced as though about to cross at Raccoon Ford and the fords in front of the Sixth corps. The ruse of threatening to cross the river by the two corps, succeeded in calling the rebel infantry back to check our advance; and at night, after building large fires, the two corps hastily withdrew toward Culpepper, which we reached at daylight, after a severe march. After a brief halt for breakfast, the corps, with the whole of the infantry, was on its way toward Brandy Station, leaving the cavalry force under Pleasanton to cover the retreat. A rapid march, in which the army moved in several parallel columns, brought the infantry all safe across the Rappahannock at Rappahannock Station. But the cavalry were not allowed to retreat without some hard fighting. Their guns could be heard by us during the afternoon, and toward evening the firing became more rapid and nearer. Indeed, the rebels advanced almost to the banks of the river.

Gregg, with a brigade of cavalry, was overtaken by a considerable force of the enemy, near Jefferson, early in the day, and after a severe engagement of two hours, fell back, crossing the river at Sulphur Springs.

Kilpatrick with his brigade, following the trail of the infantry, and designing to form a union with Gregg, found, on passing Brandy Station, that his way was blocked by a whole division of rebel cavalry, which had slipped in between him and the rear of the infantry. Halting for a moment to take a single glance at the situation of affairs, the dashing general shouted to his men, "Boys, there are the cusses!" Then, springing to the head of the column, he led his men to such a charge as has rarely been witnessed even in our cavalry service.

The road was strongly guarded by three regiments of cavalry in solid column, flanked on either side by a regiment in line. Directly upon this strongly posted force, the gallant general and his brave fellows rushed with shouts and oaths, and sabre thrusts, trampling down everything in their way. Unable to withstand this impetuous and unexpected onset, the rebels gave way, allowing the Union brigade to pass between their broken ranks. Dead men and horses lay thickly scattered upon the ground when the victorious brigade left the field to join the infantry at the river.

Thus, hotly pursued, General Meade determined to offer battle to the pursuing army, making the Rappahannock his immediate base of operations. Accordingly, early the following morning, a large portion of the infantry and artillery was countermarched across the river, where, within a mile of the stream, the line of battle was formed, and we waited the onset of the enemy until past noon. Then, Buford's cavalry having engaged the enemy in front, three corps, the Second, Fifth and Sixth, commenced to advance in line of battle. It was a grand spectacle. During two years of service we had not seen its like. Our line of battle stretched across the vast plain, nearly three miles in length, straight as the flight of an arrow. At each flank were several battalions *in echelon*. In the rear of the center of each wing of the line, was a heavy reserve in solid square, and, following in the rear of each square, a large column, stretching back to the river and across the pontoon bridges to the farther side of the stream.

Thus the line of battle moved forward across the plain, never for a moment losing its perfect form. Brisk cannonading and musketry were kept up by the cavalry in front, and the army earnestly hoped that General Lee

might accept our challenge to an open field fight, but the
rebel general was too wary to accept battle on such equal
terms, and pushed on toward Sulphur Springs, hoping to
reach Centreville before us.

Our line of battle halted at dark, at Brandy Station.
But there was no time to be lost; resting there until
eleven o'clock, we were ordered to retrace our steps to
the river; this time not in line of battle, but in all haste.
The night was dark, and the troops had already made long
marches; so when they reached and crossed the river at
daylight, they were fairly worn out. An hour for sleep
and breakfast was allowed, the railroad bridge was blown
up, and again we were on a grand race northward.

It was a great medley; baggage wagons, pontoons,
ambulances, artillery and troops, all thrown together in
splendid confusion. Drivers cursing, cannon rattling, soldiers singing and shouting, horses racing, and all that
sublime confusion which can never be seen except in a
hasty but well directed retreat of a vast army.

We passed Warrenton Junction and Bealton Station,
and at eight o'clock halted near Kettle Run, having
marched more than thirty miles within twenty-four hours.

We had not long to rest, for at daylight, October 14th,
we were again on the road, making quick time. We
passed our old camp at Bristoe, and the familiar scenes at
Manassas Junction, and crossed Bull Run at Blackman's
Ford. We reached Centreville at three P. M. The booming of cannon in the rear, the huge clouds of smoke, and
the heavy rattle of musketry, told us there was hot work
on the ground we had lately passed over; and as we
formed in line of battle in front of Centreville, the soldiers
said, "Here is the third Bull Run, but this time the run
will be on the other side."

To the Second corps had been assigned the duty of
guarding the rear of the army. About twelve o'clock, as

the rear of that corps was crossing Broad Run, a wide and muddy stream at Bristoe Station, the rebel corps of A. P. Hill suddenly appeared from the cover of the woods in the vicinity, and, running out a battery, opened a severe fire of artillery and musketry upon the column, which was in a degree of confusion, owing to the difficult crossing of the stream.

In a moment order was restored, and the troops so placed as to defy the advance of the enemy.

The rebels, finding that their attack upon the advance was fruitless, now turned their attention to the rear division, which was advancing toward the run. Opening upon the column a fierce cannonade and a storm of bullets, they hoped to throw the division into confusion, but again they were disappointed. After a severe fight, the rebels were forced to flee across the run in great disorder, leaving in the hands of the Second corps five pieces of artillery, two stands of colors, and four hundred and fifty prisoners. Such was the battle of Bristoe Station.

At dark that evening the Sixth corps moved to Chantilly, where we rested for the night. Next morning we took a new and stronger position, where we waited, listening to the roar of cannon where the cavalry was contending with the advance of the enemy, and wondering how soon our own turn would come. Suddenly, at three o'clock, the doubts seemed to be removed. An officer came dashing along the line, with the order to "Strip for the fray! the enemy are coming down upon us!" The men stood to arms, and again we waited for the attack, but none was made: our cavalry had arrested the advance of the enemy. At night the firing died away, and we pitched our tents and slept undisturbed.

In the afternoon of the 16th, the Seventy-seventh being on picket, a horseman suddenly rushed in front of the head-quarter tents, saying that the left of our picket line

36

was attacked. It proved that a body of rebel cavalry had discovered some wagons outside the picket line, and had made a dash upon them. Our boys drove them back in haste, but the line was strengthened in the expectation of a more important demonstration. This, however, was the last we saw of the rebels on our part of the line.

Lee, finding himself too late to occupy the works around Centreville before us, and hopeless of the success of any flank movement, turned his army again towards the Rappahannock.

On the following morning, October 17th, our army started in pursuit, the rain falling upon us in torrents, rendering the mud deep and the marching hard. We halted that night at Gainesville, marched the next day through New Baltimore, and reached Warrenton at night. On our march we had passed the bodies of many of our cavalrymen, who had been killed in the constant skirmishes which had been going on since our advance. Near New Baltimore, where Kilpatrick's brigade had been forced back, the bodies of his men lay scattered along the roadside, nearly all of them stripped of their clothing by the rebels.

The army encamped in the vicinity of Warrenton; the Sixth corps occupying a pleasant ridge just in front of the town. Here we remained a fortnight.

Our first week at Warrenton was anything but agreeable. The cold northwest winds swept through our camps, carrying chilly discomfort everywhere. The men shivered over their log fires; but while the fitful wind drove the smoke and fire into their faces, it froze their backs. At our head-quarters, as we drew closely about our fire, dreading equally the chilly winds and the provoking clouds of smoke, one of the party, perhaps reading for the amusement of the others from a volume of Saxe's poems, a stranger, had one chanced to drop in among us, would have imagined that Saxe must have written most grievous tales of woe, and that our hearts and eyes were all melted by the sad stories. At length, having suffered these disagreeable exposures for a week, the men of the corps fell to work to erect comfortable quarters, and thinking that the present camp might possibly become winter quarters, they made for themselves much more comfortable huts than had served them in their winter's camp at White Oak Church. Generals Neill and Grant reviewed their brigades, and then Generals Howe and Wright reviewed their divisions, and last of all, General Sedgwick had a grand review of the whole corps, which was a very splendid affair.

The weather became again mild and agreeable. Pontoons were arriving and there were many indications that we must soon leave our comfortable quarters. At length, at ten o'clock at night, November 6th, came the order, "Reveille at half-past four; move at daylight." So goodbye, fine quarters and comfortable fire-places, we must be off.

We were in line and commenced moving from camp at daylight, November 7th. We marched rapidly, taking the road to Rappahannock Station. The Sixth and Fifth corps only had taken this road, the remaining corps were, however, either on the move or under orders to move, the Third corps having taken the road to Ely's Ford, and the others following. General Sedgwick was placed in command of the Fifth and Sixth corps, while General Meade accompanied the left wing.

At noon we halted within a mile of the Station, and the corps was immediately thrown into line of battle. The men were allowed to rest on their arms for an hour or two, wondering what was to come.

In front of us was a line of low hills, stretching parallel with our line of battle, and on the slope toward us, and within pistol shot of us, were rebel cavalry pickets, sitting upon their horses and facing us with the coolest impudence; but not a shot was fired at them. We had not rested here long before we heard the booming of cannon on our left, where, three miles down the river, the Third corps had already engaged the enemy. At length the order came to move forward. The Second division, under General Howe, held the right, the Third brigade constituting its front line, the Vermont brigade its second, the Forty-third New York as skirmishers. On the left, was the First division, the Sixth Maine on the skirmish line, the Second and Third brigades in the advance, the New Jersey brigade in the reserve; and in the center the Third division, under General Terry.

In this order the corps pushed forward up the hills, the rebel horsemen whirling and flying before our advance. As our skirmishers gained the summit of the hills, the rebel infantry delivered their fire upon them, but the brave boys of the Forty-third and of the Sixth Maine pushed on, never halting or wavering for a moment, driving the enemy before them until they had pushed the rebel skirmishers close upon their line of battle.

The First division at once became hotly engaged, the rebels disputing the advance with unavailing obstinacy. That noble division bore the brunt of the battle. While the Second and Third divisions behaved with great gallantry, doing all that was required of them, and doing it with that fighting joy so characteristic of the whole corps, the First division, from its position, was called upon to perform unusual feats of valor. As General Sedgwick was that day in command of the right wing of the army, General Wright, of the First division, commanded the corps, and General Russell, the brave, unassuming and beloved commander of the Third brigade, commanded the division.

The skirmishers of our Second division, the Forty-third New York, pushed gallantly forward, their brave Colonel

Baker riding rapidly from one end of the line to the other, his white horse making a prominent mark for the rebels. The line of battle of the whole corps followed closely upon the skirmishers. As we reached the summit of the hills, a grand panorama of the battle opened before us. The whole battle-field could be seen at a single glance; a rare occurrence. On one side were the eminences occupied by our own line of battle, and on the other, a line of hills of equal elevation, covered with swarms of rebels. Between the two ranges of hills, stretched a plain one-fourth of a mile wide and from one to two miles long, which was occupied by the skirmishers of the opposing forces.

The rebels were posted in strong positions behind extensive earthworks, forts, redoubts and rifle pits; and their artillery was posted so as to sweep the plain and the sloping grounds confronting them. Their gray lines of infantry were pouring out from behind the earthworks to meet us at the edge of the plain.

As our line of battle appeared on the crest of the hills, the rebel batteries opened a terrific fire upon us. The air was filled with the shriekings of these fearful projectiles, which exploded with startling frequency above our heads and just behind us; but, fortunately, the rebels aimed high, and many of the shells ploughed the ground in our rear or burst about our hospitals. The First division was pressing toward the rebel works at double quick, under a terrible fire of musketry and artillery, the boys with the red crosses pushing everything before them. They neared the rebel works, and the skirmishers along the whole line threw themselves upon the ground waiting for the line of battle to come up. The rebel skirmishers did the same. Each moment the scene became more exciting. Rebel infantry crowded the opposite side of the plain, the slopes of the hills and the rifle pits. The whole line was ablaze with the fire of musketry, and the roar of battle constantly increased.

At length, toward evening, the rebels having been driven back to the cover of their rifle pits, the Third brigade of the First division, consisting of the Sixth Maine, the Fifth Wisconsin, the Forty-ninth and One Hundred and Nineteenth Pennsylvania, regiments whose fame already stood high in the army, was ordered forward.

First the Maine and Wisconsin regiments rushed forward, the intrepid Russell riding at the very front. At his order to "charge," the two regiments quickened their pace to a run, and, with bayonets fixed, without ever stopping to fire a gun, the gallant fellows ran forward. They seized the fort, but the rebels rallied and drove them out. Again they charged; a hand to hand encounter followed. The boys leaped over into the fort, using their muskets for clubs, and, when the work was too close for that, dropping their guns and pommeling their adversaries with their fists. The general had sent back for the remaining regiments of the brigade, but, in the ten minutes that elapsed before the Pennsylvanians could come up on a run, half the men of the Sixth Maine, and nearly as many of the Wisconsin regiment, had fallen. The whole brigade leaped over the embankments, capturing hundreds of the rebels.

Not less gallant was the charge of the Second brigade, led by the young, ambitious Colonel Upton. His regiments were the One Hundred and Twenty-first New York, his own, the Fifth Maine, and the Ninety-fifth and Ninety-sixth Pennsylvania. The brigade occupied the left of the Sixth corps, joining the Fifth corps. Under cover of the growing darkness, the courageous Upton led the One Hundred and Twenty-first New York and Fifth Maine within a few yards of the rebel rifle pits, when the order to charge was given. Instantly the rifle pits were ablaze, and a destructive volley was poured into the two regiments.

Another moment and the Union boys were leaping into the rifle pits, sweeping everything before them. All this while not a shot had been fired by Upton's men, but, charging with the bayonet, they carried all before them.

The confederates took to their heels, and attempted to flee to the other side of the river, but their pontoon bridge was in possession of our troops, and hundreds of panic-stricken rebels leaped into the rapid stream and attempted to swim across. Some succeeded, but many were drowned in the attempt. Sixteen hundred prisoners, eight pieces of artillery, four battle-flags, and more than two thousand stand of small arms, were the trophies of this splendid victory.

The credit of this brilliant success belongs mainly to the First division; yet the Second and Third divisions, while less actively engaged, performed their part with alacrity and bravery, and the many dead and wounded from these two divisions attested the severity of the fight along their portions of the line. The loss to the corps, in killed and wounded, was about three hundred, among whom were many choice spirits. The commander of the Fifth Wisconsin, Captain Walker, was killed. Captain Ordway succeeded to the command. He leaped upon the parapet, and fell dead inside the rebel fort.

All this time the Third corps was actively engaged at Kelly's Ford, three miles to our left. It had found the rebels strongly posted on the opposite side of the river, well protected by forts and rifle pits. The artillery of the corps was taken to the river side and brought to bear upon the rebel works. At length a storming party was selected and massed on the banks. At the word, the brave fellows plunged into the stream, and rushing across, charged the strong works of the rebels with great fury. The occupants were obliged to flee, but five hundred of them were left as prisoners.

Owing to the depth and force of the stream between the works the Sixth corps had taken, and those still occupied by the rebels on the other side, it was impossible to push our victory further that night. The confederates, finding our troops in possession of their pontoon bridge, had set it on fire at the end still held by them; thus all pursuit was for the time cut off. But on the following morning the rebels had retreated, leaving us to rebuild the bridge and cross at our leisure.

Without further delay we pushed on toward Brandy Station, which we reached toward evening, the cavalry having preceded us.

The whole of Lee's army, except the forces stationed at Rappahannock Station and Kelly's Ford, had been encamped in the vicinity of Brandy Station, and their recently deserted camps, where they had erected comfortable huts and made many other preparations for a winter's stay, showed that their hasty leave was entirely unexpected to them. In many instances officers had forgotten to take their valises and trunks with them, and Union soldiers strutted about in the garb of rebel brigadiers and colonels.

It was said, by the rebel prisoners taken by the cavalry, that while the fights were in progress on the Rappahannock, General Lee was holding a grand review of his army, when suddenly the information reached him that the Yankees were coming. The review was broken off, and there was hurrying of regiments to their respective camps, each regiment, independently of its division or brigade, making hot haste for its own quarters. Baggage was quickly thrown into wagons, and a general stampede toward the Rapidan commenced at once.

CHAPTER XXII.

THE ARMY AT BRANDY STATION.

THE Sixth corps went into camp on the right of the army, two miles from Brandy Station. We occupied land belonging to John Minor Botts. Mr. Botts boasted that he owned six hundred miles of fence when we came upon his possessions. He could not say that when we had been there a week! His fences were burned, and his forests cut down; and it was generally known that our chief quarter-master was paying him immense sums of money for the wood used by our army.

At the end of a week it became pretty evident that our stay at Brandy Station might be of considerable duration, possibly for the winter. Accordingly, the men proceeded once more to build houses for the winter; and never, since we had been in service, had they constructed so comfortable quarters as they now built. All about us were the rebel camps, in which they had vainly hoped to spend the winter; and these furnished timbers already hewn, fine stones ready for use in making chimneys, and hewn saplings ready prepared for bunks. The Sixth corps was encamped in a fine forest, which should have furnished not only great abundance of timber for use about the quarters, but for fuel for the winter; but owing to the wasteful manner in which the wood was at first used in building log fires in the open air, the forest melted away before the men had

37

fairly concluded that there was any necessity for using it economically.

Preparations were hurried forward for another advance. The railroad, which had been destroyed by the rebels at the time of the raid to Centreville, from the Rappahannock to Bristoe Station, was to be rebuilt, and the bridge across the Rappahannock, which we had ourselves destroyed, was to be replaced, before the army could safely undertake another advance. It is one of the mysteries which people who have never been connected with a great army have greatest difficulty in comprehending, that an army advancing into such a country as we were now threatening, must have ample and easy communications with its base of supplies. Could such people for a moment realize the vast amount of material consumed by such an army as ours, the mystery might be solved. To attempt to advance into a desert country without first either providing a supply for many days, or opening ready communications with our base of supplies, would have been suicidal. General Sherman might lead his army through a fertile country, where the ravages of war had not appeared, and, by sweeping across a territory forty miles wide, collect abundant supplies for his men; but our army was now to march into a wilderness where even a regiment could not find subsistence. The newspapers at the north that condemned the delay at Brandy Station, and sneered at the idea that the army needed a base of supplies, simply exhibited their profound ignorance of the first principles of campaigning.

By the 25th the road was completed as far as Brandy Station, the bridge rebuilt, and a large amount of supplies brought up; and the army was ordered to move at an early hour on the 26th.

The hour for moving was assigned each corps, and the order in which it was to march, that no delay or confusion might occur. The Third corps was to start as soon as daylight, and the Sixth was to follow it.

Our Sixth corps was moving at sunrise, the hour designated, toward Brandy Station. Presently the head of the column halted in the midst of the camps of the Third corps, which were yet undisturbed. According to the order for marching, the Third corps was to precede the Sixth, and should have been out of camp before we arrived, but as yet not a tent was struck nor a wagon loaded, and most of the men were asleep in their quarters. The Sixth corps was obliged to halt and stand in the mud for hours, waiting for the delinquent corps to get out of the way. Here was the first blunder of the new campaign.

At length at eleven o'clock we moved again, taking the road to the Rapidan. Our march was slow and tedious, and instead of reaching the river at noon as was expected, and as General Meade's orders contemplated, the head of the Third corps only reached the river at Jacobs' Ford long after dark, and here again a delay was occasioned by a mistake of the engineers, who had not brought a sufficient number of boats to this point to complete the pontoon bridge; a part of the bridge had therefore to be extemporized out of poles.

The road for several miles was merely a narrow passage cut through the forest; a dense growth of stunted pines and tangled bushes, filling up the space between the trees of larger growth. Our corps moved along very slowly, halting for a moment, then advancing one or two rods, then standing still again for perhaps several minutes, and again moving forward for a few steps. This became very tedious. The men were faint and weary, and withal discouraged. They were neither advancing nor resting.

From one end of the column of the Sixth corps to the other, through the miles of forest the shout, coffee! coffee! passed from one regiment to another, until there could be heard nothing but the vociferous demand for coffee. At eleven o'clock at night the order "ten minutes rest for coffee," passed down the line and was received with shouts of approval. Instantly the roadside was illuminated with thousands of little fires, over which the soldiers were cooking their favorite beverage.

We crossed the Rapidan at Jacobs' Ford at midnight, leaving Upton's brigade on the north side as rear-guard, and in another hour the men had thrown themselves upon the ground without waiting to erect shelter tents, and were sleeping soundly notwithstanding the severity of the cold. The Fifth and First corps had crossed at Culpepper Ford and the Second corps at Germania Ford about noon, and were in the positions assigned them.

The position assigned to the Third and Sixth corps was not reached. These corps were ordered to proceed to Robertson's Tavern, a point some seven miles beyond the ford, but the night was far advanced, the men exhausted and the country little known, so these two corps did not seize this very important point as directed. Of course the responsibility for this delay was not with the Sixth corps or its commander, who was directed to follow the Third.

Next morning the Third corps commenced the advance, and we of the Sixth were drawn out in line of march to follow; but it became evident that the advance was not unobstructed. Sharp picket firing and the occasional booming of cannon revealed to us the fact that that corps had fallen in with the enemy. Thus the day passed; the Sixth corps resting quietly, while the Third was skirmishing with the enemy in front, until about three o'clock, when the firing increased and there was evidently a severe engagement in front.

The First and Second divisions of the Sixth corps were now hurried along the narrow and winding path to the support of the Third corps—our Third division being left near the river to cover the bridges and trains. That corps was now fiercely engaged. The sulphurous smoke filled the woods, and the roar of musketry became so general, and the forest echoed and reëchoed the sound, so that it lost the rattling usually heard, and became a smooth, uniform roll. Our corps at once took its position in line of battle, so as to support the Third corps and protect the interval between the Third and Second corps, with Ellmaker's brigade on the right, and Neill's and Upton's on the left, while the Vermonters and Torbert's Jersey brigade were held in reserve; but the corps was not called into action. The dense growth of young timber completely obscured all view of the operations at a little distance, and, indeed, rebel scouting parties were able to hang close upon our flanks, and even penetrate our lines, protected from view and from pursuit by the tangled forest.

On our right, the Second corps also encountered a force of the enemy, and became engaged in the vicinity of Robertson's Tavern. They succeeded in driving the rebel force, which was small, back to the cover of the wilderness. Gregg, also, with his cavalry, became engaged, but drove the rebels back.

It now appeared that the fight of the Third corps was brought on by a blunder. General French, in attempting to lead his corps to Robertson's Tavern, had mistaken the road, and, by bearing too far to the west, had encountered Ewell's corps, which was hastening to intercept our progress. The rebels made repeated charges upon the corps, but were each time repulsed, and under cover of the night they fell back, leaving their dead on the ground. The loss to the Third corps was between three and four hundred; that of the rebels, judging from the dead left upon the ground, must have been greater.

While the fight was in progress, General Sedgwick and

his staff dismounted and were reclining about a large tree, when the attention of all was directed to two soldiers who were approaching, bearing between them a stretcher on which lay a wounded man. As the men approached within a few rods of the place where the general and his staff were, a solid cannon shot came shrieking along, striking both of the stretcher bearers. Both fell to the ground — the one behind fatally wounded, the other dead. But the man upon the stretcher leaped up and ran away as fast as his legs could carry him, never stopping to look behind at his unfortunate companions. Shocking as was the occurrence, neither the general nor the members of his staff could suppress a laugh at the speedy restoration of the man who was being borne disabled from the field.

The two corps moved during the night to Robertson's Tavern, the destination which they should have reached twenty-four hours before.

The unexpected encounter with the rebels in the Wilderness had hindered the two corps thus long, and as might have been expected the time was not left unimproved by General Lee. On moving in the morning on the road to Orange Court House, Lee's whole army was found strongly posted along the banks of a muddy stream called Mine Run. Our army was brought into position on the north side of the stream, and arrangements commenced for a general assault. Sharp picket firing and the occasional roar of artillery, warned us that we were on the eve of a great battle. A cold storm of rain rendered the situation cheerless and uncomfortable, but the excitement of getting into position, regiments and brigades marching from one part of the line to another, now approaching where the bullets of the rebel skirmishers whistled about them, and then withdrawing a little to the rear, kept up the spirits of the men notwithstanding the tedious storm.

The greater part of the lines of both armies were in the

midst of forests. Between the two lines and in the midst
of a deep valley, was the little stream Mine Run, bordered
on each side by marshes in which were luxuriant growths
of reed grasses. The marshes and slopes on either side
were thickly set with low pines and scrub oaks, offering
concealment to both parties.

Darkness closed over the two armies, neither of which
was yet prepared for battle. The night was spent by both
parties in throwing up earthworks, and the morning
revealed several strong lines of rifle pits on the rebel side
of the stream, one commanding another so that in case
they should be driven from one the next would afford an
equally strong or even stronger position.

Thus the two armies remained during Sunday. General
Meade still waiting to perfect his arrangements.

During the day the disposition of the line was completed. General Warren with his Second corps occupied
the extreme left of the line. His position fronted a very
strong position of the enemy, where the hills rose abruptly
to the rear. This being considered by far the strongest
portion of the enemy's line. Warren was supported by
the Fifth corps, two divisions of the Third corps, and the
Third division of the Sixth corps, under General Terry.
In the center was the First and Fifth corps, and, forming
the right, were the two remaining divisions of the Sixth
corps and what was left of the Third. Our Second division
constituted the extreme right of the line; the Third brigade
the right of the division; and the Seventy-seventh New
York the right of the brigade.

At two, A. M., the Sixth corps and the division of the
Third, covered by the woods, moved about two miles to a
position on the left flank of the enemy. The dense thicket
and a gentle eminence concealed the corps from the view
of the rebels, who were but a few yards distant; and in
order to insure secrecy, orders were issued that the men

should avoid all noise, as far as possible, and refrain from lighting fires.

It was arranged that the grand attack should be made on Monday; and early in the evening the commanders of corps were summoned to General Meade's head-quarters, where the plan of the battle was laid before them.

At a given signal, very early in the morning, General Warren with his strong force was to press forward on the right of the rebel line. At the same time forces in the center were to open a fierce fire upon the enemy, while the Sixth corps, at the same moment, was to rush from its concealed position and turn the left flank of Lee's army.

The commanders of the divisions of the Sixth corps summoned the commanders of brigades and regiments, and communicated to them also the plan of the battle, and assigned to each his part.

The night was bitter cold, and the men of our corps were without fires. It was vain to attempt to sleep, and the men spent the night in leaping and running in efforts to keep warm.

No one doubted that the morning was to bring on one of the most terrific struggles in the history of warfare. No man knew what was to be his own fate, but each seemed braced for the conflict. It was a glorious moonlight, and the stars looked down in beauty from the cold skies upon the strange scene. Thus all waited for the day.

The morning dawned; and soon after daylight the signal gun for the grand attack was heard near the center of the line, and an active cannonade commenced there.

In a short time the order came for the commencement of the movement on the right. The men were ordered to fall in; they were faced to the right, to move a little farther in that direction before making the direct assault; they stood, with their muskets on their shoulders, their hearts beating violently in anticipation of the onset to be made in another moment, when an aid rode hastily to General Howe with directions to suspend the movement!

Warren, on advancing his line of skirmishers, and viewing the strong works thrown up by the enemy during the night, had sent word that he could not carry the position before him. And General Meade had ordered the whole movement to be discontinued for the time.

Never before, in the history of our army, had such elaborate preparations been made for an attack. Every commander and every man knew exactly the part he was expected to take in the great encounter, and each had prepared himself for it. At the hospitals everything was in a state of perfect readiness. Hospital tents were all up, beds for the wounded prepared, operating tables were in readiness, basins and pails stood filled with water, lint and dressings were laid out upon the tables, and surgical instruments spread out ready for the grasp of the surgeon.

All day the men remained suffering with cold, their hunger but partially satisfied with hard bread without coffee. It was a day of discomfort and suffering long to be remembered. It chanced that the hard bread issued to our division was old and very wormy. It was, in some cases, difficult for a man to know whether his diet was to be considered principally animal or vegetable. Our General, Neill, sat with his staff munching some of these crackers of doubtful character, when he was handed one unusually animated. The general broke the cracker, examined it for a moment, and, handing it back to the servant, said, " Jim, give us one that hasn't so many worms in it." Many of the men who were on the picket line that day and the night before, were found, when the relief came arounds, dead at their posts, frozen.

During the night of December 1st and 2d, the army withdrew from Mine Run. The pickets were directed to build fires and keep up a show of force. Our Seventy-

38

seventh being that night on the picket line, formed the rear of the rear-guard of the army on its retreat. It was three o'clock in the morning of December 2d when the picket line was silently withdrawn. After a rapid march, it crossed the pontoon bridge at Germania Ford at ten o'clock. Scarcely had the troops crossed the bridge, when the cavalry of the enemy made its appearance on the south side of the river. The Seventy-seventh New York, the Third Vermont and a battery of artillery were directed to remain and guard the ford, while the remainder of the army continued the march to the old camps. Next morning the two regiments and the battery started for Brandy Station, and that night slept in their old quarters.

It was now evident that we were in permanent winter quarters. It is not our purpose to discuss the merits of this fruitless campaign, but it may not be out of place to recall some of the facts relating to it. The orders for marching on the 26th, were issued to all the corps commanders on the evening previous, indicating the time for leaving camp. The Sixth corps was to follow the Third, yet when the Sixth corps reached the camp of that corps, there were no signs of moving. Several hours were thus lost on the start. General French declared that the order to move did not reach him on the previous evening, yet he knew that the movement was expected that day. As the result of this and other delays, two corps did not reach the position assigned them on the 26th.

When, on the morning of the 27th, General French moved his corps again, he took the wrong road, and thus brought on a premature engagement, which caused another delay of twenty-four hours. By this time Lee had ample opportunity to concentrate his whole army in a strong position on Mine Run. Had General Meade's orders been promptly obeyed, Lee could have offered no opposition to us at that point, and must have accepted battle much nearer Richmond.

Our campaigns for 1863 were now finished ; the last two of these had certainly been remarkable episodes in the fortunes of our stout-hearted army. In October, the rebel army had followed us from the Rapidan to the defenses of Washington, and in turn we had pursued the confederates back to the Rapidan, all without a battle of any magnitude. Now, in November, our whole army had crossed the river and confronted the rebel army face to face for days, and again we were back in our old camps without an engagement, except the fight of the Third corps, and some skirmishing on the part of others.

During the month of December, general orders were issued from the war department offering to soldiers of the army, who had already served two years, and who had still a year or less to serve, large bounties, a release from the term of their former enlistment and thirty-five days' furlough, as inducements for them to reënlist for three years from that time. Much excitement was created by the order throughout the army, and thousands accepted it, nearly all claiming that they cared little for the large bounties, but that the thirty-five days' furlough was the great inducement.

The only military movement of the winter was Kilpatrick's great raid upon Richmond, in which the lamented Dahlgren lost his life.

Simultaneous with this great raid, General Custer, with a division of cavalry, made a movement on Charlottesville, and the Sixth corps was ordered to move in that direction as support to the cavalry. On Saturday, February 27th, the corps, leaving its camp and sick in charge of a small guard, marched through Culpepper and proceeded to James City, a Virginia city of two or three houses, where the bivouac for the night was made. Next morning the corps marched slowly to Robertson's River, within three miles of Madison Court House, the New Jersey brigade alone crossing the river and proceeding as far as the latter village. Here the corps lay all the following day, and as the weather was pleasant, the men passed the time in sports and games, but at evening a cold storm of rain set in, continuing all night and the next day, to the great discomfort of all. Custer's cavalry returned at evening of the 1st of March, looking in a sorry plight from their long ride in the mud. Reveille sounded at five o'clock on the morning of March 2d, and at seven the corps turned toward the old camp, at which it arrived, after a severe march through the mud, at sunset the same day.

There were, connected with our camp near Brandy Station, many pleasant remembrances; and notwithstanding a few severe experiences, this was the most cheerful winter we had passed in camp. One agreeable feature of this encampment was the great number of ladies, wives of officers, who spent the winter with their husbands. On every fine day great numbers of ladies might be seen riding about the camps and over the desolate fields, and their presence added greatly to the brilliancy of the frequent reviews.

Great taste was displayed by many officers in fitting up their tents and quarters for the reception of their wives. The tents were usually inclosed by high walls of evergreens, woven with much skill, and fine arches and exquisite designs beautified the entrances to these happy retreats. The Christian Commission, among other good things which it did for the soldiers, and, indeed, this was among the best, made arrangements by which it loaned to nearly every brigade in the army, a large canvas, to be used as a roof for a brigade chapel. These chapels were built of logs and covered with the canvas, and were in many cases large enough to hold three hundred people. Here religious services were held, not only on Sunday, but also on week day evenings. A deep religious interest prevailed in many of the brigades, and great numbers of soldiers professed to have met with a change of heart. In our Third brigade, this religious interest was unusually great; a religious organization was formed within the Seventy-seventh, and Chaplain Fox baptized eleven members of the regiment in Hazel river. A course of literary lectures was also delivered in the chapel of our Third brigade, and Washington's birthday was celebrated in it with appropriate ceremonies and addresses. The chapel tent was also a reading room, where, owing to the energy of Chaplain Fox, all the principal papers, secular and religious, literary, military, pictorial, agricultural and scientific, were furnished; and these were a great source both of pleasure and profit to the men.

Our corps was reviewed by General Grant; by the Russian admiral and suite, who for the amusement of the soldiers, performed some most ludicrous feats in horsemanship; and by a body of English officers. Never had such general good health prevailed among our camps, and never were the men so well contented or in so good spirits.

CHURCH CALL.

CHAPTER XXIII.

THE WILDERNESS CAMPAIGN.

Preparing to leave camp—General Grant in command—The last advance across the Rapidan—The battle-ground—Battle of the Wilderness—Noble fight of Getty's division—Hancock's fight on the left—Rickett's division driven back—The ground retaken—The wounded—Duties of the surgeons—The noble dead.

MANY pleasant recollections cluster around the old camp at Brandy Station, which will never be effaced from the memory of the soldiers of the Army of the Potomac.

But at length preparations were commenced for opening the spring campaign, and one of the first orders, looking toward the breaking up of our camps, was one directing that our lady friends should take their departure, then another to send all superfluous camp equipage to the rear.

Our army had been reorganized, its five corps being consolidated into three. The three divisions of the First corps were transferred to the Fifth, retaining their corps badges. Two divisions of the Third were assigned to the Second, preserving their badges, while the Third division, Third corps, was transferred permanently to the Sixth corps, and became the Third division of that corps. Our old Third division was broken up, the brigades of Wheaton and Eustis being transferred to the Second division, and Shaler's brigade to the First. Our corps, as reorganized, consisted of three divisions, comprising eleven brigades.*

---

* The corps, as reorganized, was commanded as follows:
Major-General John Sedgwick commanding the corps.
First division, Brigadier-General H. G. Wright, commanding. First brigade, Colonel W. H. Penrose; Second brigade, Colonel E. Upton; Third brigade, Brigadier-General D. A. Russell; Fourth brigade, Brigadier-General A. Shaler.
Second division, Brigadier-general George W. Getty, commanding. First brigade, Brigadier-General Frank Wheaton; Second brigade, Colonel L. A. Grant; Third

During the winter, congress, recognizing the great ability of General Grant, had conferred upon that officer the rank of Lieutenant-General, giving him, under the President, command of all the armies of the United States. General Grant at once proceeded to adopt a plan for harmonious movements of all the armies. General Sherman, in the west, was directed to push vigorously southward, penetrating the enemy's country as far as possible, and prevent reinforcements being sent to Lee's army in the east. General Butler, on the Peninsula, was to advance on Richmond, taking Petersburgh, and, if possible, Richmond itself, while the Army of the Potomac was to attack Lee's army in the front, and force it back upon Richmond or destroy it.

These coöperative movements having been all arranged, each commander of an army or department informed not only of the part which he was expected to perform himself, but what all were expected to do, the Army of the Potomac was ready to move. General Grant had established his head-quarters with that army.

At length the order for moving came. On the morning of the 4th of May, reveille was sounded at half-past two o'clock, and at half-past four the Sixth corps moved, taking the road to Germania Ford.

It was a lovely day, and all nature seemed rejoicing at the advent of spring. Flowers strewed the wayside, and the warble of the blue bird, and the lively song of the sparrow, were heard in the groves and hedges.

The distance from our camps to Germania Ford was sixteen miles. This distance we marched rapidly, and long before sunset we had crossed the ford on pontoon

brigade, Brigadier-General Thomas H. Neill; Fourth brigade, Brigadier-General L. A. Eustis.

Third division, Brigadier-General James B. Ricketts, commanding. First brigade, Brigadier-General W. H. Morris; Second brigade, Brigadier-General Truman Seymour; Third brigade, Colonel Keiffer.

bridges and marched to a point three miles south of the river, where we bivouacked for the night.

The Second corps, at an earlier hour, had crossed at Ely's Ford, and had reached a position near the old Chancellorsville battle-field, and the Fifth corps had led the way across Germania Ford.

The infantry had been preceded by the cavalry divisions of Gregg and Wilson, under Sheridan. They had fallen in with a small picket force which, after exchanging a few shots, had beat a hasty retreat.

Before night the army and the greater part of our trains had effected a crossing without opposition; and, doubtless, much to the surprise and chagrin of General Lee, we were holding strong positions, from which it would hardly be possible to force us.

Except slight skirmishes in front of Hancock's Second corps, there was no fighting on the fourth of May. At seven o'clock on the morning of the fifth, the Sixth corps moved southward about two miles on the Wilderness plank road. Here the corps rested until eleven o'clock, while artillery and cavalry passed along the road in a continuous column. At eleven o'clock the corps faced to the front, and advanced into the woods which skirted the road.

The Sixth corps now occupied the extreme right of the line, General Warren's Fifth corps the center, and Hancock's Second corps was on the left, near Chancellorsville. Between Warren and Hancock was an unoccupied space — a point of vital importance to our line. Thither General Getty, with the First, Second and Fourth brigades of our Second division, was sent to hold the ground till Hancock, who was ordered to come up, should arrive. Our Third brigade being all that was left of the Second division, it was assigned to the First division. General Meade's headquarters were just in rear of the Fifth corps. The wood through which our line was now moving was a thick growth of oak and walnut, densely filled with a smaller growth of pines and other brushwood; and in many places so thickly was this undergrowth interwoven among the large trees, that one could not see five yards in front of the line. Yet, as we pushed on, with as good a line as possible, the thick tangle in a measure disappeared, and the woods were more open. Still, in the most favorable places, the thicket was so close as to make it impossible to manage artillery or cavalry, and, indeed, infantry found great difficulty in advancing, and at length we were again in the midst of the thick undergrowth.

Warren's corps, on our left, was already fighting, and forcing the enemy to retire from his front, when our own corps struck the rebel skirmishers, who steadily fell back, disputing the ground. As our line advanced, it would suddenly come upon a line of gray-coated rebels, lying upon the ground, covered with dried leaves, and concealed by the chapparal, when the rebels would rise, deliver a murderous fire, and retire.

We thus advanced through this interminable forest more than a mile and a half, driving the rebel skirmishers before us, when we came upon their line of battle, which refused to retire.

Neill's brigade and the New Jersey brigade were in the first line of battle, at the foot of a slope, and in the rear of these two brigades were Russell's, Upton's and Shaler's. On the left of the First division were Seymour's and Keiffer's brigades, General Morris with his brigade remaining on the right.

The enemy now charged upon our lines, making a desperate effort to turn our right flank, but without avail. Again and again the rebels in columns rushed with the greatest fury upon the two brigades in front, without being able to move them from their position. At half-past three o'clock our sufferings had been so great that General Sedgwick

39

sent a messenger to General Burnside, who had now crossed his corps at Germania Ford, with a request that he would send a division to our assistance.

The assistance was promised, but an order from General Grant made other disposition of the division, and what remained of the noble old Sixth corps was left to hold its position alone. At four, or a little later, the rebels retired, leaving many of their dead upon the ground, whom they were unable to remove. In these encounters the Seventh Maine and Sixty-first Pennsylvania regiments of Neill's brigade, who were on the right flank, received the heaviest onsets, and suffered most severely. At one time the Maine regiment found itself flanked by a brigade of rebels. Changing front the gallant regiment charged to the rear and scattered its opponents in confusion. The opposing lines were upon the two slopes of a ravine, through which ran a strip of level marshy ground, densely wooded like the rest of the wilderness. The confederates now commenced to strengthen the position on their side of the ravine, felling timber and covering it with earth. The woods resounded with the strokes of their axes, as the busy workmen plied their labor within three hundred yards, and in some places less than one hundred yards of our line, yet so dense was the thicket that they were entirely concealed from our view.

Meanwhile the battle had raged furiously along the whole line. The rattle of musketry would swell into a full continuous roar as the simultaneous discharge of ten thousand guns mingled in one grand concert, and then after a few minutes, become more interrupted, resembling the crash of some huge king of the forest when felled by the stroke of the woodman's axe. Then would be heard the wild yells which always told of a rebel charge, and again the volleys would become more terrible and the broken, crashing tones would swell into one continuous roll of sound, which presently would be interrupted by the vigorous manly cheers of the northern soldiers, so different from the shrill yell of the rebels, and which indicated a repulse of their enemies. Now and then the monotony of the muskets was broken by a few discharges of artillery, which seemed to come in as a double bass in this concert of death, but so impenetrable was the forest that little use was made of artillery, and the work of destruction was carried on with the rifles.

Warren's corps, first engaged, had nobly withstood the fierce assaults upon the center of the line, and had even advanced considerably. Hancock's command was also hotly engaged. In the commencement of the battle, three brigades of the Second division, the First, Second and Fourth, with our commander, General Getty, were taken from the Sixth corps and sent to the right of Warren's corps, to seize and hold the intersection of the Brock road and the Orange county turnpike, a point of vital importance, and which, as Hancock's corps was still far to the left near Chancellorsville, was entirely exposed. Toward this point Hill was hastening his rebel corps down the turnpike, with the design of interposing between Hancock and the main army. No sooner had the division reached the crossing of the two roads than the First brigade, General Wheaton's, became hotly engaged with Hill's corps, which was coming down the road driving some of our cavalry before it. The Vermont brigade quickly formed on the left of the plank road, and the Fourth brigade on the right of the First. The engagement became general at once, and each brigade was suffering heavy losses. The men hugged the ground closely, firing as rapidly as possible.

Hancock's corps was advancing from the left, but thus far the division was holding the ground alone. An attack by the three brigades was ordered, and the line was considerably advanced. Again the men hugged the ground, the rebels doing the same.

Thus, holding the ground against vastly superior numbers, the division sustained the weight of the rebel attacks until long after noon, when some of Hancock's regiments came to its support. With the heroic valor for which the division was so well known throughout the army, it withstood the force of the rebels until its lines were terribly thinned. The First brigade had held the ground with desperate valor, and our friends, the Vermonters, fought with that gallantry which always characterized the sons of the Green Mountain State. Their noblest men were falling thickly, yet they held the road.

As Hancock joined his corps on the left of Getty's division, he ordered a charge along the whole line, and again the carnage became fearful. For two hours the struggle continued, and when the sounds of battle became less, and as darkness finally came over the wilderness, it brought a season of respite to the hard fought divisions.

A thousand brave men of the Vermont brigade, and nearly as many of Wheaton's brigade, with hundreds from the Fourth brigade, had fallen upon that bloody field.

In the evening the contest was renewed, especially along the line of the Sixth corps, and the dark woods were lighted with the flame from the mouths of tens of thousands of muskets.

Charges and counter-charges followed each other in quick succession, and the rebel yell and northern cheer were heard alternately, but no decided advantage was gained by either party. At two o'clock at night the battle died away, but there was no rest for the weary soldiers after the fatiguing duties of the day. Each man sat with musket in hand during the wearisome hours of the night, prepared for an onset of the enemy. Skirmishing was kept up during the entire night, and at times the musketry would break out in full volleys, which rolled along the opposing lines until they seemed vast sheets of flame.

The position of the two armies on the morning of the 6th was substantially that of the day before; the Sixth corps on the right, its rear on Wilderness Run near the old Wilderness Tavern, the Fifth corps next on its left, and the Second corps with three brigades of the Second division Sixth corps, on the left; the line extending about five miles. Besides these corps, General Burnside was bringing his troops into the line.

Between the two armies lay hundreds of dead and dying men whom neither army could remove, and over whose bodies the fight must be renewed.

The battle was opened at daylight by a fierce charge of the enemy on the Sixth corps, and soon it raged along the whole line. The volleys of musketry echoed and reëchoed through the forests like peals of thunder, and the battle surged to and fro, now one party charging, and now the other, the interval between the two armies being fought over in many places as many as five times, leaving the ground covered with dead and wounded. Those of the wounded able to crawl, reached one or the other line, but the groans of others, who could not move, lent an additional horror to the terrible scene whenever there was a lull in the battle. At ten o'clock the roar of battle ceased, and from that time until five P. M., it was comparatively quiet in front of the Sixth corps, but from the left where Hancock's corps and Getty's braves were nobly battling, the war of musketry was incessant. There, Hancock had formed his troops in several lines of battle, and advanced them upon the plank road. Getty's troops, their ranks having been so terribly shattered the day before, were allowed to form in the rear. The attack was commenced, but presently the enemy came down in terrible fury upon Hancock's lines. One after another was swept away, leaving no Union troops in front of Getty. Now the exulting rebels came with stunning force against the Sixth corps men. They had prepared breastworks of logs and decayed wood, and against these light defenses the' rebels charged, but only to meet with a deadly repulse. Again and again the charge was renewed, and as often the brave men who had seen nearly three thousand of their comrades fall on the day before, sent the confederates back from the road. At length, the divisions on the right and left of Getty having fallen back to the Brock road, the division was forced to fall back to the road also, but only after exhibiting a steadiness and valor rarely equaled by any troops.

The road was held, in spite of every effort of the enemy to take it; but the noble soldier and patriotic gentleman, General Wadsworth, lost his life while striving to rally his division to hold the ground against the confederates.

Although the storm of battle had abated in our front, the rebels had stationed sharpshooters in the trees and other advantageous positions, who kept up an incessant and annoying fire, and now and then a shell from a rebel battery would drop into our ranks. By these, the corps lost many men.

Until the evening of the 6th, our Third brigade of the Second division, and the New Jersey brigade of the First division of the Sixth corps, had occupied the right of the line of battle along the base of our slope of the ravine. Other portions of the First division, and the Third division, occupying a position in our rear, on the summit of the slope, had been engaged during the day in throwing up earthworks. At 5 p. m., the two advance brigades received orders to fall back to the cover of these breastworks.

For thirty hours the Sixth corps, stripped of three brigades of its veteran troops, weary from fighting and fasting, had been patiently waiting for the relief promised it long ago, and steadily holding its ground until half of the advance brigades and almost half of the corps was destroyed.

Thirty hours before, General Sedgwick had sent word that the rebels were trying to turn our flank, and begged that support might be sent; but no support had come. These breastworks had been prepared to give the exhausted corps a little protection, that they might, by falling back to their cover, occupy a stronger and less exposed position.

Soon after five o'clock, the brigades commenced falling back to these works. The rebels discovered the movement, and thought it was a retreat. They were evidently already prepared for a desperate assault upon our flank; and now that there seemed a retreat, there was no longer any hesitation. Cheer after cheer arose from the rebel ranks, and, in fifteen minutes after, their yells were mingled with terrific volleys of musketry, as they poured in overwhelming numbers upon our flanks.

A brief description of the position will explain the nature of the movement, which lost to the Sixth corps the position it had held for a day and a half.

When the brigades which had occupied the base of the slope fell back to the breastworks, the line of battle was arranged thus: on the extreme right was the Third division — a division but a few days before joined to the corps — a division composed mostly of new troops who had never before faced an enemy, and none of them had ever had any connection with the already historic fame of that glorious corps. Next on the left was the First division, and joining this division on the left was our own Third brigade of the Second division.

The assault of the rebels fell upon the green troops of the Third division, who, seized with consternation, fled in confusion without attempting resistance. General Seymour whose gallant conduct up to this time had won for him the admiration of all, made desperate attempts to rally his panic-stricken brigade and refused to go to the rear with them. While thus striving vainly to restore order to his shattered command, rushing to the front and attempting by his own manner to inspire courage in his men, he was surrounded by the enemy and captured. He had but just returned from the rebel prisons where he had been since the unfortunate battle of Olustee.

The hasty flight of the Third division opened the flank and rear of the First division to the charge of the rebels, who now rushed on with redoubled fury and with demoniac yells, carrying everything before them. The First division fell back, but not in the disorder and confusion of the other. General Shaler, with a large part of his brigade, which held that part of the line joining the Third division, was captured while vainly striving to resist the onset of the rebel forces.

The regiments of our Third brigade were forced from the rifle pits, leaving the Seventy-seventh regiment and a part of the Forty-third alone contending the ground, exposed to a galling fire on front, flank and rear. The gallant regiments remained in the breastworks, pouring their fire into the enemy's ranks until ordered to withdraw, to save themselves from capture.

The right wing, if not the whole army, was now in danger. It was at such times that the great spirit of the noble Sedgwick rose to the control of events. It seemed to require adversity to bring out all the grand qualities of his nature. We had witnessed his imperturbable bravery and determination on the retreat to Banks' Ford, his unsurpassed heroism at Antietam, when he kept the field after he was thrice wounded, was familiar to the nation, and now we were to see another manifestation of his indomitable courage.

Rushing here and there, regardless of personal safety,

he faced the disordered mass of fugitives of the Third division, and with threats and entreaties prevailed upon them to halt; then turning to the veterans of the First division, he shouted to them to remember the honor of the old Sixth corps. That was an irresistible appeal, and the ranks of the First division and of our Third brigade were formed along the turnpike, which was at right angles to our former position. The corps now charged upon the exultant foe, and forced them back until our breastworks were recaptured; but our flank was too much exposed, and again the enemy charged upon our front and flank, forcing the corps to wheel back to the turnpike, where it had first rallied.

General Sedgwick now ordered another charge, and bravely the men rushed forward, ready to obey any order from the revered lips of " *Uncle John.*" The enemy was again forced back, and again the corps occupied the breastworks. It was now dark, but the roar of musketry mingled with the deep toned artillery shook the ground, and the dense forest was lighted by the scores of thousands of flashing rifles which sent death to unseen foes.

The corps had not recovered its line of works without sacrifice, for the ground in our rear was covered with our fallen comrades, while many more had been captured by the enemy. But we were now able to hold the ground. The temporary disorder had arisen, and had been mostly confined to the new troops, and even these, when rallied from their momentary confusion, had fought with heroic valor. Although, for a time, forced back by the surprise of the rebel onset, the old troops of the corps had shown no want of courage. *The Sixth corps proper had not lost its pristine glory.* Something of a panic had been created among the teamsters in the rear, and before dark the trains were hurrying toward Chancellorsville.

40

Leaving the excitement of the battle, let us now turn where the results of this carnage are seen in their sober reality. While we stand in line of battle we see little of the frightful havoc of war. The wounded drop about us, but, except those left on disputed ground and unable to crawl away, they are carried instantly to the rear. The groans and cries of the wounded and dying, of which we so often read as filling up the grand discord of sounds on the battle-field, are things scarcely known in actual war. Rarely, as in the present battles, wounded men, unable to get away, are left between the lines in such numbers that, when the musketry dies away, their groans become heart-rending. But this is not usual.

But at the field hospitals, the work of destruction is seen in all its horrors. There, wounded men by thousands are brought together, filling the tents and stretched upon every available spot of ground for many rods around. Surgeons, with never tiring energy, are ministering to their wants, giving them food, dressing their wounds or standing at the operating table removing the shattered fragments of limbs. Men wounded in every conceivable way, men with mutilated bodies, with shattered limbs and broken heads, men enduring their injuries with heroic patience, and men giving way to violent grief, men stoically indifferent, and men bravely rejoicing that it is *only a leg*. To all these the surgeons are to give such relief as lies in their power, a task the very thoughts of which would overcome physicians at home, but upon which the army surgeon enters with as much coolness and confidence as though he could do it all at once. He has learned to do what he can. Contenting himself with working day and night without respite, and often without food, until, by unremitting but quiet toil, the wants of all are relieved. No class of men in the army perform so great labors with so little credit as the surgeons.

Lest the author should be accused of undue partiality for his own staff, he will quote the words of an unprejudiced witness, who, in speaking of the labor, the anxiety and the responsibility imposed upon the surgeons after a great battle, says:

"The devotion, the solicitude, the unceasing efforts to remedy the defects of the situation, the untiring attentions to the wounded, upon their part, were so marked as to be apparent to all who visited the hospitals. It must be remembered that these same officers had endured the privations and fatigues of the long forced marches with the rest of the army; they had shared its dangers, for one medical officer from each regiment follows it into battle, and is liable to the accidents of war, as has been repeatedly and fatally the case; that its field hospitals are often, from the changes of the line of battle, brought under fire of the enemy, and that while in this situation these surgeons are called upon to exercise the calmest judgment, to perform the most critical and serious operations, and this quickly and continuously. The battle ceasing, their labors continue. While other officers are sleeping, renewing their strength for further efforts, the medical are still toiling. They have to improvise hospitals from the rudest materials, are obliged to "make bricks without straw," to surmount seeming impossibilities. The work is unending both by day and night, the anxiety is constant, and the strain upon both the physical and mental faculties unceasing. Thus, after this battle, operators had to be held up while performing the operations, and fainted from exhaustion the operation finished. One completed his labors to be seized with partial paralysis, the penalty of his over exertion.

" While his duties are as arduous, his exposure as great, and the mortality from disease and injury as large as among other staff officers of similar rank, the surgeon has no prospect of promotion, of a brevet or an honorable mention, to stimulate him. His duties are performed quietly, unostentatiously. He does his duty for his country's sake, for the sake of humanity."*

The labors of the medical officers had never been so great as at these battles. Thousands of wounded men were stretched in and about the several field hospitals, and long trains of ambulances, loaded with more bleeding victims, were constantly bringing in new subjects of care.

The hospitals of the Sixth corps were located, that of the First division about a large house near the turnpike, in rear of the position of the division; that of the Third division was near by, and the hospital of our Second division was placed on the banks of Wilderness Run, near the old gold mine, and within a few rods of General Meade's head-quarters. The hospitals of the Fifth corps were also within a short distance, on the left.

At the hospital of our Second division, the scene was one of activity and sadness. Never had so many of our choice spirits been brought to the rear, and never had the division been bereft of so many of its brightest ornaments by death.

All the hospital tents belonging to the division were filled to overflowing with the unfortunate victims of the battle. There, all the space between the different rows of tents, and for many yards in front and rear, was covered with others, for whom there was no room under the canvas, and, finally, long rows of them were laid upon the ground at a little distance from the hospitals as close as they could lie, covering many rods of ground.

In the operating tents, the surgeons assigned to the duty of performing operations plied their work without rest from the time the battle commenced until its close, day

---

* J. H. Douglass, Assistant Secretary Sanitary Commission.

and night, while dressers, and those whose duty it was to supply the wounded with food, were untiring in their zeal.

At midnight of the 6th, the operators were directed to cease their work. Ambulances and army wagons in great numbers were loaded with the wounded, and the whole train, accompanied by the surgeons, moved toward Chancellorsville, taking the turnpike along the rear of the army. But, with all the ambulances and army wagons at command, hundreds of these unfortunate heroes were left behind; and as it was known that our line of battle was to fall back within a few hours, preparations were made for their care when they should fall into the hands of the enemy. Four assistant surgeons from each division, a number of hospital tents, a supply of hard bread and beef, with dressings and instruments, were left behind; and with sad hearts, their companions bade them farewell. Like preparations were made by the other corps, for those of the wounded who must be left to their fate. The long train bearing the wounded reached the left of the old battle-field of Chancellorsville toward morning, and at once the labor of reëstablishing the hospitals commenced. Tents were erected, the ambulances unloaded, and the surgeons, already worn out by forty hours of incessant toil, resumed their work.

When the Sixth corps reoccupied the breastworks at dark on the 6th, it was desirable that the right flank should be protected by old and reliable troops. Neill's Third brigade was assigned to that position, the Seventy-seventh being upon the extreme right, the Sixty-first Pennsylvania thrown out at right angles to protect the rear. On the left of the Seventy-seventh was the Forty-ninth New York, the Seventh Maine was next, then the One Hundred and Twenty-second, and the Forty-third New York was on the left of the brigade.

All was now quiet. No sound was heard except now and then the suppressed tones of officers in command. The stars shone through the openings among the trees upon a long line of dusky forms lying close behind the sheltering breastworks, as silent as death but ready at an instant to pour out a storm of destruction. A row of bayonets projected over the breastworks; an abattis of steel awaiting the momentarily expected onset of the enemy.

At ten o'clock the low tones of command of the rebel officers were heard as they urged their men against our rear and flank. Colonel Smith of the Sixty-first Pennsylvania, ordered his men to lie down, for they had no breastworks, and to reserve their fire. Nearer and nearer came the dark line, until within twenty feet of the recumbent Pennsylvanians, but not a sound from them. Still nearer the rebel line approached, to within a distance of ten feet, when the sharp command rang out, " *Fire ;*" and rising the Pennsylvanians delivered a withering fire into the rebel ranks that sent them reeling back into the darkness from whence they came; but a line of prostrate forms where the fire from our line had met the advancing column, told of its terrible execution. Twenty minutes after this repulse they advanced silently but in stronger force, directly in front of our breastworks. They advanced slowly and in silence until within a few feet of the Union line, when with wild yells they leaped forward, some even mounting the breastworks. But a sheet of flame instantly flashed along the whole line of our works; the astonished rebels wavered for a moment and then beat a hasty retreat, relinquishing with this last desperate effort the attempt to drive back the old Sixth corps.

Scarcely a man of the Union force was injured by this charge, but the dead and wounded from the rebel ranks literally covered the ground. There was no help for them. Our men were unable even to take care of their own wounded which lay scattered through the woods in the rear. So the rebel wounded lay between the two armies, making the night hideous with their groans.

The battle of the 6th was now at an end, neither party having gained any decided advantage.

At midnight the Sixth corps fell back upon the plank road to the vicinity of the old gold mine mill, where our hospitals had been. Intrenchments were thrown up and the position was held without much annoyance from the rebels all the next day. The whole line of the army remained quiet on the 7th, only a few skirmishes along different parts of the line, relieving the monotony of the day.

The two days of fighting had told fearfully upon our ranks. Our regiments which a few hours before were well filled, were now but fragments of regiments; and our hearts were weighed down with heavy grief when we thought of the many grand spirits who had left us forever since we crossed the Rapidan.

We thought of the young colonel of the Forty-third, Wilson, beloved and admired throughout the corps. His death was a heavy blow to us all. We should miss his soldierly presence on the parade; his winning pleasantry in our social circles; we were no longer to enjoy his beautiful example of unswerving christian morality. His manly form was no longer to be our pride, and his heroic valor would never again be manifest on the field of battle.

Major Fryer had received his mortal hurt. Fryer was young and gallant; his handsome form and brilliant eye were in fine harmony with those of his friend and superior. "In their lives they were beautiful, and in their death they were not divided."

Captain Hickmot, too, of the Forty-ninth was among the slain. Surely death loves a shining mark, and with what terrible precision had he chosen his victims. Hickmot's bright eye was glazed in death. His gayety was hushed forever. We remembered now his hearty laugh, his friendly words and his purity of character, and knew that they were ours only in memory.

Wallace of the Forty-third and Terry of the Forty-ninth, too, were gone. Colonel Ryerson, the gallant commander of the Tenth New Jersey, was mortally wounded.

In the Seventy-seventh we had lost Craig; a youth of rare qualities and of stern patriotism.

The Vermont brigade had lost many of its brightest ornaments. Colonel Barney of the Sixth was one of Vermont's best men. A kind yet faithful commander in camp, gallant and fearless on the field. He was the highest type of a man; a christian gentleman. Colonel Stone had been killed instantly on the 5th. His urbane manners were remembered by all who frequented our division head-quarters, and his bravery had endeared him to his men. Colonel Tyler, too, of the Second was among the mortally wounded, and all felt his loss deeply.

Captains Bixby, of the Second, Bartlett and Buck, of the Third, Carpenter and Farr, of the Fourth, Ormsbee and Hurlburt, of the Fifth, and Bird and Randall, of the Sixth — all men of bravery and patriotism, all beloved as companions and valued as officers — were among the dead or dying. But among Vermont's fallen sons was no more ardent patriot or gallant soldier than Captain George D. Davenport, of the Fifth. His manly bearing, his brilliant intellect, his ready wit, his social virtues and his well known bravery, combined to render him a favorite officer in his brigade, while to those who were bound to him by the ties of fellowship, his disinterested love and noble generosity rendered his friendship of inestimable value.

These were a few among the many noble names of fallen heroes. Never were grander men sacrificed for a noble cause than they.

General Getty and General Morris and Colonel Keiffer were among the wounded, and we had lost General Shaler and General Seymour, captured by the enemy.

General Neill succeeded to the command of the Second division, and Colonel Bidwell assumed the command vacated by General Neill.

41

CHAPTER XXIV.

SPOTTSYLVANIA.

By this time General Grant, finding the rebel position too strong to force in front, and finding, by reconnoissance, that the enemy had fallen back to strong works where he awaited attack, determined to throw the army between Lee's army and Richmond, and accordingly ordered the first of that wonderful series of flank movements that have become the admiration of the world. The Fifth and Sixth corps withdrew with secrecy from the line held by them, and falling into the rear of the rest of the army, marched rapidly from the right to the left flank toward Spottsylvania. The Sixth corps, taking the Chancellorsville road, reached the old battle-field at daylight, and halted for breakfast near the ruins of the historic Chancellor House. The Fifth corps taking a more direct road to Spottsylvania, and being unincumbered with the train, marched rapidly and reached Piney Branch Church, a little hamlet in the midst of the woods, about five miles north of Spottsylvania Court House, at nine o'clock in the morning. These two corps were quickly followed by the Ninth and Second corps, leaving the old wilderness field entirely in the hands of the enemy.

Another of those distressful necessities of war occurred on withdrawing from the Wilderness. Wounded men of the Fifth and Sixth corps had already been left on the site of the hospitals near the old gold mine mills, and now hundreds more from every corps were abandoned for want of sufficient transportation. Let it not be thought that the Army of the Potomac was deficient in ambulances. Our hospital train was immense, yet insufficient for such an emergency as the present. To have provided a train sufficient for such a time, would have been to incumber the army with an enormous establishment, which would so interfere with its movements as to defeat the very object in view. The present was one of those terrible but unavoidable contingencies which must sometimes occur in war.

Trains had returned and brought away some of the wounded left at the old gold mine, but many were still there; and now, again, as we loaded ambulances and army wagons to their utmost capacity, making a train of many miles in extent, some two hundred of the wounded of our Sixth corps were left upon the ground. It was, indeed, a sickening thought that these noble fellows, who had nobly fallen in their country's cause, must be abandoned to the enemy, many of them, perhaps the majority of them, to die in their hands. All communication with their friends at home hopelessly cut off, and with no expectation of any but the roughest treatment from their enemies, it was a sad prospect for the unfortunate ones. Medical officers from each corps were directed to remain and care for those thus left behind, and a limited supply of rations and medicines were also left. Surgeon Phillips, of the Third Vermont, and Assistant Surgeon Thompson, of the Seventy-seventh New York, were the detail to remain behind from the Second division. They stayed with our wounded among the rebels for several weeks, faithfully ministering to their wants, until nearly all had been removed to Richmond, when, one day, learning that those remaining were to be sent south on the following day, they made their escape by

night. By traveling throughout the night and hiding in
the woods by day, they made their way across the Rapidan,
and finally reached Washington in safety.

The Fifth corps, having taken the most direct road to
Spottsylvania, arrived at Piney Branch Church at nine
o'clock on the morning of the 8th, where the infantry skirmishers of the enemy were encountered. Gregg's division
of cavalry had been for some time engaged with the rebel
cavalry; but the cavalry had not discovered the infantry
of the enemy before the approach of the Fifth corps. Two
divisions of the Fifth corps were at once formed in line of
battle, Bartlett's brigade of Griffin's division being sent
ahead as skirmishers. As the corps advanced, the skirmishers of the enemy steadily withdrew, until they reached
a large clearing, called Alsop's Farm, along the rear of
which ran a small stream, the river Ny, about three miles
north of Spottsylvania. Here the enemy was formed in
force, with a line of strong earthworks. An attack was
ordered, and bravely Warren's men advanced against
the breastworks of the enemy; but their efforts to drive the
rebels were unavailing. The field was composed of a succession of ridges, dotted here and there with clumps of
pines and oaks, while the country in rear, through which
the corps had already pressed the opposing skirmishers,
was a wilderness of trees. The rebels had their artillery
well posted, and they hurled a fierce storm of shells among
the advancing lines, arresting their advance. The enemy
in turn charged upon the Fifth corps, but the Union boys
fought with desperation, repelling every charge and holding their ground. Our troops behaved magnificently, yet
they were unable to push their advance further.

It was now evident that Lee, anticipating Grant's
strategy, had set about thwarting it. As soon as our
troops were withdrawn from Wilderness Run, Lee had
hastened Ewell's corps and a part of Longstreet's on an

inner road to Spottsylvania, and these troops now confronted us and disputed our advance.

Such was the situation when the Sixth corps arrived on the field at two o'clock in the afternoon. The day had been the most sultry of the season, and many of the men, overcome by the intensity of the heat, and exhausted by the constant fighting and marching since the morning of the 4th, had fallen by the wayside. The corps halted for about two hours, and was then ordered to the front to the assistance of Warren's corps, which was again hotly engaged with the enemy. We pressed forward along a narrow road leading through a thick growth of timber, until we came where the Fifth corps was contending the ground. The corps was drawn up in line of battle, but did not at once commence an attack.

Before us the ground was rolling and partially wooded, admirably adapted for defensive warfare. A wooded ravine, at a little distance from our front, concealed a rebel line of battle, and in our rear, were dense woods extending to the road along which our line was formed. These woods were on fire, and the hot blasts of air which swept over us, together with the burning heat of the sun, rendered our position a very uncomfortable one. Before long, however, the corps was ordered to the left, and took its position in the woods on the left of Warren's corps. Our Second division was formed in three lines with the view of attacking the enemy.

Soon after dark all things being ready, the division moved forward to the attack, but after some desperate fighting on the part of both the Fifth corps and our own division, finding the enemy too strongly posted, the attack was relinquished.

Toward midnight some changes of position were ordered, but, in the darkness, regiments lost their brigades, and wandered about in the woods until daylight, some narrowly escaping capture within the lines of the enemy.

There was little hard fighting on Monday the 9th, though skirmishing was briskly kept up along the whole line throughout the day. Our line of battle was now extended from northwest to southeast with Hancock's Second corps on the right, Warren's Fifth corps on the right center, Sedgwick's Sixth corps on the left center, and Burnside's Ninth corps on the extreme left. Our Second division was formed in a clearing on the side of a hill which sloped gradually until it reached a swamp, which, however, turned and passed through our line at our left. About three hundred yards in front of us was a strip of woods one-fourth of a mile wide, and beyond the woods an open field where the rebel forces were posted behind formidable earthworks. Just in our rear and on the crest of the hill, our batteries were posted so as to fire over our heads. On our right was a dense forest where the Fifth corps were posted, and on our left Burnside's troops occupied a more open country.

The whole line of the army was strengthened with breastworks of rails and logs, which the men procured in many cases from almost under the rebel guns, while the heavy mist of the morning concealed them from the view of their enemies. Over the logs and rails earth was thrown in quantity sufficient to protect the men from the shot and shell of the enemy.

Although there was little fighting on the 9th, it was a sad day for the Sixth corps and for the army; for on that day our corps lost its beloved commander, and the army a a most distinguished soldier.

General Sedgwick, while standing behind an outer line of works, personally superintending and directing, as was his custom, the posting of a battery of artillery at an angle which he regarded as of great importance, was shot through the head by a rebel sharpshooter, and died instantly. The ball had entered his head just below the left eye, and passed out at the back of the head.

Never had such a gloom rested upon the whole army on account of the death of one man as came over it when the heavy tidings passed along the lines that General Sedgwick was killed.

Major-General John Sedgwick, who had so long been identified with the Sixth corps, was a native of Connecticut. He graduated at West Point on the 30th of June, 1837, and was at once assigned to the Second artillery, as second-lieutenant. In 1839, he was promoted to first-lieutenant. He served in Mexico, and was brevetted captain for gallant and meritorious conduct, in the battles of Contreras and Cherubusco. He was soon afterward brevetted major for gallant conduct, and greatly distinguished himself in the attack on Cosino gate, Mexico city. In 1845 he was made major of the First United States Cavalry, and served in Texas until the breaking out of the rebellion. In March, 1861, he was commissioned lieutenant-colonel, Second United States Cavalry; and in April promoted to the colonelcy of the Fourth Cavalry. He was made a brigadier-general of volunteers in August, 1861, and assigned to the command of a brigade in the Army of the Potomac.

He was afterward assigned to the command of the Third division, Second corps, then under General Sumner. He participated in the siege of Yorktown, and greatly distinguished himself in many battles on the Peninsula. He was particularly noted at the battle of Fair Oaks, Savage's Station, and Glendale. His division was one of the few divisions of the Army of the Potomac that rendered any assistance to General Pope in his unfortunate campaign.

At Antietam he led his men repeatedly against the rebels, and was as often forced back, until the ground over which his division had fought was covered with dead. He was thrice wounded, but refused to be carried from the field until faintness from loss of blood obliged him to relinquish his command.

In December, 1862, he was nominated by the President a major-general of volunteers, and was confirmed in March, 1863, with rank from the 31st of May, 1862.

In January following his promotion, he was assigned to the command of the Ninth corps, and, on the 5th of February, was transferred to the command of the Sixth corps, relieving General Smith, who was assigned to the Ninth corps.

Soon after taking command of our corps, the famous charge upon Fredericksburgh Heights was made, in which both the corps and its commander acquired lasting renown. General Sedgwick was especially commended by General Meade for the manner in which he handled his corps at Rappahannock Station, and, in General Meade's absence, he was several times in command of the army. He was, on several occasions, offered the supreme command of the army, but his excessive modesty forbade him to accept so important a command.

No soldier was more beloved by the army or honored by the country than this noble general. His corps regarded him as a father, and his great military abilities made his judgment, in all critical emergencies, sought after by his superior as well as his fellows. The command of the Sixth corps now devolved upon General Wright, who had long been well known in the corps as the commander of our First division, and who held the command of the corps from this time until it was disbanded in the autumn of 1865.

Monday night passed quietly. An occasional volley on the picket line would rouse us to arms, but there was no general assault, and the tired soldiers would throw themselves again upon the ground to catch a few moments more of rest.

Our position on Tuesday morning, May 10th, was the same as it had been the day previous. During the lull of battle on the 9th, both armies had gathered their strength and perfected their plans for a renewal of the contest, on a scale of magnificence seldom if ever witnessed by any army before. This was destined to be a day of most fearful carnage, and desperate attempts on the part of each antagonist to crush the other by the weight of its terrible charges.

Active skirmishing commenced along different portions of the line early in the morning, and continued to grow more and more general until the rattle of the skirmishers' rifles grew into the reverberating roll of battle. From one end of the long line to the other the tide of battle surged, the musketry continually increasing in volume, until it seemed one continuous peal of thunder. During all the battles in the Wilderness, artillery had been useless, except when here and there a section could be brought in to command the roadway; but now all the artillery on both sides was brought into the work. It was the terrible cannonading of Malvern Hill with the fierce musketry of Gaines' Mills combined, that seemed fairly to shake the earth and skies. Never during the war had the two armies made such gigantic struggles for the destruction of each other.

At first the heavy assaults were made against the right wing — Hancock's and Warren's corps sustaining the principal shock of the enemy's repeated charges. Massing their forces against particular points of the line held by these two corps, the rebel generals would hurl their gray legions like an avalanche against our breastworks, hoping by the very momentum of the charge to break through our lines; but a most withering storm of leaden and iron hail would set the mass wavering, and finally send it back to

42

the cover of the woods and earthworks in confusion, leaving the ground covered at each time with an additional layer of their dead. In turn, the men of the Fifth and Second corps would charge upon their adversaries, and in turn they too would be forced to seek shelter behind their rifle pits. Thus the tide of battle along the right of the line rolled to and fro, while the horrid din of musketry and artillery rose and swelled as the storm grew fiercer.

Meanwhile the Sixth and Ninth corps were quietly awaiting events, and it was not until six o'clock in the afternoon that the Sixth corps was called into action. Then it was to make one of the most notable charges on record.

At five o'clock the men of the corps were ordered to unsling knapsacks and divest themselves of every incumbrance preparatory to a charge. Colonel Upton commanding the Second brigade of the First division, was directed to take twelve picked regiments from the corps and lead them in a charge against the right center of the rebel line. The regiments which shared the dearly purchased honor of this magnificent charge were, in the first line, the One Hundred and Twenty-first New York, the Fifth Maine, the Ninety-sixth and One Hundred and Nineteenth Pennsylvania; in the second line the Seventy-seventh and Forty-third New York, the Fifth Wisconsin, Sixth Maine and Forty-ninth Pennsylvania; and in the third line, the Second, Fifth and Sixth Vermont. It was indeed an honor to be selected for this duty, but it was an honor to be paid for at the cost of fearful peril.

The twelve regiments assembled on the open space in front of our works, then silently entered the strip of woods which was between our line and that of the rebels. Passing through to the further edge of the woods, the twelve regiments were formed in columns of three lines, each line consisting of four regiments.

The regiments of the Second division, not included in the charging column, formed in the rear, to act as support, but did not advance to the charge.

As the regiments took their places, they threw themselves upon the ground, and all orders were given in suppressed tones, for the rebels were but a hundred yards distant, in the open field, and the minies of their skirmishers were whistling among the trees and brushwood.

The other corps of the army were prepared, in case this charging party succeeded in breaking the enemy's line, to rush in and turn the success into a rout of the rebels. Generals Meade, Hancock, Warren and Burnside stationed themselves on eminences, from which they could watch the success of the perilous enterprise.

At six o'clock all things were ready, and the artillery from the eminences in our rear opened a terrific fire, sending the shells howling and shrieking over the heads of the charging column, and plunging into the works of the enemy. This was the signal for the attack, and Colonel Upton's clear voice rang out, "*Attention, battalions! Forward, double-quick!* CHARGE!" and in an instant every man was on his feet, and, with tremendous cheers, which were answered by the wild yells of the rebels, the column rushed from the cover of the woods. Quick as lightning, a sheet of flame burst from the rebel line, and the leaden hail swept the ground over which the column was advancing, while the canister from the artillery came crashing through our ranks at every step, and scores and hundreds of our brave fellows fell, literally covering the ground. But, nothing daunted, the noble fellows rushed upon the defenses, leaping over the ditch in front, and mounting the breastworks. The rebels made a determined resistance, and a hand to hand fight ensued, until, with their bayonets, our men had filled the rifle pits with bleeding rebels. About two thousand of the survivors of the struggle surrendered, and were immediately marched to the rear, under guard.

Without halting for breath, the impetuous column rushed toward the second line of works, which was equally as strong as the first. The resistance here was less stubborn than at the first line, yet the gray occupants of the rifle pits refused to fly, until forced back at the point of the bayonet.

Our ranks were now fearfully thinned, yet the brave fellows passed on to the third line of defenses which was also captured.

It was but a shattered remnant of that noble column that rushed from the woods against the hostile works, that reached this advanced point, and now, finding that reën-forcements were reaching the enemy, while our column was every moment melting away, a retreat was ordered.

There was not even time to bring away the six pieces of artillery which we had captured; they were filled with sods and abandoned.

What remained of the twelve regiments retreated to the cover of our rifle pits, leaving the dead and most of the wounded in the enemy's hands.

The corps lost, in this charge, some of its ablest men. In the First brigade of the Second division Lieutenant-Colonel Hamilton, of the Sixty-second New York, was killed. Captain Carpenter, of the Seventy-seventh, one of its first and best officers, and Lieutenant Lyon, a young officer of great bravery, were killed in the interior line of works, and many other noble fellows of that regiment were left on that fatal field. The regiment crossed the Rapidan six days before with over five hundred men, and now, after this charge, less than ninety men were left, and this is but an example of the losses to most of the regiments in that division.

The noise of the battle gradually died away as night threw her mantle over the fearful scene of carnage, and both armies were glad of a respite from their severe labors.

The 11th of May passed in making new arrangements and in sending the thousands of wounded to Fredricksburgh. Immense trains of ambulances and army wagons freighted with the mangled forms of wounded men were running day and night to Fredricksburgh, and returning with supplies.

Skirmishing was kept up along the line, but no general engagement was brought on. During the night the Second corps, General Hancock, silently withdrew from the position it had occupied on the right of the line, and marching along in the rear of the army occupied a position between the Sixth and Ninth corps, which was not before occupied. With great caution and silence preparations were made for a desperate attack upon that part of the enemy's line fronting this position. This line made here a sharp angle and by seizing this angle, it was hoped to turn the right flank of Lee's army. Between the position of the Second corps and the rebel works, the ground was covered with pines and underbrush, and as it neared the defenses ascended abruptly to a considerable height.

As soon as the gray light of the morning began to streak through the mists, all was in readiness for the charge, and with strictest orders of silence the corps in mass advanced rapidly across the field, the thick fog concealing the movement. As the column neared the rifle pits a storm of bullets met it; but charging impetuously up the hill and over the works, the rebels, surprised and overpowered, gave way; those who could escaping to the second line in the rear, though thousands were obliged to surrender on the spot, so complete had been the surprise. The victorious column now pushed on toward the second line of works, but here, the enemy by this time fully prepared for the attack, the resistance became more stubborn.

The battle now raged with greatest fury. The Sixth corps was withdrawn from its position, leaving a strong picket line to guard its front, and marching along the rear of its works joined in the attack with the Second corps. The works taken by Hancock's corps, were occupied by the men of the Sixth corps, and the enemy commenced the most desperate efforts to retake them. Forming their troops in heavy columns they hurled them against our line with tremendous force. Russell's division held the center of the line of the corps at a point known as "the angle." This was the key to the whole position. Our forces held the rebel works from the left as far as this "angle," and the rebels still held the rest of the line. Whoever could hold "the angle" would be the victors; for with the angle, either party could possess themselves of the whole line of works. Hence the desperate efforts to drive us from this position. The First division being unable to maintain the position alone, the Second division was sent to its aid. And now, as the boys of the Second division took their places in the front, the battle became a hand to hand combat. A breastwork of logs separated the combatants. Our men would reach over this partition and discharge their muskets in the face of the enemy, and in return would receive the fire of the rebels at the same close range. Finally, the men began to use their muskets as clubs and then rails were used. The men were willing thus to fight from behind the breastworks, but to rise up and attempt a charge in the face of an enemy so near at hand and so strong in numbers required unusual bravery. Yet they did charge and they drove the rebels back and held the angle themselves. It was in one of these charges that the gallant Major Ellis of the Forty-ninth New York, was shot with a ramrod through the arm and in the side, from the effects of which he afterwards died. The trees in front of the position held by the Sixth corps during this remarkable struggle, were literally cut to pieces by bullets. Even trees more than a foot in diameter, were cut off by the constant action of bullets. A section of one of these was, and doubtless still is, in Washington, with a card attached stating that the tree was cut down in front of the position of the Second corps. Our gallant brothers of that corps won undying honors on that glorious day, but it was the long-continued, fearful musketry battle between the Sixth corps and the enemy which cut down those trees. We have no desire to detract from the well-deserved honors of the brave men of the Second corps, but this is a simple matter of justice. The conflict became more and more bloody, and soon the Fifth corps was also engaged, and at ten o'clock the battle rolled along the whole line. The terrible fighting continued till eleven o'clock, when there was a lull in the musketry, but the artillery continued its work of destruction. Thus the second line of works was taken, but not without fearful loss to both armies. Our corps had fought at close range for eight hours. Behind the works the rebel dead were lying literally piled one upon another, and wounded men were groaning under the weight of bodies of their dead companions. The loss to the rebels in prisoners and guns was also great.

Major-General Edward Johnson with his whole division, General Stewart, a brigade from Early's division and a whole regiment, including in all between three and four thousand prisoners and between thirty and forty guns, were the trophies of this glorious but bloody morning's work. These captures were nearly all made by the Second corps in the first assault in the morning.

The losses to the Sixth corps were great, but far less than on the 12th. The Seventy-seventh lost one of its finest officers. Captain O. P. Rugg was shot in the breast and died while being carried to the hospital. The captain was

a young man of great promise, of genial and lively temper-
ament and greatly beloved by his regiment. He had been
married but a few months before his death, and had
parted from his bride at Elmira just before the spring campaign opened.

The corps remained near the scene of action during
the next day. Reconnoissances were made, and another
attempt was made on the 14th to turn the right flank
of the enemy. The Sixth corps, at three o'clock on
the morning of that day, moved off to the left of our
line about two miles and encamped about the Anderson
House, but our pickets soon found the enemy in force in
our front, and no attempt was made to bring on an
engagement. The time passed quietly along the line, only
occasionally the roar of artillery kept up something of
excitement of battle. On the night of the 17th, the Sixth
corps moved back to the scene of the battle of the 12th.
At daylight three corps moved forward to attack the
enemy's line. The Second corps forming the center of
the line, the Sixth corps the right, and the Ninth corps the
left. The first line of rifle pits were those which had
been abandoned by us on the 12th. These were filled with
rebel skirmishers, who readily gave way, leaving the works
in our hands.

Our line of battle advanced till it confronted the second
line of the rebel works. This was a strong line behind a
thick impenetrable abattis and held by a powerful force.
The three corps pressed this formidable line, and a sharp
engagement ensued, but without advantage to our forces,
and .it was concluded that an attempt to dislodge the
enemy could only result in a fearful waste of life. Accordingly the troops were quietly withdrawn, though submitted
to a galling fire, having lost in the morning's work about
eight hundred men.

In the afternoon the enemy attacked the Fifth corps on

the left, but was driven back. The same afternoon the Sixth corps returned to the vicinity of the Anderson House, from which it had started on the evening previous; and orders were issued to be ready to march toward the North Anna.

General Grant, deeming it impracticable to make any further attempt to carry the rebel position at Spottsylvania by direct assault, had determined upon another flank movement; and his preparations were made for moving around the left flank of the enemy during the night of the 19th, and seizing a position on the North Anna. But late in the afternoon of the 19th, Ewell's rebel corps made a fierce assault upon the right of our line. Our forces gave the rebels a warm reception, and forced them back to the cover of their earthworks.

On the 20th, Aaron B. Quincy, a young soldier, beloved by all who knew him, was shot through the breast, and died in a few minutes. His faithful christian character, his undoubted bravery, and his ardent patriotism, had endeared him to all.

On the night of the 21st, the flank movement was commenced. Withdrawing in silence, and first throwing the right corps in rear of the rest of the army and to its left, as at the Wilderness, the troops marched rapidly all night, halting for a few moments for breath once or twice, and then pressing forward again. During the next forenoon a halt of some hours occurred at Quincy Station, near the house where Stonewall Jackson died the year before. Then the march was renewed and continued till dark.

The Fifth and Sixth corps reached the banks of the North Anna on the evening of the 23d, and was soon followed by the Second and Ninth corps. Again the enemy, aware of our intentions, and having the shortest line, confronted us, and disputed the crossing; but, after considerable artillery practice, the Fifth corps succeeded in

43

throwing their pontoon bridges and obtaining a position on the south bank. The enemy now attacked the corps with great vigor, but were repulsed with equal slaughter. The Sixth corps followed at four o'clock in the morning, and a little later the Second and Ninth corps also joined us. Strong breastworks were thrown up, and parties were sent to the front to reconnoiter the position.

A further advance of a few miles was made on the 25th, but finding the enemy in a stronger position than he had occupied either in the Wilderness or at Spottsylvania, General Grant determined again to withdraw and try his favorite flank movement. Accordingly, on the night of the 26th, the army was withdrawn to the north bank of the river. The night was very dark, and the mud deep. Several days' rain had rendered the roads, proverbial for their mud, almost impassable; but heeding no difficulties, the army followed without hesitation wherever our great leader directed. The Sixth corps, with two divisions of cavalry under Sheridan, who had now rejoined the army from his great raid on which he had started from Spottsylvania, took the advance. On Saturday, the 28th, the corps and the cavalry divisions, after a good deal of hard fighting, crossed the Pamunkey river, at Hanovertown. The cavalry, at once advancing several miles beyond the river, encountered a large force of rebel cavalry, which was driven back. The army encamped at Hanovertown, stretching from the river several miles southward.

CHAPTER XXV.

THE HOSPITALS AT FREDERICKSBURGH.

The journey from the battle-field — Sufferings of the wounded — A surgeon's letters — Rebel hatred — Assistance from the north — A father in search of his boy —
The wounded sent to Washington.

Let us turn now from the field of battle to Fredericksburgh, that great depot for wounded men.

It will be recollected that, from Piney Branch church,
the trains, with the wounded from the Wilderness, were
sent to Fredericksburgh. Over a rough road, nearly fifteen
miles, these unfortunate men, with shattered or amputated
limbs, with shots through the lungs or head or abdomen, suffering the most excruciating pain from every jar
or jolt of the ambulance or wagon, crowded as closely
as they could be packed, were to be transported. Already
they had been carted about over many miles of hard road,
most of them having been carried from the old gold mine
to Chancellorsville, and now again loaded and brought to
Spottsylvania. They were worn out with fatigue and suffering, and yet there was much misery in store for them.
Slowly the immense train labored over the rough road,
now corduroy, now the remains of a worn out plank road,
and anon a series of ruts and mud holes, until, at three
o'clock on the morning of the 9th of May, the head of the
train arrived in Fredericksburgh.

The train had been preceded by some three hundred
men who were wounded but able to walk. Mayor Slaughter and other rebel citizens surrounded these unarmed men,
made them prisoners and delivered them to some rebel
cavalry, who took them to Richmond.

The process of unloading the wounded at once commenced; all the churches and other public buildings were first seized and filled. Negroes who could be found in town were pressed into the work, yet, with all the help that could be obtained, it was a slow process. All night and all the next day the work went on. The churches were filled first, then warehouses and stores, and then private houses, until the town was literally one immense hospital.

The surgeons were too much engaged in transferring the men from the wagons to the houses to find time that day to dress many wounds, and many an unfortunate soldier whose stump of an arm or leg had not been dressed since the first day of the fighting, became the victim of gangrene, which set in as the result of this unavoidable want of care. No sooner were the men removed from the ambulances than surgeons and nurses addressed themselves with all the strength that remained to them to relieve the immediate wants of the sufferers. Never before had such herculean labors been thrown upon so small a body of men, yet nobly did they accomplish the task. All the buildings in town were full of wounded men, the walks were covered with them, and long trains of ambulances were filling the streets with more. Yet to relieve the wants of all these thousands of suffering men not more than forty surgeons had been sent from the field.

It was one grand funeral; men were dropping away on every side. Large numbers of nurses were detailed as burial parties, and these plied their work day after day with hardly time for their needed rest.

Surgeons were completely worn out, and many of them had to be sent to Washington, fairly broken down with their labors.

The following extract from a letter of a surgeon at Fredricksburgh to his wife, written on the 11th, may convey something of an idea of the experience of the medical officers during those terrible days. He says: "We are almost worked to death; my feet are terribly swollen; yet we cannot rest for there are so many poor fellows who are suffering. All day yesterday I worked at the operating table. That was the fourth day that I had worked at those terrible operations since the battle commenced, and I have also worked at the tables two whole nights and part of another. Oh! it is awful. It does not seem as though I could take a knife in my hand to-day, yet there are a hundred cases of amputations waiting for me. Poor fellows come and beg almost on their knees for the first chance to have an arm taken off. It is a scene of horror such as I never saw. God forbid that I should ever see another."

Again, the same officer writing a day or two later, says, "It is fearful. I see so many grand men dropping one by one. They are my acquaintances and my friends. They look to me for help, and I have to turn away heartsick at my want of ability to relieve their sufferings. Captain Walker of the Seventh Maine is dying to-night. He is a noble good man, and he looks in my face and pleads for help. Adjutant Hessy and Lieutenant Hooper of the same regiment died last night. All were my friends, and all thought that I could save them. General Sedgwick is dead, and General Getty and General Torbert are my patients. * * * Mrs. Lewis has just come; what a blessing her presence will be to the colonel, who bears the loss of his arm so bravely. Colonel Barney of the Sixth Vermont died yesterday, and Major Fryer of the Forty-third is dying. The major says, "Doctor, can nothing be done?" Major Dudley lies in the room where I am writing, seriously wounded. * * * I have to-day sent sixty officers of the Sixth corps to Washington. * * * Oh! can I ever write anything beside these mournful details? Hundreds of ambulances are coming into town now, and it is almost midnight. So they come every night."

For a time it was almost impossible to obtain sufficient supplies either of food or dressings. Everything that could be spared from the field had been sent, but in the field they were still fighting terrible battles, and there was little to spare. Food was obtained in very limited quantities in town, and men went to the houses of citizens and demanded sheets, which were torn into bandages.

But large supplies were sent from Washington by the government in a few days, so that all necessary articles were furnished in abundance, with a profusion of lemons, oranges and canned fruit. The Sanitary Commission was also on hand with large supplies of delicacies, which were joyfully received by the wounded heroes, who not only relished the luxuries, but remembered that they were the gifts of friends at home, who had not forgotten the soldiers.

Many of the people of Fredericksburgh exhibited the most malignant spite against the " Yankee wounded ;" but others, while they claimed no sympathy with our cause, showed themselves friends of humanity, and rendered us all the assistance in their power. No men, except negroes and white men unfit for military duty, were left in town, but the women were bitter rebels. Some of them made fierce opposition to the use of their houses as hospitals, but they were occupied notwithstanding their remonstrances.

At one fine mansion a surgeon rang the door bell, and in a moment saw the door open just enough to show the nose and a pair of small twinkling eyes of what was evidently a portly women. "What do you want?" snarled out the female defender of the premises. "We want to come and see if we can place a few wounded officers in this house." "You can't come in here!" shouted the woman slamming the door together. A few knocks induced her again to open the door two or three inches. "Madam, we must come in here; we shall do you no harm." "You can't come here; I am a lone widow." "But I assure you no harm is intended you." Again the door was closed, and again at the summons was opened. "Madam, it will be much better for you to allow us to enter than for me to direct these men to force the door; but we must enter." The woman now threw the door wide open and rushing into the yard with as much alacrity as her enormous proportions would admit, threw her arms out and whirled about like a reversed spinning top shouting for help. She was again assured that no harm was intended her, but that unless she chose to show us the house we should be obliged to go alone. Concluding that wisdom was the better part of valor, she proceeded to show us the rooms.

At another mansion, one of the finest in Fredericksburgh, a red-haired woman thrust her head out of the side window, in answer to the ring of the door bell:

"What do you want here?"

"We wish to place some wounded officers in this house."

"You can't bring any officers nor anybody else to this house. I'm all alone. I hope you have more honor than to come and disturb defenseless, unprotected women."

"Have you no husband?"

"Yes, thank God, he's a colonel in the confederate service."

"Well, if your husband was at home, where he ought to be, you would not be a defenseless woman."

The woman refused to unbolt the door, in spite of all persuasion, but while she railed at the "detestable Yankees," a soldier climbed in at a window in the rear, and unbolted the door. Her splendid rooms and fine mattresses furnished lodgings for twenty wounded officers. Day after day, the gloom of death hung over the town.

Hundreds of our brave fellows were dying. Some of the finest officers of our army were daily yielding to the destroyer.

Among the severe losses to the Sixth corps were, Colonel Barney, of the Sixth Vermont, who had been shot through the head. He died on the 10th. He was one of the noblest of the sons of Vermont, a pattern of a brave soldier and christian gentleman, respected for his ability as a commander, and loved for his social virtues; he was lamented by the whole corps. Major Fryer, of the Forty-third New York, one of the most promising young officers in the corps, died on the 12th, from wounds through the left arm and lungs. Captain Walker and Adjutant Hesse, of the Seventh Maine, and Lieutenants Hooper and Vining, of the same regiment, all died within a few hours of each other. Lieutenants Follensbee and Cook, of the Thirty-seventh Massachusetts, and Captain Kirkbride, of the One Hundred and Second Pennsylvania, were also among those who died. Major Dudley, of the Fifth Vermont, after suffering untold agony for many days, finally yielded, and died in the embraces of his youthful wife, who had arrived in Fredericksburgh just in time to be present during his last hours. The major had gone into the fight sick with a fever, but his determined bravery forbade him to remain quiet. Receiving a severe wound while thus depressed by disease, he gradually sunk, until his brave spirit took its departure.

These were a few of the sad, sad scenes, which brought sorrow to our hearts day after day, of the hospitals at Fredericksburgh.

Physicians and nurses from civil life came to our assistance in large numbers. Some were earnest men, wholly devoted to the object of relieving the distress which they saw on every side. Others had come for selfish purposes.

Physicians who had never performed an important surgical operation came armed with amputating cases, and seemed to think that there was but one thing to be done, *to operate* as they said.

Distressed fathers and brothers wandered about the town, in search of information regarding some son or friend who had been wounded, or perhaps, as they feared, killed.

The following is but an example of many sad incidents of this kind: H. A. Bowers, of the Seventy-seventh New York, a young man much beloved and respected in his regiment, was wounded through the chest on the 5th of May, and with the other wounded brought to Fredericksburgh. His father, who resided in Albany, received the intelligence that his son was dangerously wounded, and hastened to Fredericksburgh in search of him. He arrived at that immense hospital, and at once commenced his inquiries after his soldier boy. Failing to learn anything of him, except the assurance that he had been placed in the ambulances, he sought out the quartermaster of the Seventy-seventh, who was with the army train just out of town. The quartermaster readily lent his aid in the search, and both at once sought the surgeon of that regiment for information, but he, having the care of a multitude, could tell them nothing of the object of their search. Thousands of wounded men were here, filling the city, but, thus far, the important duties of relieving their immediate necessities had occupied the attention of surgeons and attendants to the exclusion of everything else; and no record or register had been made by which a particular wounded man might be found. Unless some friend or acquaintance could direct to his place, the search was often long. The nurses were instructed to afford the anxious father every assistance in finding his son. Two more long weary days were spent in the fruitless search,

44

when word was sent to the father that his boy might be
found in a certain church.   Overjoyed at the thought
that at last his search was to be crowned with success,
he hastened to the place.   Who shall attempt to tell the
anguish of that father, when, on reaching the hospital, he
found that his son had expired half an hour before!

At length, by the 26th of May, all the wounded men
were sent by transports to Washington, and the hospitals
broken up.   The surgeons, escorted by a squadron of cavalry, crossed the country by way of Bowling Green, and,
after a three days' journey, rejoined the army at Hanover.

CHAPTER XXVI.

COAL HARBOR.

At Hanover Court House — The Eighteenth corps joins the Army of the Potomac — The armies meet at Coal Harbor — Battle of June 1st — Battle of June 3d — Terrible exposure — The army strikes for Petersburgh — Charles City Court House — A centenarian — Review of the overland campaign.

EARLY on the morning of the 30th, the army was again moving, advancing with heavy skirmishing toward Hanover Court House. Remaining here some hours the column retraced its steps a short distance, the rebels meanwhile opening a severe artillery fire upon our hospital trains.

Toward evening the enemy attacked our left vigorously but were repulsed, and an attack was in turn made by our own troops which resulted in forcing the rebels from a part of their intrenchments. Except some changes of position and ascertaining that of the enemy, our army lay quietly confronting the rebels during the 31st, but on the 1st of June we were again on the road marching toward Coal Harbor. The march was a hard one. The day was sultry, and the dust, ankle deep, raised in clouds by the column, was almost suffocating. It filled the air and hung upon the leaves of the trees like snow. Seldom had our men experienced so severe a march. As we neared Coal Harbor our Sixth corps in advance, we fell in with the column of General Smith's command, the Eighteenth and Tenth corps. It was a relief to the old soldiers of the Army of the Potomac to see these full regiments, and they felt that with such large reinforcements our success must now be insured. It was also a source of much gratification to the old Second division to meet

again our friends Generals Smith and Brooks, whose
names were so intimately connected with the division, and
who still held a large place in the affections of the men.

These two corps were a part of General Butler's command, which had advanced up the Peninsula as far as
Bermuda Hundreds, but were unable to make further progress. General Grant had, therefore, directed General
Butler to send them forward by way of transports to
White House Landing, to join the Army of the Potomac.
They reached us tired and almost discouraged by their
unusual march of nearly sixteen miles, their trains and
baggage being left behind.

In the afternoon we had fallen in with ambulances
returning with wounded cavalrymen, and learned from
them that Sheridan had engaged the rebel cavalry at Coal
Harbor early in the morning, and that he was now fighting
both infantry and cavalry. Toward that point the troops
pushed on rapidly, reaching the cavalry line at about four
o'clock. The men halted a few moments, and then were
ordered to fall in and advance against the enemy. Skirmishers, as usual, had advanced and prepared the way for
the lines of infantry and the artillery. The shots of the
skirmishers had become more and more frequent, till
the sharp rattle of musketry told of the actual presence
of the enemy. The artillery of the Sixth corps was at once
run out, and a brisk fire opened upon the rebels, who replied
with their guns, but with less vigor than that exhibited by
our own. The commands of Wright and Smith were at
once formed in line of battle, our Sixth corps on the left in
line, Rickett's Third division holding the right of the line,
Russell's the center, and Neill's Second division the extreme
left of the whole line. On our right was Smith's command
in single line.

In front of our line was an open space two-thirds of a
mile in width, beyond which was a strip of pine woods.

In these woods the enemy had intrenched, and was holding the position in strong force. Lee, again anticipating
the design of Grant, had sent Longstreet's corps and other
troops to occupy Coal Harbor, and now, with their rear
resting upon the Chickahominy, at this point a shallow
and easily forded stream, the rebels occupied a strong
position between our advance and Richmond.

The order for the charge was given, and these two commands, weary and exhausted, the veterans of the Sixth
corps from many days and nights of most severe labor,
and both corps by the tedious march of the day, dashed
impetuously across the ploughed field with shouts and
cheers, making for the rebel works.

The storm of battle seemed suddenly to have broken
without the usual warning. It was less than an hour
since the Union troops had arrived on the field, and
already a most bloody struggle was in progress. Volleys
rang out upon the evening air, crashing louder and still
louder. The First and Third divisions of the Sixth corps,
in heavy columns, rushed across the field, cleared the abattis, and seized the rebel works, while the Second division,
on the left, discovering a strong force of the enemy planting a battery on our flank, engaged them and forced them
back. Smith's command, also, by a desperate charge,
seized nearly the whole line in the front, that on the
extreme right, in front of Brooks' command, alone remaining in the hands of the rebels. The whole line thundered
with the incessant volleys of musketry, and the shot and
shell of the artillery shrieked and howled like spirits of
evil. The sun was sinking, red, in the west, and the
clouds of dust and smoke almost obscured the terrible
scene. Hundreds of our brave fellows were falling on
every side, and stretcher bearers were actively engaged in
removing the wounded from the field. The First division,
after a stubborn resistance of a few minutes, was forced

to give up the line of works it had captured and fall back; only the Third division held its ground. The others had advanced as far, but the ground was unfavorable, and in spite of most determined efforts to hold the line, they were forced to swing back.

This was the first experience of Smith's command in a great battle, and well did his men earn the confidence of the veterans who fought by their side. Their courage and impetuosity were the subjects of admiration of the boys of the old Sixth corps, who declared that Baldy Smith could make any troops fight like veterans.

The gallantry shown by our Third division in taking and holding the enemy's works, was acknowledged with true soldierly generosity by the other divisions of our corps, who thus far had not regarded the new division as their peer.

As darkness came on, the conflict still raged, and sheets of flame rolled from one end of the line to the other as the discomfited rebels strove desperately to regain their lost ground. But as the sound of battle died away at nine o'clock, the advantages gained by us were still held, and our men set to work to strengthen the works they had captured from the enemy and to throw up new ones. Again and again the rebels rushed against the Union line hoping to regain their lost ground, but without success. The battle, although of brief duration, had been a most sanguinary one. The loss to the Sixth corps was about two hundred killed and nine hundred and sixty wounded, while the Eighteenth corps lost one hundred and twenty-five killed and six hundred and fifty wounded.

Meanwhile the Second, Fifth and Ninth corps were holding the position occupied by them the day before, and against these corps most desperate assaults were repeatedly made by the enemy, but they were as often repulsed with great slaughter.

The movement at Coal Harbor, while it had not succeeded in forcing the enemy across the Chickahominy,
had secured our communications with White House Landing, which now became, after two years, for the second
time, the base of supplies for the Army of the Potomac.
General Grant now determined to renew the attempt to
dislodge the rebels on the following day.

Accordingly, after the fashion of all the movements of
the army, the Second corps, which now occupied the
extreme right of the line, withdrew during the night, and
falling behind the other corps, marched rapidly to the left
and took position in that flank on the road leading from
Dispatch Station to Coal Harbor. The corps did not
secure this position without considerable fighting, and it
was not in condition to take part in the expected advance
until the afternoon. Then a most violent thunder shower
set in, putting a stop to all movements for the remainder
der of the day.

The men of the Sixth and Eighteenth corps, tired and
worn out from marching, fighting, and the hard night's
work in throwing up intrenchments, had spent the early
part of the day in quietly watching the enemy, or lounging
behind the breastworks, glad of an opportunity for rest.

Orders were now given for a simultaneous attack along
the whole line, to take place at half-past four on the morning of the 3d. Our line of battle extended from Coal
Harbor to Tolopotamy creek, in the following order, from
left to right: Second, Sixth, Eighteenth, Fifth, and Ninth.
This line was nearly parallel with the Chickahominy, and
from a mile and a half to two miles north of it.

The rebels had not left the day unimproved, in concentrating their troops and strengthening their works. They
now held three lines of breastworks, all of great strength;
the first occupied by their skirmish lines, the others by
strong lines of battle. Between the two armies the

ground was low and swampy, while the positions occupied by both were sandy plains.

At half-past six on the morning of the 3d, our army was astir; and the skirmishers, leaving the cover of the rifle pits, were advancing. Presently they fell in with the skirmishers of the enemy, and the sharp cracking of rifles betokened the storm of battle.

As soon as the skirmishers were engaged, our artillery opened upon the rebel works, and the conflict now commenced in earnest. Amid the deafening volleys of musketry, the thunders of the artillery, and the wild yells of battle, our brave fellows pressed rapidly across the space between the hostile lines of works, and the whole Union force was thrown against the rebel breastworks almost simultaneously. But the works were too strong, the abattis too troublesome, and the rebel forces too numerous. Their line could not be taken.

The vigorous and gallant assault made by the Sixth corps, resulted in carrying the first line, where the rebel skirmishers had been posted, and our troops got within two hundred and fifty yards of the main works, but Martindale's division of Smith's corps, which advanced with the Sixth corps, and on our right, found the task before it too great; the troops of that division became disarranged and were repulsed. Although General Smith, who was always up to the front, made several attempts to relieve Martindale's division, it failed to take the rifle pits.

The right flank of the Sixth corps, thus exposed, the whole corps was forced to fall back.

Thus this grand assault, in which General Grant hoped to force his enemy across the Chickahominy, failed with immense loss to us and comparatively little to the confederate army, which as usual was defended by earthworks, while our men advancing to the charge were unprotected. But our brave fellows were to have their revenge.

The battle was over, and again the occupants of the opposing lines of defenses watched each other, the quiet being only disturbed by the occasional shots of sharp-shooters. Darkness closed over the plains of Coal Harbor, and even the sharpshooters desisted from their work. The stars shed a mild light upon the two armies which had so lately been engaged in fierce conflict, each now securely resting behind its line of earthworks, and the plain which lay between them, which the hurricane of battle had so lately swept, was as still as though the noise of war had never been heard there.

Suddenly, at eight o'clock, the rebels in front of our Sixth corps and of the Second corps, leaped over their works and rushed with a yell toward our lines. At the same time their artillery opened upon us. The course of their shells was marked by long curves of fire upon the dark sky, while the flashes of the guns and bursting missiles made a sublime display of pyrotechnics.

On came the charging column, against the left of the Sixth and the right of the Second corps; but nothing pleased our brave boys more than to see their enemies come out from the cover of their works to fight.

It had, during all these long days of battles, been ours to charge well defended earthworks almost invariably; and whenever the rebels chose to assume the offensive, our men were glad to show them the difference between being the assailants and the assailed.

Now the rebels came on with determination, but their attack was met by volley after volley of musketry aimed for effect; and our well directed fire of artillery made great gaps in the advancing lines. The attack was nobly repulsed, and many grey-coated soldiers who advanced to the charge, were left by their retreating comrades, dead between the two lines, while others were ordered in as prisoners. The rebels returned to their place, and again

45

all was still. From this time we had no more battles at
Coal Harbor, yet we daily lost many men by the shots of
the sharpshooters who were perched in trees, and who
kept up a fire at every moving thing which showed itself
within our lines.

Never before had our army been in a position where
there was such constant danger as at Coal Harbor. Men
in the front line dared not leave the cover of the breastworks except in the darkness of night, and even then the
movement of a company to the rear might bring on a
storm of shells. High breastworks were thrown up at all
angles with the main line, and deep trenches were dug, in
which the men might pass to and from the front without
being observed. Even with all these extraordinary precautions, no man was safe in venturing to go to the rear
by daylight. If a soldier collected the canteens of his
companions and started to the rear for water, he was
obliged to crawl along the trenches with the utmost
secrecy, and even then he was liable to be shot. Not a
day passed, even when there was no battle, in which
scores of men were not killed or brought to the hospitals
with severe wounds.

The whole plain occupied by our army was dug over.
Far to the rear the men had intrenched themselves. General officers had their tents erected in deep excavations
surrounded by embankments of earth, and special duty
men had each prepared for themselves burrows in the
ground, many of which were creditable specimens of
engineering. One was reminded, in riding over the plain,
of the colonies of prairie dogs with their burrows and
mounds. Although we had but two days' actual fighting
at Coal Harbor, our losses were more than thirteen thousand
men, while the rebels suffered comparatively small losses.

Thus the army lay upon the burning sands of that
arid plain, the greater part of the line without the

friendly shelter of a tree, weary, yet not discouraged; grimmy and dirty, and choked with dust, yet uttering no words of complaint, for twelve days.

Troops commenced moving toward the rear on the morning of the 11th of July, and it became known that we were to make no more attempts to force the formidable position. General Grant had ordered another flank movement. This time to the James river. Preparations for withdrawing went on actively on the 10th and 11th; all the wounded were sent to the White House, and the long trains of forage, ammunition and commissary supplies which had been allowed to come far toward the front, began to pass to the rear. On the 12th, Smith's corps was ordered to the White House, thence to embark to City Point, while the remainder of the army was to cross the Chickahominy far to the right of the rebel position, and march to the James river.

At three o'clock in the afternoon, the long hospital train of the Sixth corps moved out toward the left a few miles and halted for the corps, which withdrew from the works after dark, and marched with great rapidity toward the left. The other corps also withdrew from their positions, and the whole army moved off down the Chickahominy, the Second corps in advance. The march was kept up all night, a short halt only being allowed in the morning near Dispatch Station. Then the column pressed on again, the men almost suffocated with the dust, which hung over the column like a huge cloud; no halt was made at noon, and the men, deprived of their coffee, choked with dust, and burned with heat, marched wearily toward night. The sun was sinking in the west, tinging the clouds with purple, and crowning the distant hills with gold, when we crossed the historic Chickahominy. Two years before we had crossed the same stream not far from this very spot. Through how many vicissitudes of army life had we passed since that time.   The stream was not wide, and its banks were well defined where we crossed.   Indeed, at this point, there was nothing in the appearance of the stream that would convey any idea of the difficulties which it had once presented to the Union army.   The corps bivouacked on high grounds a mile from the river, glad to rest from the toiling march.

We were early astir on the morning of the 14th; taking our line of march through a delightful section of country where the comfortable farm houses and fine residences presented a striking contrast with the desolations to which we had become accustomed.   As we began to descend from the high lands toward the plain, on which stands the little cluster of houses called, in southern fashion, Charles City, we beheld, in the distance, the James river, lying in all its loveliness, spreading widely between its banks.   A magnificent prospect opened before us.   The river in the distance bordered by green fields, one undulating slope four or five miles wide, and twice as long, presenting a scene of surpassing beauty.   There were large fields of grain already yellow and nearly ripe for the harvest, green meadows lay in the beautiful valleys, the gentle breeze dallied with the tassels of the long rows of corn, which gave rich promise of an abundant harvest; fine groves upon the hillside, in the valleys and on the plain, gave a charming diversity to the scene, and the old mansions, embosomed in vines and trees, and surrounded by colonies of outhouses, reminded us of the ease and comfort which had reigned here before the ravages of war had desolated Virginia.   To the right was Charles City, almost hidden by trees, a little town, in prosperous days, the home of a few hundred people, now almost deserted.

In the vicinity of Charles City we halted a little before noon.   The Second corps, which was in the advance, had already reached the James at Wilcox's Landing, and was preparing to cross. The men of our corps were delighted with the opportunity of once more spreading their tents over clean grassy turf, and each quickly pitched his shelter tent preparatory to a refreshing rest.

Within two miles of our camp was the residence of the late ex-president, John Tyler, which was visited by many of our officers. It was a charming spot, with everything about it to please the eye of a lover of the beautiful. But except the grounds immediately surrounding the house, everything was in the wildness of nature.

The house was stripped of almost everything. The cabinet was carried off. The large library had lost many of its choicest volumes, while the remainder, with heaps of letters, lay thrown in wild confusion about the floor. The pile of sheet music which had been left on the piano by the family, had been culled over and nearly all taken away. In fact such a sad scene of destruction was rare, even in the track of a great army.

On the morning of the 15th, the corps moved to the river side, where it remained while other troops were crossing by ferry and on an immensely long pontoon bridge. The river was full of shipping, the forests of masts making strange contrasts with the native forests on the river banks.

Near the crossing was a superb old mansion, the residence of a rebel general, surrounded by its little village of negro cabins. Here many officers of the corps resorted, to spend the time in walking among the grand old trees, or to stroll through the garden, admiring the elegant and rare exotics which adorned the grounds. Here was the magnolia grandiflora in full bloom, its immense cup-like flowers filling the whole place with delightful fragrance, and the American agave, also loaded with a profusion of elegant flowers; roses of the most rare and superb varieties, jasmines, honeysuckles, clematis, spice woods, and a great variety of other choice plants, were also in lavish abundance. There were locust trees of enormous size, and everything that was inanimate filled us with surprise and delight. But, within the mansion, we were met with the accustomed bitterness and want of civility. Among the slaves on the premises was a white-haired negro, who was one hundred and eight years old. His wife, who lived upon a neighboring plantation, was one hundred and four years of age. When asked his age by the boys, he was accustomed to answer, " Well, massa, I'se going on *two hundred* now." The old fellow manifested no sympathy for the cause of his master, and even he sighed for freedom. When asked of what value freedom could be to him now, he answered, impatiently, " Well, massa, isn't a hundred and eight years long enough to be a slave ?"

The army, which had thus fought its way at fearful cost from the Rapidan to the James, was now to change its base, and threaten the rebel capital from the south. Petersburgh was now the objective point, and this was regarded as the door to Richmond.

Our army had, during the period of a little more than a month, fought the most extraordinary series of battles, and executed some of the most remarkable movements on record. Never was heroic valor exhibited on a grander scale than had been manifested by the Army of the Potomac throughout this long struggle, in which every man's life seemed doomed. The stubborn perseverance of the general was equaled by the persistent determination of his soldiers. Day after day they had been called upon to assault earthworks of formidable character, defended by veteran troops; and it was usually the case that they had seen, as the only fruits of their daring, almost reckless, charges, the ground in front of the hostile intrenchments strewed with the lifeless bodies of their comrades, while the enemy still held the coveted line of works.

The battle of the Wilderness was a strange, deadly struggle, which no man could see. A battle in which both armies were hidden in thickets and forests, impenetrable to vision, each making gigantic efforts for the overthrow and destruction of the other. It had resulted in no decisive advantage to either party. Lee was as ready to meet us at Spottsylvania as he had been in the Wilderness, and Grant was determined in his attack along the Ny, as though he had met with no repulse on Wilderness Run. The soldiers, too, of each army were as ready at Spottsylvania to test their relative valor as they had been in the Wilderness.

At Spottsylvania we had lost thousands of our best men, and hundreds of our ablest officers in futile attempts to drive our enemy from impregnable positions; yet, notwithstanding all our losses, and our hitherto unsuccessful assaults, our men rushed against the strong defenses at Coal Harbor with as much resolution and fortitude as though they had met with no reverses.

From the Rapidan to the Chickahominy the advance had been almost a continuous battle, in which our army fought at a disadvantage. The men had for more than a month engaged the enemy in mortal combat by day and made fatiguing marches by night only to find themselves again face to face with the enemy in the morning. Sixty thousand of our comrades were either killed, wounded or missing. Of these more than thirteen thousand had been lost at Coal Harbor, about thirty-two thousand in the Wilderness, and nearly fifteen thousand at Spottsylvania and on the North Anna.

It is true that our enemy had suffered great losses, yet not half as many rebels as Union men had fallen. At Coal Harbor the disproportion was much greater than elsewhere. There the rebel loss had not been one-tenth as great as our own. Notwithstanding our frequent repulses, and despite the fact that our road was continually blocked by an army behind powerful defenses, our march had been straight on toward the goal of our ambition, the rebel capital.

From the crossing of the Rapidan to the halt at Coal Harbor, in all our battles and all our flank movements, we had not swerved from the direct line to Richmond; and now, with unimpaired vigor and still relentless determination, the Army of the Potomac, and the imperturbable leader of the Union armies, were ready to undertake the capture of Richmond, by way of Petersburgh, fully assured that their illustrious valor and never failing courage must sooner or later meet with their award.

CHAPTER XXVII.

PETERSBURGH.

AT sunset on the 16th, the Sixth corps gathered upon the banks of the James river, and while the First and Third divisions embarked on steamers for City Point, the Second division crossed on the pontoon bridge. The division marched all night toward Petersburgh, from which direction we had heard cannonading all day. The column moved rapidly, leaving scores of stragglers, who quietly rolled themselves in their blankets and lay down behind the hedges to sleep till morning. The following day was sultry, and the dust was very annoying. The men were weary from want of sleep, and the march was a severe one; but at sunset the division arrived at our lines before Petersburgh. Smith's corps had preceded us, and by assaulting the rebel position on the evening of the 16th, had carried the lines northeast of the town for a distance of over two and a half miles, capturing fifteen pieces of artillery and three hundred prisoners. General Smith was then reinforced by Hancock's corps, which had just arrived by land, but no further advance was made that night. This neglect to take advantage of the absence of any large force of rebels in the works about Petersburgh was severely censured by General Grant, who could not understand why General Smith, now reinforced by a large corps, had not at once taken possession of the town. The day that the Second division, Sixth corps, arrived in

46

front of Petersburgh, the two divisions of that corps which had taken transports up the river, were ordered to reinforce General Butler at Bermuda Hundreds, where his command had gained some advantages, which were, however, lost before night. All the corps having got up, attacks upon the rebel positions were renewed on the 17th and 18th. The attack on the 17th was made by Smith's command, and resulted in the loss of a few men, when the lines were withdrawn.

Our Second division now relieved Brooks' division of the Eighteenth corps on the front line, the Seventy-seventh taking possession of a powerful redoubt, the other regiments taking their places in close proximity. The Vermont brigade was placed in rifle pits, as was also the First brigade. In order to secure unity of action, General Neill, commanding the division, was directed to receive orders from General Martindale of the Eighteenth corps.

Standing in the redoubt occupied by the Seventy-seventh, which was upon a high bluff, and commanded a fine prospect of the surrounding country, we could trace the line of defenses which had already been captured, and those yet in the hands of the enemy. The defenses of Petersburgh consisted of a line of strong earthworks, in the form of a semicircle. Immense redoubts, like the one we now occupied, were placed at frequent intervals, upon commanding positions, and these were connected by a line of rifle pits and high breastworks. At all advantageous points, also, were well constructed rifle pits, in front (now in rear) of the main works. Smith's corps had captured eleven of these forts and redoubts in the first assault, and they were now occupied by our forces, and the strong works which were intended for the defense of the town now bristled with cannon pointing toward it.

The line of powerful forts and breastworks commenced about two and a half miles below Petersburgh, on the

Appomattox, and, circling the city, terminated two or three miles above.

Before us stretched the valley of the Appomattox in all its beauty, the level plain between us and the river clothed in the verdure of summer, the green fields of corn yet untrodden by the troops of either side. Below the heights, stretching far to the right and left, was the line of rifle pits now occupied by our men, and beyond these could be traced the outlines of the new works which the rebels were throwing up. Still beyond all these, the spires of Petersburgh towered grandly, and by the help of a glass the streets and houses were distinctly visible.

On the 18th, another advance was made by the divisions of Smith's corps, a part of the Second corps, and our own Second division. Smith's troops advanced spiritedly across the plain, facing a withering fire of grape and canister, but were unable to come up to the rebel works.

They were ordered to lie down, and at once every man commenced to throw up a little mound of earth in front of him, using his cup or plate, or even his hands or jackknife, in place of a spade.

Under this destructive fire the troops were forced to remain for some time, but they at length retired, having lost several hundred of their number. Neill's division was on the left of Smith's troops, and did not advance as far. Our losses were therefore slight.

Owing to some unfortunate misunderstanding, the surgeons of the Eighteenth corps were ordered to the right of the line to establish field hospitals; consequently, when the wounded of that corps began to come in, there were none of their surgeons at hand. The surgeons of our own division, however, quickly proceeded to establish a hospital for them, in which they were all received and cared for, their wounds dressed, the shattered limbs removed, and all their wants attended to. The medical officers of the Eighteenth corps expressed their warmest gratitude for this act of kindness on the part of the Sixth corps surgeons, this being the second time that we had found an opportunity of assisting them in an emergency.

Our lines were daily drawn more closely around Petersburgh, but no other general action was brought on for some time. There was constant firing of artillery from both sides, and now and then the rattle of musketry would pass along the lines.

On the 22d, Colonel Bidwell's brigade occupied the front line of rifle pits. The sun was shining brightly, and our men, unprotected by shelter, were striving to pass the time with as little discomfort as possible. A group of men of the Seventy-seventh were behind the breastwork, stretched out upon the sand, resting upon their elbows and amusing each other with jokes, when a shell came shrieking into their midst. Its explosion threw them in every direction. One went high in the air and fell twenty feet from the spot where he was lying when the shell exploded. Strange to tell, not a man was killed, yet three had each a leg crushed to jelly, and two others were seriously wounded. The three whose legs were crushed were Sergeant James Barnes, James Lawrence, and James Allen, all of company A. The poor fellows were taken to the field hospital completely prostrated from the shock, cold sweat stood upon their pallid brows, and life seemed but to flicker before going out. The surgeons were making haste to load the wounded and sick into ambulances to send to City Point, for we were ordered to march at a moment's notice. "You can do nothing for those men," said the wide awake, enterprising Doctor Hall, who was superintending the loading of the ambulances, as he saw the surgeon who had charge of the operations prepare to remove the mangled members. "Better put them into ambulances and let them have a chance for their lives! There is no time now to wait for operations." "How long will it take you to load your ambulances, doctor?" "Twenty minutes, at least." "Then I will have the men ready for you." The surgeon gave to each of the unfortunate ones a glass of brandy, then administered his chloroform, and in less than thirty minutes had amputated the limbs, dressed the stumps, and placed the men in ambulances. They were taken at once to City Point, where they were placed together. Their cases excited great interest among the attendants in the hospital and the visitors, for each had lost a leg just above the knee, the name of each was James, they were all from one company, all wounded by a single shell, and all as cheerful as were ever wounded men. They were afterward removed to Washington and again placed side by side, and here, also, they were subjects of great interest to visitors. The writer has frequently heard the case of the three Jameses related by persons in different States, who never mistrusted that they were men of his own regiment. The boys are each well now, each walks with his artificial limb, and each is a worthy member of society.

General Grant, finding that his expectation of taking Petersburgh by surprise had failed, prepared for a systematic investment of the town. Accordingly, the Sixth and Second corps were directed to proceed to the left of the present line, so as to envelop the town, and also with the view of striking the Weldon railroad, and thus cutting off an important source of supplies for the rebel army.

On the 21st of May, the two corps marching in the rear of the rest of the army went into position on the left flank, the Second corps on the west of the Jerusalem plank road, and the Sixth to the left and rear of that corps, its line nearly at right angles with that of the Second corps. The cavalry divisions of Wilson and Kautz were, at the same time, ordered to proceed still farther to the left, and, cutting the Weldon road, continue the march across the country, until they should strike the Southside railroad, which they were directed to destroy.

On the morning of the 22d, General Birney, who, during the temporary absence of General Hancock, was in command of the Second corps, was directed to move his corps forward, so as to press upon the left flank of the enemy. This he proceeded to do, without giving notice of his intention to General Wright. The result of the movement was to leave a wide gap between the Second and Sixth corps.

To the great surprise of the Third division of our corps, which was just getting into position, the rebels advanced in strong force upon the flank and rear. A sharp skirmish occurred, in which that division and a part of the Second division lost some prisoners; but the principal loss fell upon the Second corps, for that corps, having thrown its left far in advance, was greatly exposed. The principal attack fell upon Barlow's division, which occupied the left. That division was driven in confusion upon the other divisions of the corps. The whole corps was forced back, but after some spirited fighting the rebels were forced back, carrying with them a battery belonging to the Second corps, and more than two thousand prisoners. From our own corps they had captured about six hundred men and a stand of colors.

The responsibility for this unfortunate surprise rests with the commander of the Second corps; for General Wright, being entirely ignorant of any design to advance that corps, had, of course, made no disposition to keep the line intact. The men of the Third division did all that men could do under the circumstances, and are entitled to much credit for the repulse which they gave the enemy.

From that day, except that at times the roar of artillery shook the earth for miles about, we remained quiet until the 29th of June. The light sandy soil soon became reduced to powder, and the continual passing of mules and army wagons raised huge clouds of dust, which completely enveloped the army. At sunset this cloud would settle down and become so dense that one could not see objects twenty yards from him. The heat was almost intolerable, yet the health of the men was better than usual for the summer months.

The surgeons had their hospitals neatly fitted up, and nurses and attendants took great pride in adorning the hospital tents with the boughs of the magnolia and other beautiful shrubs and flowers. The government and the agents of the Sanitary Commission supplied us liberally with lemons and vegetables, so, notwithstanding the intense heat, and the constant watchfulness of the men behind the earthworks, there was comparatively little illness.

In the afternoon of the 29th of June orders came for the Sixth corps to march at once to Reams' Station, far to the left, where the cavalry of Kautz and Wilson, which had been on an extensive raid, was expected to arrive. At four o'clock we left camp, marched all the remainder of the day and all night. We found ourselves in the morning at Reams' Station, on the Weldon Railroad. The men at once commenced tearing up the track and burning the ties. Thus they toiled all the morning, but no cavalry made its appearance. Late in the day the corps retraced their steps, and arrived that night within two and a half miles of the position we had left the day before. We made our bivouac on the Jerusalem plank road, and in the morning rejoined the main army before Petersburgh and resumed our old position.

The story of the great raid of Kautz and Wilson, which we now learned in detail, was one of thrilling interest, full of wild adventure, untold hardship and great peril. The two divisions had penetrated far to the rear of Lee's army,

had destroyed miles of the Weldon railroad, and then,
reaching the Southside road, the great artery for the supply of the rebel army, had torn up the track and burned
the ties for dozens of miles. In their return they had
fallen in with the cavalry of the enemy, and, when near
Reams' Station, had come upon a strong force of cavalry
and infantry. An engagement ensued, which resulted in
the Union cavalry being driven, and hundreds from the
immense throng of colored refugees, which was following
the cavalry towards the Union lines, were ridden down
by the rebel cavalry and killed. The cavalry at length
succeeded in reaching our lines by making a circuit farther
south, and many of the negroes also succeeded in escaping
from rebeldom.

CHAPTER XXVIII.

SIXTH CORPS TRANSFERRED TO WASHINGTON — BATTLE OF FORT STEVENS.

The Shenandoah Valley — Hunter's advance to Lynchburgh — The retreat — Rebels advance into Maryland — Battle of Monocacy — Sixth corps goes to Washington — Battle of Fort Stevens.

THE Shenandoah Valley, which had been the scene of such varied fortunes to our army during the war, again became a field of great interest.

Simultaneous with the opening of the spring campaign by the army of the Potomac, General Sigel, who then commanded in the valley, commenced to move his army. On the 15th of May he met the enemy at New Market, and was defeated. He withdrew his army to Harper's Ferry, where, by order of General Grant, who was dissatisfied with his management, he was relieved of his command by General Hunter.

General Hunter at once resumed offensive operations, moved up the valley and encountered the enemy at Piedmont and routed him, capturing fifteen hundred prisoners, three pieces of artillery and three thousand stand of small arms. He then pursued the routed army to Lynchburgh, which place he invested. To meet this movement of Hunter, Lee had sent General Early with his corps to the assistance of the rebel garrison. This force arrived just before the Union army came up. General Hunter, finding that he was confronted by a large force, his ammunition being nearly exhausted, the difficulties of transporting over so long a march sufficient ordnance stores being very great, he determined to withdraw without risking a battle. His want of ammunition forced him to make his retreat by that route which would afford most natural obstacles to pursuit and attack of the enemy. Accordingly, instead of retiring directly down the Shenandoah, he drew his forces off through the Kanawha Valley, leaving the Shenandoah open to the rebel army. The march of Hunter's men through the Kanawha, harassed by the enemy and destitute of food, was one of great severity. The rebels finding the Shenandoah open to them, at once pushed northward with a view of ravaging Maryland and Pennsylvania, and, if possible, entering Washington.

Owing to the great difficulties encountered by General Hunter's army, in reaching Harper's Ferry in time to oppose Early, it became necessary to send other troops to meet the invading force. Accordingly, about the 1st of July, the Third division of our Sixth corps, under command of General Ricketts, was sent to Baltimore, and from thence marched toward Frederick, Maryland, where, on the banks of the Monocacy near the railroad bridge, the enemy was encountered. The Union forces consisted of the division from the Sixth corps, and a few thousand green troops collected about Baltimore, all under command of General Wallace. The force of Early greatly outnumbered those of the Union general, and after a hard fought battle our men were driven back. Although General Wallace had met with defeat, he had succeeded in arresting the progress of the invasion for a time, and enabled the remainder of our corps and a division of the Nineteenth corps to reach Washington in advance of the rebels.

Such was the state of affairs in Maryland, when, on the evening of the 9th July, the First and Second divisions of the Sixth corps were ordered to march to City Point at once. The order came at nine o'clock, and without delay the troops were in motion. We had become too much accustomed to sudden movements, to require long preparations for breaking up camp. The march of fourteen miles to City Point made during the night, was far more tolerable than it could have been by day. For although the roads were composed of dry beds of dust, in which the men sank almost ankle deep at every step, and the cloud which rose as the column moved along filled their throats and eyes and nostrils, yet they were not forced to endure the misery of a long march under a burning sun, such as for many days past had scorched these sandy plains.

It was daylight when the Sixth corps reached the James river at City Point, and the process of embarking commenced at once. Before noon the two divisions, with the horses and baggage, were on board transports, which were in readiness when we arrived. The staff of Bidwell's brigade, with the Seventy-seventh and part of the Forty-ninth New York, with the brigade band, where on board the steamer Escort. We had also on board a hundred horses.

Great satisfaction was felt by all at the prospect of leaving the region whose natural desolation was heightened by the devastation of war, and going to a country of plenty, with which so many pleasant remembrances were associated. Each man breathed more freely as the steamer swung out upon the river, and our brigade band sounded a good-bye to the scenes of our recent labors and privations.

Our fleet was soon steaming down the river, passing scenes of interest, many of which were intimately connected with the memories of other campaigns. There was Harrison's Landing, the camping ground of two years ago, the last one on the Peninsula, where our Union army crowded together on the banks of the James, sweltering beneath the oppressive heat of a southern sun; Fort Powhattan, where we had crossed the river on pontoons a month ago; the iron-clad Atlanta, once a rebel ram, now doing service in the Union cause; the ancient settlement of Jamestown; the three-turreted monitor Roanoke; Sewell's Point; Hampton, the scene of our earliest Peninsula experience; the bay at Newport News, made famous by the conflict of the Monitor and Merrimac, the masts of the Cumberland still towering above the waters of the bay as monuments of the wonderful contest; the old haunts of the Teaser, which had so unceremoniously introduced herself to our division; and, as evening came on, we passed Fortress Monroe, where the many lights of the fleet gave the harbor the appearance of a city in the waves.

The wind was blowing freshly when we rounded Old Point Comfort, and our little steamer ploughed the white caps bravely. We made good time, and found ourselves the next morning steaming up the Potomac. Aquia creek was passed, recalling to mind the encampment at White Oak Church; Mount Vernon claimed its tribute of thought, and at two o'clock we touched the wharf at the foot of Sixth street, Washington. The rest of the two divisions had already reached the wharves, and there, too, were some immense sea steamers, crowded with troops of the Nineteenth corps, fortunately just arrived from New Orleans.

The process of disembarking occupied but little time. President Lincoln stood upon the wharf chatting familiarly with the veterans, and now and then, as if in compliment to them, biting at a piece of hard tack which he held in his hand.

The column was formed and we marched up Seventh street, past the Smithsonian Institute, the Patent Office and the Post Office, meeting on our way many old friends, and hearing the people who crowded upon the sidewalks exclaiming, "It is the old Sixth corps!" "Those are the men who took Marye's Heights!" "The danger is over now!" We had never before realized the hold which the corps had upon the affection of the people. Washington, an hour before was in a panic; now as the people saw the veterans wearing the badge of the Greek cross marching through their streets, the excitement subsided and confidence prevailed.

Thus we made our way to the north of the city, the sound of cannonading in our front stimulating and hastening the steps of the men. Families, with a few of their choicest articles of household furniture loaded into wagons, were hastening to the city, reporting that their houses were burned, or that they had made their escape leaving the greater part of their goods to the mercy of the rebels.

We reached a fine grove in rear of Fort De Russey and made our bivouac for the night.

Now we learned the true position of affairs. Early, having defeated the small force under General Wallace, pushed on toward Washington, carrying destruction in the path of his army. His cavalry reached Rockville, a little town twelve miles north of Washington, on the 10th, detachments having destroyed portions of the Baltimore and Ohio railroad, seized trains of cars, in one of which was General Franklin, formerly commander of the Sixth corps, who was made a prisoner, but who managed to escape, and now, as we reached Washington, his advance was knocking at the defenses of that city. The forts were manned by a small force of heavy artillery, hundred days' men, and detachments of the Invalid corps; and, as we reached the rear of the defenses, regiments composed of clerks and employes of the quartermaster's department, with convalescents from the hospitals, marched past us to take their places on the front. These hasty levies were placed in the forts for the night, to be replaced by veteran troops in the morning.

July 12th came bright and glorious. The First brigade of our Second division, and our sharpshooters, were on picket in front of Fort Stevens; the Second and Third brigades still enjoying the delightful shade of the groves in rear of Fort De Russey. From the parapets of Fort Stevens could be seen the lines of rebel skirmishers, from whose rifles the white puffs of smoke rose as they discharged their pieces at our pickets. The valley beyond the fort presented a scene of surpassing loveliness, with its rich green meadows, its fields of waving corn, its orchards and its groves. To the right was Fort Slocum, and on the left Fort De Russey.

The residence of Hon. Montgomery Blair was within the line occupied by the confederates, and we heard that the fine mansion had been the scene of plunder and destruction, in revenge, as the rebels declared, for havoc wrought by our troops in Virginia.

The principal force of the enemy seemed to be in front of Fort Stevens, and here it was determined to give them battle. The barracks just in rear of the fort were converted into a hospital for our Second division, and all preparations were made for receiving our wounded men.

Four o'clock came, but, except that the rebel skirmishers were sending their bullets whizzing over the fort, all was quiet. President Lincoln and his wife drove up to the barracks, unattended, except by their coachman, the superbly mounted squadron of cavalry, whose duty it was to attend upon his excellency, being left far behind. The carriage stopped at the door of the hospital, and the President and his affable lady entered into familiar conversation with the surgeon in charge, praising the deeds of the old Sixth corps, complimenting the appearance of its veterans, and declaring that they, as well as the people of the country, appreciated the achievements of the wearers of the Greek cross.

Thus, for nearly an hour, they chatted of various things, when General Wright and his staff arrived on the ground, accompanied by several ladies and gentlemen from the city.

All now repaired to the fort, and presently the portly form of Colonel Bidwell, followed by his Third brigade, was seen approaching. The brave colonel and his brave brigade marched past the fort into the valley beyond, the President, the members of his cabinet and the ladies praising the hardy, soldierly bearing of the men as they passed. They formed in two lines of battle, in rear of the skirmish line of the first brigade, the Seventy-seventh on the right of the line, then the Seventh Maine, and then the Forty-ninth. The Forty-third New York, Sixty-first Pennsylvania, and One Hundred and Twenty-second New York forming the second line. The advance line was in charge of Colonel French.

According to preconcerted arrangements, Colonel Bidwell was to signify to General Wright, who remained in the fort, his readiness for the attack by a signal from the new flag of the Seventy-seventh, which had not yet been baptized in battle; then the great guns in the fort were to open a storm of shells upon the rebel position, especially upon a house behind which and in which numbers of rebels had all day found refuge; then General Wright was to signal from the fort the command to advance and the brigade was to rush to the charge.

Thus, with a perfect understanding on the part of all concerned, the brigade took its place.

The flag of the Seventy-seventh waved the signal of readiness, the heavy ordnance in the fort sent volley after volley of thirty-two pound shells howling over the heads of our men into the midst of the rebels, and through the house where so many of them had found shelter, and then at the command of Sedgwick's "man of iron," the brave fellows started eagerly forward. They reached and passed the skirmishers, and the white puffs of smoke and the sharp crack from their rifles became more and more frequent, first the rattle of an active skirmish, and then the continuous roar of a musketry battle.

In magnificent order and with light steps they ran forward, up the ascent, through the orchard, through the little grove on the right, over the rail fence, up to the road, making straight for the first objective point, the frame house in front. The rebels at first stood their ground, then gave way before the impetuous charge.

The President, the members of his cabinet and the ladies, as well as the military officers in the fort, and the crowd of soldiers and citizens, who had gathered about it to witness the fight, watched with breathless interest the gallant advance as our boys pushed forward, keeping their line of battle perfect, except when now and then some regiment having the advantage of ground, in its eagerness got a little in advance of others, until they saw the rebels take to flight. Then the crowd at the fort rent the air with exultant cheers, and as the boys reached the house, the people were wild with excitement, shouting and clapping their hands, leaping and dancing with joy.

But the rebels did not yield without resistance. They met our men bravely, and though forced to seek safety in flight, turned and poured their volleys into the ranks of the pursuers.

Lieutenant-Colonel Johnson, commanding the Forty-ninth, a brave man, who had never shrunk from danger, and who had shared all the varied fortunes of the brigade since its organization, fell mortally wounded. Colonel Visscher, of the Forty-third, who had but lately succeeded the beloved Wilson, was killed. Major Jones, commanding the Seventh Maine, was also among the slain; and Major Crosby, commanding the Sixty-first Pennsylvania,

BATTLE OF FORT STEVENS.

who had but just recovered from the bad wound he
received in the Wilderness, was taken to the hospital,
where the surgeon removed his left arm from the shoulder.
Colonel French, of the Seventy-seventh, was injured, but
not seriously. The commanding officer of every regiment
in the brigade was either killed or wounded.

The fight had lasted but a few minutes, when the stream
of bleeding, mangled ones, began to come to the rear.
Men, leaning upon the shoulders of comrades, or borne
painfully on stretchers, the pallor of their countenances
rendered more ghastly by the thick dust which had settled
upon them, were brought into the hospitals by scores,
where the medical officers, ever active in administering
relief to their companions, were hard at work binding up
ghastly wounds, administering stimulants, coffee and food,
or resorting to the hard necessity of amputation.

At the summit of the ascent, the confederates were
strengthened by their second line of battle, and here they
made a stout resistance ; but even this position they were
forced to abandon in haste, and as darkness closed in upon
the scene, our men were left as victors in possession of the
ground lately occupied by the rebels, having driven their
adversaries more than a mile.

The Vermont brigade now came to the relief of the boys
who had so gallantly won the field, and the Third brigade
returned at midnight to the bivouac it had left in the
morning. But not all returned. Many of those brave
fellows who went with such alacrity into the battle, had
fallen to rise no more. In the orchard, in the road, about
the frame house and upon the summit, where the rebels had
made so determined a resistance, their forms were stretched
upon the green sward and in the dusty road, stiff and cold.
Many more had come to the hospital severely injured,
maimed for life or mortally wounded.

The little brigade, numbering only a thousand men

when it went into action, had lost two hundred and fifty of its number.

During the night the raiders made their escape toward Rockville. The prisoners left in our hands told us that they had anticipated an easy victory in front of Washington, believing that the forts were defended only by convalescents and quartermaster's men, and, when they saw the white crosses of the old Sixth corps, they were seized with consternation. They now understood that the city was guarded by veterans who had acquired, in the rebel army, a disagreeable reputation.

While the battle was in progress, President Lincoln stood upon the parapet of the fort watching, with eager interest, the scene before him. Bullets came whistling around, and one severely wounded a surgeon who stood within three feet of the President. Mrs. Lincoln entreated him to leave the fort, but he refused; he, however, accepted the advice of General Wright to descend from the parapet and watch the battle from a less exposed position.

Cavalry was sent in the morning to ascertain the direction of the flight of the enemy, but the infantry remained quietly awaiting events.

We gathered our dead comrades from the field where they had fallen, and gave them the rude burial of soldiers on the common near Fort Stevens. None of those high in authority, who had come out to see them give up their lives for their country, were present to pay the last honors to the dead heroes. No officer of state, no lady of wealth, no citizen of Washington was there; but we laid them in their graves within sight of the capital, without coffins, with only their gory garments and their blankets around them. With the rude tenderness of soldiers, we covered them in the earth; we marked their names with our pencils on the little head-boards of pine, and turned sadly away to other scenes.

But though no concourse of citizens followed the patriots to their humble resting place, though no bands wailed the solemn dirge, and no casket but the earth inclosed their remains, their deeds were not forgotten. Their memory was enshrined in the hearts of the people ; and after a few weeks their remains were exhumed from their scattered graves, they were placed together in a little inclosure on the sunny slope in front of the fort, and a beautiful monument tells the story of their noble sacrifice.

CHAPTER XXIX.

THE SHENANDOAH VALLEY.

The Sixth and Nineteenth corps follow the enemy—Crossing the Potomac—
Averill's fight at Snicker's Gap—Return of the Sixth corps to Washing-
ton—March back to Harper's Ferry—Return to Maryland—Death of Major
Ellis—General Sheridan assigned to command—Back in the Valley—Charles-
town—John Mosher—March to Fisher Hill—Return to Charlestown—Fight at
Charlestown.

At one o'clock the column of the Sixth corps moved
away from Fort Stevens, marching through the little village of Tanleytown, following in pursuit of the rebels.
We moved rapidly till ten o'clock, then halted, much
fatigued, at Potomac Cross Roads. At five o'clock, next
morning, we were once more on our way, and after a march
of twelve hours through a pleasant country, we made our
bivouac at Poolsville, having marched thirty-six miles
since leaving Fort Stevens. Our Sixth corps, with the
two divisions of the Nineteenth corps, now constituted a
new army, under command of General Wright, General
Getty having command of the Sixth corps. At Poolsville
we lay all day, waiting for our small cavalry force to find
out the course which Early's army had taken, but on Saturday morning, the 16th, we were moving at daylight.
We marched toward the Potomac, which we forded near
the scene of Ball's Bluff slaughter. The spectacle at the
ford was novel and exciting. The stream was wide, but
not more than two or three feet deep. The bottom was
rough and stony, and the current was strong. For nearly
a mile up and down the river the brigades were crossing;
the stream filled with infantry wading with difficult steps

over the uneven bottom, mounted officers carefully guiding their horses lest they should stumble, trains of artillery and wagons slowly toiling through, and groups of pack animals scarcely able to keep their footing under their huge burdens. The laugh of hundreds sounded up and down the river, as some unfortunate footman, slipping from a smooth stone, would, for a moment, disappear beneath the surface of the river, or as some overloaded mule or pack horse, losing his footing, would precipitate his load, and peradventure the small negro boy, who, in order to secure a dry passage across the ford, had perched himself on the top of the bags and bundles, into the rushing waters.

The troops gathered upon the southern bank of the river, and the infantry proceeded to empty the water from their boots and shoes, and to wring it from their stockings. This short task over, the march was resumed.

Passing through a section where some very interesting conglomerate rocks attracted the attention of those scientifically inclined, we left the little town of Leesburgh behind, and at eight o'clock in the morning encamped in a ploughed field, tired and hungry, and, it must be confessed, a little dissatisfied at the idea of sleeping on ploughed ground while fresh meadows were on every side of us. In this bivouac we spent the Sabbath, and services were held by the chaplains in the various brigades.

Early Monday morning the march was resumed, our little army passing through the delightful hill scenery of Loudon county, and through the diminutive villages of Hamilton and Purcellville. As the afternoon advanced, we found ourselves toiling up the ascent of the Blue Ridge, pleasant farm houses and fine orchards greeting our sight on either side of the road. Darkness was upon us before we passed through Snicker's Gap, a deep gorge in the mountains, through which winds a rough, unkept road; and by the moonlight we spread our blankets for another night's rest.

The morning revealed the lovely Shenandoah Valley spread out before us, its river lying at our feet.

The troops of the "Army of Virginia," under Averill, had engaged the enemy with doubtful success before our arrival. Indeed, the troops on both sides seemed to have become demoralized. The rebels were retreating, and Averill's men had made their way back to the east side of the river in such hot haste as to leave some of their flags floating in the stream.

We remained during the 19th in apparent uncertainty as to what course to pursue, whether to give chase to the enemy, who it was now supposed had made good his retreat up the valley, or to return to Washington. But an order from General Grant, directing General Wright to get back to Washington at once with the Sixth corps, that the troops might be at once returned to the Army of the Potomac before Early could reinforce Lee, determined our course, and at night we were again passing through Snicker's Gap, the infantry and teams crowded together in the narrow defile to the great inconvenience of the footmen and annoyance of the artillerymen and teamsters. Marching rapidly all night and the next day, halting only a short time for coffee in the morning and at noon, we retraced our steps to Leesburgh, then following the turnpike we reached and passed Drainsville, and halted near Difficult creek. July 23d, the corps marched through Lewinsville and Langley, passed Camp Griffin, the memory of which was indissolubly connected with our first winter in the service, crossed Chain bridge and went in camp near Tanleytown, five miles out from Washington.

Transports were waiting on the Potomac to convey us to City Point, but as matters in the valley still seemed unsettled, the corps remained at Tanleytown, and on the

25th, it became certain that Early with his army was again moving down the valley, threatening Maryland and Pennsylvania. The Sixth corps received orders to move at once toward Harper's Ferry, but by some delay it was noon of the 26th when it turned back from Tanleytown toward the scene of our future brilliant operations.

The day on which the corps moved had been hot, and many of the men, weary with long marches, had been forced to fall out, but, most of all, bad whisky from Washington had demoralized great numbers, and these, with the sick and weary, made up a great crowd of stragglers. The task, which was assigned to the rear-guard, the Seventy-seventh New York, of urging these inebriated and discouraged ones toward their commands, was not an easy or agreeable one. The corps made all haste in the direction of Frederick, which city it reached on the 28th, crossing the field of General Wallace's battle with Early.

Without halting at Frederick, except to get our coffee near Monocacy creek, we pushed on to Jefferson, getting into camp at midnight. The next day we marched through Knoxville, Newton and Sandy Hook, through that wonderful gorge in the mountains at Harper's Ferry, and arrived at evening footsore and weary at Halltown, four miles south of Harper's Ferry. Then, next day we were ordered back again. The whole command poured into the deep valley at Harper's Ferry, the day was sultry even for that locality, not a breath of air seemed to be stirring, and the high mountains on every side reflected the heat and kept off the breeze. Into this hot, dusty inclosure among the hills, the whole army poured, and as there was only a single pontoon bridge to serve as an outlet, there was of course great delay. Horses stood harnessed to the cannon or under the saddle, the sweat literally pouring off their sides like rain, while men panted for breath and seemed almost on the point of suffocation. It was late in the night when our corps was all over the bridge, and the march was continued without rest during the whole night and all next day till we arrived again near Frederick City, where we had a night and a day of rest. We now learned that the cause of our sudden countermarch was the raid of Early's cavalry, who had burned the city of Chambersburgh, and caused much destruction of property elsewhere.

By this time the Sixth corps was, in army parlance, "about played out." Even our famous marches on the Gettysburgh campaign were eclipsed by this perpetual series of forced marches for nearly a month. The men were very much worn from their campaigns before leaving Petersburgh, but now we had had a month of traveling, night and day.

Hardly were the troops settled in camp for a night of rest, before the bugle called them to go again. Now when we marched, horses would drop down by dozens along the road, unable to rise again. Their riders would strip them of their saddles, and leave the worn out steeds to their fate. If, by chance, one of these deserted horses, after a few hours of rest, could muster strength to rise to his feet, he was doomed to be seized by some drummer boy, or other wight of the "bummer" tribe, mounted and rode till his strength again failed. Then the dismounted bummer would coolly remove his hempen bridle, shoulder his drum, and seek for another steed. For two or three days past the weather had been excessively hot, and men could be seen lying all along the roadside, as we marched, suffering from sunstroke.

Wednesday, August 3d, the Sixth corps marched to Buckeystown, a little village on the Monocacy, about five miles south of Frederick.

The different brigades of the corps were scattered about on the hillsides which bounded the pleasant valley of the

Monocacy, where pure fresh air was in abundance, and the men gladly availed themselves of the privilege of bathing in the delightfully clear waters of the river. For a distance of nearly two miles the river was filled with bathers at all hours, except in the hottest part of the day and in the night, and even then some might be seen enjoying the luxury of the bath.

At Buckeystown we remained two days, in the enjoyment of a pleasant bivouac; yet, as though no place was free from evil, an event occurred here afflictive to our brigade and to the corps.

Among the most energetic and brave officers of our Third brigade, was Major Ellis, of the Forty-ninth New York. He had been wounded at Spottsylvania while leading a charge against the enemy at the terrible "angle." A ramrod had passed through his left arm, and bruised the chest near the heart. He was taken to Fredericksburgh, from whence he went to Washington, and thence home. Returning to his command before he had fully recovered, he was advised by medical officers not to attempt any severe duty. But being detailed to the staff of General Russell, commanding the First division, he at once resumed active military duties. On these recent marches, the major, weary of inaction, had taken command of a body of men who acted as additional provost-guard to the division.

In this position he had exhibited his usual energy, though it was thought by some he executed his duties with too great severity. Ever since receiving his wound, he had complained of severe neuralgic pains in the region of the heart. Except that this pain was slightly more acute than usual, the major retired to his tent on the night of the 3d, in his accustomed health.

In the morning he sent his servant from the tent for a moment, and when the man returned the major was dead. An autopsy was made by the writer of these pages, in the

49

presence of about twenty of his professional brethren. A sharp splinter of bone from one of the ribs was found with its acute point piercing vital organs.

The funeral display was the most imposing ever witnessed in any corps of the Army of the Potomac. We had seen military pageants on a large scale, but nothing to compare with this in its solemn sublimity.

The remains were laid in state in a large tent near General Russell's head-quarters, wrapped in a silken flag, and the tent itself was draped with the Stars and Stripes. Presently the major's regiment, the Forty-ninth New York, came as mourners, unarmed, and formed in two ranks facing each other near the tent. Then the chaplain of the Forty-ninth, led in a short religious service, very appropriate and very impressive, while the whole of the First division was being formed in two parallel lines facing each other, and about eighty paces apart. The service over, a regiment of heavy artillery came to act as escort. The remains, inclosed in a rude coffin, wrapped in the flag under which he had so often fought, were placed in an ambulance, and the funeral cortege began its slow march through the long lines of sunbrowned veterans who stood on either side. First in the procession was the escort, the muskets of the men reversed, preceded by a band playing a solemn dirge. Then the ambulance with the remains, the major's hat, coat and sword lying upon the coffin; then his riderless horse, saddled and bridled, and led by a servant; then the regiment as mourners; and finally General Russell and the staff of the First division with the division flag, and the staffs of the three brigades of the division, and our Third brigade, Second division, each with its flag, with a large concourse of officers, personal friends of him whose remains were thus honored.

As the cortege proceeded with slow steps between the lines of soldiers, they stood with arms presented, and the colors of the regiments drooped as the procession passed. Thus attended the remains were conveyed to the railroad station, three miles distant, where they were placed on board a train for Washington.

Lieutenant-General Grant visited our army on the 5th of August, and, in consultation with General Hunter, determined upon a course for our future operations. So quietly was this visit of the Commander-in-Chief of the armies made, that very few in our little army knew of the presence of General Grant.

Among other things determined upon at this time was a change of commanders. General Hunter, who had commanded the "Army of the Shenandoah," with credit to himself and honor to our arms, was to be relieved, and General Philip S. Sheridan, who had, since the commencement of the spring campaign, commanded the cavalry corps of the Army of the Potomac, was to take command of all the forces operating against Early. The department of West Virginia, Washington, Susquehanna and the Middle Department, were to constitute the "Middle Military Division," to be under the command of General Sheridan. To this middle military division the Sixth corps was temporarily assigned. This was a new era in the history of that corps. Hitherto it had been, from the beginning, connected with the noble Army of the Potomac. Its history and its fame were inseparably connected with the history of that army, and when the corps had come to the rescue of the capital, it came as a detachment of the Army of the Potomac. Now, for the first time, the corps was to be identified with another army. But great as was the fame and honor which the corps had, by noble deeds, won for itself, it was now, by heroic achievements in the new field, to crown itself with glories even more dazzling than those in its proudest days in the old army.

We were ordered, on the evening of the 5th, to march

immediately. The troops of the Sixth corps proceeded at once to Monocacy Junction, where they took cars for Harper's Ferry. The quartermasters, and hospital trains followed rapidly by the wagon roads.

Troops and trains reached the heights beyond Harper's Ferry at night, and on the following morning the line of battle was established at Halltown.

General Sheridan now assumed command. We knew little of him except that he had very successfully commanded the cavalry of the Army of the Potomac for the last three months, but we were satisfied that General Grant trusted to his generalship, and we had already learned enough of General Grant's knowledge of human nature to place confidence in the general of his choice.

One thing pleased us at the start. Our new general was visible to the soldiers of his command; wherever we went he was with the column, inhaling the dust, leaving the road for the teams, never a day or two days behind the rest of the army, but always riding by the side of the men. His watchful care of the details of the march, his interest in the progress of the trains, and the ready faculty with which he brought order out of confusion when the roads became blockaded, reminded us of our lamented Sedgwick. Another feature of the new administration pleased us. When the head-quarter tents of the commander of the Middle Military Division were pitched, there was one wall tent, one wedge tent and two flies. This modest array of shelter for the general and his staff was in happy contrast with the good old times in the Army of the Potomac, when more than eighty six-mule teams were required to haul the baggage for head-quarters of the army.

At Halltown we remained for a few days, gaining what we so much needed, rest. The air was delightfully cool and refreshing, and it seemed as though each particular breath was laden with health and strength.

We were rejoiced to see some of our Army of the Potomac cavalry joining us, and our army began to assume dimensions which filled us with confidence. We had now the Sixth corps, General Wright, two divisions of the Nineteenth corps under General Emory, and Hunter's "Army of Virginia," usually called the Eighth corps, under command of General Crook. Our cavalry consisted of Averill's force which had been in the valley, and we were now receiving two divisions from the Army of the Potomac, one in command of General Torbert, the other of General Wilson. The cavalry force was soon afterward organized, with General Torbert in command of the whole force, and Generals Custer, Averill and Merritt, each in command of a division.

On the tenth of the month we commenced our march up the Shenandoah Valley. No sooner had the sun made its appearance above the Blue Ridge than we found the day to be most intensely hot. Soldiers were falling along the roadside in great numbers overcome with the heat, and what added to the hardships of the day's journey was the want of water. The turnpike along which we marched was parallel with a fine stream of water on either side, but the water was so far distant as to be useless to the soldiers. Yet there were a few springs and wells at some distance from the road which supplied those who could leave the column.

We passed through Charlestown, the scene of the trial and execution of John Brown. There was the court house to which he was brought on his couch to receive his trial for treason, and there the jail in which he spent his last days, and from which he was led to execution. How had all things changed! The people who stood about the gallows of John Brown, and gnashed their teeth in their bitter hatred, were now themselves guilty of treason. The court house was in ruins, and the jail was but a shell of tottering walls. The town also had suffered fearful ravages from war, and now a Union army was marching through its streets, every band and every drum corps playing the stirring but to southern ears hateful air, " John Brown's body lies mouldering in the grave," and we may anticipate our narrative to say that whenever our army or any part of it had occasion to pass through this town, the bands always struck up this air, as if to taunt the inhabitants with the memory of their victim, and played it from one limit of the town to the other. So John Brown was revenged!

The Shenandoah Valley has been often called the "Garden of Virginia," and truly it is a lovely valley, yet as we marched along we could see but little cultivation. The groves of oak were delightful. Teams with wagons might be driven anywhere among them. But the fields were mostly desolate. Here and there a field of corn promised a medium crop if left to ripen untrodden by our army, but there was no luxuriance of vegetation. The mountains, the Blue Ridge on one side and the North mountains on the other, rose abruptly from the valley in parallel lines, and looked as though a race of Titans had been at war, and had thrown up these long ridges as breastworks for opposing forces.

A little beyond Charlestown was a lovely meadow, lying between two groves of oak. At the further end of the meadow was a neat white cottage, where there seemed more comfort than we had seen elsewhere in the valley. The place was away from the direct line of march, and partly concealed by the groves.

Those who left the column were furnished by the family with pure sweet water from a well, which the family asserted was sunk by order of General Braddock. Such places were so rare that our men and animals suffered from thirst. Few who were on that march will forget a spring which we passed near the close of that day's march. A large white frame house stood upon an elevation, surrounded by trees, and at foot of the elevation, a large spring, under the shade of a huge willow, and surrounded by other trees. The water gushed out from a fissure in the rock, clear as crystal, and in such volume that a large brook was formed at once. Over the spring was the usual "spring house." Soldiers filled this building, covered the great rocks, crowded the grove, and for many yards around a dense mass of men pressed to get near the tempting fountain, all eager to fill their cups and canteens, and hasten on with the column. No one can know with what delight the soldiers quaffed the sparkling fluid from their sooty coffee pots, who has not suffered the torture of extreme thirst.

We halted near Clifton, and resumed our march on the following morning, to suffer, if possible, more from heat and thirst than ever. At night we bivouacked near Opequan creek. We threw ourselves upon the grassy sward, with the beautiful canopy of heaven with its mottled clouds and twinkling stars and flying meteors, for our tent. For many of us, this was the only tent we had slept under since leaving Petersburgh, and we were satisfied with it. The air was purer and the breeze fresher than when we were inclosed by canvas.

Again, on the morning of the 12th, we were marching. We passed through the villages of Newtown and Middletown, and halted at night on the banks of Cedar creek.

We were startled in the morning by the announcement of the death of a good soldier. John Mosher had marched with the column the day before, but owing to the overpowering heat was obliged to fall a little behind. Toward evening, finding himself too much exhausted to walk further, he applied for and obtained permission to ride in an ambulance of the First division.

During the night he was found to be dying. The kind hearted surgeon in charge of the hospital of the First division, Dr. Crehore, and one of his assistants, spent some hours with him, using every means to restore him, but without avail. He died before morning. A letter in his pocket told his name and regiment. We made a grave near Cedar creek, and a few of his comrades stood around it while he was lowered to his bed of earth, wrapped in his blanket. The chaplain offered a brief prayer; his fellows in arms fired a parting salute, and we left him to sleep in the valley where, a few weeks later, some of his companions were to rest by his side.

On the 13th all the troops were across on the south side of Cedar creek. The pickets of our Second division occupied one end of the village of Strasburgh, while those of the enemy held the other. We were sure that we must fight here, and we were not unwilling. Our cavalry was scouting on the flanks, skirmishing with rebel cavalry and searching for a way to outflank Early's army. The rebels held a position of great strength, and to make a direct assault would be to run a great risk of a repulse. The walls of the valley, the Blue Ridge and the North Mountains, came close together here, and, to render the position stronger, Fisher Hill, a commanding eminence, a prominent object in the landscape, to be seen from one end of the valley to the other, rose directly in our front and obstructed our passage. Upon the declivities of this hill the enemy had planted batteries so as to command our approach from any direction.

We remained gazing at this strong position till nightfall, and then recrossed the river, and made our position strong for defense. General Sheridan had been instructed by General Grant not to bring on a general engagement unless it was forced upon him. General Grant regarded our army rather as one of defense than for offensive operations. Should we suffer defeat, the capital and the rich fields of Pennsylvania and Maryland would again be open to the rebels. So we were to watch their movements and hold them in check, but we were not to risk a battle with them.

Meanwhile, the ubiquitous Mosby was at work in our rear, at Berryville, with a band of guerrillas. He had made a bold dash upon a long train, belonging principally to the cavalry, and guarded by almost a brigade of hundred days' men; had dispersed the inexperienced guard, which was scattered along the road for miles; had captured the mules, and burned the wagons and supplies. Seventy-five wagons had fallen a prey to the adventurous bandit, while the hundred days' men had made good their escape. Old men, women and children, joined in the work of destruction, setting fire to the wagons, and carrying off whatever articles they could easily remove from them. Prisoners whom they captured were murdered, either by Mosby's band, or by the more merciless citizens, and left unburied.

This raid upon our communications led General Sheridan to fear a more general advance of the rebels beyond the mountains, with a view of coming with force upon our rear.

So, on the evening of Tuesday, the 16th, the army marched northward down the valley again. All night and all the next day the weary march was kept up. We went through Winchester, where the rebel women came out by hundreds to rejoice at our retreat, and halted on the banks of the Opequan for the night. Then, when the morning came, we were off again, and, after a severe march, formed in line of battle a mile south of Charlestown.

The Jersey brigade, under Colonel Penrose, was left as rear-guard and support to the cavalry on the retreat. At Winchester the brigade, flanked by cavalry, made a

50

stand. The enemy came down upon the brigade in large force, handled it roughly, and sent the Jersey boys through the town in confusion. Their resistance had been all that could have been asked; but the brigade, staunch as it was, was not enough for the force that came against it.

Our Sixth corps guarded the turnpike leading from Harper's Ferry to Winchester. On the left of the pike, facing southward, was our Second division, and on the right our First division.

The Eighth corps held the center of the line, and the Nineteenth corps the left, its flank resting on Berryville.

On Sunday morning, the 21st of August, our cavalry was driven back upon the infantry, and we suddenly discovered the enemy coming down upon the Sixth corps in three heavy columns. With scarcely any warning we found shells pitching into our camp among the standing tents, and bullets whistling among the trees that afforded us shelter from the sun.

The corps was quickly in line, the tents struck and everything in fighting trim. Our boys received the onset of the rebels with cool bravery, giving them back volley for volley. The fight was kept up for several hours, the Eighth corps being but slightly engaged, and the Nineteenth corps not at all. Our Second division, Sixth corps, receiving the weight of the attack. Our men threw up breastworks along the front, and at length the Vermont brigade was ordered to charge upon the enemy. The charge was executed with the usual brilliancy and fighting joy of that brigade and the confederates were glad to leave us in undisputed possession of the ground.

CHAPTER XXX.

BATTLE OF WINCHESTER.

THE rebels were repulsed; but as our position at Charlestown was one that might easily be flanked, our army fell back during the night to the strong position at Halltown, where defensive works were thrown up, and again we awaited the advance of the enemy; but except some skirmishing on the left of the line, no attack was ventured by Early; and after two or three days he withdrew to the vicinity of Winchester, and established his line along the west bank of Opequan creek, so as to cover the three roads leading from Martinsburgh, from Harper's Ferry and from Berryville to Winchester. We followed and established our line on the east side of the creek, and some miles from it, at Berryville.

Our encampment at Berryville was one of the most delightful of our resting places, even in the Shenandoah Valley. We passed the days pleasantly, strolling or riding among the groves of black walnut, visiting among the various regiments, amusing ourselves with chess and books. Nothing occurred to interrupt these pleasant pastimes and the monotony of picket duty until the 13th of September, when the Second division was directed to make a reconnoissance to the Opequan. We marched to the creek very early in the morning, found the enemy in force, lost a few men by the shells from the rebel batteries, and returned to camp.

On the 15th our army was visited by Lieutenant-General
Grant. The story of his visit we give in his own words:

"I left City Point on the 15th to visit him (General
Sheridan), at his head-quarters, to decide, after conference
with him, what should be done. I met him at Charlestown, and he pointed out so distinctly how each army lay;
what he could do the moment he was authorized, and
expressed such confidence of success, that I saw there
were but two words of instruction necessary — *Go in!*
* * * I may here add that the result was such that I
have never since deemed it necessary to visit General
Sheridan before giving him orders."

Thus the two armies lay face to face, with the stream
and a narrow strip of country between them, either able
to bring on an engagement at any time. The quiet was
broken on the morning of the 19th, when we advanced to
win the first of that series of brilliant victories which
startled Europe and America; which gave to our little
army an enviable renown among the armies of the Union,
and established the reputation of our chief as one of the
foremost generals of the age.

Early had taken the initiative. On Sunday the 18th, he
had sent General Gordon's division toward Martinsburgh,
with orders to drive out the Union forces, and destroy
the government property. Gordon was met by Averill's
cavalry and driven back to Drakesville. Sheridan, discovering the mistake made by Early in separating his
forces, was quick to avail himself of the advantage of
his enemy's blunder. Orders were issued to move at once,
but, for some reason, several hours elapsed before the army
was ready.

We left our pleasant camps at Berryville, at two o'clock
Monday morning, the Sixth corps in advance, moving in
two columns, one on either side of the road, the ammunition wagons, artillery and ambulances taking the pike.

The Third brigade, Second division, led the infantry. The Nineteenth corps followed the Sixth, marching in similar order, its infantry in the fields and its artillery and wagons on the pike, while Crook's Kanawha corps moved further to the south, with orders to connect with the Sixth corps at Opequan creek. Two divisions of cavalry, under Merritt and Averill, were directed to amuse the enemy near Bunker's Hill, and draw the attention of the rebel generals in that direction as much as possible. It was the design of General Sheridan thus to amuse the enemy on the left while he should march his army up the Berryville and Winchester pike, strike the right flank of Early's army, and by a sudden and unexpected attack, to get in the rear and cut off the retreat of the rebel forces. By one of those inexplicable mistakes, which sometimes upset the plans of our generals, this design was not fully realized, and had General Sheridan been less determined and less dashing, he might have abandoned the idea of attacking Early at all.

At five o'clock Wilson's cavalry had crossed the creek before us, having dispersed the pickets of the enemy, driving them back to their line of field works, and then, by a dashing charge, had leaped their horses over the breastworks of the first line of defenses, and routed the rebels, capturing about fifty of their number.

Immediately after this gallant exploit of the cavalry, the Sixth corps crossed the creek and advanced on the turnpike about a mile, where the enemy was found in force. As we moved along, through the deep ravine, following the pike, we were warned of the active work we might expect in front, as we saw cavalrymen coming to the rear, some leading their wounded horses, others with their heads bound in bloody handkerchiefs, some with arms hanging in slings, others borne on litters. Here by the roadside might be seen the prostrate, lifeless form of some soldier of the Union; there, where a silvery brook babbled along across the pike, on its grassy banks, and beneath the shadow of a large tree, was gathered a little group of boys in blue, performing the last acts of kindness to a comrade in whom the vital spark was almost extinguished, and a surgeon bending over the dying soldier striving to render less painful the few lingering moments of life.

We moved up a steep ascent and formed in line of battle in a cornfield; the Third brigade on the left, the First in the center, and the Vermonters on the right; then on the left of the Second division the Third division got into position, and the First division came up in the rear as reserve. Our artillery was brought into position and a vigorous shelling commenced on both sides.

The Sixth corps was now ready for a charge upon the enemy, but it was discovered that, by some misconception of orders, the Nineteenth corps, which should have been on the ground, was left far behind. Orders were dispatched to hasten it to the field of action, but two hours, precious hours to that army, elapsed before it was in position.

Those two hours of delay enabled Early to strengthen his right; to throw up strong earthworks, and bring Gordon's division on the run, to his assistance. We had been fortunate only in seizing the position on the west side of the stream, or the battle would, from this delay, have been worse for us.

Merritt and Averill, by skillfully maneuvering their troops in front of Bunker's Hill, had enabled us to seize this advantage.

The Nineteenth corps was formed on the right of the Sixth, in four lines of battle; Wilson's cavalry was on our left. It was eleven o'clock when the advance was sounded. In our front were undulating fields, traversed by deep ravines, almost stripped of timber, except where the rebels had formed their line of battle in a belt of woods that skirted the turnpike. It was an imposing spectacle to watch that line of battle, stretching three miles across the fields, as it moved toward the rebel lines, the men as composed as though on parade, the line straight and compact, the various division, brigade and regimental flags floating gaily in the sunlight. Away in our front we could see Winchester; its gleaming spires and shining roofs, bright with the warm glow of mid-day, and we proudly felt that before night it would be ours. Onward, through the cornfields and over the grassy knolls, now descending into a ravine and now rising upon the open plain, where the rebel artillery swept with terrible effect, the long line pressed forward, regardless of the destructive fire that constantly thinned our ranks. At every step forward, men were dropping, dropping; some dead, some mortally hurt, and some with slight wounds. Now on this side, now on that they fell; still the line swept forward, leaving the ground behind it covered with the victims.

Thus we pushed onward, the rebels falling back, desperately disputing every step, when a murderous fire, from batteries which the enemy had skillfully placed, suddenly swept our right with fearful slaughter.

Thus far all had gone well. Now our hearts were sick as we looked far to the right and saw the Nineteenth corps and our Third division falling back, back, back, the grape and canister of the hostile cannon crashing through the now disordered ranks, and the exulting rebels following with wild yells of victory.

The retreat of the troops on the right of the Second division left its flank, held by the Vermonters, exposed, and they, too, were forced to fall behind the Third brigade, which still held its ground, the fire in its front being at the moment less severe. Our batteries were rushed forward, and the gallant First division, the noble Russell at its head, came bravely up to the rescue.

As the noble soldier brought his division into position a cannon ball swept him from his horse—dead. A great spirit had fallen, and in a moment we were made an army of mourners. "I have lost my captain," said Sheridan, as the work of the day closed.

We all remembered the modest, almost bashful, demeanor of the fallen general among his friends, and his glorious heroism in the presence of his enemies, and many tears moistened the brown cheeks of rough soldiers as they thought of the loss of one of our best beloved leaders.

But, notwithstanding the loss of their hero, the brave division pushed straight on. Nothing could withstand them; and now, joined by the other troops of the corps, the boys with the red crosses press on, and as the peals of musketry and artillery roll through those valleys, it tells of victory for the Union. The lost ground is regained, and now the fire in front of the Sixth corps slackens.

We rested, throwing ourselves on the ground, waiting for orders. Some of the men, fatigued from the early march and severe morning's work, slept; while others regaled themselves from their well filled haversacks; and many gathered in groups to talk over the doings of the morning, and to speak of those who had been stretched upon the sod, who had fallen with their faces to the foe.

We were waiting for Crook's corps. It had halted on the eastern bank of the river as reserve for the army. Now it was brought forward at quick pace and placed, a part on the right of the Nineteenth corps, where the rebels could be seen massing troops on their left, with a view of turning our right flank, the other part in rear of the Nineteenth corps. Averill and Merritt, too, were with the army, and our whole force was together. It was nearly three o'clock when Crook's forces were brought into position. His right was in a thick forest, and against him were heavy columns of rebels.

At length we, of the Sixth corps, heard rapid firing away on the right of the forest. All was attention. Every man stood to his arms ready to advance. Sheridan came to our part of the line. His face all aglow with excitement, the perspiration rolling down his forehead, his famous black steed spotted with white foam, a single orderly at his back. He rode straight to General Getty, exclaiming, " General, I have put Torbert on the right, and told him to give 'em h—l, and he is doing it. Crook, too, is on the right and giving it to them. Press them, General, they'll run!" and then, using one of those phrases sometimes employed in the army to give additional force to language, he shouted again, " *Press them, General, I know they'll run!* " And then the shout that went up from the men drowned all the other noise of the battle.

We did press them, and they did run. Over the long stretch of open plain, down into the deep hollow, up again and over the rolling ground, past the white farm house, on we went. The rebels would run, then reaching a commanding position, they would turn their artillery upon us and sweep our line with iron hail. On our left was Wilson, with the cavalry charging through the growing corn, the sabres gleaming in the sunlight, the iron scabbards clanging against iron spurs, the horses dashing madly forward in seeming disorder, but all rushing, like an avalanche, against the right wing of the enemy. Now the retreat became a rout. The cheers of the Union boys rose strong and clear above the roar of artillery and the harsh rattle of musketry, and Early's scattered and demoralized divisions were rushing through Winchester in consternation and unutterable confusion. Frightened teamsters were lashing their animals through the streets in greatest alarm ; riderless horses were galloping here and there, and pack mules were on a general stampede. Some streets became entirely blocked up by the disordered mass, and even foot-

51

men could not press through; a squad of cavalry coming to one of these obstructions leaped from their horses and made their escape on foot. Our cavalry, taking advantage of the confusion, rushed among the panic stricken fugitives and gathered hundreds of them; captured fifteen battle-flags and five guns.

The remnants of the rebel army collected some miles beyond the town, and reformed; but after a short rest made haste to get farther up the valley. As we advanced we found the mountains full of fugitives, and in the town were thousands of their wounded.

The infantry halted upon the high grounds at the borders of the town, leaving the cavalry to follow up the pursuit of the flying foe; and as Generals Sheridan, Wright, Emory and Crook rode along our front, we made the welkin ring with lusty cheers. Glorious leaders of a victorious army!

At our feet was Winchester, the scene of Washington's early military experience. Here he was stationed during the French war, and shared in the perilous sentinelship of the frontier. For then the valley was ravaged by French and Indians, and fearful massacres were of frequent occurrence; and when Washington demanded of Governor Dinwiddie reinforcements, and was refused, he offered to resign; and when the governor could not allow him to resign he sent him men.

Here, on the ground occupied by the Seventy-seventh New York regiment, near the ruins of an old church, was the grave of General Daniel Morgan, the hero of Quebec and Saratoga, the friend of Washington. A plain marble tablet, broken across, now covered the grave, with a simple inscription, his name and the date of his death, 1802.

In the cemetery, still north, we saw, as we passed, the resting place of Thomas, Earl of Fairfax; a great tory in his day, and the owner of immense tracts of land in this part of Virginia, and from whom Fairfax county took its name.

The sun had sunk to his golden rest behind the wall of hills on our left when we arrived at the outskirts of Winchester; and, as darkness set in, the infantry of our victorious army stretched themselves upon the ground to sleep. It had been a hard day's work, and the men were faint. It required no unusual inducements to woo the angel of sleep.

If the day had been an active one on the field, it had been no less so in the hospitals. First, early in the morning, came ambulance loads of men with white crosses; they were from the Third brigade, Second division, all from the Seventy-seventh New York. Then came others from the Forty-ninth New York, from the Seventh Maine, and from the One Hundred and Twenty-second and Forty-third New York. Then came men from the Vermont brigade, and from our First brigade, and soon the hospitals of the Third division began to be filled. Then, last of all, came the men of the red crosses, bleeding and mangled. Surgeons worked all day and all night. There was no rest as long as a wounded man was uncared for. Yet, when morning came, and the medical officers were ordered forward with the army, there was much to do, and faithful men were left to finish the needful task. Next morning Winchester was full of rebel wounded and rebel prisoners. Five thousand men in gray were under guard in the court house yard and other public places, and Colonel Edwards' brigade of the First division was left to take care of the prisoners and the town. Many brave men had fallen. Russell was gone; the gallant Upton was wounded; Colonel Elright, of the Third division, was dead, and many, many brave boys were lying with their blackened faces to the sun, a slip of paper or a letter envelope pinned to the breast of each to tell the buriers his name and regiment.

The term of service of one of our regiments, the Fourth Vermont, had expired, and on the day after the battle the small remnant of the regiment, a company of about forty men, under command of Colonel Foster, started for Harper's Ferry, on their return home. They had suffered heavily, and they left many of their brave comrades dead upon the battle-field, or suffering in the hospitals. How had those noble boys, whose lives had, at the very expiration of their three years of toil, danger and privations, been given for their country, rejoiced at the prospect of a speedy reunion with the loved ones at home. How had they written, even the day before the battle, "we are going home!" and then how had the loving ones, away among the beautiful green hills of Vermont, exulted at the thought that now, after three long years of suspense and anxiety, the danger and toil were over. And we can picture to our thoughts the mother who watches with eager interest the smoking train as it dashes along at the base of the old

"WHY DON'T HE COME?"

hills, wondering if her patriot son will not come to-day; but instead, a letter comes with the heavy news, a great battle has been fought and her son lies in the Valley; or, on the banks of the sunny Champlain, some young sister or lover gazes from the window of the cottage among the trees, at the steamer as it glides over the surface of the beautiful lake and touches at the wharf near by. But her soldier boy is not on board, and she watches in vain to see his familiar form coming toward the cottage. She sadly leans her head upon her hand and sighs, "Why don't he come?"

CHAPTER XXXI.

FISHER HILL.

WE started very early in the morning in pursuit of Early's defeated army, which it was supposed would halt at the strong position at Strasburgh. On the battle-field which we left, the lifeless bodies of many of our men were awaiting the office of the burial parties. They lay, not in thick clusters, but here and there over a great extent of ground, showing that they had fallen while the lines were in motion; but in places, six or eight mangled bodies would lie in close proximity, showing the fatal effects of some well directed shell.

In Winchester were nearly five thousand prisoners, and more were constantly coming in, and hundreds of rebel wounded were being cared for by sympathizing friends and confederate surgeons.

We reached the vicinity of Strasburgh, the Sixth corps in advance, at three o'clock on the 20th, and, as we expected, found the rebels awaiting us in a position, which the citizens of the valley assured us could be held by Early's army against one hundred thousand men. The position was indeed a formidable one, but nothing daunted our spirited leader set about devising a way of taking it.

At Strasburgh the two chains of mountains, the Blue Ridge and the Alleghanies, approach each other, making the valley quite narrow. As if to interpose an impassable barrier to the advance of an army, a mountain, Fisher Hill, stretches across from the Blue Ridge to the branch of the Alleghanies called the North Mountains. At the foot of this mountain, on the north, is the village of Strasburgh, and still north of Strasburgh Cedar creek runs almost directly across the valley. We took possession of the northern part of the village of Strasburgh, the Union pickets occupying one part of the town, and the rebels the other. The night passed with little of interest.

On the morning of the 21st squads of rebel prisoners were coming in to army head-quarters, and as brigade after brigade of cavalry passed, each carrying a large number of confederate flags at the head of the column, it looked as though our cavalry had adopted the confederate banner and had paraded in gala day splendor.

The mists and fogs melted away, and we discovered that our enemy, lately routed and disorganized, now with confidence confronted us and awaited our advance. During the night the mountain had been the scene of busy labors, and now, breastworks of earth and stones, and lines of troublesome abattis, rendered the position, so strong by nature, apparently too formidable for any army to attempt to force. But, notwithstanding the brilliant success at Winchester, neither the rebel army nor our own fully appreciated the fertile resources of our gallant leader. Starting with his staff early in the day, he rode from one end of the picket line to the other, carefully noting the character of the ground.

To attempt to storm those heights, now strengthened with earthworks and bristling with cannon, would be presumptuous; but away on the right seemed the vulnerable point of the enemy's line. Returning to his quarters, Sheridan determined at once upon his plan of attack. The Nineteenth corps was thrown farther to the left, and our Sixth corps occupied the position in the center, facing now to the south.   Crook's corps was thrown well to the right, where the North Mountain formed a precipitous wall for the valley.   All day the sharp crack of the skirmishers' rifles, and the ring of the pioneers' axes were heard as the two lines faced each other, each watching the movements of the other, and each actively engaged in felling trees from which breastworks were made.

During the night Crook's corps and our Third division were toiling along the side of the mountain unseen and unexpected by the rebels.   All night and the following morning these two commands labored to drag artillery along the precipitous mountain side, executing every movement in silence and with utmost secrecy.   The Nineteenth corps and the First and Second divisions of the Sixth were all this time keeping up a show of determination to attack in front.

At length, just as the sun was sinking behind the mountain barrier, a wild shout was heard from the hillside where Crook's corps and our Third division were rushing down from the cover of the forest, upon the flank and rear of the astonished confederates.   The shout was taken up by the troops in front, and at the same time the two remaining divisions of the Sixth corps and the Nineteenth corps advanced against the rebel front. Completely surprised by the movement on the flank, the rear of the rebel army was quickly thrown into a panic. Still resistance was kept up along the front.   Steadily the troops of Wright and Emory pressed forward, the rebel gunners firing their shells over the heads of our men, our line advancing over ditches and fences, over fallen trees and stone walls, each man his own commander and each pressing eagerly forward.   In the foremost line rode Phil. Sheridan, the men cheering him lustily as they pressed hastily forward.   "Let us take the guns," shouted the men; and forward at double-quick they rushed.   The panic in the rear had by this time reached the front, and the whole rebel army was rushing in unutterable confusion and rout, up the valley. They left with us sixteen guns, of which Bidwell's brigade captured six. We gathered up the prisoners, and they numbered eleven hundred.* The hill was strewed with small arms, and cannon and caissons met our view wherever we passed.

We had lost, as the cost of this brilliant victory, less than forty men in the army; and the confederate loss in killed and wounded was scarcely greater.

We followed the routed army through Mount Jackson, where were large hospitals, occupied by wounded confederates, and attended by confederate surgeons; then pressed on to New Market, keeping up a running fight with the rear-guard of the rebel army.

On the 25th we reached Harrisonburgh, a village more than sixty miles above Winchester.

Our march had been a grand triumphal pursuit of a routed enemy. Never had we marched with such light hearts; and, though each day had found us pursuing rapidly from dawn till dark, the men seemed to endure the fatigue with wonderful patience. Our column, as it swept up the valley, was a spectacle of rare beauty. Never had we, in all our campaigns, seen anything to compare with the appearance of this victorious little army. The smooth, wide turnpike was occupied by the artillery, ambulances and baggage wagons moving in double file. The infantry marched in several parallel columns on either side of the pike, and a line of cavalry, followed by a skirmish line of infantry, led the way. Cavalry, too, hung on

---

* The prisoners taken thus far, at Winchester and Fisher Hill, including the wounded, numbered more than seven thousand. The absurdity and falsity of Early's statement, that his effective force at Winchester amounted to only eight thousand five hundred men, is readily seen. The rebel surgeons at Mount Jackson, and the citizens, while claiming that we outnumbered Early's forces, acknowledged that he retreated from Winchester with more than twenty thousand men.

either flank, and scouted the country. It was intensely
exciting to watch the steady progress of the advancing
skirmishers.   Now, as they reached the base of some sloping eminence, the rebel skirmishers would confront them;
then, as they advanced, never halting nor slackening their
pace, the confederates would surrender the ground, to
appear in our front on the next commanding ground.   So
we marched up the valley—a grand excursion—skirmishing only enough to maintain a constant state of pleasant
excitement.

At Harrisonburgh we remained until the 29th, then
marched farther up the valley to Mount Crawford, while
the cavalry penetrated as far as Staunton.   The rebel
army was broken up and demoralized, yet considerable
force was in the vicinity of Lynchburgh, and Early
devoted himself to reorganizing it.

Guerrilla warfare was a favorite resort of the rebels in
the Shenandoah Valley, and many of our men were murdered in cold blood by the cowardly villains who lurked
about our camps by day as harmless farmers, and murdered our men at night dressed in confederate uniform.
Among those who lost their lives by this cowardly species
of warfare, were Surgeon Ochenslayer, Medical Inspector of
our army; Colonel Tolles, Chief Quartermaster, and Captain Meigs, son of the Quartermaster-General, U. S. A.

We fell back from Mount Crawford to Harrisonburgh,
burning barns, mills and granaries, driving before us cattle and sheep, and bringing white and black refugees
without number.   From Harrisonburgh we again fell
back, retracing our steps through New Market, Mount
Jackson and Woodstock, and encamped on the evening of
the 8th of October on the north bank of Cedar creek.
Each day as we marched, dark columns of smoke rose
from numberless conflagrations in our rear and on either
flank, where the cavalry was at work carrying out the

edict of destruction of the valley. A certain number of mills with the grain contained, a specified number of wheat-stacks and granaries, and cattle and sheep sufficient for the wants of the people of the valley were saved; all other mills, barns, stacks and granaries were burned, and all other cattle and sheep driven away. Seventy mills, with the flour and grain, and over two thousand barns filled with wheat, hay and farming implements were thus committed to the flames, and seven thousand cattle and sheep were either driven off or killed and issued to the men. This destruction, cruel as it seemed, was fully justified as a matter of military necessity. For so long as a rebel army could subsist in the valley, so long a large force must remain to guard the frontier of Maryland.

Hundreds of refugees accompanied us from Staunton, Mount Crawford and Harrisonburgh: Unionists who had endured persecution until it was no longer endurable, and who now left houses and farms to find relief in the north from their sufferings for loyalty; and negroes who sought freedom from their ancient bondage.

Among the latter class was a group which had followed the cavalry from Staunton, and which now took a place in our Sixth corps hospital train, which attracted universal attention. The party rode in one of the huge Virginia wagons, so familiar to those who have spent much time in those parts, and consisted of an aged colored woman, probably more than ninety years old, one or two younger women, a black man of fifty, who was a cripple, a boy of twelve or fifteen years, and a very large number of small children, varying in hue from jet black to dark brunette. The load was drawn by four broken down, spavined animals, the crippled man riding one of the horses of the rear span, the boy one of the leaders. The soldiers manifested great interest in this curious load of refugees, and

freely divided with them their hard tack and coffee. The
writer of these pages, reining his horse to the side of the
vehicle, addressed the aged negress, "Well, aunty, are all
those your children?" "Lor, no massa, dey's only eighteen ob 'em." Doubtless she designed to say that there
were only eighteen of the children, not that "only
eighteen" were her own.

As our army neared Fisher Hill the cavalry of the
enemy became annoying to our rear-guard. General Sheridan said to General Torbert, that the annoyance must be
stopped at once. Accordingly Custer and his horsemen
lay in wait for the rebel cavalry, attacked them, drove
them away beyond Mount Jackson, and took eleven pieces
of artillery and three hundred prisoners from them. They
gave us no more trouble at that time.

Monday, October 10th, the Sixth corps, leaving the
Eighth and Nineteenth guarding the line of Cedar creek,
turned toward the left and proceeded to Front Royal.
The Seventy-seventh was made provost guard of the town,
and the brigades were stationed along the mountain passes.
Here, in the enjoyment of lovely weather, pleasant associations, a bountiful supply of lamb and honey, and untold
quantities of grapes of delicious flavor, the corps remained
several days, and the men even flattered themselves that in
the enjoyment of these luxuries they were to pass the winter.
But, as usual with bright anticipations, these were suddenly dispelled by the order to march, on the morning of
the 13th, toward Ashby's Gap.

From the direction of our march it was evident that
we were on the road to Washington, and rumor had it
that we were to be shipped at once for Petersburgh. We
reached the bank of the Shenandoah, where we expected
to cross to the gap; the corps was massed by the river
side, and the men looked dismally into the cold, dark
waters, and shivered at the thought of wading through

"GOING NORF."

the stream whose waters would reach nearly to their necks. But while we waited to get ready for crossing, a courier came to General Wright with a message from Sheridan to return to his army in haste. We heard that Longstreet's corps had reinforced Early, and that an attack had been made, but with no important result. We turned about, encamped for the night among the hills, started again at three o'clock in the morning, and joined the army again on Cedar creek, in the afternoon of the 14th, where we remained in the enjoyment of undisturbed quiet for several days.

CHAPTER XXXII.

BATTLE OF CEDAR CREEK.

Position of the Union forces on Cedar creek — Demonstrations by Early — The morning of October 19th — Eighth corps straggling — Nineteenth corps routed — The Sixth corps to the rescue — Death of General Bidwell — The Sixth corps holds the enemy — General Wright prepares for another attack — Arrival of Sheridan — The charge — The rout — Guns, wagons and prisoners — The victors in camp.

OUR army was thus resting in apparent security along the banks of Cedar creek. The men were amusing themselves in visiting the numerous caverns in the vicinity, strolling among the pleasant groves or wandering by the shady borders of the stream. Sheridan had left the army and returned to Washington for a day or two, to make arrangements for his future movements, and General Wright had temporary command of the army.

Our infantry force was arranged from left to right along the creek, first, on the left of the turnpike, General Crook's "Army of Virginia," or as it was more generally known, the Eighth corps, holding the left flank, facing eastward and southward; then, the Nineteenth corps, holding the pike and facing toward the south, its line occupying high bluffs which overhung the creek. On the right of the Nineteenth corps, and almost at right angles with it, was the Sixth corps, its line extending far toward the north. The corps faced the stream, looking directly west. The divisions of the corps were posted, on the right the Second, in the center the First, and on the left the Third division.

On the flanks of the infantry, cavalry was posted; Custer on the right of the Sixth corps, and Averill's division, now under Colonel Powell, on the left of the infantry line, near Front Royal. Our line thus extended from North Mountain, on the right, almost to Front Royal, on the left, following nearly the course of Cedar creek, and that part of the north branch of the Shenandoah which crosses the valley at right angles.

The enemy had been trying our line at various points, during the last two or three days, and in one instance had captured or dispersed a small squad of cavalry on the right, and captured some signaling instruments. These demonstrations were little heeded; our line had been posted by General Sheridan, and these slight attacks seemed of little account. In Early's army, however, they were considered of more weighty import. That army had recently been reinforced by Longstreet's corps of sixteen thousand men, and the immediate defeat, and, if possible, destruction, of Sheridan's army was regarded, by both General Lee and the authorities at Richmond, as absolutely necessary to the safety of Lee's army. Hence every preparation had been made for a most determined attack, and these lighter demonstrations had been made to ascertain the exact position of our troops.

When, at two o'clock, on the morning of the nineteenth of October, we heard rapid firing where Custer, with his horsemen, held the right, and on the left, where Averill's cavalry was posted, we turned over in our blankets and said, "The cavalry is having a brush," and went to sleep again. And then, at a later hour, at four o'clock in the morning, when we of the Sixth corps heard brisk picket firing in front of the Eighth and Nineteenth corps, we were scarcely aroused from our slumbers, for we thought it to be a mere picket skirmish, in which none but those directly engaged had any particular interest. But when the firing became general along the whole line of these two corps, and we saw hundreds of men going with hasty steps and lengthy strides to the rear, we were at length aroused to the truth that a battle was really in progress.

From a Sixth corps point of view, the scene was at first extremely ludicrous, we did not know and could not have believed at that time that the flank of our army was turned, and that the enemy was actually in possession of the camps of one whole corps; and when we saw stragglers filling the fields, taking rapid strides toward the rear, scarce any two of them going together, some without hats, others destitute of coats or boots, a few with guns, many wearing the shoulder straps of officers, all bent on getting a good way to the rear, never stopping to answer a question or explain what was going on at the front, the spectacle was to us of the Sixth corps one of infinite amusement. None of these hundreds and thousands of stragglers were so undignified as to run, but such walking was never seen before. None of them deigned to look to the right or left, they were bent only upon getting as far on the road to Winchester as possible.

At length the truth flashed upon us. More than half of our army was already beaten and routed, while the remainder had been in ignorance of the fact that anything serious was transpiring. Now the rebels were pouring down toward the Winchester and Strasburgh turnpike, sending a perfect shower of bullets whistling about the vicinity of the head-quarters of the army, into the Sixth corps hospital camp and into the trains, which were by this time joining in the stampede.

Staff officers now came riding furiously through the camps of the Sixth corps, with orders to fall in at once, and proceed at double-quick to the left.

We may now turn back and trace the cause of this unexpected state of affairs. Early had, without doubt, assured himself of the exact position of our army through information conveyed by spies, who were able to comprehend the whole situation. He then prepared for a bold and sudden movement, which should take by surprise one flank of our army. Kershaw's rebel division advanced along the sides of the mountains, and, at midnight, crossed the north branch of the Shenandoah, still observing the most complete silence. Even the canteens of the soldiers had been left behind lest the sound of them should betray the movement.

The whole division over, it was massed on the left of General Crook's command. A dense fog enveloped the whole surrounding country, and so thick was it that no man could see an object a few feet from him. Under the cover of this fog, the rebels succeeded in quietly capturing a large part of the picket force and nothing now interposed between the rebels and General Crook's camps. Toward these they hastened, and so complete was the surprise, that the men of the Eighth corps were, for the most part, quietly sleeping in their tents. The few who had got into the breastworks were subjected to a fierce fire in the flank, and were soon forced to abandon the line. The rebels seized the Union batteries along that part of the line, and turned them upon the camps of the Nineteenth corps, and at the same time a rebel line of battle advanced against that corps from the front. The confusion became every moment greater. Daylight was just merging from night, the thick mists hung like an impenetrable veil over the field, and the men of the Nineteenth corps were unable to tell whence came all this storm of missiles; but, trailing their guns in the direction from which the shells seemed to come, the gunners worked their pieces at random. A general stampede was commenced. The men of the Eighth corps were mostly fugitives; and those who strove to keep in line were forced back. Both the fugitives and the disordered line of battle, were rushing through the camps of the Nineteenth

53

corps. The officers of that corps were, with shouts and wild gesticulations, striving to collect their disordered commands, but with little success. Riderless horses were galloping here and there, cows, with which the army was well supplied, were bellowing, mules were braying, bullets whistling and shells howling. The Eighth corps having left the way clear, the rebels came down upon the Nineteenth, which gave way and was doubled upon the Sixth corps, but although thrown into confusion it was not in the panic with which the Eighth corps yielded the ground.

It was at this critical moment that the warning was given to the Sixth corps. General Wright being in command of the army, the corps was in charge of General Ricketts. He at once faced the corps to the rear, and moved it over the plain in face of the advancing hosts of the enemy. General Ricketts was wounded very early in the engagement of the corps, and the command fell upon General Getty.

The Second division held the left of the new line, the First the center, and the Third the right. Bidwell's brigade was the left brigade of the Second division, the Vermonters held the center, and Warner's First brigade the right. The Second division was posted in the edge of an open oak grove. General Grant, of the Vermont brigade, was in charge.

We now awaited the onset of the victorious columns, which were driving the shattered and disorganized fragments of the Eighth and Nineteenth corps, beaten and discouraged, wildly through our well formed ranks to the rear.

The hope of the nation now rested with those heroes of many bloody fields. Now that peerless band of veterans, the wearers of the Greek cross, whose fame was already among the choicest treasures of American history, was to show to the country and the world, an exhibition of valor which should tower above all the grand achievements of the war.

The corps, numbering less than twelve thousand men, now confronted Early's whole army of more than thirty thousand men, who, flushed with victory, already bringing to bear against us the twenty-one guns which they had just captured from the two broken corps, rushed upon our lines with those wild, exultant yells, the terror of which can never be conceived by those who have not heard them on the field.

With fearless impetuosity the rebel army moved up the gentle rise of ground in front of the Sixth corps, and the attack, from one end of the line to the other, was simultaneous. It was like the clash of steel to steel. The astonished columns were checked. They had found an immovable obstacle to their march of victory.

The Second division, on the left, nearest the pike, had received the most severe shock of the attack, while Bidwell's brigade, which held the extreme left, and the key to the pike, had sustained the attack of the whole of Kershaw's rebel division, which came up in compact order to within very close range. The gallant brigade received the onset with full volleys, which caused the right of the rebel line to stagger back, and the whole line was, almost at the same moment, repulsed by the corps. The cavalry on our flank — and never braver men than the cavalry of our little army mounted saddles — were doing their best to protect the pike leading to Winchester, and it was the great aim of both the cavalry and the single organized corps of infantry to hold this pike; for on this depended the safety of the whole army, and more, of our cause.

The rebels checked, General Bidwell ordered his brigade to charge. Rising from their places in the little graveyard and the grove, the brigade rushed forward, the rebels breaking and running in confusion down the declivity which they had but just ascended with such confidence, and across the little stream. But the rebel artillery sent our men back to their places, to the shelter of the roll of ground. The charge cost us dearly. Major Brower, of the One hundred and twenty-second New York, lost his life. Captain Lennon, of the Seventy-seventh, was mortally wounded, Lieutenant Tabor was killed. Captain Taylor, commanding the Sixty-first Pennsylvania, was also killed, and many other valuable lives were lost, but the most severe blow to the brigade and the corps, was the loss of our gallant General Bidwell. He fell, while bravely directing the charge, with a frightful shell wound. He was at once borne to an ambulance. The general sent one of his staff for the writer of these pages. When he reached the general's ambulance, the wounded man said: "Doctor, I suppose there is no hope of recovery." When told that there was none he exclaimed, "Oh, my poor wife!" Then after a moment he said, "Doctor, see that my record is right at home. Tell them I died at my post doing my duty." A few hours of intense suffering and the brave man was relieved by death.

The fall of General Bidwell left Colonel French, of the Seventy-seventh, in command of the brigade. The line was quickly reformed in the position from which the charge was made, and again the rebels came on with cheers and yells. They were as bravely met as before, and a second counter-charge sent them again in disorder across the creek, leaving the ground covered with their dead and wounded. The greatest shock of the second charge of the rebels had fallen upon our Third brigade, and nobly had it been met. A third time Early's forces came on; this time with less spirit. His men now knew the troops they had to contend with. They had been informed that the Sixth corps had been sent to Washing-

ton, on its way to Petersburgh. Now they discovered
the mistake, and all of Early's authority was insufficient
to bring them up to a spirited charge. We had repulsed
them three times with terrible damage to their ranks, as
well as sad loss to our own. But now we looked toward
the right, and we saw rebels passing around our flank,
and the Third and First divisions falling back. We were
but twelve thousand. They were thirty thousand, and
their line far overlapped ours. When Early could not
drive us he went round us. And now it was necessary
to take another position, which should protect the road to
Winchester, and General Wright directed General Getty
to fall back, with his corps, to a more commanding position, unless he saw good reason for desiring to hold his
present position. So the order was given to take the new
position.

The Sixth corps was not driven back. It had thrice
repulsed the most desperate charges of the whole rebel
army, and now that the rebels were turning our flank, it
was necessary to interpose an organized force, and
there was no organized troops except the cavalry.

Certain erudite historians, who have sent broadcast over
our land, compilations of newspaper paragraphs under the
sounding titles of historians of the rebellion, powerful gentlemen, who, from their comfortable quarters in northern
homes, watched our battles from afar, quiet citizens whose
sensibilities were never shocked by the sight of a battle-field,
and whose nerves can hardly withstand the shock of fire
crackers on the morning of a Fourth of July, have gravely
informed their readers that our whole army, including the
Sixth corps, was driven pellmell six miles to the rear; and
one of these grave historians very quietly assures those
who have leisure to peruse his queer accumulations of
absurdities, that we were driven all the way to Winchester, a distance of more than twenty miles. For the

comfort and encouragement of these historians, so prolific of martial literature, and so barren of any ideas of military movements, it is conceded that their accounts of this battle are quite as correct as any which they are accustomed to give to the public.

We took position just north of Middletown, which was about two miles in the rear of the position held by the Second division of our corps early in the morning. We went back quietly and in good order, a single regiment, the Second Vermont, holding without difficulty the position we abandoned. We carried with us all our wounded, all our shelter tents and all our personal property of every description, and the rebels did not dare to attack us. When we had taken our new position in the same order that we had formed in the morning, the Second division on the left, the First in the center, and the Third on the right, other troops also took position in the line. The cavalry, which had never for a moment faltered, took position, Custer on the right, Merritt on the left and the Nineteenth corps, which had now succeeded in restoring order to its broken ranks, was massed on the right and rear of the Sixth.

With this new line of battle in the strong position we now held, General Wright determined that not only should the retreat stop here, but that the rebels should be driven back across Cedar creek. Their career of victory was ended. The grand old Sixth corps, directed by our own loved General Getty, had turned the fortunes of the day. It was now ten o'clock; far away in the rear was heard cheer after cheer. What was the cause? Were reinforcements coming? Yes, Phil. Sheridan was coming, and he was a host. He had ridden from Winchester at amazing speed, and now, as he passed the long trains of ambulances in which were the hundreds of bleeding victims of the morning's work, the wounded men whose shattered limbs or mangled bodies attested that they had not run away, raised themselves and cheered with wild enthusiasm the hero of the valley. On he rode; most of his staff left far to the rear, his famous war-horse covered with foam and dirt, cheered at every step by hundreds of men in whom new courage was now kindled. Dashing along the pike, he came upon the line of battle. "What troops are those?" shouted Sheridan. "The Sixth corps," was the response from a hundred voices. "We are all right," said Sheridan, as he swung his old hat and dashed along the line toward the right. "Never mind, boys, we'll whip them yet; we'll whip them yet! We shall sleep in our old quarters to-night!" were the encouraging words of the chief as he rode along, while the men threw their hats high in air, leaped and danced and cheered in wildest joy.

Sheridan at once completed the arrangements already commenced and nearly finished by General Wright. The men of the Sixth corps meanwhile busied themselves in cooking their morning meal.

None but soldiers can realize the contending emotions we experienced as we waited for the development of the new arrangements. We had, with the pride which none but soldiers can feel, regained for northern troops the prestige for brilliant achievements and open field fighting in this valley, so often, in times past, the scene of humiliation to our arms. Were we now, notwithstanding all our brilliant successes and our proud consciousness of superiority, to see our prestige fade in an hour? Sheridan said, "No;" and we trusted him. Had Sheridan never reached the field, General Wright would have led us against the foe, whose ardor was already lost after the repeated repulses from the single corps. But there was a charm about the real commander of the army, and his opportune arrival inspired fresh hope and zeal in the breasts of all.

Even a considerable portion of the Eighth corps was collected and placed on the left of the Sixth, and then, with cavalry on either flank, Custer on the right and Merritt on the left, we were ready to assume the offensive.

Thus, all things being arranged, we were prepared to test the question whether our army was to fall back to Winchester beaten and humiliated or return to our old camps.

At one o'clock, the rebels advanced against the right of our line, but were repulsed. A brisk fire of artillery was for a time kept up, but even this died away and nothing but the scattering fire of skirmishers was heard.

Early had, without doubt, now relinquished the idea of any further offensive operations, and he as little thought that any were designed on our part. The rebels quietly proceed to bring their baggage wagons and ambulances across the river, and they set themselves about fitting up our camps for their own use.

At three o'clock, Sheridan gave the order to move; wheeling from right to left, as a gate swings upon its hinges. The Third division on the right of our corps became for a moment embarrassed in passing through a strip of woods, the First division moved slowly but firmly, gaining a strong position. The Second division also advanced, but it was ordered to go very slowly, and this was far more difficult than to rush quickly over the ground. Yet the division obeyed the order and forced the rebels to fall back. In front of the First and Second brigades was a stone wall. This they seized and were at once partially sheltered; but there was no such protection for the Third brigade. In its front was a meadow and a gradually inclined plane, and behind a wall which skirted the crest, was the rebel line. Between that line and ours, in a hollow, stood a brick mill, from the windows of which the enemy's sharpshooters picked off our men. The galling fire from the line of battle, and the fatal shots of the sharpshooters in the mill, made it impossible to advance slowly, and the line fell back. Our best men were falling fast. The color-sergeant of the Seventy-seventh fell dead; another sergeant seized the flag and fell. Adjutant Gilbert Thomas, a youth of rare beauty and surpassing bravery, seized the fallen flag; he cried, "forward, men!" and fell dead with the staff grasped in his hand.

"I cannot take my brigade over that field, slowly," said Colonel French; "then go quickly," responded General Getty. The word was given, and with a bound and a shout the noble brigade went across the field, quickly driving the confederates from their strong position.

By this time the right of the army had started the rebels, and their whole line was giving way. The three divisions of the Sixth corps bounded forward, and commenced the wildest race that had ever been witnessed even in that valley so famous for the flight of beaten armies. The rebel lines were completely broken, and now in utmost confusion, every man was going in greatest haste toward Cedar creek. Our men, with wild enthusiasm, with shouts and cheers, regardless of order or formation, joined in the hot pursuit. There was our mortal enemy, who had but a few hours since driven us unceremoniously from our camps, now beaten, routed, broken, bent on nothing but the most rapid flight. We had not forgotten our humiliation of the morning, and the thought of it gave fleetness to the feet of our pursuers.

From the point where we broke the rebel ranks to the crossing of Cedar creek, was three miles, an open plain. Over this plain and down the pike the panic-stricken army was flying, while our soldiers, without ever stopping to load their pieces, were charging tardy batteries with empty muskets, seizing prisoners by scores and hundreds, every Union soldier his own commander, bent on nothing but the destruction of the flying foe. As we reached Cedar creek, the pursuit was given over to the cavalry. The gallant Custer, now in his wild joy, could be heard shouting to his impetuous men, "Charge them! Charge them!" and then we could hear words, hard to print, but which added startling emphasis to the commands.

Crossing the river, he came upon the pike, crowded with men and cannon, caissons and ambulances, wagons and pack animals. With one mighty sweep, forty-five pieces of artillery, many wagons and ambulances, and hundreds of prisoners, were taken. Merritt, too, captured seven guns, many battle-flags, and prisoners without number. Indeed, the prisoners could not be numbered, for there were not enough of the cavalry to guard them, and as soon as they had thrown down their arms they were passed to the rear, and in the darkness hundreds of them escaped to the mountains. Through the darkness the cavalry kept up the pursuit until Mount Jackson was passed.

The infantry returned to the camps, and as we took our old places, cheers made the welkin ring; and then as we heard constantly of new trophies, the wild huzzahs rang from one end of our army to the other. Such wild joy has rarely been felt by an army. What cared the men of the Nineteenth corps that they were forced to lie upon the ground without tents or blankets? Our army was victorious and our honor saved.

The moon shining brightly over the battle-field revealed the camps of the living side by side with the resting places of the dead. All the way from Middletown to Cedar creek the debris of battle was scattered over the fields. Here and there were seen the remains of our comrades of the morning, their lifeless bodies stripped by vandal rebels of almost every garment. They lay like specters in the pale moonlight; here, still in death, under a cluster of bushes, was stretched a group; there, by the side of a wall, a row of inanimate bodies marked a spot where brave men had fallen at their posts; in the ravine where the little creek wound its way, and beneath the boughs of the chestnut trees of the grove, many slept their last sleep. Among our camps, the spades of the pioneers were heard as they hollowed out the shallow graves; and as we threw ourselves upon the ground to rest, we mourned for our comrades, and we rejoiced for our victory.

Sad, sad it was to think of the noble ones who had left us. Never again were we to see the form of the great-hearted Bidwell at the head of his brigade. We remembered his heroic bravery in all the terrible fights of those bloody days, from the Rapidan to Petersburgh; we thought of him when, at Winchester and Fisher Hill, he directed the movements of his brigade with such consummate coolness and skill; we remembered his cordial smile and friendly words, and then we thought of his heroism in the morning, and our hearts were heavy to think that he was gone.

Adjutant Thomas, too, had left us; our noble, beautiful boy. Could he have died a grander death had he been spared longer? Could his last words have been better chosen had he expired in the embrace of loved ones at home? "Forward, men; forward!" Were they not grand dying words? Rest, brother; thy death was as grand as thy life was lovely.

Lennon's bright eye must soon close forever. We should never again hear his hearty laugh or listen to his sparkling wit. He had fallen as a hero falls, and his life had been the life of a hero and patriot. Belding and Tabor, too, brave captains of brave men, each had fallen in advance of his friends.

Major Brower of the One Hundred and Twenty-second, Captain Taylor, commanding the Sixty-first Pensylvania, Lieutenant-Colonel Kohler of the Ninety-eighth Pennsylvania and Major Borman of the Fifteenth New Jersey, all brave and competent officers, were lost to our corps; while among the wounded were General Ricketts, Colonel Penrose, commander of the New Jersey brigade, Colonel Dwight of the One Hundred and Twenty-second, Captain Orr of Bidwell's staff, and Lieutenant Mitchell of the Seventh Maine.

Our army remained along Cedar creek for several days, the cavalry only scouting up the valley in search of remnants of Early's shattered army. Then, we fell back to the vicinity of Winchester, where our men built comfortable quarters, and here we remained until General Grant called us back to Petersburgh. Many of the regiments in the meantime were mustered out of the service as regiments, the recruits and reënlisted men remaining as battalions with the name of the original regiments, except the substitution of the battalion for the regiment. Among other regiments whose time expired was the one whose early career formed the subject of the first chapters of this narrative, and whose honorable and indeed brilliant course we have never lost sight of. The returning veterans left camp on the 19th of November, leaving two hundred and fifty men still to represent the organization. We will not pause to speak of the parting of those so long companions in arms, of the trip homeward or of the brilliant reception and magnificent entertainment extended by the patriotic citizens of Saratoga to the veterans of a hundred battles. These were fitting testimonials of appreciation of the service of patriot soldiers.

CHAPTER XXXIII.

THE FINAL CAMPAIGN.

Sixth corps returns to Petersburgh — Condition of the corps — Sheridan joins the grand army — Capture of Fort Steadman — The last grand charge — The pursuit of Lee's army — Tributes to the Sixth corps — Disbanding.

On the 9th of December, the Sixth corps was recalled to Petersburgh. We need not describe the journey to Washington, nor the steamboat ride to City Point; the scenes along this route have already been described.

We took our position on the Weldon railroad, erected more comfortable huts than we had ever built before, our sick were placed in hospitals fitted up with great taste, and everything which the government or our friends at home, through the agencies of Sanitary and Christian Commissions, could do for their comfort was gladly done.

During our absence in the Shenandoah Valley, the army under General Grant had been making steady progress in the siege of Petersburgh, and our war-worn brothers of the other corps showed upon their faces the marks of overwork. We were in fresh vigor. We had marched through a blooming valley literally abounding in milk and honey. The fruits of the vine, the orchard and the fold had been ours, and our camps had been in green fields and pleasant groves, we had marched over wide roads, and through rolling meadows, and we had fought in the open field. We returned to our old comrades, proud of our own achievements, and of the praise we had won from the nation. We could point to the valley, and to the memory of Early's army, now no more; and we proudly claimed that it had been ours to rid the country of one of the most troublesome of the rebel columns.

Now that we were again in the trenches, we felt a confidence in our own valor which made our corps eminently fitted for the last grand duty, the crowning act in the glorious history of this superb corps, the breaking asunder of Lee's lines at Petersburgh, and as the result, the overthrow of the rebellion.

Grant's army had, during our absence, extended the line much farther to the west and south. When we left for Washington, our line extended only a little beyond the Jerusalem plank road. Now, it crossed the Weldon railroad, and reached Hatcher's Run, nearly eight miles from the position occupied by us when we left the lines. The military railroad, too, had been constructed, and now all supplies were brought from City Point to the rear of our camps by rail cars.

The famous mine had exploded, and with it the project of taking Petersburgh by surprise. Events of importance had transpired on the north of the James, and the Dutch Gap canal was in progress. Yet, Lee's army held us at arm's length, and Petersburgh was still to be taken.

In the latter part of February, our friend, Sheridan, was ordered to leave the valley with his superb body of horsemen, and cross the country through Lynchburgh, destroy Lee's communications with the west, pass through Danville and join Sherman in his grand march to the sea. But the James river, swollen by heavy rains, forbade a crossing, and Sheridan, nowise disconcerted, turned the heads of his horses toward the White House, and after many adventures, having wrought much mischief in the rear of the rebel army, he joined Grant's army before Petersburgh, on the 26th of March. The result was better than though he had been able to accomplish the original design.

Now, the Army of the Potomac was one again. The Sixth corps, and Sheridan with his cavalry, were important elements in that grand army; and now, as the glorious spring-time was drying the depths of the mud, and opening the way for a fresh campaign, we were in most superb condition to administer the last blows to the already tottering fabric of the rebellion.

We need not dwell long upon the particulars of this final campaign.

Lee took the initiative. Knowing that it would be impossible to hold his present line much longer, he determined to retreat to Danville; but wishing to cover his retreat by a bold movement in front, he sent a strong column to attack Fort Steadman, a point toward the right of the line where the two opposing lines were very close. The fort was guarded by troops of the Ninth corps. The attack was made very early on the morning of the 25th of March, and resulted in the complete surprise and capture of the fort and of many of the men of the Ninth corps. It was a short-lived triumph; the work taken was commanded by the guns of other forts on either flank, and the enfilading guns with strong bodies of infantry soon compelled a retreat of the enemy.

Meanwhile the opportunity had not been lost by General Meade for advancing his line on the left. The Sixth corps was to do the work. The Third brigade, Second division was sent forward to take and hold the rebel picket line near the Squirrel Level road, for the double purpose of withdrawing the attention of the enemy, and of advancing our line for future operations. The brigade gallantly executed the order, and, notwithstanding the rebels brought nine pieces of artillery to bear upon it, and sent reinforcements to the point, the ground was held. Colonel Dwight of the One Hundred and Twenty-second

was killed; Captain Oakley and Lieutenant Pierce lost
their lives, and many others of the brigade were killed or
wounded.

The 29th of March was the day fixed for the opening
of the grand final campaign. The Twenty-fourth corps
relieved the Second and Fifth corps from the intrenchments
in front of Petersburgh, and these two corps were loose
to join Sheridan in an expedition on our left with the view
of turning the enemy's right flank.

Leaving camp early on the morning of the 29th, the
two corps and the cavalry proceeded to the southwest,
crossed Hatcher's Run, and marched toward Dinwiddie
Court House, the infantry reaching the Quaker road,
the cavalry continuing the march to Dinwiddie. We had
now an unbroken line from the Appomattox to Dinwiddie
Court House. The corps were posted from right to
left, as follows: Ninth, Sixth, Twenty-fourth, Second,
Fifth, and on the left of all, Sheridan with the cavalry.

On the morning of the 30th, the infantry and cavalry
on the left were ready for the grand blow upon the flank
and rear of the enemy, but a heavy rain storm set in,
rendering the roads impracticable, and except some man-
neuvering to get nearer the enemy's position, no
movements were made. On the following day, the
rebels made a fierce onset upon the corps of Warren, but
failed to dislodge him. April 1st, Sheridan, with infantry
and cavalry, engaged the rebels at a place called Five
Forks, a position of vital importance to the enemy.

While Sheridan was thus dealing heavy blows upon
the flank, we in front were preparing for a general
advance.

The position occupied by the Sixth corps formed a sali-
ent, the angle approaching very near the rebel line.
Here, in front of Fort Welch and Fort Fisher, the corps
was massed in columns of brigades in *echelon*, forming a

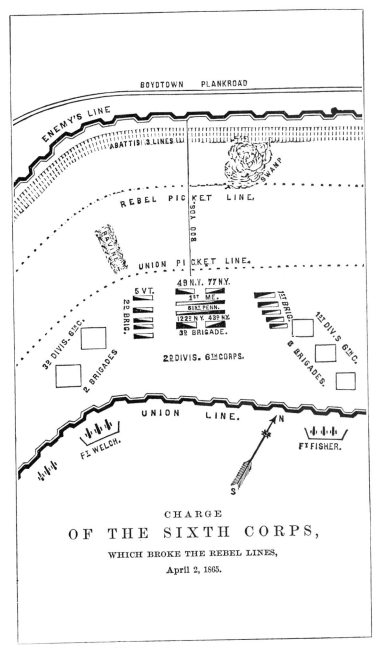

CHARGE

OF THE SIXTH CORPS,

WHICH BROKE THE REBEL LINES,

April 2, 1865.

mighty wedge, which should rive the frame-work of the confederacy.

The corps was formed in the rear of the picket line; the Third brigade, Second division, being the point of the wedge. On the right of that brigade was the First brigade of the same division, and on the left, the Vermont brigade. The First division of three brigades was in *echelon* by brigades on the right of the Second, and the Third of two large brigades also in *echelon*. Each brigade was in column of battalions. Axemen were ready to be sent forward to remove abattis, and Captain Adams had twenty cannoneers ready to man captured guns. Every commanding officer of battalions was informed what he was expected to do, and thus all was in readiness.

At half-past four in the morning of April 2d, the signal gun from Fort Fisher sounded the advance. Without wavering, through the darkness, the wedge which was to split the confederacy was driven home.

The abattis was past, the breastworks mounted, the works were our own. Thousands of prisoners, many stands of colors and many guns were our trophies, while many of our friends, dead or wounded, was the price of our glory. The rebel line was broken, and now the troops of Ord, and those of the Ninth corps pressed on after us. Humphries, too, of the Second corps, hearing of our splendid success, stormed the works in his front away on the left and carried them. The confederate army gathered close around Petersburgh, but we followed closely. We will not stop to tell all the splendid achievements of that glorious day.

That night our corps rested on the Appomattox, just above Petersburgh, and General Grant, of the Vermont brigade, had his head-quarters in the house which General Lee had occupied all winter, and had left only a few hours before. During the night Lee made his escape with his army. He had already sent word to Richmond that he was to retreat, and the fatal message reached Davis while in church.

We all joined in the pursuit next morning. The Second and Sixth corps hastening to the help of Sheridan, who was following hard after the flying army. We confronted Lee at Jetersville, and on the morning of the 6th we moved up to attack, but there was no army to attack. Why need we tell of the forced march that followed; of the gallant fight at Sailor's creek, where we whipped Lee's army; of the wild joy of the surrender? These are all too well known to repeat, and the details would be tiresome.

The grand old Sixth corps, the pride of the army and the delight of the nation, had crowned all its former record of glory by breaking the famous "backbone" of the rebellion, and all that follows is tame.

General Grant did us the credit to say, "General Wright penetrated the lines with his whole corps, sweeping everything before him, and to his left, toward Hatcher's run, capturing many guns and several thousand prisoners."

General Meade, too, says: "Major-General Wright attacked at four A. M., carrying everything before him, taking possession of the enemy's strong line of works, and capturing many guns and prisoners. After carrying the enemy's lines in his front, and reaching the Boydtown plank road, Major-General Wright turned to his left and swept down the enemy's line of intrenchments till near Hatcher's run, where, meeting the head of the Twenty-fourth corps, General Wright retraced his steps and advanced on the Boydtown plank road toward Peters-burgh, encountering the enemy in an inner line of works immediately around the city."

The march and halt at Danville, the rapid journey through Fredericksburgh to Alexandria, the separate

review of the corps under the scorching rays of one of
the hottest days ever known even in Washington, when
hundreds of our men fell down from sunstroke and
exhaustion, the return to camp and the disbanding, finish
the story of the grandest corps that ever faced a foe.

Library of Congress Cataloguing in Publication Data

Stevens, George T. (George Thomas), 1832-1921.
Three years in the Sixth Corps.
(Collector's library of the Civil War)
Reprint. Originally published: Albany, N.Y.: S. R. Gray, 1866.
1. Stevens, George T. (George Thomas), 1832-1921.
2. United States—History—Civil War, 1861-1865—Personal narratives.
3. United States. Army. Corps, Sixth—History. 4. United States. Army. Corps, Sixth—Biography.
5. United States—History—Civil War, 1861-1865—Regimental histories.
6. Soldiers—New York (State)—Biography.
I. Title. II. Title: 3 years in the 6th Corps. III. Series.
E493.1 6th.S85   1984   973.7'447'0924   83-17904
ISBN 0-8094-4267-1 (library)
ISBN 0-8094-4266-3 (retail)